The Outbreak of the Irish Rebellion of 1641

The Outbreak of
the Irish Rebellion
of 1641

M. PERCEVAL-MAXWELL

Gill & Macmillan

Published in Ireland by
Gill & Macmillan Ltd
Goldenbridge
Dublin 8
with associated companies throughout the world
© McGill-Queen's University Press 1994
0 7171 2173 9

Printed in Canada

Published in North America by McGill-Queen's
University Press   .

A catalogue record for this book is available from the
British Library.

This book has been published with the help of a
grant from the Social Science Federation of Canada,
using funds provided by the Social Sciences and
Humanities Research Council of Canada.

Typeset in Baskerville 10/12
by Caractéra production graphique inc., Quebec City

For Maria

Contents

Maps, Figure, Tables

Preface

My purpose in this book is to try to explain how the rebellion that broke out in Ireland in 1641 began. This rebellion, viewed from a long-term perspective, is one incident in a process which started with the creation of the early modern English nation-state. As the English crown withdrew from the continent, a sense of English identity developed which found one of its strongest expressions in the creation of a distinctly English form of Christianity. The crystallization of the English nation coincided with a period of technical changes in ships and sails that enhanced communication, which, in turn, necessarily extended the importance of sea power. Thus, at precisely the moment that England was becoming culturally more isolated from the continent, it became physically more susceptible to attack by continental forces. If it was to maintain its independence, the security of its western flank, and thus its control over Ireland, became imperative. Once before Ireland had become a strategic liability to a government in England. The nature of the threat during the twelfth century differed from that in the sixteenth in that Henry II feared, not that Ireland would become a base for a continental invasion, but that it would furnish one of his own nobles with an opportunity to create a separate and rival kingdom. Significantly, he and his immediate successors dealt with the problem by invasion, conquest, and settlement.

Similarly, if Henry VIII at one stage in his reign could declare that Ireland was best governed by "sober ways, politic drifts and amiable persuasions," by the end of his life he had abandoned a policy of non-interference. Under his successors, whether Catholic or Protestant, England intruded into Irish affairs to an increasing degree, and this intrusion led to a repetition of Henry II's tactics of conquest and colonization. The major difference between the two waves of settlers was that the sixteenth-century incursion brought not a continental form of Christianity but one identified with the English state, and it was the adherents of this doctrine which, step by step, took over Irish and Old English institutions of government.

If we believe the shape that Anglo-Irish relations have taken over the last four centuries to have been inevitable, the rebellion of 1641 has little significance as it simply got in the way of the prevailing trend for a moment until inevitability restored itself as a tide flows over a sand bar. Such a sweeping interpretation suggests a historical process which ignores the cumulative effect of numerous decisions taken within a short period of time, sometimes without Ireland in mind, and often with results that were not intended by those who made them but which had a profound effect on what happened. Conditions in Ireland that had developed since the sixteenth century undoubtedly contributed to the outbreak of the rebellion and to the course that it took once it had started, but it is my view that the rebellion was primarily the consequence of a series of decisions made by a relatively small number of men in England, Ireland, and Scotland during the years immediately preceding it. Therefore these decisions command considerable significance because they have left an indelible mark upon Irish and, to a lesser extent, English and British history. The broad outline of these events has long been known, but less attention has been given to how they came to be. I have tried, therefore, to trace in detail the formation of these decisions and their intended and unintended interactions.

It may be asked if we need another monograph on the period of the late 1630s and early 1640s after the substantial contributions made by Conrad Russell, Anthony Fletcher, David Stevenson, and others. Russell, in particular, in *The Fall of the British Monarchies*, has devoted considerable attention to Ireland. I would respond that, while my own work is heavily indebted to that of others, particularly to those I have mentioned, and I am convinced that we can only understand the outbreak of the rebellion in the context of the three kingdoms, there is no other recent book which looks at this overall picture from a primarily Irish perspective. I have, moreover, given considerable space to the sessions of the Irish parliament held during 1640–41, which, by comparison with English parliaments of the period, has been neglected. This is not to diminish the contributions of Aidan Clarke and H.F. Kearney, whose works remain the foundation for understanding Irish history during this period. However, here, in contrast to such historians, I have adopted a more "British" orientation. In short, I have placed more emphasis on Ireland than is common among historians of England and Scotland, and more emphasis upon England and Scotland than is usually found among historians of Ireland.

My use of the term "rebellion" to describe the conflict does not, however, reflect a particular point of view so much as a reluctance to split hairs over words. The term "rebellion" has been used in most of the literature about the war, and one alternative, "commotion," sometimes used at the time, sounds quaint. Most of those in early modern Europe who fought their monarchs claimed to be doing so as loyal subjects, and this applied to the Irish as much as to the Scots and English. I have also used other terms such as "Old English," "Puritan," and "constitutionalist" which could breed endless (and fruitless) dispute over meaning. I use such terms, often with a brief explanation, as a concise way of identifying a particular group, but most such groups have fuzzy edges, and it is my hope that the context as well as the explanations make my meaning clear.

Anyone who has written a book of this kind is well aware of what a joint effort it becomes as assistance is given from all quarters. In thanking those who have helped me, I would like to begin by expressing particular appreciation to three scholars. Conrad Russell, quite apart from the influence of his writing, which has been considerable, has read and commented on one chapter in draft and has directed me to valuable sources which I would not have found without his assistance. His generosity in this respect, particularly as he was writing his *British Monarchies* at the time, has been an inspiration. Similarly, Raymond Gillespie has given me frequent guidance, often while I have been staying with him and his wife, Bernadette Cunningham, as I searched the Dublin archives. He has been a source of many ideas, and I have learned as much from our discussions as from the particular items to which he has directed me. To John Morrill I also owe a major intellectual debt, as do so many other scholars in the field. From his reading of the entire typescript I gained not only invaluable advice, which I have tried to follow, but also great encouragement.

I should also thank two scholars whose identities I do not know: namely, the readers for McGill-Queen's University Press and the Social Science Federation of Canada, the latter having generously provided a subsidy to assist publication. The revisions which have been made in response to their comments have, I know, substantially improved the text, but I should make clear that what failings remain are mine and mine alone. It is impossible to relate in each case how assistance has been given, but Toby Barnard, Nicholas Canny, Aidan Clarke, Donal Cregan, Stephen Ellis, Anthony Fletcher, John Guy,

Robert Hunter, Rolf Loeber, Michael MacCarthy-Morrogh, Lee Mat-thews, Jane Ohlmeyer, Vera Rutledge, and Kevin Sharpe have all provided help of one sort or another for which I am deeply grateful.

I thank the staff of all the libraries and archives listed in the bibliography, but the librarians in one library, which is not listed because I did not use manuscript material in its keeping, deserve special mention. The staff of McGill's McLennan Library has pro-vided continuous and essential support over many years. In this context I thank Kendall Wallis particularly for his patience, diligence, and learning as I prepared the bibliography.

Before venturing into book form, I tested two aspects of this work as articles. I have incorporated substantial, though modified, portions of these articles into this text, and I thank the editors of the *Canadian Journal of History* and *The Historical Journal*, as well as the Syndics of Cambridge University Press, for permission to re-publish those por-tions of these articles which I have used. I also thank His Royal Highness, the duke of Cornwall, His Grace, the duke of Devonshire, His Grace, the duke of Northumberland, the earl of Rosse, and Viscount De Lisle, v.c. k.g., for permitting me to consult their muni-ments.

Perhaps the most precious commodity to the historian is time, and I thank McGill University for granting me two leaves during which I could visit the necessary archives and work on the text. Travel money and other research funds are, however, also necessary, and here I thank not only McGill, but the Social Sciences and Humanities Research Council of Canada, which gave me a research grant in 1987, and the Huntington Library of San Marino, Cali-fornia. This financial support has been essential, but its effectiveness has been much enhanced by the long suffering hospitality of Susan Horsman, Pat Perceval-Maxwell, Polly Hughes, and Selina Gun-Cuninghame as I moved about Charles's three kingdoms searching for evidence. I cannot adequately express thanks to Carol LeDain, secretary to the dean of arts at McGill, who has faced more drafts of this text on her word processor than I am sure she cares to remember, and has helped in innumerable other ways. To Marion Magee, who has edited the manuscript and guided me through the last labour of preparing it for publication, I owe a special word of gratitude. Her skill and thoroughness in commenting on the text have been matched only by her sensitivity to its contents. Joan McGilvray, coordinating editor of McGill-Queen's University Press, has also been most helpful as the book has gone to press, and to her too I express my appreciation.

Finally, I thank my wife, Maria, to whom this book is dedicated, who has both borne the excitements and disappointments of this project with me and borne with me during the frustration occasioned by their interruption.

Montreal, 1993   M.P.M.

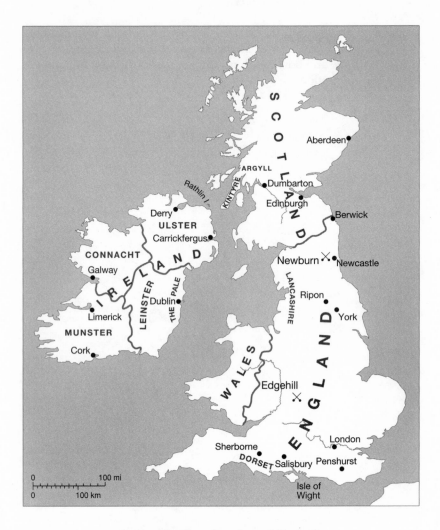

Map 1   The Three Kingdoms of Charles I

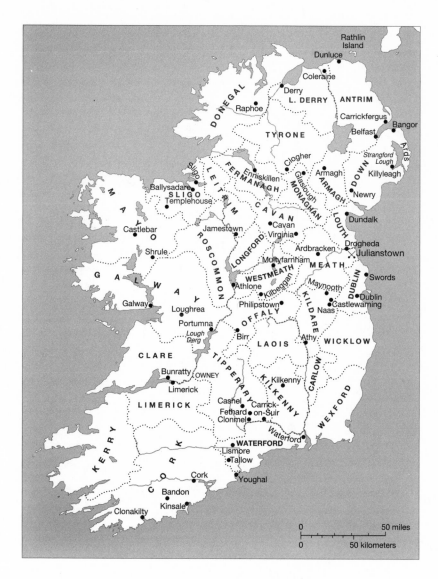

Map 2 Ireland – Counties and Principal Places

The Outbreak of the Irish Rebellion of 1641

Ireland's Political Components, 1603–41

The Irish parliament was summoned early in 1640 to provide money for a specially raised army. This was intended to assist Charles I against his Scottish subjects who, since 1637, had demonstrated increasing defiance in asserting their own form of church and worship in opposition to that preferred by their monarch. As the first session of this parliament began in March of 1640, the speaker of the Commons, Maurice Eustace, member for Athy, County Kildare, delivered a speech describing the state of the country and praising Thomas Wentworth, who had served as lord deputy of Ireland since 1633 and who had recently been promoted to lord lieutenant and created earl of Strafford. Sycophantic the speech definitely was, but much of what was said was true and must have rung true to most of those who heard it, even those who hated Wentworth because of his high-handed methods. "The time was," Eustace said:

and not very long since, when the Judges of our land were, as it were, impaled within the *English Pale* ... but now their Circuit is like the Sun, from one End of the Kingdom unto the other, and there is no Place therein where their Voice and Sound is not heard ... If we look abroad, is not all the world in combustion round about us? Is not *Germany*, poor *Germany* as I may now say, which was the Garden of *Europe*, all turned [to] waste ... ?

Is not *France* and *Spain* entered in the List of War, and striving in sweat and blood for a doubtful Conquest? How long have the States of *Holland* and the House of *Austria* been hacking each other with the swords of war both by Sea and Land?

Then he recalled the past civil wars in Ireland, and continued: "But these black and sad Times are in Manner forgotten by Reason of that long and happy Peace, which we have enjoyed ... for every one of us now doth sit in Safety at Home under his own Roof; our Swords turned into Plow-shares, and we have wholly forgotten the Use of War."[1]

Within eighteen months of the delivery of this speech Ireland was engulfed in a war that was to continue for a decade and which was as bitter as any that affected other European nations. The explanation of how the state of harmony described by Eustace degenerated into conflict lies in the day-to-day decisions taken in the months just before the Irish parliament met and the events that followed its sitting. Nevertheless, we must glance back at the "black and sad times" which Eustace recalled because it was then that the various elements which participated in the conflict were defined. Together they created the particular environment of political imbalance in which conflict-causing agents could flourish.

Modern historians have generally agreed with Eustace that Ireland's fate during the reign of Elizabeth was, indeed, black and sad. There is also general agreement that the strife that is such a prominent feature of Ireland's sixteenth-century history arose largely from English policies involving religious coercion, military conquest, and territorial colonization. The discussion about religion in late Tudor Ireland has tended to be dominated by the issue of when (and even whether) the Reformation had failed.[2] This debate has been valuable in that it reflects a certain fluidity in the religious convictions of the population that can be detected even into the seventeenth century. Yet what needs to be stressed about Irish religious history, and what distinguishes it from that of both England and Scotland, is that it was tied to the issues of conquest and colonization. Here, perhaps, the contrast with Scotland is more instructive than that with England.

Scotland, like Ireland, posed a strategic threat to the newly Protestant English state, and during the 1540s there were signs of an intention to deal with this threat by force.[3] However, the advent of a native Scottish reform movement rendered such action unnecessary. English intervention could be restricted to temporary protective moves; the Scots instituted a relatively non-violent Reformation on their own despite the presence initially of a Catholic monarch, and England's northern border remained secure from continental intrusion. By contrast, England had to introduce the Reformation into Ireland, and although it is evident that during the 1540s the new faith encountered little hostility within Ireland's population, it failed to become a popular movement, and policies that might have enabled it to do so were overtaken by the imperatives of English strategic security.

Similarly, Tudor political policies in Ireland ultimately became heavily determined by the same strategic considerations that drove those relating to religion. At times, indeed, political and religious policies became almost indistinguishable in that their common aim was the survival and security of the English state. During the 1540s, under the lord deputyship of Sir Anthony St Leger, policies were followed in Ireland which could have served as an alternative to those ultimately adopted under Elizabeth. These policies had tried to draw the leaders of the entire population of Ireland into the governance of the realm. Thus many Gaelic Irish lords were given English titles to their land and some were raised to the English nobility in Ireland; for instance, the O'Neill, who controlled much of Ulster, received the title of earl of Tyrone in 1542. St Leger also tended, in operating the English institutions in Ireland, to rely on those English who possessed Irish estates and whose families had long associations with the country.[4]

We can detect some continuation of such policies of accommodation under Elizabeth, but they were not pursued with either determination or consistency. Resistance to the Dublin government broke out time after time, and the leaders of these risings frequently attempted to obtain assistance from England's foreign rivals. Before the Reformation in Scotland, the English administration in Ireland perceived the strongest threat to come from that country, but during the 1560s Shane O'Neill called on the French for aid. Subsequently, after 1570 when Elizabeth was excommunicated, those opposing English authority sought papal and, ultimately, Spanish assistance. During the 1590s, Ireland became as much a target for Philip II's naval expeditions as was England. One of these succeeded in landing troops at Kinsale in 1601 and attempted to link up with Hugh O'Neill, earl of Tyrone, the Irish leader during the Nine Years' War. Elizabethan administrators, fearful of Ireland being turned into a base from which to conquer England, tended to opt for a policy of obedience imposed by force, often ruthlessly exercised, and such force was frequently followed by forfeiture of land.[5]

The very measures used to attain this goal of obedience often created conditions that diminished the chances of its voluntary adoption. Traditionally, English authority in Ireland had rested upon the support of those who had colonized Ireland during the mediaeval period, and in particular under the Normans. These settlers, whose estates were concentrated in the Pale counties round Dublin and the Anglo-Irish lordships controlled by such families as the Butlers (earls of Ormond) and the Fitzgeralds (earls of Kildare and Desmond), perceived themselves as English and distinct from the Gaelic Irish. These Anglo-Irish, or Old English, had occupied the offices of the English administration in Ireland, and it was on them that St Leger had tended to rely. However, one of the most distinctive features of late Tudor government was the shift from dependence on these families to the use of English-born personnel.

We can find instances of English officials being sent to lead the government of Ireland before the Reformation. The earl of Surrey served in this capacity from 1520 to 1522, but those who staffed his administration continued to consist very largely of men from the Old English community. After the Reformation, however, when the Old English failed to embrace the new faith even if they did not actively oppose it, they became suspect in the context of the strategic threat. Thus the Irish administration's civil and military establishment became increasingly the preserve of the English-born, a trend accelerated after the passage in 1560 of the act requiring all holders of ecclesiastical and state offices in Ireland to swear the Oath of Supremacy. The men who crossed to Ireland to fill these positions soon acquired the name of New English, and a fissure developed between the majority of the mediaeval colonists and the new arrivals.[6] Some of Elizabeth's most determined opponents in Ireland bore Old English names such as Fitzgerald or Fitzmaurice, and those who did not enter rebellion did not hesitate to oppose her government in parliament. The idea of a "Puritan" opposition in the English Elizabethan Commons is no longer accepted, but in Ireland as early as 1569 an opposition made up of pre-Reformation settlers was already evident, and as the century progressed the Old English gentry took on an increasingly Catholic hue.[7]

Surrey was among the first to propose a new wave of settlement. Colonization, therefore, was as much a product of the assertiveness of the early modern English state as it was the product of the reformed religion. Significantly, the first major plantation project, that in Laois and Offaly, began to be implemented under Mary, and had she lived longer the process might have been identified with the Counter-Reformation and not with Protestantism. Yet because it was under Elizabeth that most of the early projects were attempted, in the popular Irish mind they came to be associated with the reformed faith.[8]

The details of Elizabethan colonization need not concern us, but it may be remarked that just as the discovery of the New World fired the imagination of Englishmen, so Ireland appeared in somewhat the same light. Richard Grenville, Francis Drake, and Walter Raleigh all had Irish experience before venturing farther west, and both the push to America and English policy in Ireland were linked to the growing conflict with Spain. In the 1570s Englishmen tried to start settlements in Ulster, but the ventures failed. The plantation of Munster, based on the forfeiture of land following the Desmond rebellion of the 1580s and begun at the same time as the Roanoke settlement in Virginia, enjoyed more success. It has been estimated that some 4,000 English persons had settled by 1598, but in that year this scheme also failed as it became caught up in the upheavals of the Nine Years' War and most of the English inhabitants fled or were killed.[9]

Only under James I and VI did settlement from Britain begin to make a long-term impact upon Ireland. The Munster plantation was revived and by 1622 contained some 2,700 English households. Other Jacobean settlements were also more successful than Elizabethan ones, in particular those in the province of Ulster. English and Lowland Scots began to move into Down and Antrim on their own initiative almost as soon as James ascended the thrones of England and Ireland. Subsequently, after the "flight" of the earls of Tyrone and Tyrconnell in 1607, the government devised a much more ambitious project involving the partial settlement of six additional Ulster counties with English and Scots, who were frequently referred to in contemporary documents as "British." By 1630 some 14,000 Lowland, and primarily Protestant, Scots adults were living in the province, and it is likely that there was a similar number of English settlers. Finally, under James, the government also started smaller settlements in the counties of Leitrim, Longford, and Wexford.[10]

As in the case of the appointment of Englishmen to Irish office, colonization as a policy divided the New English, who generally favoured it, from the Old English, who opposed it. The New English leaders valued plantation because it supplied them with wealth in the form of land and tenants on whom they could rely politically and militarily. The Old English, for their part, were bound to resent a process in which they participated little and which further diminished their influence. Moreover, the formal plantation schemes were accompanied by a private investigation into weak titles. In 1568 Sir Peter Carew, an Englishman, laid claim to land in Meath on the basis of a Norman grant to one of his ancestors and the courts upheld the claim. As many Old English estates rested on old and uncertain titles, plantation appeared to be just one more mechanism to undermine the influence of this group. This influence had rested on the relationship of the English crown to Ireland, and for this reason we must look briefly at the constitutional relationship between England and Ireland in the sixteenth century.[11]

By the end of the century the Irish constitution, in theory though not always in practice, rested on three pillars: English common law, though with some Irish variations, and two Irish statutes, the act passed in 1541 changing Ireland from a lordship to a kingdom, and Poynings's Act as amended. Under the 1541 act, the king acquired "the name, style, title and honour of king of this land of Ireland," a title which brought with it "all prerogatives whatsoever to the majesty of a king imperial belonging." The Irish crown, therefore, was an imperial crown, "but united and knit to the imperial crown of England."[12] The passage of the act brought about little change as Ireland already possessed most of the trappings of a kingdom in the form of courts of law, a council, and a parliament, but the act defined the relationship between the English and the Irish crowns. Poynings's Act, passed in 1494 when Ireland was still a lordship, had much more practical significance. Ireland required an executive of its own because of its distance from the king, but sometimes this executive had shown separatist leanings. Poynings's Act was intended to deal with this problem and, as its historians have stressed, it was not aimed at the legislature, but only by limiting the power of the executive to legislate could the king ensure ultimate control over his Irish servants.[13]

Under Poynings's Act as originally passed, the Irish executive could only call a parliament after obtaining a licence from the king, and all proposed legislation had to be "affirmed by the king and his [English] council."[14] Despite the 1541 act, therefore, Ireland was, in law, still administered by the English council to some extent. In 1557, however, Poynings's law underwent substantial amendment, by which the English council was excluded from the formal process of approving draft bills.[15] There was little or no change in practice because the English council continued to participate in the administration of Ireland, and it must be said that during the sixteenth century the Irish constitution was seldom discussed. Often, during the course of rebellions, officials applied martial law and some features of the Reformation and Counter-Reformation were imposed in the 1540s and 1550s by proclamation rather than statute. Nevertheless, a statement by the speaker of the Irish Commons in 1586 to the effect that Ireland was autonomous from England indicates an awareness of the legal relationship between the two states.[16]

With this background in mind, we may examine the position of the various political constituents of Ireland during the decades leading up to 1641. There were at least seven political interests. Besides the native Irish, the Old English, and the New English, we must look at the Catholic church, the crown, the Protestant or state church, and, finally, the Scottish settlers. Obviously the interests of some of these groups overlapped. Both native Irish and Old English, with a few exceptions, identified with the Catholic church, and the planters, again with a few exceptions, with the Protestant faith, and virtually the entire population would have claimed loyalty to the crown. But the interests of the Old English were not identical with those of the Catholic church, and the planters did not hesitate, on occasion, to undermine the interests of the church to which they were supposed to be attached. Each of these groups or institutions, therefore, warrants separate consideration.

THE NATIVE IRISH

As the Irish are associated with the first armed action in the 1641 rising, it is appropriate to start with them. Even within this group there was wide variation in attitude between those who had gone into exile in reaction to English penetration of Ireland, some of whom in 1627 envisaged establishing a republic of Ireland under Spanish auspices, and such nobles as Ulick Bourke, fifth earl of Clanricard, the Catholic but anglicized half-brother to the Puritan earl of Essex.[17] Clanricard was as at home in the English court as he was at Portumna, County Galway, his Irish house. The attitudes of the vast majority of the Irish, however, lay somewhere between these extremes. A more useful distinction to draw in assessing their position is between those who lived in the areas subjected to plantation and those who did not. Despite the implementation of the various plantation schemes, Irish landowners controlled approximately one-third of the area of the country, and many Irish lived untouched by the process of colonization. Some of these last were anxious to assert strong loyalty to the crown. In 1626, for instance, when England was at war with Spain, thirteen leading Irish gentry from Leinster and Munster, provinces where the Irish had not been seriously affected by plantation, issued a "loyal address" declaring their devotion to the king and repudiating the rule of any foreign prince.[18] No such declaration, it may be remarked, came from the Ulster Irish.

The hard core of Irish culture and attitude lay in Ulster, along with the adjoining counties of Longford and Leitrim. It was from Ulster that the exiles derived their leadership, initially from Hugh O'Neill and Rory O'Donnell, the earls of Tyrone and Tyrconnell, who, after the failure of the their long military struggle against Elizabeth, had gone into exile themselves in 1607 and thus opened the way for the English government to initiate the plantation in Ulster. By 1641 this leadership had descended to John, Hugh O'Neill's son, and on his death in that year without issue, to Hugh's nephew, Owen Roe. Important though these exiles were, it is a mistake to place too much emphasis upon them. In Ulster itself, many of the Irish gentry who remained in Ireland benefited from the plantation. Sir Phelim O'Neill, who would be one of the leaders of the Irish in 1641, attended Lincoln's Inn for three years as a young man, may have been a Protestant briefly, owned an estate of some 4,500 acres in County Armagh by 1624, lived in a strong, freestone house, and in 1627 purchased a knighthood.[19] Similarly, the Maguires, also to be deeply involved in the rising, received very large grants of land in County Fermanagh at the time of the plantation.[20] Moreover, not only did many of the Irish leaders own large estates, but they also participated in the government of the country. "Men like the O'Neills," Aidan Clarke has written, "had not only come to terms with the new order in Ulster, but were a part of it, and they were not excluded from the degree of participation for which their rank and possessions qualified them."[21] Lord Maguire, Sir Phelim O'Neill, and Philip O'Reilly, another leader of the Ulster Irish during the rebellion, all sat in the 1640 parliament.

Indeed, the separation of Irish political interests into seven categories tends to obscure the co-operation that occurred between them at some levels. In 1628 a committee of gentry from Ireland crossed to England to discuss defence measures to counter the Spanish threat. The committee was designed to provide representation from each of Ireland's four provinces and consisted of eleven men. Eight of these were Old English Catholics and three were Protestant planters, two from Ulster and one from Munster.[22] At first sight it appears that the Irish played no part in the process, but an examination of the committees that made the provincial selection shows that they consisted of men from each major political group. Thus the Old English and Irish predominated among the selectors in Connacht, Leinster, and Munster though there was planter participation, and in Ulster, although the planters commanded a majority, the selection committee included two men with Irish names.[23]

It may be objected that the influence of the Irish did not reflect their numerical importance and that this type of analysis takes no account of those below the social level of the gentry. Even though seventeenth-century representative institutions set less store by majoritarian principles than do those of the twentieth century, the first objection has some validity because, as we shall see, when the Irish sought political change from which they alone would benefit, they were less successful in attaining their ends than when pursuing goals that enjoyed the support of other groups. The second objection is anachronistic in that throughout Europe only the relatively wealthy participated fully in the political process at this time. Nevertheless, it is worth noting that the Irish at the lower social levels seem to have borne a far deeper resentment against the colonists than did their leaders, and this feeling became of significance once the rising had started. They were less anglicized than the gentry and they had less stake in the existing system, but even they had sufficient regard for the king that their leaders thought it worthwhile to pretend that Charles had given his blessing to the rising.[24]

THE OLD ENGLISH

The Old English have been well studied. They included some 2,000 land-owning families, with a heavy concentration in the counties of Dublin, Kildare, Kilkenny, Louth, Meath, Westmeath, Wexford, and Galway, though present in most counties south of Ulster.[25] They, like the Irish, controlled about one-third of the land area of the kingdom. Although it is possible to point to some of their leaders as Protestant, most notably, James Butler, twelfth earl of Ormond, George Fitzgerald, earl of Kildare, and Lords Kerry, Howth, Courcy, Mayo, and Kilmallock, the overwhelming majority adhered to the Roman church despite the material and political disadvantages of doing so.[26] Because they possessed property they retained influence, in the towns as well as in the counties, but they were excluded from office because of their religion and even their influence had been slipping in that their representation in parliament was less in 1634 than in 1615 and less in 1640 than in 1634. Thus, whereas the Irish had increased their level of political participation, if only marginally, the Old English had lost ground to the colonists, and whereas the Irish had never held office, the Old English had and now resented their exclusion.

Religion was not the only issue which threatened to undermine the political influence of the Old English. As already noted, their land titles were often open to challenge because they dated back to mediaeval times and were vaguely worded or might even have been lost. This was not a problem confined to Ireland, and legislation had been passed in England in 1624 guaranteeing titles to land held for sixty years or more.[27] Thus, when the crown needed the support of all landed elements in Ireland to resist the foreign threat of the late 1620s, the opportunity arose both to prove Old English loyalty and to acquire the same security as those in a similar position in England.

The result of negotiations between the English government and the committee of Irish landowners who went to England in 1628 was the declaration of fifty-one Graces, or royal promises, remedying various grievances in return for sufficient funds to increase the size of the Irish army from 1,500 to 5,000 men.[28] It is important to stress that the benefits of the Graces extended well beyond the interests of the Old English. The titles of the recent planters could be challenged too, if for different reasons, because many had failed to fulfil building or other conditions that were stipulated in their grants and the twenty-sixth and twenty-seventh Graces were intended to secure their titles. Some of the Graces, moreover, were of a general nature, such as the forty-eighth, which set limits on what sheriffs might charge for carrying out their duties. The negotiation of the Graces showed how all Irish landowners – Old English, planter, and even Irish – could work together for mutual benefit. Nevertheless, it is probably true that the Old English set more store by the promises, particularly the twenty-fourth which secured their titles, than other groups. Associated with this concern was the fifteenth Grace, which permitted Catholic lawyers to practice in Ireland by allowing them to take the Oath of Allegiance instead of the Oath of Supremacy.[29] If the Old English were to resist encroachments on their property, they required not only the protection of the law but the services of Catholic lawyers on whom they could depend, such as Patrick Darcy and Richard Martin.

The intention in 1628 had been to call a parliament and transform the Graces from mere royal promises, not enforceable through the courts, into law. A parliament was called, but it was found to have been summoned incorrectly because of a failure to follow properly the complex procedures of Poynings's law.[30] By the time the muddle had been detected the foreign threat had retreated and with it the need to make concessions to the taxpayers. When a parliament was next called and met, in 1634, under Thomas Wentworth, it was on the understanding that taxes would be levied in return for the passage of the Graces into law. Once again the Old English were thwarted, for no sooner were the subsidies granted than it appeared that the government intended to exclude the key Graces from the confirming legislation. This act of bad faith, which affected all landed interests, reinforced the growing hatred of Wentworth and tended to create a "country" interest against the government which spanned religious differences.[31] It also explains why, when the passage of the Graces into law was again delayed in 1641, the loyalty of the Old English was stretched to breaking point.

THE CATHOLIC CHURCH

There remains considerable dispute about whether Protestantism had failed in Ireland by the end of the sixteenth century. Certainly the popular religion of Ireland in 1600 was not Protestant, but nor, in the words of John Bossy, did it "correspond to the criteria of modern catholicism." Probationary marriage was common, and married priests could be found in Ulster as late as 1620. The strictures of David Rothe, the Catholic bishop of Ossory (southwest of Dublin), in condemnation of Irish customs sounded like those of English Protestant officials, and in a sense the social aims of the English state and the Roman church in Ireland were the same: to make the Irish conform more closely to the codes of behaviour found elsewhere in Europe. Between 1600 and 1641 some progress was made in this respect, but Bossy has concluded, nevertheless, that by the latter date "Ireland was only beginning to struggle towards the change of life which came with systematic religious instruction."[32] This suggests that the population as a whole may have remained open to a determined missionary effort by the reformers, had one been launched as late as the 1630s. However, no such campaign arose, and in any case, the more wealthy elements in the country remained aloof from the reformers and adhered to the older faith, much as the gentry of Lancashire did in England. It was under such Old English influence that seminaries were established in Europe, first at Paris in 1574 and later at Salamanca (1592) and Douai (1595). In the seventeenth century more such schools were founded; Franciscan seminaries were started at Louvain in 1607 and Rome in 1625, and other schools were set up at Bordeaux and Rouen.[33]

While this educational network was being established abroad, Hugh O'Neill, as part of his struggle against Elizabeth, insisted on the appointment of Catholic bishops in Ireland, the most prominent of these being Peter Lombard, who became archbishop of Armagh in 1601. Lombard, of Old English stock from Waterford, sought accommodation with the Protestant state and on the whole the state under James reciprocated, even though instances of persecution can be cited (four Franciscans were executed in 1607) and the Act of Uniformity remained on the statute books.[34] Accommodation served the church well because, by 1623, there were four Catholic archbishops in Ireland, five bishops, some 860 secular priests, 200 Franciscans, and 40 Jesuits, and a network of schools was being set up from which the better students went to the European seminaries to complete their education before returning to Ireland to reinforce the church that had educated them. The Franciscans in particular won the hearts of the common people, in part because they had never left the country and in part because they were organized around the monastic system, which was the traditional Irish ecclesiastical structure. There was, indeed, considerable rivalry between the secular and regular elements of the church.[35]

Under Lombard, church appointments had tended to be from the secular clergy and the Old English, but he died in 1625, just when England and Spain were at war, which gave the Irish exiles an influence in church appointments they might otherwise not have had. Thus Hugh O'Reilly became archbishop of Armagh in 1626, and subsequent appointments tended to favour the regular, pro-Spanish clergy, who fostered anti-Protestant, anti-plantation, and anti-English sentiment.[36] Such attitudes were particularly prevalent among the Franciscans. Thus we find Father Thomas McKiernan, formerly vicar-general of the diocese of Clogher and in 1641 guardian of the friary at Dundalk, actively involved in the pre-rebellion conspiracy.[37] In the words of their historian, once the rebellion broke out, the Franciscans considered it "a holy crusade for homes and altars, and did everything they could to unite the Irish and the Anglo-Irish [Old English] in the common cause."[38]

The English government was not unaware of the dangers of having a powerful institution in Ireland over which it had no control. In 1639 Francis Windebank, secretary to Charles I, endorsed a proposal that the queen should use her influence with the pope to permit Charles to nominate the Catholic bishops of Ireland.[39] The scheme, had it ever been adopted and become public, would have been as unpopular in English parliamentary circles as in Rome, but it is of interest as it reflected the official English recognition of the influence of the Roman church in Ireland and the desire to control it through episcopal appointments. Yet it may be doubted that even this would have been enough to control the Franciscans and, to a lesser extent, other priests whose role in the rebellion environment may be compared with that of the ministers in Covenanting Scotland. Strongly motivated ideologically, generally well educated, beyond the control of the hierarchy, and with a strong popular following, they moved freely about the country and served both as communicators and as agents who could supply theological justification for armed action. Even had Charles acquired some influence in the appointment of Catholic bishops in Ireland, it is unlikely that they would have been any more successful in stemming the popular feeling than the Protestant bishops were in Scotland.

THE NEW ENGLISH

Whereas the Old English were probably the most cohesive political group in Ireland, the New English were probably the least so. They possessed the virtues and defects of those who began from low social positions and sought to better themselves. The richest and most successful of them, Richard Boyle, first earl of Cork, had arrived in Ireland with virtually nothing in his pocket.[40] On the whole they professed the Protestant religion, but even here there were many exceptions and one of them, the earl of Castlehaven, served as a general to the Confederate Catholics. Even their common Protestantism could prove divisive as they did not always agree on the form of this faith to be followed. Some of them, most notably Sir John Clotworthy, an Antrim planter, held strong Puritan sympathies (in the sense of opposition to episcopal jurisdiction) and regarded the Irish Protestant bishops as a front for Catholicism. They sought to expand their estates, not only at the expense of the Irish and sometimes the Old English, but also in competition with each other and the Protestant church which they were supposed to defend.

As might be expected, given this lack of solidarity, the attitudes of the New English to their adopted country and its people ranged from contempt to a sympathy and acceptance which led them to marry their children to Old English and Irish, and even occasionally to take this step themselves. Sir Hardress Waller, for example, who had land in Munster and who was sufficiently Puritan to become a regicide in 1649, married into the Old English Dowdall family.[41] Sympathy for and identity with Ireland tended to be stronger among those born in the country than among those who arrived in mid-life, but even those born in England could develop strong antipathies to later arrivals. Wentworth, for instance, acquired extensive Irish estates along with the implacable hatred of the veteran settler, the earl of Cork.[42]

This last example illustrates another major division within the New English community, namely, between those in and out of office. Because office (though not unpaid positions such as justice of the peace or sheriff) was limited to those who had taken the Oath of Supremacy, it was the New English who dominated the administration. They commanded power out of all proportion to their numbers and sought to extend it by increasing the number of seats they controlled in parliament. Of course not all the New English obtained office or even wanted it. Thus we can detect three categories: those who had no aspirations to office and whose interests often overlapped with the Catholic gentry; those who had aspirations to office but did not possess it; and those who possessed both. There was, in short, competition not only for land but for place, and the two were closely connected as the possession of the latter led to the former. Yet such a picture is perhaps overly neat. Even among those who held office strong divisions over policy arose, and these divisions often overlapped with more personal ones.

It is upon those of the New English who held office or wanted to that we must concentrate because they had the most influence in shaping the policies which contributed to the outbreak of the rebellion. It would be neither possible nor useful to look at all the political issues that concerned the New English governors in the decades before the rebellion. Two will illustrate the way in which matters of policy and personal advancement interacted: first, the organization of the army in the face of the foreign threat during the 1620s, and second, the continuation of plantation.

The army was an issue which crossed religious lines yet also highlighted them. On the one hand, no less than five of the Graces of 1628 concerned abuses stemming from the army and these aroused resentment as much among the planters and their tenants as among the Old English and the Irish. On the other hand, the army also raised the question of political control. When it was first proposed that the size of the Irish army be increased in the face of the foreign threat, the Old English had suggested that this should be accomplished by the creation of a militia of the type available in England. This would have been paid for and officered by the gentry, including the Old English. The attitude towards this scheme of the lord deputy, Henry Cary, Viscount Falkland, may be deduced from a comment he made about the Galway gentry in 1625, before the proposal came forward. "I confess," he wrote, "that papists in this county are men of the best estates, and govern best when they hold offices of trust. But the constitution of this time makes it dangerous to trust them."[43]

We may assume that the idea of such a militia failed to win official sanction because of attitudes similar to those expressed by Falkland, but not all on the Irish council agreed with him. Viscount Loftus of Ely, the lord chancellor, seems to have supported the Old English proposal – at least he was accused by some of his colleagues on the council of having made "common cause with the nobility of the country" (a term worth noting) in order to win popularity.[44] Ely vigorously denied the charge and may have been misinterpreted, but another senior official, Sir Francis Annesley (subsequently Lord Mountnorris), the vice-treasurer, openly supported the Old English plan. In March 1628 he wrote a report in which he deplored the oppression suffered by the population at the hands of the soldiers, some of whom he described as the "dregs" of the Irish, and recommended the formation of an army based on the model of the English trained bands. This would, he suggested, incorporate "loyal natives and English." He concluded: "if the soldiers are taken away, if justice is honestly administered and if parliament is speedily called, all may yet be well." Lord Wilmot, marshal of the army, also favoured the placing of Old English and Irish gentry in positions of trust although he opposed the formation of trained bands.[45]

Such views illustrate the spectrum of opinion within governing New English circles. Some officials clearly envisaged a society based on accommodation, sound government, and gentry rule without religious distinction. This did not mean a movement towards official toleration. The suspicion of the possibility that this might be considered during the negotiations leading to the Graces aroused strong Protestant reaction in Dublin.[46] Even Annesley, whom we find lending his silver plate to a priest so that the Catholic bishop of Ferns could be entertained in a manner be fitting his position, considered that the laws against Catholics should be executed "moderately" and that all mass houses should be suppressed by degrees.[47] Except for the clause permitting Catholics back into legal practice, the subject of religion is noticeable by its absence in the Graces, and in April of 1629 a proclamation was issued against Roman Catholic activities.[48] On Falkland's recall in the same year the two lords justices, Cork and Ely, agreed on little else save that the army should in future be financed by the levy of recusancy fines.

If the religious issue could not be addressed formally, the land issue could and was. Had the Graces been passed into law, the Old English would have been protected from the effects of further planter expansion. Unlike religion, the policy of extending plantation does not seem to have aroused strong planter reaction. It was here that accommodation could have been achieved and, as Annesley had noted, if parliament had been called, all might have been "well." But parliament was not called, or, when it was, failed to address the land issue, and a powerful group of government officials, associated, initially, with Falkland and, after he departed in 1629, with Cork, held the cause of the continuation of plantation as dear as the preservation of Protestantism.

The most important members of this group during the 1620s were Sir William Parsons, Roger Jones, Sir Charles Coote, Richard Bolton, Sir Adam Loftus of Rathfarnham, and we may add Sir Henry Docwra, though he died in 1631. Parsons had succeeded his uncle, Sir Geoffrey Fenton, as surveyor-general. Fenton had befriended Cork, who became his son-in-law, and as early as 1614 we find Parsons writing to Cork in a manner that shows that he was continuing the alliance. Parsons subsequently became master of the court of wards, which placed him in an ideal position to favour those whose interests he wished to advance. Roger Jones became Viscount Ranelagh in 1628 and lord president of Connacht in 1630. By the end of that year his son, Arthur, had married Cork's fifth daughter,

Katherine. Sir Charles Coote also had his base in Connacht, being made vice-president of that province, and he also had business connections with Cork. Richard Bolton was attorney to the court of wards, thus close to Parsons. Sir Adam Loftus (not to be confused with Viscount Loftus of Ely, his cousin), unlike the others, did not sit on the privy council during the 1620s, but his link with the group is clear. His eldest daughter married Sir William Parsons's son and heir, a second daughter married Sir William's nephew, and his son married Ranelagh's daughter. Sir Adam, along with Parsons and Ranelagh, served as pallbearers at the funeral of Cork's wife in 1630. In the same year we find Sir Adam and Ranelagh drawing up charges against Lord Mountnorris.[49]

The opposition to Falkland and his friends in the council consisted primarily of Ely, Wilmot, and Mountnorris. The reasons for this division went beyond plantations.[50] Mountnorris had benefited from them in the north and the south of Ireland and had praised their effects in 1628. Yet his approach to plantation seems to have been to preserve what existed rather than to extend the process. He opposed Falkland's efforts to seize the lands of Phelim McFeagh O'Byrne in County Wicklow and initially served as an intermediary between the next lord deputy, Wentworth, and the Old English. Later Wentworth turned against him, but he did so after he, too, had decided to extend plantation, and Mountnorris's words in 1628 and subsequent actions are consistent with a desire to foster a sense of one political community within which Protestantism would dominate but not in an aggressive way.

That personal gain motivated Parsons and his friends need not be doubted, but personal enrichment was a fortunate concomitant to a policy which they perceived to be in the English national interest. In view of Parsons's later prominence as lord justice in 1641, it is worth noting his statements about policy in 1625 when he answered an attack on the court of wards over which he presided. His aim, he declared, was to mix English with native landlords "by which policy under two good deputies more was done in one year for the English empire than in near 300 years before." The king's revenue had been substantially increased and the sheriffs and justices of the peace could now be chosen "from the older established planters." It was not, he stressed, the Irish army that must be subdued, but "the Irish manner of living." "We must change their course of government, apparel, manner of holding land, language and habit of life. It will otherwise be impossible to set up in them obedience to the laws and the English empire." Already, he argued, considerable change had been wrought as the Irish now build "storehouses, make enclosures and put their children to school ... Where before they purchased men, now they purchase lands." Plantation, he continued, was the best means of reducing the Irish to subjection, "which we must do, as we cannot, without too great an effusion of blood, avoid their presence here."[51] A similar perception was expressed by Cork some five years later. If there were a few more years of peace, he wrote to the earl of Dorchester, the king ought to be able to command a levy of English and Irish, "reformed in manners and religion," more powerful than any an opposing side might raise. He too stressed the improvement in farming and buildings and the loyalty of the Old English whom, he claimed, preferred peace to war "which is good for their trade and estates."[52]

In concrete terms, the extension of plantation meant the settlement of Connacht, hitherto, with the exception of County Leitrim, untouched by confiscation. The prospect of a plantation here had loomed since the beginning of the century and had grown towards the end of James's reign, but it had aroused such strong opposition from the leading Irish landowner of the province, the earl of Clanricard, that the project had been put aside.[53] One of the inspirations for the land clauses in the Graces derived from a desire to protect Connacht, but the failure to call parliament successfully left the way open for the scheme to be revived, and by 1631 Cork's group had begun planning for the project. To avoid Clanricard's wrath, the planters excluded County Galway from their plans, where most of the Bourke estates lay, and they tried to give the idea broader political support by incorporating some of the Old English as beneficiaries. Nevertheless, opposition arose in England as it appeared that the undertakers and their Old English allies would gain at the expense of the poorer existing landlords and the crown.[54] Before any more progress could be made in developing the plantation, Thomas Wentworth had succeeded Falkland as lord deputy, and on his arrival in Ireland in 1633 it fell to Wentworth to decide what further plantations, if any, would be pursued.

THE CROWN

The interests of the crown are best considered in the context of Wentworth's administration, but it may be noted that the crown had traditionally faced the problem in Ireland that those who served it tended to interpret its interests and their own as identical. This had been true in the pre-Reformation era when the Old English were the only English in Ireland, and the plan of Cork and his friends for Connacht provides one of a number of possible examples of similar behaviour on the part of the New English.[55] Their desire to enforce recusancy fines to pay for the army is another example, for it was unlikely to endear the crown to the majority of the population, however much it may have appealed to Protestants.

It has been remarked that Thomas Wentworth's policy in Ireland amounted to "nothing less than the reversal of the work of the last forty years of Irish history: the destruction of the settler system and the establishment of a strong royal authority supported by a powerful church."[56] In some senses this is correct and is summed up in his celebrated determination to "bow and govern the native by the planter, and the planter by the native."[57] He quarrelled with the earl of Cork, he quarrelled with Lord Mountnorris after using him – indeed, he had him condemned to death after an incident which the lord deputy chose to interpret as mutiny. He infuriated the city of London by pressing the case against the city in Star Chamber under which it lost its entire investment in Londonderry on the grounds that it had failed to fulfil all its plantation obligations. He alienated the county gentry, Catholic and Protestant, in the 1634 parliament when he denied passage into law of some of the most important Graces, and he infuriated the Scots in Ulster when he made them take an oath that isolated them from their Covenanting compatriots in Scotland. He also supported the endowment of the Protestant church, which sometimes could only be achieved at the expense of the planters. Undoubtedly he did increase royal authority and he did so at the expense of any popular base the crown might have had in the country. All of this is true, but if we look at the policies he pursued in the two major areas of religion and plantation, there was more continuity than change between what he did and what had been done in the reign of King James.

On the issue of religion, Wentworth, like James, pursued a policy of tacit toleration. Initially, he used Mountnorris to establish an understanding with the Old English. As part of this understanding he reversed Cork's policy of forcing the Catholic population to bear the full burden of maintaining the army. Unspoken toleration had been the policy of the 1620s, and it was Cork, not Wentworth, who had tried to innovate by placing the full burden of supporting the army on Catholics. Nor did Wentworth hesitate to bring Catholics into the new Irish army formed in 1640 to counter the Scottish Covenanters, though he was careful to ensure that most of the offi- cers were Protestant. His religious position was probably cynical, in that he would not have been so tolerant had he had the means to enforce a more stringent policy. Archbisop Ussher, the Protestant primate of Ireland, testified in 1641 that Wentworth had told him early in his administration that the crown could not be well secured in Ireland without reducing the Irish "to conformity in religion with the church of England," but such was the strength of the Catholic church, it is unlikely that a time would have come that he would have felt himself strong enough to take measures against it.[58]

On the issue of plantation, Wentworth pursued a more determined policy than Falkland, Cork, and their friends. From the first year of his deputyship Wentworth had shown an interest in the plantation of Connacht, but he could not reveal his true intentions until the subsidies had been passed in the 1634 parliament. In the month that he dissolved parliament, April 1635, he took the first steps to initiate the plantation of Connacht, but his scheme, unlike the earlier one devised by Cork and the planters, incorporated the estates of the earl of Clanricard in County Galway along with Counties Roscommon, Sligo, and Mayo.[59] By the end of the year, these last three counties had been surveyed. The incorporation of Galway took longer and required the imprisonment of the jury that had refused to find a land title for the king and political pressure in England to overrule the objections of Clanricard who, as a resident at court, had powerful allies. In overcoming this last obstacle, the death at the end of 1635 of the fourth earl of Clanricard was providential. Ulick Bourke, who succeeded to the title, found that he had inherited huge debts and had therefore to reach an accommodation with the lord deputy. By April 1637 the king's title to Galway had been established.[60] At the same time it was recognized in Ireland that the king possessed as a good title to large sections of County Meath as he did to Connacht and, in England, Thomas Howard, the earl of Arundel, was pressing a land claim in southern Leinster. The implications of Wentworth's plan, therefore, extended well beyond Connacht.

The threat of war with the Holy Roman Empire (usually referred to as Austria by correspondents of the day) delayed the plantation of Connacht during 1637, and by the next year the king's dispute with Scotland prevented implementation of the scheme. By 1641 eleven Protestants possessed land in the counties of Mayo, Sligo, and Roscommon. These included Sir George Radcliffe, Wentworth's close friend, and the earl of Ormond, also a Wentworth ally, but none of the others stood close to the deputy; indeed four of them, including Cork, Ranelagh, and Coote, would appear as witnesses against him at his trial. It is unlikely, therefore, that the presence of any of these individuals as landowners represents the beginning of the plantation. Had it taken place under Wentworth's direction, it is reasonable to assume that those who obtained estates would have been among his friends and would probably have included Wentworth himself. The lord deputy was described by a contemporary as a "servant violently zealous in his master's ends and not negligent of his own." He held the tobacco monopoly, and by 1640 had acquired estates in Counties Kildare and Wicklow amounting to almost 34,000 profitable acres and had built a house larger than that at Hatfield. Some of the land was acquired by purchase, but 14,000 acres was a royal plantation grant in Wicklow.[61]

Wentworth quarrelled with planters of earlier generations, but there was no stronger advocate of plantation as a policy, and like his predecessors, he had no qualms about advancing his own interests along with those of the crown. In short, he continued policies that were well established. What distinguished him was that he imposed them without the support of any existing political group in Ireland. It was as though he was about to introduce yet another layer of colonization, which would be superimposed over the Irish, the Old English, and the New English alike, but he did not last long enough for more than the outlines of his plan to appear. This plan, perhaps, looked beyond Ireland. It has been suggested that Wentworth was not really interested in Irish affairs but saw them as a mechanism for establishing a centralized system of government in England and Ireland (and we may add Scotland). By the time the Scots challenged this centralizing direction, there was already in place in Ireland a regime that provided a model for what might be applied elsewhere, but there were also many in Ireland and England who were prepared to use the occasion to thwart this larger vision. Some of Wentworth's opponents in Ireland, however, were aware that his departure did not necessarily mean an end to the plantation of Connacht, simply a change in management and therefore a change in the persons who would profit. Thus, once again, we see political and personal motives being mixed, but those seeking these dual goals of political change and personal advantage weakened the entire structure upon which the plantation system rested.

THE PROTESTANT CHURCH

Whereas the contribution to the rebellion of the Catholic church was active, that of the Protestant church was passive. The Protestant clergy occupied the physical manifestations of the church, such as the churches themselves, and the Irish had to pay tithes to the Protestant clergy, which undoubtedly caused resentment. It was not what the church had done, however, which helped create the climate for rebellion; it was what it had not done. Alan Ford's recent study of this church in the pre-rebellion period emphasizes its failings. By the 1630s, he has written, the Irish Protestant church was "an elitist, anglicized church, whose commitment to a state-aided reformation remained despite, or perhaps because of, the lack of progress in spreading the reformation."[62] He generally blames these deficiencies on the link between the Protestant church and British colonization. In failing to convert the Irish, the church became content to serve the needs of the planter, therefore ensuring its inability to reach into the majority of the population who associated it with an alien and hostile culture.

The Protestants may have had more success than Ford is willing to allow. The refugee reports, or depositions, taken down after 1641 remain untapped as a source to determine the extent of Protestant penetration of the populace as a whole.[63] These show Irish resentment against Protestants, but in doing so reveal a prevalence of Irish Protestants beyond what Ford's analysis would lead us to expect. More substantive evidence lies in the report by Father Robert Nugent in 1636 that the Catholic bishop of Raphoe had pleaded to be transferred to Derry "because the diocese of Raphoe is full of Protestants and Puritans, both English and Scottish, so that between them he has scarcely enough to live on, nor can he have a single family to receive him."[64] As there were many Irish families in the diocese, this remark suggests that here, at least, the plantation religion had extended beyond the planters.

Nevertheless, it remains true that by 1641 the Protestant church had failed to put down roots among the Irish people. It was slow to set up an educational network to match that created by the Catholics, and Trinity College, which was supposed to help meet this need, remained aloof from Irish society. Yet the problems of the church did not end here. Although it was associated with plantation in the eyes of the Irish, even planter-church relations could be tense. The planter believed that the church was supposed to create a secure environment for plantation, yet the church frequently found itself in competition with the planters for resources without which it could not do its job. In turn, it looked to the state for protection, both against its rival church and against those who were supposed to be its allies. The English state, however, tended to prefer civil order to Protestant advancement and expected those in power in Ireland to follow policies accordingly.

Wentworth's religious policy was determined to a large degree by these considerations; hence his reluctance to enforce the recusancy laws. This did not mean that he intended to neglect the interests of the Church of Ireland. On the contrary, the state church constituted an essential part of the political structure he envisaged. His aim was to force Ireland into a mould so that it became another England. He took pride that by the legislation passed in 1634, "I might truly say, that Ireland was totally become English."[65] Thus he and his political ally at court, Archbishop William Laud, sought to create in Ireland a church similar to the one Laud was fashioning in England in which outward uniformity in ritual was linked to an attempt to regain for the church an influence on social policy not enjoyed since the Reformation. John Bramhall, who became bishop of Derry, was sent to Ireland by Laud as his primary agent, and with Wentworth's help, he tried to re-endow the Irish church and so re-create in Ireland the type of church he was trying to fashion in England. Loss of church property to laymen, Laud complained to Bramhall soon after the latter's arrival in Ireland, had been "bad enough" in England, "and therefore I can easily conceive Ireland has been much worse." Bramhall set about his task with diligence, and within four years the annual revenue of the state church had risen by £30,000 per annum.[66] The emphasis on endowment meant that the evangelical side of the church, as represented by Bishop William Bedell, received little encouragement. It also created a greater gulf between the planters and the church because endowment could often only take place at the expense of Protestant landowners who had procured doubtful rights over church property. At the heart of the dispute between Cork and Wentworth, for instance, lay a conflict over church property rights, and Cork's chaplains, reported one of the earl's agents, were "daily like to be devoured by the bishop [of Cloyne's] as Pharaoh's fat kine, by his lean."[67]

The emphasis upon uniformity led to an entirely different type of division within Protestant ranks. One of the most striking consequences of James VI's accession to the thrones of England and Ireland had been the addition of substantial numbers of Scots to the population of Ireland through the plantation process. Some of these Scots brought to Ireland a variety of the Protestant religion which had the same attributes as the revived Catholic one. It appealed not only to the clergy and the gentry, but to persons at all levels of society. With the Scottish settlers came committed clergy, such as Robert Blair and John Livingstone, who built up considerable popular followings, particularly in the counties of Down and Antrim.[68] Under James, such congregations had operated within the general auspices of the official church, and Andrew Knox, the Scottish bishop of Raphoe, had permitted sections of the official prayer book which offended the Scottish Calvinist mind to be left out of the ordination service. But with the rise of Laud in England and Wentworth in Ireland, such latitude could not continue, and through the efforts of

Bramhall and other bishops in Ireland, including the Scot, Henry Leslie, ministers who refused to conform suffered deposition and excommunication.[69]

This type of pressure led Livingstone to attempt twice, once in 1634 and again in 1636, to migrate to New England with some of his more devoted followers. Both expeditions failed, though the last only after the rudder of the ship carrying the non-conformists broke in mid-Atlantic forcing the vessel to return home. As a result, Livingstone had to return to Scotland, but many who thought like him remained in Ireland.[70] These Scots were not Presbyterians: indeed, Livingstone seems to have been more of a Congregationalist than anything else. Nevertheless, Laud, Wentworth, and Bramhall regarded them as a threat to the type of body politic they wished to create. When, therefore, the Scottish crisis struck, the Scots, particularly those in Ulster, which could quickly have become a beachhead for an expanding Covenanting force, appeared to be more of a threat to the state than the Irish. For this reason the Scots in Ireland have to be considered as a separate group.

THE SCOTS

There had been ties between the north of Ireland and Scotland since before the arrival of the Angles and Saxons in Britain. During the sixteenth century, Islanders and Highlanders had entered Ulster both as mercenary soldiers on the invitation of the Irish leaders and of their own accord. It was primarily these last who settled, and by the end of the century the MacDonnells dominated what today is the county of Antrim. The Tudors had tried to resist this inward flow of Scots; indeed, under Mary, the Irish parliament had passed a law declaring Scots in Ireland to be outlaws. This policy, as might be expected, changed when Ireland acquired a Scottish king. Lowland Scots, most of them Protestant, began to migrate to Ulster with official encouragement, initially to the counties of Down and Antrim, and after the implementation of the broader plantation of Ulster in 1610, to other counties in the province. The 1613–15 parliament repealed the Marian legislation, and by 1641 we find evidence of Scottish settlement beyond Ulster's borders in such counties as Wexford, Cork, Limerick, Longford, Roscommon, Mayo, and Sligo.[71]

Although no longer outlaws, and in spite of their Protestant faith, the political position of the Scots in Ireland in some respects resembled that of the Irish though they were far less numerous. As in the case of the Irish, they sat in parliament, but no Scot acquired office and, like the Irish, they lacked influence at court. It is true that

Randal MacDonnell, earl of Antrim, married the widowed duchess of Buckingham, lived at the English court during much of the 1630s, and enjoyed the friendship of the marquis of Hamilton, but Antrim was a descendant of the pre-1603 settlers and his Catholic faith led him to identify more with the Old English than with the Lowland settlers.[72] Other Catholic Scots intermarried with the Irish. Jean Gordon, Lady Strabane, turned down Sir Phelim O'Neill's proposal in 1641 but married him later, and Sir Robert Knight was somehow related by marriage to Sir Phelim's brother, Turlough.[73] There were Scottish Protestant nobles in Ireland, such as James Hamilton, first Viscount Clandeboye, and the second viscount of the Ards, but these men, influential though they may have been in their own districts, commanded little political weight in either Ireland or England.

This isolation was more marked below the social level of the gentry. Here there was little identity with London or Dublin and much with Scotland. Despite the success of the policy instituted by Laud and implemented by Bramhall and Leslie in rooting out non-conformist clergy, the Scottish people in Ireland maintained a loyalty to the faith taught to them by their persecuted ministers. Thus, when the Covenanting crisis began in Edinburgh in July 1637, it was only a matter of months before popular support for the Scottish cause began to be manifested in Ulster – in one instance by depositing customs collectors into the sea.[74] In February 1638 Bramhall complained that "anabaptistical prophetesses" were "gadding up and down" his diocese, and by April Scots who owned land in Ulster were reported to be departing for Scotland to take the Covenant.[75]

Initially, Wentworth was unable to do much to prevent this type of support, particularly when, in September, Charles I granted the Scots both a parliament and a church assembly. Nevertheless, the lord deputy began to send troops into Ulster in October, and by January 1639 he had begun to declare his determination to force the Scots in Ireland to conform or return to Scotland. This attitude led to what has become known as the Black Oath, according to which Scots in Ireland were to abjure the Covenant. Once Charles had signed the Treaty of Berwick in June 1639 with his Scottish subjects, however, it became extremely hard to impose this oath. A campaign of civil disobedience developed, in many instances taking the form of flight to Scotland, no doubt to the satisfaction of the deputy, but to the consternation of landlords who were left without tenants just before the harvest.[76]

It is striking that resistance was passive rather than violent, a reflection of the absence of the type of leadership enjoyed by the Covenanters in Scotland and by the Irish in 1641. A man like

Clandeboye may have sympathized with his tenants, but he was in no position to flout the government, and Bramhall and Leslie had effectively purged the clergy of those who could supply Covenanting leadership. The only minister recorded to have supplied this type of leadership was blind. Yet, if Wentworth had succeeded in keeping the Scottish threat at bay, he had only reinforced the Ulster-Scottish sense of separateness from the rest of the country.

By the following year Sir Thomas had been able to call the Irish parliament at which Eustace delivered his speech glorifying the peace that Ireland had enjoyed for a generation. That peace was first shattered, not in Ireland but in Scotland, and it is vital to recognize the Scottish component in the crisis. The outbreak of the Scottish war wrought a fundamental change in Wentworth's position. He had to raise an army, which created financial pressure and which in turn forced him to accommodate men like Cork and Clanricard. The blend of fragmentation and cohesion that we have observed within the Irish body politic did not inevitably mean that further fragmentation would take the form of civil war, but the stress imposed by the conflict in Scotland and its repercussions in England placed additional, and ultimately unbearable, stress upon a vulnerable system. Some of that stress arose from economic disruption. In Ireland's economy we find a mixture of positive and negative features, but here too the negative became predominant to a large extent as a consequence of the Scottish challenge to Charles I.

CHAPTER ONE

Ireland before
the Rebellion

Just as Maurice Eustace could extol political peace before the rebellion broke out, many of those who lived through it extolled their memory of Ireland's economy before 1641 as they recollected the flourishing, harmonious, and prosperous community which had been shattered by the war. This impression of good times crossed both religious and cultural divisions. It is not surprising to find Sir William Parsons, given his office as master of the court of wards and his opinions on the English empire, remarking that before the war the kingdom had "grown in wealth and substance."[1] He had grown likewise. Another Protestant, albeit anonymous, painted an even more glowing picture as he looked back during the interregnum through nostalgic royalist eyes to the pre-war past:

in this blessed condition of peace and security the English and Irish, the Protestants and Roman Catholics lived mingled together ... [T]he wealth of the kingdom was exceedingly increased by the importation of great store of money [and] wonderful increase of trade, several new and profitable manufactures were introduced ... and the land [was] generally improved by applying to it several new sorts of good husbandry which that people had been utterly unacquainted with.[2]

Both these writers, Parsons explicitly and the anonymous royalist implicitly, ascribed the prosperity to plantation. Here we might expect to find the Old English and Catholic Richard Bellings holding a different view as the Old English had seldom benefited from plantation and had sometimes been threatened by it. Yet his words echo those of the Protestants:

The colonies (setting aside their different tenets in matters of religion,) were as perfectly incorporated, and as firmly knit together, as frequent marriages, daily ties of hospitality, and the mutual bond between lord and tenant could unite any people ... The land, by the blessing of peace ... was so well inhabited, and so much improved, that farms in all parts of the kingdom were set at a marvellous increase of rent, and yet the tenants grew rich by holding them at those rates, especially in the government of the earl of Strafford, who had it in his care.[3]

The *Aphorismical Discovery*, a contemporary pamphlet which represented the native Irish point of view, extolled neither plantation nor Strafford, but did accept that in 1641 Ireland was "one of the best islands in Europe [and] stood in fairer terms of happiness and prosperity than ever it had done these 500 years past."[4] Nor were these opinions confined to the gentry. William Skelton, an English brewer who lived in Armagh, commented soon after the rebellion began that the English and the Irish had been living peacefully together.[5]

These idyllic images may be contrasted with the picture portrayed by Ireland's members of parliament just a year before the rebellion broke out. Again, Catholics and Protestants, Irish, Old English, and planters spoke in unison as the Commons issued its Remonstrance in November 1640 protesting against the four subsidies extracted by Strafford to finance the new army which had been raised to suppress the Scottish Covenanters. After listing the various sums of money demanded by the state since Falkland's deputyship, the Commons complained of "extreme and universal poverty," as well as a "general and apparent decay of trade," and concluded that "the gentry, merchants and other his majesty's subjects are of late by the grievances and pressures aforesaid ... very near to ruin and destruction."[6] Similar sentiments appear in the Schedule of Grievances drawn up in February 1641 by the Irish Lords, which then forwarded them to England for redress.[7] The Remonstrance and the Grievances were intended to relieve men of taxes and the complaints they contain cannot therefore be accepted at face value, but they cannot be dismissed entirely.

There is little in the secondary literature to help reconcile these contrasting views. H.F. Kearney stresses the pastoral nature of the Irish economy. He plots the customs records and describes the increase in customs receipts during the 1630s as "remarkable," but he ascribes this more to Strafford's efficiency in collecting them than to any improvement in the economy, and he is at pains to show that, when there is evidence of an increase in production, as in the case of wool, it reflected more England's economic interest than a growth in Irish prosperity. He does allow that some of the increase in customs receipts must be credited "to forces which were beyond the deputy's control," but he does not tell us what these forces were.[8] Aidan Clarke also emphasizes Ireland's pastoral economic base, and, like Kearney, he stresses the elimination of smuggling in explaining the increase in wool exports. He accepts that the period before the rebellion was one of "recovery and expansion" but does not believe that plantation had anything to do with this recovery while nonetheless remarking that what gains were obtained were at the cost of the "conquered community."[9]

Nicholas Canny and Michael MacCarthy-Morrogh give a much more positive picture of the effects of plantation.[10] Canny argues that through plantation new agricultural techniques were introduced which affected the efficiency of the industry well beyond the planted areas, though his perception of this positive effect is limited to Munster. Ulster remained backward, he thinks, because those British who settled there possessed skills not much in advance of the Irish inhabitants. Philip Robinson sees the northern plantation in more complex terms. He accepts that there was some continuity between the pre-plantation society and that which followed it but also cites much evidence pointing to the introduction of improved techniques and changed conditions.[11] Raymond Gillespie is one of those who disputes Canny's argument about the failure of the Ulster planters to change the economy of the province, yet he agrees with Clarke that whatever change was wrought did not benefit the Irish. Indeed, he explains the rebellion primarily in terms of economic grievances.[12] Such opinions, of course, are not necessarily mutually exclusive, but they point to the need for some overall picture of the Irish economy before the rebellion broke out.

POPULATION

The most authoritative modern assessment concludes that Ireland's population rose considerably after 1603 and that, by 1641, it supported 2.1 million people.[13] This estimate is obtained by working backwards from fairly reliable eighteenth-century demographic data, though such a technique faces the formidable problem of estimating from very little evidence the effects on population of the decade of upheaval that followed the outbreak of the rebellion. The duke of Ormond, looking back after the Restoration and using Sir William Petty's figures, reached the more conservative conclusion of a population of between 1.2 and 2 million. We should not dismiss lightly the opinion of a man whose knowledge of Ireland derived from a lifetime (on and off) of running it, but more interesting than his assessment of the total population was Ormond's estimate that in

1641 Catholics outnumbered Protestants fifteen to one, thus giving us a figure of between 80,000 and 125,000 Protestants.[14] This accords fairly well with what we know about emigration to Ireland up to 1641, almost all of which was Protestant.

The most recent study of the plantation of Munster suggests an immigrant population by 1641 of approximately 22,000 connected with this scheme.[15] Contemporary estimates of the Scottish population of Ulster ranged from 40,000 men to 150,000 "of that nation." These estimates are far too high as the Scottish population of that province in 1630 amounted to approximately 8,000 males. Yet we must also recognize that considerable emigration from Scotland occurred during the decade after 1630 and that there seems to have been considerable natural increase among the Scots in the province.[16] To the figure for the Scots must be added the significant English population of the area. It seems, therefore, not unreasonable to set the total British population of Ulster in 1641 at about 40,000 to 45,000 adults.[17] Canny has noted that native as well as planter land-lords settled English tenants on their land,[18] including, it may be remarked, the leader of the Ulster rising, Sir Phelim O'Neill. There were, therefore, pockets of British (mainly English) settlements in areas not officially designated for plantation.[19] If, within such areas, within officially planted counties outside Ulster and Munster (such as Laois, Offaly, Longford, and Wexford), and within the towns, there were at least an additional 25,000 British adults, we reach a figure that falls within the bracket suggested by Ormond.

Most of the Irish population lived in rural conditions, as did most of all populations in early modern Europe. Seventeenth-century maps of Ireland show that towns tended to be concentrated in the southern half of the country, with the main ones, save for Kilkenny, located on the coast. Dublin had a larger population (by 1641 approximately 20,000 inhabitants and a fourfold increase since 1600) than any city in England with the exception of London and therefore was a very large urban centre by contemporary standards. Other towns came nowhere near to Dublin's size or importance. Cork fol-lowed with a population of about 5,500, then Limerick with 3,500. Youghal had a population of 1,600 persons, about half of whom were New English, and by 1641 there were about 2,300 persons, mostly New English, in Bandon, which had hardly existed in 1600. These figures may be contrasted with the largest centre in the north, Londonderry, whose population in 1641 numbered about 1,000 adults.[20] If the northern towns were small, twenty-five new boroughs, including Belfast, were incorporated from 1603 to 1629, thus laying the foundation for urban development later in the century.[21]

REVENUE AND TRADE

Growth in population without subsequent famine and rapid urban development point to a prosperous economy, and most of the evidence reinforces this impression. It is striking, for instance, that whereas the English treasury had to supplement the Irish government's income by £48,000 a year between 1611 and 1613, by 1619–23, the annual supplement had been reduced to about £3,333, and from then onwards Ireland was self-supporting to 1640. Indeed, during the 1630s, money flowed in the reverse direction; in 1638, £10,441 passed from the Irish treasury to England, and at his trial Strafford boasted that by 1639 he was able to claim a surplus in the Irish treasury of £100,000, a boast subsequently confirmed by the lords justices. In 1640 £50,000 had to be sent from England to help to levy and equip the new army, but it was clearly intended that this should be repaid once the four subsidies granted by the Irish parliament in the spring of 1640 had been collected.[22]

As noted, Kearney described the increases in customs revenue during Strafford's government as "remarkable." Figure 1 shows these revenues for three periods: 1619–20 to 1631–32, 1632–33 to 1636–37 and 1637–38 to 1640–41. The three periods cannot be compared directly because of changes in the rates in 1632 and 1637, but trends within the periods may be compared. Kearney explained the post-1632 increase primarily in terms of growing efficiency in collection. This may have been one variable, particularly in 1636, though we may note that George Monck undertook a survey of the Ulster ports in 1637 and the total customs revenue declined after that year. Thus administrative attention did not necessarily lead to increased yield. If greater efficiency was a factor, it was certainly not the only one at work, as it does not, by itself, explain the changes in the graph curves. The first period, for instance, shows rises and dips, the latter occurring during the bad harvest years of 1621 to 1623 and the period of the Spanish war – 1626–29. These variations reflect known conditions of trade, not variations in collection efficiency. Similarly, while Strafford's harsh government may account for some of the improvements after 1632, increased efficiency alone does not explain the variations in the curves, which in fact reflect real increases and decreases in trade.[23]

This interpretation of the evidence does not have to rely on deduction alone. Sir George Radcliffe, who was responsible for the collection of customs and might have been expected to take credit for any increased efficiency in collection, did not make this claim when explaining to Wentworth the rise in customs revenue in 1634. He

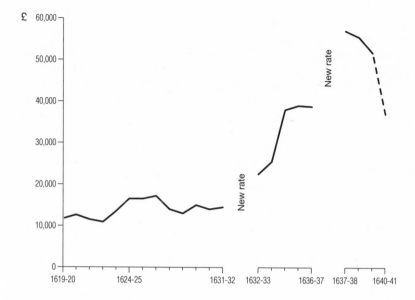

Figure 1   Revenue from Irish customs, 1619–20 through 1640–41 (to nearest £100). SOURCES: Treadwell, "Irish Financial Reform," 404; SCL, Wentworth Woodhouse MSS 24–5: no. 174; PRO, SP 63/258: 260. Also Gillespie, *Transformation of the Irish Economy*, 62.

gave three reasons: first, the session of parliament in Dublin during 1634, which had increased consumption of imports; second, the fact that the pilchard fishery was "more plentiful that year than any other within the memory of man"; and third, the "security of the merchants from piracy," which ensured that "they lost little or nothing all that year."[24] Government efficiency, therefore, was a factor, but as an agent in stopping loss of goods not as an agent of collection. Nor were these customs revenues primarily derived from import duties. In 1634 and again in 1641 the value of Ireland's exports exceeded that of its imports – in the latter year, by a factor of two.[25]

Once it has been established that the increments in the customs revenues represented a real increase in trade, we may look at specific commodities, and again the increases in export volume were substantial over time. The number of packs of linen yarn rose from 627 in 1621–22 to an average of 1,257 for the years 1635–36 to 1639–40. Wool exports rose from 57,889 great stones in 1632 to a peak of 185,857 great stones in 1637. In 1621–22, 4,000 cows and oxen left Ireland; by 1640–41 the figure had risen to 46,000. At a more local level, we see a rise in horse exports from the Ards peninsula from

590 in 1621–22 to 1,600 in 1635 and to 2,484 two years later. There were, it is true, declines in some commodities, for instance hides, and in another case exports of linen yarn dropped from 1307 packs to 823 when an attempt by Wentworth to improve quality proved disastrous. This attempt failed, in part, as the report on the problem revealed, because the labour force engaged in spinning was unable to adapt to technical innovation. Once the experiment was halted, however, linen yarn exports recovered to an all-time high.[26]

Most of this trade was, as Kearney and Clarke stress, derived from a pastoral economy. But if we compare the list of goods exported in 1621–22 with that of 1640–41, we find the number of commodities had more than doubled (from nineteen to fifty-five) and by the latter date included such items as small amounts of brass, iron, rapeseed oil, and "train oil" along with other manufactured items. It is just possible that, if we had similar figures for 1638, the variety of products exported might be even more impressive because this year marked the high point of trade growth, 1640–41 being, comparatively, a disastrous year. Indeed, the single most important feature of Figure 1 is that it shows that there was a substantial decline in trade from the onset of the Scottish crisis to 1641.

THE DISTRIBUTION OF WEALTH

The next challenge is to try to determine the way in which this new prosperity – up to 1638 – was distributed within the country. This issue may be approached from two levels. First, we may look at the share of the trade enjoyed by particular towns at different times. This provides some sense of the geographic distribution of the benefits of the trade increase. Second, we can examine the evidence there is about how people were living at the local level. This method is obviously more impressionistic than the first one because we are subject to the accidents of record survival and the information is not sufficiently plentiful to be sure that it is representative of more than a small element of the population. Yet because the evidence comes in a variety of forms, these deficiencies are, to some extent, diminished, if not eliminated.

Table 1 shows the average percentage of customs collected at nine of the more important ports during four different blocks of years, along with similar figures by province. The use of blocks of years is adopted partly because this is the way the information for 1634–40 has come down to us and partly because such averaging diminishes the impact of events that had a strong effect on only one year. That

Table 1
Total Irish Customs Revenue for Five Periods, 1619–40 (%)

	1619–24	1624–28	1628–32	1632–33[a]	1634–40
Ports					
Dublin	23.0	31.9	32.7	27.2	41.0
Drogheda	10.0	6.0	6.6	6.3	3.0
Waterford	12.0	8.0	6.4	7.5	7.0
Youghal	6.0	11.7	10.1	8.4	5.0
Cork	7.0	6.3	8.2	7.8	10.0
Limerick	6.0	5.6	7.1	7.2	5.0
Galway	9.0	4.7	6.2	6.1	7.0
Derry	n.a.	n.a.	n.a.	6.3	3.0
Carrickfergus	2.0	2.5	2.7	3.4	3.0
Provinces					
Connacht	13.0	5.3	6.8	6.7	8.0
Leinster	41.0	42.0	44.0	36.8	47.0
Munster	38.0[b]	44.0	40.8	40.9	33.8
Ulster (less Derry & Coleraine)	8.0	8.5	8.2	9.9	4.6
Ulster (with Derry & Coleraine)	n.a.	n.a.	n.a.	15.7	7.6

Sources: Treadwell, "Irish Financial Reform," 404; scl, Wentwork Woodhouse mss 24–5: no. 174; "Comparing ... the duty for six years ... from the several ports of Ireland ..." pro, sp 63/276: 30. This last is not dated, but it could refer to no period other than 1634–40.

[a] This year, 1632–33, is treated separately because this was the year the new rates took effect. Percentages from this date onwards include Derry's customs in the total.

[b] In 1619–24 an entry called "western ports" accounted for 6 per cent of the total. This has been divided equally among Munster, Connacht, and Ulster.

there could be wide variation from year to year is shown by comparing the figures for 1632–33 with those before this date and later.

It will be evident that some quite striking changes took place in the relative positions of particular towns over the period. Cork, for instance, began with a slightly greater share of the customs than Youghal, lost its lead, and then regained and surpassed its earlier position. Waterford lost a strong lead over all other ports save Dublin, but the most striking feature of the table is the dominance, and increasing dominance, of Dublin. This is certainly in accord with what we know about the growth of Dublin's population. The figures do not necessarily reflect an increase in the prosperity of the capital at the expense of the outlying areas because a drop in the share of the market brings little suffering if the market is expanding sufficiently rapidly to permit all to increase their volume of business, if unequally. Nevertheless, while the share of customs declined in all provinces save Leinster, in Ulster the decline was more marked than elsewhere. This trend finds an echo in the figures for Drogheda which drew much of its business from the northern province despite its location in Leinster. What was happening in Ulster can be explained to some extent by what happened at Derry, yet, by itself, this is not an adequate explanation. If we exclude Derry and Cole- raine from the picture, Ulster's share of customs revenues still dropped. Clearly, Ulster's economy and any possible links between it and the outbreak of the rebellion warrant examination.

When we look at the less systematic data, we find that prosperity was by no means confined to Dublin, or to Leinster, or to the colo- nists. Canny, by using the post-rebellion depositions, has demon- strated the considerable investments in agricultural improvements in Munster which followed, but were not confined to, the plantation enterprise.[27] MacCarthy-Morrogh has also remarked on the estab- lishment of orchards and gardens amongst "all communities" in Mun- ster, on the presence of a municipal tennis court at Cork, and on the importation of books, including those for children.[28] Similarly, the plantation in Ulster led to many improvements such as windmills, lime kilns, more efficient water mills, improved ploughs, improved livestock, and orchards, not to mention many buildings, even if some planters adopted Irish techniques such as ploughing by the tail.[29] The royal silver mines at Tipperary and the presence of nearly forty iron works in Ireland by 1640 (thirteen in Ulster, fifteen in Munster, and most of them started in the seventeenth century) are other indications that new means of production were being established in many parts of the country.[30]

There are relatively few surviving pre-1641 estate records, but there are three sets of such data, one from the south, one from mid- Ireland, and one from the north, which, when compared, reveal a similar pattern of economic conditions. The correspondence of the earl of Cork from 1634 to 1641 shows that from 1639 his estate began to face increasing economic difficulties. At the beginning of 1639 a note by the earl on one of the letters sent to him by his agent, John Walley, reveals his acquisitive optimism. He was about to pur- chase another £20,000 worth of land and required another £5,000 for other purposes. To raise this money, his agent was instructed to use his "utmost endeavours to gather in and collect all my debts, rents and arrears, without sparing any man." These instructions were to extend even to his relative, John Boyle, "for I must prefer my own good before any man's particular favour in so unjust detention of their rents."[31] In short, though rents might not be paid from time to

time, the blame lay with the improvidence of particular men, and
non-payment was not the result of any general conditions.

The first hint of a changed situation came in September of the
same year when Walley apologized for "so many arrears." For these
he blamed not only the backwardness of the harvest, caused by the
"foulness of the weather," but also the shortage of money, an issue
that appeared repeatedly in subsequent correspondence. A year later
the earl was informed of "much discontent" among the people and
of a fear of the effects of the taxation approved by parliament, and
in April 1641 Walley informed his employer that "I did never hear
the like complaining of all men generally for the want of money, or
how to pay their rents as now, when the commodities they have of
corn and cattle can not be sold except at such under rates as will
undo all farmers."[32] The implication is that the want of money was a
consequence of a drop in demand, which in turn led to a decline in
prices.

Walley's view that there were general economic difficulties is supported by official opinion. In June the lords justices reported to Sir
Henry Vane, Charles's secretary, that there was a "universal cry of
poverty and extreme want," but it needs to be added that the subsidies
cannot be held responsible for this situation because, as we shall see,
little of the money granted by parliament was, in fact, collected. By
15 October 1640 half of the first subsidy was still not collected, though
it had been due by 1 June, and this was the only subsidy that came
close to raising the revenue intended.[33] The problem arose more
because of the general decline of the economy, a trend already detected
in the customs records, which had reduced demand dramatically.

The records of the estate of William Parsons, a nephew of the lord
justice, at Birr, County Offaly, give the same impression of economic
decline, starting in 1638, though in a different way from the records
of the earl of Cork. For this estate we have rent records which show
when the rent was paid and when it was not. Table 2 sets out the
number of rents that were unpaid by each half-year (rents were
collected at Easter and Michaelmas). It is evident that unpaid rents
began to pose a problem during the second half of 1638, and by the
autumn of 1640, not only had the number of unpaid rents risen to
a peak, but the number of tenants had declined significantly. Moreover, those who failed to pay rent were those who held small plots of
land, the rent for which was seldom more than £1.10.0 for half a
year. It looks, therefore, as though the poorer tenants were leaving
the land.

The situation at Birr may be compared with that on the Balfour
estate in Fermanagh. What is striking here is the increase in rents

Table 2
Unpaid Rents at Birr, 1637–40
(Easter and Michaelmas)

Year	Entries	Tenants	Unpaid	Yearly unpaid
1637	82	68	5	
1637	81	68	5	10
1638	75	58	2	
1638	78	66	11	13
1639	78	63	14	
1639	76	62	18	32
1640	75	62	10	
1640	69	52	20	30

Source: BIRR Castle, Rosse MSS A/4.

during the 1630s. The Balfour records do not permit us to follow the story up to 1640, but the prosperity during the earlier period is evident: the population increased, as did rents and landlord income, and the land became more productive.[34] This information does not coincide with the impression derived from the trade records of Ulster's slow growth relative to the rest of the country, but we must bear in mind that the Balfour data do not record the situation after the Scottish crisis had begun. What the 1634–40 figures in Table 1 may well be reflecting is that Ulster was more heavily affected by the Anglo-Scottish confrontation than other parts of Ireland. This might be expected from Ulster's strong trade links with Scotland, and we know that in 1640 the archbishop of Armagh could not collect his rents because of the general depression. Thus, the Ulster situation also tends to support the view that there was general prosperity up to 1638 and serious economic decline from that date to the outbreak of the rebellion.[35]

So far, because there are more records available for the planters than for either the Irish or the Old English, the discussion about the pre-rebellion economy at the local level has had to draw mainly upon their experience. The depositions, for instance, which contain many inventories of goods lost, have been used effectively in determining the general wealth of the New English, even if these documents provide only self-assessments of losses. But there are virtually no such inventories for the Irish or the Old English. It may be assumed that these other groups both benefited to some degree in good times and suffered in bad, as each of them still controlled approximately one-third of the land in Ireland and some of the profits of the agricultural exports must have accrued to them.[36] It is surely significant that 107 new markets were established in Munster during the early seventeenth century, and these markets must have served more than the planter community.[37]

We may, however, go beyond this speculation as there is some direct evidence that at least one Irish noble was able to develop his estate on the same lines as the planters. A detailed inventory of the estate of Henry O'Brien, earl of Thomond, was compiled in 1639 at the time of his death, and because this was done by four men who were not members of his family it is more reliable than the inventories found in the depositions. It is true that O'Brien was unusual in that he was a Protestant and he had adopted more English ways than his religion in that he served as godfather to two of the earl of Cork's children, but with his home at Bunratty Castle and his forebears substantially of Celtic origin nobody could accuse him of being New English.

The total value of O'Brien's movable goods, apart from his clothes, which included twelve suits, amounted to £2,139.3.4, in addition to which he left £1,153.6.3 (we are not told of any debts). The castle contained items of silver, mainly produced in Dublin, and therefore showing that silversmiths were at work there, but also including a silver basin worth £294 with the "London touch." The dining room was hung with eleven pieces of tapestry "which have lost their colour," and there was a Turkish table carpet, also somewhat the worse for wear. Some of the rest of the furniture was described as Spanish or Portuguese, and one of the bedrooms contained an "Arras curtain, a chimney piece of tapestry," and two "Turkey work foot carpets." The furniture of the main hall included a shuffleboard table, a "drawing table," four rough-hewn benches, and several old muskets. Other items of interest were a "new red cloth bed trimmed with yellow silk," two long "holland" towels "for the sewer," and 200 books, surely an impressive number, but also a tantalizing entry as the inventory takers did not list the titles.[38]

The contents of the outbuildings and the fields surrounding the castle tell us a considerable amount about the type of agriculture practised on the earl's estate. In 1638 the earl's flock had produced 182 stone of wool from 351 hoggets and wethers and 449 breeding ewes. The breeding flock, served by 22 rams, had produced 253 lambs that year, or a ratio of 1.77 per ewe, an indication of successful flock management for the seventeenth century, given that twentieth-century expectations for a flock of that size would not be much greater. The estate also supported 127 horses of various sorts, including 8 coach horses and 5 wagon horses. The only piece of machinery mentioned was the coach, but the presence of the wagon horses and 23 draft oxen implies the existence of a considerable amount of agricultural equipment. Among the cattle were 35 milk cows and we may assume most of the cattle were of the improved English variety as 36 were described specifically as "Irish beeves" and valued below the rest. There was no mention of grain, possibly because the inventory was compiled in August, but there must have been some grain production to judge by the number of draft animals on the estate.[39]

Thomond's possessions may look modest by comparison with those of Scottish peers as a whole, the average value of whose inventories between 1610 and 1637 was £10,309, and he was poor by the side of the earl of Cork who had an income of £18,250 a year, but Cork was the richest man in Ireland, and Thomond's inventory compares favourably with that of the Scottish planter, the earl of Abercorn, whose movable assets were valued at his death in 1617 at £2,679 sterling.[40] For all the modesty of the total, the inventory leaves the impression of a flourishing enterprise.

The same impression is left by the inventory of an Old English gentleman, Christopher Dowdall, of County Louth. His total inventory was valued at only £786.16.8, but his livestock included 19 labouring oxen, 20 plough horses, and 829 "big ewes." Another Old English landowner, Robert Nugent of Westmeath, was said to have an income of £1,500 a year, and we may also observe that the Old English (but Protestant) earl of Ormond had introduced "several kinds of large cattle" onto his estate as well as English tenants. Yet we should not draw the conclusion that only Protestants could benefit from the good times. During the pre-rebellion period some of the Old English gentry were expanding their estates beyond the Pale. The extent of their ownership of profitable land in the counties of Sligo and Roscommon, for instance, rose from virtually nothing in 1600 to about 20 per cent in 1641. Twelve of twenty-seven Catholic bishops came from families with estates of 2,000 acres or more. By 1641, Richard Walsh, the Catholic archbishop of Cashel, had established a property endowment that was raising 10 per cent a year and which was expected to be able to endow a college to teach fifteen students in a few years. By the same date a convent had been built at Drogheda with eighty windows on each side. Building on this scale suggests a considerable cash surplus among Catholics.[41]

It is, of course, very hard to determine what conditions were like for those below the social level of landlord and tenant among the Irish and Old English. Some Irish undoubtedly found employment on planter estates, and in the south there seems to have been no pay discrimination between English and Irish servants. On the Castle-warning estate, for instance, Nicholas Gorton (presumably British) received £6.13.4 a year as a weeder and Murrogh Doole, a labourer, £7.0.0, though it may be significant that all employees who received their "diet" and a wage had English names. Women, interestingly, seem to have received equal pay to men when doing similar work.[42] It is evident, nonetheless, that some of those who could not find employment of this sort led a precarious existence. There was a report in 1638 by Alan Cooke, vice-admiral of Leinster, of "great complaint made by fishermen in this kingdom" that "they are not able to live." In the summertime, when the herring and salmon fishing was done, "the gentry and the merchants take the trade out of the fishermen's hands" as they send boats to sea "where they employ cobblers, weavers and ploughmen."[43] We may observe here that as this was happening in Leinster, where there was little plantation, the landlords and merchants who were benefiting at the expense of the fishermen were probably Old English or Irish gentry and that if the fishermen suffered, the cobblers, weavers, and ploughmen were able to supplement their income. This comment also modifies the impression created by other sources that foreigners alone exploited the Irish fisheries.[44]

A second example which covers a general group concerns the spinners who suffered from Sir Thomas Wentworth's attempts to improve the quality of the linen yarn produced in Ireland. The old method involved knotting the yarn. The new one eliminated the knots but required numbering the threads and dividing them "into hundreds." Difficulty arose in changing from the old method to the new because the yarn was "made and winded up by thousands of old women ... that can hardly be taught to number their fingers." There was also in this case abuse by the officials in charge of introducing the new methods who, however well the yarn was made, seized it and "converted" it "into wine or ale" in front of those who made it. As a result, many women "are now starving that were able to live." Here we gain an insight into an important source of income among older women, most of whom must have been Irish; as we have seen, the experiment was halted and exports rose to a new high the following year. It may also be remarked that we know of these two abuses because government officials were concerned about an economic situation that affected the poor.[45]

THE ANGLO-SCOTTISH CRISIS AND ULSTER

Both the trade and estate records support the view of a flourishing economy till 1638, at which time an economic downturn began and continued into 1641. The poor conditions arose in part because of bad weather, but probably a more decisive factor in bringing about the situation was the growing confrontation between Charles and his Scottish subjects. Certainly, it was Wentworth's opinion that this conflict contributed to the decline in Irish trade. In May 1639 he wrote to the marquis of Hamilton to say: "These troubles have already a great operation upon the trade of this kingdom; so as I fear his Majesty's customs will fall very much this year."[46] The same opinion was expressed the next year by Christopher Lowther, who was engaged in shipping iron ore from England for manufacture into iron in Ireland. Conducting business, he remarked, was difficult because "these Scotch wars hindereth us in all things."[47]

If the strife with Scotland adversely affected Ireland's trade as a whole, it was likely, given Ulster's links with Scotland, to affect that province the most. The dramatic drop in Ulster's share of customs revenues between 1632–33 and the 1634–40 period would seem to support this conclusion. Raymond Gillespie's study of eastern Ulster concludes that the economic problems in the province began in 1635 and are reflected in the decline in customs revenues from that year.[48] Although there was a drop in that year, the serious decline began only in 1638–39. If we also bear in mind the situation in Fermanagh on the Balfour estate, and the rapid rise in the export of horses from the Ards up to 1638, more definitive proof of a major downturn before the Scottish troubles began has to be supplied before it can be accepted. Certainly, when George Monck visited Ulster in 1637 to examine the collection of customs at the various ports, the impression he left was not one of an economy in trouble.

Monck had been in Ulster at an earlier (unspecified) date and was able to compare what he found in 1637 with what he had known before. His overall opinion was that he was "very glad to see such store of shipping in the Derry and the good increase of boats and barques in all the ports by the way," and he observed that cattle were being driven from the hinterland to the ports on the east coast, and that quantities of oats were being cultivated in the Ards peninsula. It is true that he found much smuggling, and he reported a general laxness in the collection of customs, but such evasion is itself an indication of the existence of profitable commerce and suggests that Ulster may have enjoyed a higher proportion of the country's trade at this time than the customs records reflect. Monck provided half-year customs returns for some ports; if we double his figure and compare the result with the full-year returns for 1632–33, we find that, in spite of the evasion, the returns had increased at Bangor by 2.2 per cent, at Strangford by 1.6 per cent, at Donaghadee by 1 per cent, at Carrickfergus by 3.4 per cent, and at Derry by 6.3 per cent. His figures also make it clear that the province enjoyed a favourable balance of trade, as did the country as a whole.[49] Monck's account, therefore, strengthens the impression of prosperity up to 1638 in Ulster. It also reinforces the impression that the decline in Ulster's share of customs revenues from 1634 to 1640 arose from a very substantial decline from 1638 onwards.

There is no doubt that the economic situation in Ulster deteriorated dramatically from 1638. Bad harvests certainly contributed to these poor conditions, but the economic effects of the developing political crisis in Scotland and England are as well documented as they were disastrous.[50] As well, Ulster quickly began to lose population. As early as January 1639, the earl of Antrim told his friend, Hamilton, that those in Ulster who sympathized with the Covenanters "flocks [sic] over daily to them fearing the high commission court here." Wentworth's decision later that year to impose on Scottish residents of Ireland an oath dissociating themselves from the Covenant only increased the exodus. Lord Conway's agent in Antrim reported in July that, because of the oath, Scots were leaving and rents would be late, and Edward Chichester told Wentworth the same thing the following month. The "great numbers" leaving for Scotland took with them "their horses, cows, sheep and what else they have, and leave their corn standing in the ground." By December, land in Antrim had declined in value by 50 per cent. In 1640 there was a "hard spring," and the district had to bear an additional burden in that Wentworth stationed the new army in Ulster to be ready to attack the Covenanters on their western flank, and the army had to be quartered and supplied by the population of the area well into 1641 after a poor harvest the previous year.[51]

These successive blows to Ulster's economy quickly began to have an impact on the stability of its society. Wentworth reported to Sir Henry Vane in June 1639 that there had been disorder in numerous counties, including Donegal, the previous winter.[52] In April 1640 Bishop Bramhall, writing from County Tyrone, warned that "all places and all sorts of men" were "full of discontents and complaints."[53] Small wonder that by 1641 towns such as Derry, with an adult population of 1,000, were beginning to complain that the presence of 500 soldiers had increased the price of food to ruinous levels.[54] In the spring of 1641 there were outbreaks of social unrest in the Protestant areas of Down and Antrim, motivated partly by resentment against the official form of Protestantism, but also by economic distress. Just two months before the rebellion began the breakdown in order had reached the point that "forcible entry" had become so common that "it is questionable whether security lie in the law or outrage."[55]

We gain some additional sense of discontent within the British tenant community in Ulster through the statement made by a Henry Bell in 1640. Bell was almost certainly a Scottish clergyman. He looked back to James's reign as a sort of Golden Age. Since James's death, he complained, "spiritual and temporal government for this fifteen years space waxeth worse and worse." Many of his objections were directed against the advances made by the Catholic church and the deficiencies of the Protestant one. The wives and children of the Protestant ministers, he protested, attended mass. There was much pluralism, and the clergy as a whole had little education. "Popish schools," meanwhile, were "everywhere kept" to "infect children with their dregs." In particular, he scorned the Protestant bishops who, he alleged, married their children to Catholics and when absent from their sees appointed "cruel men" as their agents. Such complaints have direct bearing on the outbreak of the rising because the Irish perceived such Protestant demands for reform as threatening, but Bell's commentary extended beyond religious issues into the secular world common to Irish and British tenants. Innocents, he protested, were found guilty by the courts while the guilty went free; just jurors went to jail; interest rates of over 15 per cent were common; customs duties were too high; and, finally, blending secular with religious grievance, tenants were exploited by their landlords and feared the Catholics, who, "if occasion would serve would join hand in hand to massacre your majesty's faithful subjects."[56]

We possess no similar description of the pre-rebellion attitudes of Irish tenants, but as will be shown in a later chapter dealing with the period immediately after the rebellion had begun, we may assume that they resembled a mirror image of Bell's description of British tenant mentality in that their fear of the British equalled the British fear of them. Moreover, the economic pressures upon them would have been the same if not greater. Bell's complaint serves to balance the image of harmony among tenants of different extraction left to us by writers such as Richard Bellings, but it may be significant that Bell's experience derived from Ulster.

If some Irish outside Ulster had benefited from the period of prosperity, they do not seem to have been as fortunate within it. The reasons for this are complex. It must first be accepted that Ulster's economy differed from those of Munster and Leinster because of its geographical position. The growing season was shorter by two or three weeks as military commanders interested in fodder for horses during campaigns were well aware. This certainly affected the type of agriculture practised. Except for some areas in the south of the province, oats rather than wheat, which requires more light to ripen, had to be cultivated.[57] In pre-plantation Ulster, stress had been placed on livestock raising, and this emphasis continued after the British settlement, though quantities of oats do seem to have been cultivated and exported. What the settlement changed was not the nature of the product of the land so much as the quantity produced and the use to which it was put. Whereas the economy of Ulster before plantation was essentially a pre-market one geared towards self-sufficiency, what emerged after the plantation was closer to a market economy in which surpluses were produced and exported and the profits so derived reinvested in capital accretion either in the form of land purchases, new building, or the application of new technology in the form of improved livestock, iron works, or an innovation such as the planting of orchards. To a very large extent these exports consisted of livestock or products derived from livestock.[58]

Recently it has been stressed that the plantation created numerous Irish as well as English and Scottish landowners. The Irish received one-fifth more land than either the Scots or the English, and, indeed, many of those who led the rebellion in 1641 were beneficiaries of the redistribution of land imposed by England between 1603 and 1610. Moreover, we have been warned against "any easy identification of religious affiliation with the significant redistribution of land which occurred in seventeenth-century Ireland."[59]

It has also been argued that many of the Irish landowners had difficulty in adjusting to the new economic conditions. There is considerable evidence to support this contention. The earl of Antrim, who had an income of £6,000 a year in 1639, was £50,000 in debt. Sir Phelim O'Neill, one of the leaders of the insurrection was in debt, as was Lord Maguire, another leader. Sir Henry O'Neill and Hugh Magennis, Viscount Iveagh, both prominent Irish landowners in Ulster who died just before the rebellion, were also in debt.[60] Yet we must be extremely cautious about assuming a causation between indebtedness, Irish extraction, and rebellion. Some planters were in debt, including the earl of Cork, and Irish nobles like the earl of Clanricard and the earl of Barrymore, who did not rebel, were also in debt. Moreover, some of those of pre-plantation stock were among the modernizers. Antrim tried to introduce improvements on his estate. Sir Phelim O'Neill not only introduced British tenants onto his land because he could expect higher rents from them, but in so doing evicted Irish ones – a policy which can hardly have improved Irish-British relations at the tenant level.[61]

Like the women displaced from employment by Wentworth's attempt to improve spinning techniques, the Irish tenants found change put them at a disadvantage. Left to themselves, they might have found few outlets to express their discontent, but the Irish gentry also had economic grievances and they provided the leadership necessary for the tenantry to become a political force. No doubt indebtedness, and its accompanying sense of frustration, contributed to the motives of the Irish gentry for leading the rebellion. Rory O'More, one of the original Irish plotters, in seeking to bring Lord Maguire into his scheme, played on Maguire's worsened circumstances. Yet, at the same time, we must recognize that there was resentment not so much at the new economic system but at the special rules that were applied which prevented the Irish competing in this system on an equal footing.

As has already been stressed, one of the deep concerns among the Old English had been, and was in 1641, security of land tenure. For different reasons, this was also a concern of Protestant planters. Irish landowners in planted areas did not have the same concerns as either the Old English or the planters. Their patents were of recent origin. Unlike the Old English, therefore, they did not have to fear insecurity of tenure because their titles were old and hard to defend in law, nor were their titles subject to specific conditions of building and tenancy like those of the undertakers. Where they did suffer a disadvantage, however, was that under the plantation conditions they were not permitted to purchase land from either the British or each other.

Petitions submitted by Irish landowners resident in planted areas to the Irish Commons in the spring of 1641 made direct reference to these limitations. As one of these petitions pointed out, even when such Irish landowners had their patents renewed, they were not allowed to "sell or set" more than sixty acres to any native and then only to lease for twenty-one years, which, complained the petitioners, "in all much abate the industry of the said natives to gain any greater or further estates." Such "national distinction" and "mark of separation" could not but breed jealousy, they continued, as there were no grounds why "freeborn subjects" should be placed in "a worse condition than those born out of his majesty's dominions" and subsequently naturalized. The same complaint surfaced after the outbreak of the rebellion when the O'Farrells of Longford asserted that this restraint on purchase did more to arouse discontent than plantation itself, "for they are brought to that exigent of poverty in these late times, that they must be sellers and not buyers of land."[62] Significantly, although one of those who signed this document had joined the Irish by December 1641, another was serving in the royal forces at the same time.[63] The Irish gentry were torn between wanting to be part of the new system and the conviction that they would never be fully accepted into it. The effects of the policy to which they objected are to be found in the gradual decrease in the proportion of Irish-owned land in such counties as Armagh and Cavan between 1610 and 1641, in the former by 6 per cent and in the latter by 4 per cent.[64]

We may conclude that some Irish landowners were ready and able to compete in the new economic environment and that what angered them was the political restraints placed on their competitiveness. Here there is a striking difference between their experience in 1641 before the rebellion and that of the Old English. During the summer of this year, the Old English were given the strong impression that their economic grievances would be met; it was only after the rebellion had broken out that it appeared to many of them that the security of land tenure that they sought would never be granted voluntarily. The Irish, however, had been denied their request to be placed on an equal footing by July. On this issue, politics and economics blended, and while the context of the denial must await a later chapter, it is worth noting now that the group that began the rebellion was the first to be denied a political remedy to an economic and social grievance. This particular grievance was not the single cause of the rebellion. The process that was at work was far more complex. Nonetheless, the expression of the complaint both before and after the rising points to its importance within that element of Irish society from which the insurgents derived their leaders.

There is some indication that the Irish in Ulster below the level of landowner, in contrast to those in Munster, also faced discrimination. Sir Phelim's policy of favouring British over Irish tenants provides support for this view. On the Clothworkers' proportion in Londonderry in 1615, thirty-two English labourers were paid various amounts from 10d. per day to 8d. per day, most being paid 9d. In the same year, twenty-eight Irish labourers were employed for between 10d. and 6d. per day, a majority of them at the lowest rate.[65] The work done by the two groups may have differed, and even if the Irish were paid less than the English for the same work, it may have been an isolated case and what happened in 1615 may not have been typical of later years, but the comparison, along with Bell's remark about general conditions, alerts us to possible causes of resentment at this level of society. Indeed, the depositions reveal widespread concern over indebtedness among the lower social levels of the Irish as well as the gentry. One of the reasons that the Protestant clergy suffered attack at the hands of the insurgents was because of their "heavy involvement in money-lending transactions," and debt collectors were similarly attacked.[66]

This accumulation of evidence suggests that the economic downturn in Ulster following the outbreak of the Anglo-Scottish conflict aggravated the frustrations of those who had fallen into debt. We have, moreover, confirmation from Bishop Bramhall that in 1640 there was general discontent. Landlords complained that they could not find tenants, the "middle sort of people" complained of excessive taxes – mostly local ones which went into the pockets of local officials – and the "poor Irish" complained "grievously" at the enforcement of the penal laws against them, particularly the legislation directed at their practice of harnessing horses to ploughs by the horse's tail. The enforcement of this law prevented them from cultivating their land, which led to a shortage of winter fodder, which in turn meant their cattle died of starvation, "very many cattle being of late dead in the mountains." The bishop recommended the suspension of the penal laws against the Irish to alleviate the general malaise, but he also blamed the "Scotch troubles," thus independently reaching the same conclusion as others, including Wentworth, of the origin of the economic decline.[67]

This chapter began by juxtaposing two contrasting images of Ireland's economic condition before the outbreak of the rebellion, and it has been argued that both were accurate to a degree. The prosperous image was correct up to 1638 and remained in men's memories after the rebellion, while that which depicted the country as close to ruin reflected the situation brought on, to a large extent, by the conflict that was taking place in Britain, but aggravated by poor harvests. Undoubtedly the economic difficulties that we have observed in Ireland in general and in Ulster in particular were among the ingredients bubbling in the cauldron that boiled over in October 1641, but it has also been argued here that these economic problems were themselves the symptoms of political turbulence across the water. Ireland was part not only of an economic network but of a political one in which events beyond its shores could cause trauma within them, which, in turn, sent shock waves into Britain. This network consisted of men whose decisions responded to their interpretation of what was happening about them. In Ireland, both the Old English and Irish developed interpretations which led them to rebellion, but it was the Irish who began it. They had grievances other than economic ones, but the denial of equality for them in the economic sphere gave them no incentive to overlook the others. They then used the occasion that had contributed to their economic woes to assert a demand for equality which constitutional means had failed to supply. The following chapters will attempt to trace how the characteristics of the political network led to this failure.

CHAPTER TWO

Prelude to Parliaments

Economic conditions, and particularly the disruption of Irish commerce following the Covenanting challenge to the king, created a climate of discontent in Ireland. This in itself need not have led to civil strife. It was as much the weakness of government in England as discontent in Ireland that led to the conflict because that weakness permitted rebellion to become a viable political option. The Scots only succeeded because the largest of Charles's three kingdoms was divided within itself, and it was the Scottish success that increased those divisions to the point that English authority in Ireland could be challenged.

These divisions took a number of forms, but perhaps the most dangerous for the government, and certainly the most significant so far as the control of Ireland was concerned, was the factional strife within the king's English council. The role of faction in English politics has recently received much attention, and there is no need here to recapitulate the findings of the historians who have emphasized this aspect of the struggle. It is sufficient to say that, since the governor of Ireland controlled a substantial amount of patronage and was chosen like any other English official, Ireland became, from the sixteenth century onwards, a part of this factional web.[1] There were, as well, factions specific to Ireland as patronage there encouraged the development of a petty court around the lord deputy. Nevertheless, an Irish faction could only thrive, indeed an Irish governor could only retain office, through association with elements of the English court, and any event, particularly one of such moment as the Scottish challenge, could be used by one group or another to advance its interests at the expense of its rivals. As Archbishop William Laud remarked to Sir Thomas Wentworth in the autumn of 1637, all councillors strove for their own ends, "every one of them aiming at their own greatness if a greater were out of the way. And all agreeing in this to have him [Laud] gone."[2]

THE PLOTS AGAINST WENTWORTH

There are two, independent, seventeenth-century accounts of a plot by a leading group of planters in Ireland, who, in alliance with Wentworth's enemies in England, planned to use the Scottish challenge to Charles's authority as a means to destroy the lord deputy and acquire the profits that Ireland had to offer. The shorter of these, which dates from after the Restoration, claimed that Sir Adam Loftus, by 1637 the vice-treasurer of Ireland, Sir William Parsons, master of the court of wards, Sir Charles Coote, vice-president of Connacht, Sir Robert Meredith, chancellor of the exchequer, and Sir John Borlase, master of the ordnance, were the prime movers in this conspiracy. The second account was written by Sir George Wentworth, Thomas Wentworth's brother, sometime after 1642 and before 1649, and in cipher. Sir George claimed as his sources: Sir Charles Coote, the "late" earl of Roscommon (that is, Lord Robert Dillon, who died in 1642), and "many papers" which had, however, perished by the time Sir George wrote his account. As this document was not published till 1810, it is highly unlikely that it could have influenced the post-Restoration version of these events.[3]

What Sir George alleged was that, as the quarrel with the Scots developed, Viscount Ranelagh, Sir William Parsons, and Sir Adam Loftus plotted to use the situation "as a ready means to work his [Wentworth's] ruin." Sir John Clotworthy, the Antrim planter, and a man called Parr were sent to Scotland and England to encourage opposition. Ranelagh and his friends then approached Sir Henry Vane the elder, then comptroller of the royal household, and the marquis of Hamilton, "of whom by the Scotch faction they had assurance" to lend assistance from England. Initially, it was only intended that Wentworth should be removed from office in Ireland by being tempted with a high English office, such as lord keeper or treasurer, but once it was decided that parliament should meet in 1640, Hamilton devised a new plan. Through Vane's influence, that parliament was to be dissolved and the blame pinned on Wentworth. The city of London, which had its own quarrel with Wentworth over the way it had been fined and deprived of its land in Ulster by the Court of Star Chamber on the grounds that it had failed to live up to its plantation conditions, was to lend no money to the king and the Scots would maintain their pressure. Wentworth was to be represented as the one obstacle in the way of a settlement, a charge of treason would be brought against him, "and if that failed, the people must do it, for go he must."

The rest of Sir George's account summarizes what is generally well known about Wentworth's trial, the attacks on his friends, and the appointment of Sir William Parsons and Sir John Borlase as lords justices in Ireland. However, he made two additional points that are unique to his story. First, he implicated in the plot, not only Vane and Hamilton, but the earl of Arundel and William Fiennes, Viscount Saye and Sele. Second, he alleged that the ultimate aim of Ranelagh and Parsons was to control the plantation of Connacht, "for now the Connacht plantations were in their power" and "these great proportions should have been shared to themselves and their undertakers," who included Arundel. The Irish customs were to be divided among Parsons, Ranelagh, and Loftus, though Vane and Saye were to receive £10,000. The Irish tobacco monopoly, hitherto farmed by Wentworth, was to pass to Hamilton.[4]

Sir George's accusations – though not the post-Restoration account – have been remarked by at least one of Wentworth's biographers. They have not, however, been treated very seriously, even though it is well known that Arundel, Hamilton, and Vane (along with the earl of Holland) were Wentworth's enemies.[5] Such plots are, of course, virtually impossible to prove or disprove beyond question because we lack the records of the private communications between those alleged to have been involved in them. Certainly scepticism is in order, as Sir George had ample motive to blacken the reputation of his brother's rivals. Yet, as we trace the events from the time the Scots overtly defied the king, the available evidence tends to reinforce the credibility of Sir George's account, or a set of circumstances which resembled it. We have seen that there were close kinship and friendship ties among the Irish planters accused by Sir George. Thus all official decisions and actions taken before the outbreak of the rebellion have to be placed in the context of this atmosphere of intense factionalism.

THE COVENANTERS
AND IRELAND

The conflict between Charles and his Scottish subjects broke upon the political stage on 23 July 1637 with the arranged riots in Edinburgh against the introduction of the new prayer book. David Stevenson has argued that an organized opposition to the royal policies in Scotland had begun to develop before 1637 and that some of

those involved were in touch with Charles's opponents in England.
These links are difficult to document, but it is possible to show the
8xtype of contact that developed by looking at the small branch of
the Scottish opposition which had penetrated Ireland.[6] Before John
Livingstone made his second attempt to emigrate to America in 1636,
he went to London to seek help in developing his venture. There he
met such men as Sir Nathaniel Rich, who was closely associated with
the Puritan earl of Warwick, Dr Richard Sibbes, the Puritan clergyman, Sir Philip Stapleton, Sir William Constable, Sir Richard
Salonstall, and Dr Alexander Leighton, the Scottish physician whose
attack on bishops led to his imprisonment during the 1630s. Rich
and Sibbes had died by the time the National Covenant was signed
in 1638, but Stapleton, an MP in the Long Parliament, took Parliament's side and served at Edgehill in Essex's life guard; Constable
also fought for Parliament at Edgehill and later became a regicide,
and Salonstall also sided against the king. Leighton tried to dissuade
Livingstone from emigrating on the grounds that he was already
confident of the downfall of the bishops in Scotland. Livingstone,
nevertheless, returned to Ireland, tried to make the voyage but was
forced back by bad weather, and on his return had to flee to Scotland
under the pressure of such bishops in Ireland as Bramhall and
Leslie.[7] As Bramhall had remarked to Laud just before the Covenanting storm broke in Edinburgh, the Irish "church will quickly
purge herself of such pecant humours if there be not a supply from
thence."[8] This very strength and confidence of the authorities in
Ireland may account for Wentworth's initial lack of concern about
Scottish events.

The news of the happenings in Scotland during the summer of
1637 was slow to reach the lord deputy. He had been in the west of
Ireland making arrangements for the plantation of Connacht. When
he returned to Dublin at the end of September, he wrote to Laud
but made no reference to Scotland. What deeply concerned him was
the information that a faction at court which "find that I serve the
crown too entirely for their purpose" aimed to bring him into suspicion with the king by accusing him of using his office to enrich
himself. The primary agent being used to advance this scheme was
a Scot, Robert Barr, who in the guise of a merchant was "leaping
like a Jackanapes betwixt two stools." With special royal permission
and without Wentworth's licence, Barr had left Ireland, where he
had held "very inward intelligence with some here which wish me
ill," and carried messages to the English court, where he had access
to the king "by some very near his Majesty." The courtier with whom
Wentworth associated this scheming was the earl of Arundel, a man

who had been friendly with the previous lord deputy, Falkland, but who had fallen foul of Wentworth in 1636 when he opposed Arundel's attempts to recover a title to lands once owned by his grandfather.[9]

By 18 October Wentworth had heard something of the July events in Edinburgh, but he made light of them. Only after Laud had written on 7 and 24 October, the latter letter arriving on 11 November, did Wentworth begin to get a picture of what was happening in Scotland.[10] Yet even at the end of November he remarked to Laud that it was strange how "the great tumult" in Edinburgh "runs upon every man's tongue as if there was nothing else to be mentioned." By 26 December, however, Bishop Bramhall, who had been in London and had returned to Ireland via Scotland, was able to give the lord deputy a full account of the seriousness of the situation.[11] Before the year was out Wentworth had himself written to the English council to complain of outrages committed by Scots in Ulster against the officers of the crown. It was becoming apparent that defiance of the king's authority in Scotland was likely to spill over into Ireland.[12]

Wentworth believed that what he deemed excesses in Scotland were fomented in England, and Laud, responding to him in May of 1638, just as the marquis of Hamilton was about to be dispatched north as the king's commissioner to negotiate with the Covenanters, declared that he had no doubt that the challenge to the king's authority in the north had been encouraged in England.[13] We have no direct evidence of communication between opposition groups in Scotland and England, but it must have been taking place. As soon as the Covenant had been signed, at the end of February 1638, John Livingstone was sent down to London by the Scots nobles to renew the contacts he had established at the time of his ill-favoured attempt to settle in New England. It is hard to imagine that Livingstone was doing anything else in London but seeking support from like-minded Englishmen.[14]

The interaction between Scotland and Ireland at this time is much easier to document than links between the Covenanters and the English opponents of Charles. We can observe this process at two distinct, though not unconnected, levels. First, there was the direct influence of the Covenanters upon the Scots living in Ulster.[15] By the autumn of 1638, the Scots in Ulster were showing signs of linking up with their brethren at home even to the point of arming themselves. To counter that potential threat, Wentworth ordered weapons from the Netherlands, posted additional troops in Ulster, and by early 1639 had obtained a ruling from the judges in Ireland that, although residents of Ireland who took the Covenant could not be found guilty of treason, they could be prosecuted and fined by the Court of Castle Chamber.[16]

The second, though related, level of interaction between Scottish interests and Ireland concerned Irish land. By 1638 various proposals were being advanced for the reorganization of the lands in County Londonderry which had been forfeited by the city of London to the crown on the grounds that the conditions of plantation had not been fulfilled. One of these plans, originating with Wentworth himself, was a scheme whereby he was to act as the principal farmer of the crown's interest.[17] It is tempting to assume that the lord deputy's own interest in the Londonderry lands coloured his attitude to the projects that were proposed by others to develop the same lands, but we shall see that his opposition to one of the proposals was as much influenced by its political implications as by any personal interests.

It was in January 1638 that Wentworth first learned of a scheme being put forward by a group of Scottish promoters. The leader of this venture was Hamilton. The marquis had already shown an interest in acquiring an Irish estate through the plantation of Connacht, and in 1637 had wanted to drain Strangford Lough and plant the territory so recovered from the sea, a wild proposal which had aroused the lord deputy's strong disapproval.[18] As Hamilton began to show an interest in Londonderry, what caused Wentworth particular concern was that the marquis was employing as his agent none other than Robert Barr who had been associated with Arundel the previous September. In Wentworth's eyes, Barr represented a danger, not only because of his involvement in court intrigue but also because he could be linked to the Covenanting movement.[19]

In writing to Laud to use his influence to oppose the idea at court, Wentworth warned that, if the project was approved, it would "turn the English wholly out of Ulster" and "you shall see" the Scots "here in the very same rebellion against the clergy and discipline of the church as they are now in Scotland."[20] Bramhall was more outspoken, and it was at this point that he remarked on the Covenanting "contagion" having spread to the diocese of Derry from the eastern counties.[21] Barr, he reported, was "a maintainer of secret conventicles" and had only narrowly escaped being brought before the Irish Court of High Commission.[22] In subsequent correspondence, Wentworth described Barr and his associates as "arrant Anapaptists [sic]" and accused him of refusing to pay customs, of engineering the escape of another Scot who was sought for "causes ecclesiastical," and of defying the lord deputy's authority. In October, when Wentworth finally managed to bring Barr before the Irish council, he had to let him go with a nominal punishment because he produced "a writing" with the king's signature entrusting him with "some particular service." The following month the lord deputy warned the king that Barr would be "extremely well pleased to have all Ulster as deep in the Covenant as those in Scotland."[23]

Wentworth's fears about the Scots living in Ulster bordered on the obsessive; it was he who exaggerated their numbers, declaring in April 1639 that there were no less than 150,000 Scots in Ulster when there cannot have been more than 20,000 to 30,000 such settlers.[24] He also communicated his fears to Laud, who was as convinced as he that Scottish influence in the north of Ireland should be kept to a minimum. What aroused these fears? Fear of the spread of the Scottish form of Protestantism obviously provided one motive for resisting the Scots, but this cloaked a national antagonism. As Wentworth himself remarked, if the Scots were allowed to penetrate Londonderry, the English who were planted there would be expelled, and "we thus arm against ourselves."[25]

Robert Barr's sympathies for the Covenanters do not imply that his employers shared them. Wentworth, it is true, expressed astonishment that such men should be recommended to the king for employment, but Scots noblemen do not seem to have given much thought to the political or religious opinions of those they sought to promote. Even the duke of Lennox, whose religious orthodoxy and political loyalty have never been questioned, attempted to place a Covenanter into an Irish living. By August, Hamilton had acquired a new partner in his scheme, his friend, the bankrupt and Roman Catholic earl of Antrim, Randal MacDonnell. Antrim strongly opposed the Covenanters but also had ambitions to extend his estate into Kintyre, an area formerly occupied by his family, but now possessed by Lord Lorne, the future eighth earl of Argyll and a Covenanter leader. Antrim used Charles's Scottish difficulties to offer 2,000 men to serve the king in Scotland at his own charge, "which he is as well able to do," remarked Wentworth, "as I to take me upon the cross with so many for the Holy Land." Hamilton's scheme provided the earl with an opportunity to expand west too: "he will either have Coleraine or it shall cost him his blood." From these remarks it will be evident that Wentworth did not become any more attracted to the Scottish project in Londonderry even after Barr's religious sympathies had been balanced by Antrim's. It was to the Scots in general and the political system they represented that he was opposed. Laud expressed their mutual opinion succinctly: "I think as you do, Scotland is the veriest devil that is out of hell."[26]

Yet another proposal for the reorganization of Londonderry was put forward by the undertenants of the city of London whose leases had become void once the lands had been forfeited. The petition to the king, signed by about 500 of those affected and requesting security for their estates, was dated 23 June 1638 and reached London by early July. The undertenants' agent was Sir John Clotworthy, who in addition to his estate in Antrim held a lease from the Drapers' Company in County Londonderry. To obtain a licence to travel, Clotworthy told Wentworth that he needed to cross over to England to represent the undertenants. This he did, but he went via Scotland, and on 11 June he visited one of the leading Covenanters, Sir Archibald Johnston of Wariston, and arranged a method for exchanging information.[27] He then went south to London, where he presented the undertenants' petition later that month, but he maintained his correspondence with his Scottish friends, Livingstone in one instance serving as the bearer of a letter. That correspondence reveals a sense of religious sympathy for the Scots, and he gave warning of Antrim's plans to attack them on their flank.[28]

Clotworthy's behaviour, if more religiously motivated than Sir George Wentworth would allow, nevertheless tends to support Sir George's version of events. Clotworthy was a friend of John Pym, the king's leading opponent in the Commons, and related to him by marriage. He was also close to Puritan circles in England. John Winthrop had acquired land in Ireland before becoming involved in the Massachusetts Bay venture, and his son had visited Sir John in 1635. Sir John was closely linked with the Parsons-Ranelagh faction in Ireland because he was Ranelagh's son-in-law and, as we shall see later, had links with the earl of Holland's faction at court. Despite his residence in Ireland a seat was procured for him in the English Long Parliament, probably through the influence of the opposition peer, the earl of Warwick. It would be Clotworthy who seconded Pym's motion on 11 November 1640 to impeach Wentworth. Finally, it may be noted that he held numerous personal grievances against the lord deputy, including repeated postponement of the command of a company, punishment for opposing the government's policy on linen yarn, and the treatment of his wife, who by 12 January 1639 was being called to answer for her religious views before the Irish Court of High Commission.[29] Charles I ultimately approved none of the proposals for the reorganization of the settlement in Londonderry. Whether this decision followed from Wentworth's frequent objections to Hamilton's scheme or not, almost certainly Sir Thomas received a share of the blame for the inability of the Scottish courtiers to gain Irish property.

FACTION AND
THE ENGLISH COUNCIL

The mission of the marquis of Hamilton to Scotland in November 1638 to seek a compromise with the Scottish General Assembly failed. The assembly continued to sit in the face of Hamilton's objections and departure, and it passed legislation which included the abolition of episcopacy. By January of 1639 both the Scots and Charles were preparing for war. The Covenanters, as part of their campaign to encourage popular support and particularly English support, urged a closer union between Scotland and England; indeed, they appealed to have their case judged by an English parliament. Charles had no intention of allowing the Scots to unite with those who opposed him in England and planned instead a three-pronged military attack. Hamilton was to land at Aberdeen and Antrim in Argyll. Charles himself was to move north and threaten Scotland's southern border. By 30 March the king had reached York, but none of the other thrusts could begin to be implemented and Charles considered that his army fell short of the size and quality needed to accomplish anything by itself. Thus, while the Scots, who had their own difficulties of supply, sat close to the border, negotiations began that led to the Pacification of Berwick on 18 June.

Under this agreement, although Charles did not ratify the acts of the General Assembly of the previous November, he did agree to another meeting of the assembly in August, to be followed by a Scottish parliament. The result of these meetings was not simply the reaffirmation of the abolition of episcopacy but a substantial reduction of royal authority in the secular sphere. Charles had no intention of accepting these changes as permanent innovations and sought only to gain time as he prepared for another military solution. By the end of July the king had decided to call Wentworth over to England to manage his affairs, and early in 1640 he reinforced his minister's position by promoting him to the lord lieutenancy of Ireland and creating him earl of Strafford.[30]

As the tension between the king and his Scottish subjects increased, the competition and intrigue within the English council intensified, particularly after the Pacification of Berwick. Sir Edward Coke, the senior secretary, was informed by his assistant that, after the king's return from the north, his master and others sustained "ruder assaults here [at court] than they did ever fear at the camp."[31] Clarendon also remarked in his *History* that the factions and animosities increased at this time.[32] Perhaps it will never be possible to reconstruct completely the struggle for position within the council, but if we are to use the limited sources that are available to their best advantage, an understanding of the composition of the council is essential.

At the beginning of 1639 the English privy council consisted of thirty-five men, including such officials as Sir Henry Vane the elder, the treasurer or comptroller of the household, Sir Henry Jermyn, the vice-chamberlain, and two secretaries, Sir Edward Coke and Sir Francis Windebank. In March the king added Thomas Howard, earl of Berkshire, thus raising the membership to thirty-six. In practice, the active members of the council were a much smaller group. It would be misleading to give a precise figure describing this inner core based on attendance at meetings. Such men as Wentworth and Robert Sidney, the earl of Leicester and Charles's ambassador in France, had duties that kept them away from meetings. The use of attendance at council meetings as a measure of standing is further complicated during 1639 because some of the members of the council accompanied Charles to York, and there was a complaint to Coke, who had gone north, that the councillors who had remained in London did not know what their colleagues were doing.[33] Bearing this in mind, however, and excluding Wentworth and Leicester, we can identify some fifteen men whose attendance record suggests a strong council role from the beginning of January to 15 March, or before the king left for York. These were:

William Laud, archbishop of Canterbury
Henry Montagu, earl of Manchester, lord privy seal
William Juxon, bishop of London, lord treasurer
Thomas, Lord Coventry, lord keeper
Thomas Howard, earl of Arundel, earl marshal
Francis, Lord Cottington, chancellor of the exchequer
Edward, Lord Newburgh, chancellor of the duchy of Lancaster
James, marquis of Hamilton
Philip Herbert, earl of Pembroke, lord chamberlain
Algernon Percy, earl of Northumberland, lord admiral
Edward Sackville, earl of Dorset
Henry Rich, earl of Holland
Sir Henry Vane, comptroller
Sir Edward Coke, secretary
Sir Francis Windebank, secretary

The first three of those listed attended twenty-three of the twenty-five meetings of the council held during this period and all of the remainder save Hamilton attended ten or more.[34] It is also interesting to note that in October the committee for Ireland was drawn from the same group of men, consisting of Laud, Juxon, Arundel, Cottington, and the two secretaries.[35] Of the group as a whole, Laud could probably rely on the support of only five men: Juxon, Manchester (not to be confused with his pro-Parliament son, Henry), Coventry, Newburgh, and Coke.

Sir George Wentworth's account of his brother's fall described the hostility of the earls of Arundel and Holland, and this charge is easy to document from other sources. In their campaign they used two Irish issues in which Wentworth's prestige was involved. The first of these concerned the corrupt Irish lord chancellor, Viscount Loftus of Ely, and the second, Sir Piers Crosby, who was Holland's friend and also close to the earl of Cork. Wentworth had removed Ely from office in April 1638, but the viscount had by then appealed his case to the English privy council. Crosby, who had strong ties both with some members of the English court (particularly the queen's party) and with the Old English, had led a challenge to Wentworth in the 1634 Irish parliament. Subsequently, he accused Wentworth of causing the death of a ship's captain during interrogation. The lord deputy took the case to Star Chamber, whereupon Holland befriended Crosby.[36]

When the Ely case was heard initially by the English council in May, Laud reported in cipher that "when we had read all [the papers] and began to deliberate, Arundel spoke very largely and with much art but ... so much against [you] as any man might see they [sic] cared not to hurt one hundred men, so they might hit ... [you]." Lord Cottington, who was not close to either Laud or Wentworth, then spoke, but "spoke honestly," and "so all was well," as Laud could support what he said.[37] Laud and Wentworth interpreted (correctly) Arundel's intervention on behalf of Ely as malicious. (Arundel would later preside over the House of Lords during Wentworth's trial.) Similarly, Laud warned his friend in May 1638 that Holland was working against him. Wentworth, nevertheless, or possibly in reaction to this information, tried to force Holland to testify against Crosby, upon which the earl became "monstrously enraged." By the autumn of this year the two apostles of "thorough" government had added Hamilton's name to their cipher and a growing distrust of him emerges in Wentworth's correspondence. Thus, when in November he complained that it was "very certain indeed I [have] drawn down upon [me] a mighty court hatred," he included Hamilton along with Arundel and Holland (and the queen) among his opponents.[38]

As the new year (1639) began, the enemies of Laud and Wentworth increased their ascendancy in the council. Since Hamilton's mission in Scotland had failed and Charles had decided to resort to force, he had appointed Arundel as his commander-in-chief although, in Clarendon's words, there was "nothing martial about him but his presence and his looks."[39] Holland became general of the horse, an appointment, if Wentworth was right, resulting from Hamilton's influence.[40] These appointments were balanced by that of Robert Devereux, earl of Essex, who became lieutenant general, to the annoyance of both Arundel and Holland, but Essex did not sit on the council and bore as much ill will towards Wentworth as he did towards anyone. There was a direct quarrel with the lord deputy over Essex's estates in Ireland, and he had also been alienated by Wentworth's treatment of the old earl of Clanricard, who was Essex's stepfather.[41] When, therefore, another Howard, the earl of Berkshire, was added to the council in March, Laud wrote in sarcastic consternation: "wipe your eyes now, the king is so strong at the council table, as that to overbear his friends the earl of Berkshire is sworn a councillor." As the earl of Leicester, whom Laud also feared, was expected back from France, he concluded: "we are undone, my lord, and there is no more to be said. I am so full of indignation that I dare not let my pen go."[42] This cry of anguish was uttered as the king joined his army at York and as Wentworth heard that his rivals were using their new influence to encourage Ely to have his case heard in England. By the end of April, Holland had persuaded the king to order the release of the Irish chancellor from confinement in Ireland so that he could plead his case before the English council. Moreover, the order was written and sent directly by Holland so that it did not pass through the hands of the Wentworth's ally on the council, Coke.[43]

Holland had evidently been determined to exploit his new position of eminence. Only another change in fortune saved Wentworth from humiliation over the Ely case. The dismal performance of Arundel and Holland as military leaders undermined their standing, and after having had to accept the truce with the Scots, Charles summoned Wentworth to lead his affairs in England. By 22 September the lord deputy had begun to attend privy council meetings which transformed the political atmosphere in the council.[44] His return to England was almost certainly a reflection of Charles's need to find a capable minister whom he could trust, but such was the importance attached to the Ely case that Windebank thought that Wentworth had returned in order to be present when the case was heard.[45] The outcome of that case showed how, by this time, Wentworth had regained control. In November, the council, with Arundel and Holland present, judged Ely's appeal to be "without any just cause," and it was affirmed that he was unfit to hold office.[46]

The position of other members of the council is less easy to define. However, Northumberland and Pembroke were becoming increasingly disenchanted with the policies Charles was pursuing and identified both Laud and Wentworth with those policies. Clarendon described Pembroke as abhorring the war "as obstinately as he loved hunting and hawking," and both earls ultimately sided with Parliament. Dorset, although a firm royalist later, held a close attachment to Arundel, who appointed him executor of this will.[47] Coke, although an ally of the archbishop and the lord deputy, was over seventy-five years old by 1639 and his position as secretary had become insecure. The importance attached to this post is indicated by the determination of Leicester's wife and others to procure it for her husband. This partly explains Coke's support for Laud and Wentworth as he suspected their enemy, Holland, of pushing Leicester's candidacy. Yet the man who was most determined to get the post was actually Sir Henry Vane, who was reported to have Northumberland's support and to be willing to pay £4,000 to secure it.[48]

Hamilton's position is less clear than might be expected, given the relations between him and Wentworth the previous year. This ambiguity stems in part from the marquis's ability to give all parties to a dispute the impression of support. Laud clearly trusted him much more than Wentworth did. Hamilton, indeed, took the initiative in approaching Laud to warn him that Sir William Stewart, a leading Scottish planter in Ulster and a member of the Irish privy council, sympathized with the Covenanters and was expected to help them in their cause in Ireland.[49] However, this information turned out to be highly exaggerated or even false as Sir William and one of his sons took the oath which Wentworth imposed on the Scots in Ireland to determine their loyalty.[50] Hamilton also seems to have been behind the "vast, vain and childish" plan for Antrim to invade the west of Scotland despite the lack of the means to do so.[51] This suggests that, if Hamilton was not ill disposed to Wentworth, he was certainly inconsiderate in dabbling in Irish affairs in a manner that embarrassed the lord deputy. As well, Vane was definitely an enemy of Wentworth, and Hamilton had been quite close to Vane earlier in the decade, and in April 1639 Charles declared that he trusted only Vane and Arundel in discussing Hamilton's reports from Scotland.[52] In any case, Wentworth believed that Hamilton, Arundel, and

Holland were working together. His view of Hamilton is indicated in a letter of 11 February 1639 to Laud. Hamilton, he said, was much displeased with him and he had no doubt that Holland would use this breach to his own advantage, but, he continued, Hamilton was one of those "that hold friendship no longer than they may have all they fancy. And for my part where I find that once I never endeavour to recover them."[53] Laud, however, thought Hamilton "very right set" or, if not, "the very devil incarnate." What bothered him was that the animosity between the marquis and the lord deputy played into the hands of those who, above all, wished ill to both Laud and Wentworth.[54]

Cottington's position is interesting because it points to the number of competing factions within the council: the game was almost all-against-all. Sympathetic to the Catholics, Cottington allied himself with neither the Arundel-Holland group nor with Northumberland, yet he bore little love for Laud. This is illustrated by his position on the wisdom of calling a parliament, an issue that had become acute by February 1639. Wentworth's words to Laud on the subject suggest that a majority of the council at this time favoured a parliament because, in expressing his adamant opposition, he stressed that "it is not the number but the weight which ought to carry councils."[55] The man pushing hardest for a parliament was Cottington who, as Laud explained in May, thought that if one met, Laud and Juxon "must out," and he would gain the treasurership.[56]

THE CALLING OF
THE PARLIAMENTS

It is in the context of this conciliar intrigue that we have to place the decision to summon both the Irish and the English parliaments, which together, though in their own separate ways, were not only to destroy Laud and Wentworth but also to contribute to the outbreak of civil war in both Ireland and England. Ironically, Wentworth's first reference to the idea of calling a new parliament had been positive although he was only thinking of the Irish parliament at the time. As he informed his ally in June 1638, he had raised the matter with the king in 1636. Now he returned to the idea as the subsidies procured in 1634 had been spent, and he was convinced that he could obtain more money from the Irish parliament than he had formerly.[57] The suggestion of an English or a Scottish parliament, however, aroused a very different reaction. By July, Laud was reporting that the "main plot" in England was too fierce for the king to call a parliament. Such an event, he suggested, "may spoil all."[58]

After Hamilton had returned to Scotland in August for a second session of negotiations with the Covenanters, during which he was permitted to agree to a meeting of the Scottish parliament after the assembly had met, Wentworth expressed opposition to calling parliament in either Scotland or England. In November he associated the idea of an English parliament with the "puritan party" and urged that calling it "be avoided by all means," primarily because he saw it as a threat to the continuation of the collection of Ship Money.[59]

The idea of calling a parliament during the first half of 1639, at a time that Arundel and Holland commanded increasing influence on the council, was anathema to Wentworth. Yet the military failure in 1639, with its concomitant discrediting of Arundel and Holland, the lord deputy's return to England and his dominance on the council, as reflected in his victory in the Ely case, permitted a new flexibility borne of confidence. This, along with the shortage of funds, helps to explain Wentworth's change of heart about a parliament at this time, for, by the end of November, it had been decided that both the English and the Irish parliaments should meet. As was reported on 6 December to the earl of Bridgwater, who was in Wales, Wentworth's advice to the king was that the only way to re-establish his authority was by waging "an effectual war" and no war could "be made effectually, but such a one as should grow and be assisted from the high council of a Parliament."[60]

Wentworth's dominance in the council did not stop intrigue. It will be recalled that Sir George Wentworth believed later that the original intention of his brother's opponents had been to move him out of Ireland by securing a higher office for him in England, such as Juxon's position of lord treasurer. Only after the decision to call parliament was it considered possible to destroy him. What we know about the discussions at the time does confirm that there were suggestions that Wentworth should receive a high office in England. In late August Leicester was told of a rumour that Sir Thomas was returning to England to assume the treasurership.[61] Northumberland certainly expected the lord deputyship to be relinquished, as did the countess of Carlisle, one of the queen's friends and a person much admired by Wentworth. In October she reported that there was some dilemma about what to do with him.[62] One suggestion was that he should replace the ailing lord keeper, Coventry. By November, however, she too was reporting that he would become lord treasurer.[63] We know of these proposals because associated with the idea of Wentworth leaving Ireland was the possibility of Leicester's advancement to the lord deputyship. Shortly after he arrived in England, Wentworth told Lady Carlisle that he intended that Leicester should succeed him, and Northumberland advised the earl to stay on good terms with Wentworth as he would have much influence in determining his own successor. The queen too favoured the idea, although Leicester was not without at least one rival,[64] for Cottington coveted the position.[65] Sir George Wentworth, in his account of the plotting, mentioned nothing about Leicester, but this is not surprising. It is unlikely that at this stage the Arundel-Holland-Hamilton group hoped for anything more than the movement of Wentworth out of Ireland; indeed, this is what Sir George reported. Sir Thomas represented a major obstacle to those who wished to exploit Irish opportunities for advancement. Any change, therefore, in the government of Ireland was an improvement for such self-seekers.

It was ultimately decided not to give Wentworth an English post, but to promote him to lord lieutenant and create him earl of Strafford, a decision apparently reached early in December 1639. Wentworth still insisted to the countess of Carlisle that he would use his influence to place Leicester as deputy under him, but she doubted that such an appointment would take place for a while.[66] She was correct. Leicester was not promoted, and instead the uninfluential Christopher Wandesford, Wentworth's cousin and master of the rolls in Ireland, received the position of deputy in April 1640.

It is always possible that Wentworth was playing a double game, pretending to want to promote Leicester without having any intention of doing so. Certainly he was anxious to cultivate Leicester's brother-in-law, the earl of Northumberland, and he may have hoped to gain Northumberland's support by pretending to advance Leicester's interests.[67] Yet the evidence does not point to such a play. To see this, we have to look at the competition for another post, Coke's secretaryship. Coke's age meant that he had to be replaced sooner or later. Leicester was a contender for this position as well, and a determined effort was made by the queen in November 1639, apparently with Wentworth's support, to put Leicester in the old man's place.[68] The bid failed, in part because Charles had reservations, but more significantly because Laud did. The archbishop disliked Leicester as he believed him to be a "most dangerous practising puritan."[69] Clearly, if the queen found it impossible to secure the secretaryship for Leicester in November in the face of opposition from Laud and the king, it was going to be virtually impossible for Wentworth to place him in power in Ireland in December or January, where he would have been in a position to hurt the established church in Ireland, which was gradually acquiring a Laudian hue. Leicester, for his part, seems to have recognized Wentworth's inability to help him, or suspected duplicity, for by Christmas he had indicated to Lady Carlisle that he did not wish to be associated with the lord deputy.[70]

The failure to secure the secretaryship for Leicester had substantial repercussions. By the end of 1639 Sir Henry Vane had become one of Wentworth's strongest opponents on the council. Such a contest contained an element of the absurd as Vane, when compared with Wentworth, was small fry. A "busy and a bustling man," who "cared for no other man otherwise than as he found it very convenient for himself," he always lost in the disputes with Wentworth "which enrages him." But Vane, like Leicester, was close to the queen, and since early that year had been friendly with Northumberland, who had spurned the lord deputy's efforts to cultivate him.[71] It was typical of Wentworth's arrogance that, in accepting the earldom of Strafford in January, he requested as a courtesy title for his son the very title that all knew Vane also coveted. The insult was deliberate and politically stupid.[72] Vane turned out to be the queen's second choice for the secretaryship. The new earl of Strafford had no alternative candidate and could only plead with the king that Coke be allowed to stay on because he would not be able to do the service expected of him in Ireland without his "coadjudicator." Charles postponed but did not stop the appointment; with the queen's and Hamilton's support, and we may suspect Northumberland's, Vane became secretary on 3 February 1640. At the same time, John Finch, again with the queen's assistance, replaced Coventry, who had died, and Hamilton's brother, the earl of Lanark, joined the council as a replacement for the earl of Stirling, who had retired as Scottish secretary.[73] Despite his own promotion, Wentworth faced a difficult situation. He had lost two good friends on the council and seen one of his bitterest enemies gain a key position while Hamilton increased his influence.

In relating the events that led to the parliaments of the 1640s, Clarendon declared: "these digressions have taken up too much time and may seem foreign to the proper subject of this [history]; yet they may have given some light to the obscure and dark passages of that time, which were understood by few."[74] Similarly, it may be wondered how this English court intrigue had a bearing on Irish events. Yet what happened there must also remain "obscure and dark," if we do not take into account the shifting political sands of the English court because it was upon this unsteady foundation that Irish politics rested. As we have seen, some of the intrigue in England involved the efforts of courtiers to gain advantage in Ireland and particularly land. Those who engaged in this intrigue had no expectation, let alone intention, that their combined and accumulated actions would contribute to the outbreak of a decade of civil strife. The king might find himself at odds with his Scottish subjects, a favourite might be attacked, as Buckingham had been and as many hoped Strafford would be, but such events were perceived as opportunities to be exploited in the eternal struggle for place, not as signs that the monarchy itself and all that kept the court alive was about to be challenged and overthrown. As we pass to the Irish stage, we must bear in mind that many who played upon it took as their model the English political theatre, and given past productions, what might be expected was the replacement of one player by another over time. Nobody expected to see the play transformed into a riot.

CHAPTER THREE

The Irish Parliament in 1640

The atmosphere within the Irish parliament during the three sessions held in 1640 changed markedly from session to session. To a large extent these changes reflected the shifting of power away from the government to the various political groups in the country. Wentworth's firmness of purpose and severity had overawed political faction but had not killed it. Though robbed of their political significance for the moment, links of friendship and rivalries continued to form the basis of faction, particularly among Protestants. Apart from particular men, such as Lord Mountnorris and Viscount Loftus of Ely, the former chancellor, whom Wentworth had humiliated, we may identify five major interests that, together, constituted the Protestant political community as the Irish parliament was summoned to meet on 16 March 1640.[1]

THE PROTESTANT POLITICAL GROUPS

The followers of Strafford constituted the most influential, though not the largest, faction as parliament opened. Those closest to Wentworth were those he had brought to Ireland: men like Sir Christopher Wandesford, the master of rolls, and Sir George Radcliffe, who, though holding no office, sat in the Irish privy council and worked constantly on his behalf, and Sir George Wentworth, his brother. We must also include in this group such persons as the earl of Ormond, who entered public life during Wentworth's deputyship, and Lord Robert Dillon of Kilkenny-West, son and heir to the first earl of Roscommon. Dillon married his son and heir to Wentworth's sister.[2] In theory the lord lieutenant, as he had become, could also call upon the loyalty of the members of the Irish council. When unchallenged, practice conformed with theory, but, as we shall see, some members of the council, particularly those who had served under his predecessor, Viscount Falkland, possessed other loyalties. This brings us to the next major grouping, which may loosely be described as the friends of Richard Boyle, earl of Cork.

We have already seen that an important group of councillors, such as Sir William Parsons, Viscount Ranelagh, and Sir Adam Loftus, had advanced the cause of plantation during the deputyship of Falkland and, on Falkland's recall, had gathered round Cork.[3] Despite Cork's quarrel with Wentworth and his consequent loss of influence, he continued to command the friendship of many of his former associates. He had left Ireland in 1638 and went to court in an effort to repair the damage wrought by the quarrel, and, significantly, he had established close links with Hamilton and Arundel, the deputy's enemies, and the "popular" opposition peers, the earls of Bristol and Bedford. Nevertheless, Cork's considerable Irish interests required that he maintain close links with his planter friends. Thus, in 1639, when it looked as though the impending plantation of Connacht might "take hold" of some of his "little lands in that province," he wrote to Ranelagh and Parsons to attempt to preserve what he could. He suggested to Ranelagh, whose son, it will be recalled, had married one of the Boyle daughters, that they should correspond more often.[4] In Cork's will, Parsons was described as his "credible and constant friend," and so he was. We find the earl's land agent in Ireland consulting Parsons frequently about the best action to be taken in numerous affairs concerning the earl's estate. The agent, in reporting on this advice, remarked: "all your friends here are in very good health ... Sir William Parsons willed me to remember his best respects unto your lordship." Later that year Parsons assured the earl that he was his "faithful well wisher and servant."[5]

Parsons, indeed, had his own reasons for cultivating Wentworth's rivals. During the early years of Charles's reign he had been able to procure numerous grants of land, no doubt by exploiting his position as master of the court of wards, but this process stopped with Wentworth's arrival. Indeed, when Cork was forced to abandon his claim to the lands of the College of Youghal in 1637, Parsons seems, like his friend, to have lost assets.[6]

Cork's need to call on Ranelagh and Parsons to help him protect his land in Connacht has important implications. Here was a New English planter finding his land at risk through the extension of the plantation process. If Wentworth controlled the government during the implementation of the new plantation, some planters could expect not only to be excluded from benefiting from the scheme but also to lose part of what they had – that is, to be treated as though they were Old English or Irish.

Cork's concern with Connacht also leads us to consider another small but, from a political point of view, influential interest: that of Lord Lambert, who possessed an estate in Westmeath. Lambert quarrelled with Cork and later used parliament to advance his cause. This dispute revolved around the earl's estate in Connacht, to which Lambert laid claim. The Irish privy council considered the case in April 1639 and sided with Cork "with many good demonstrances of the lord deputy's good respects unto your lordship."[7] Very possibly it was the king's insistence on a reconciliation between Cork and Wentworth which produced this unusual spectacle of the lord deputy siding with the earl, but the council's decision was not the end of the affair. As Cork seems to have realized, parliament gave Lambert a new forum in which to press his claim, and this has to be taken into account when we assess Lambert's parliamentary interventions.[8]

Yet another interest was that of Sir William St Leger, president of Munster. He too carried on a running feud with Cork. In September 1639, for instance, he had pursued a suit against the earl in which he attempted to have Cork's weir in the river at Lismore pulled down, a suit deemed "malicious" by the earl's agent. A few months before the rebellion the agent described St Leger as favouring the Irish.[9] St Leger's closest associates were Murrough O'Brien, the Protestant Lord Inchiquin, and Sir Philip Percival, clerk of the court of wards and, from 1640, clerk of the Irish House of Lords. Percival, let it be said, retained both Wentworth's and Cork's friendship, thus illustrating the overlapping nature of these groupings.[10] Finally, we should not forget the separate interests of the Scots in Ulster despite their close ties to English planters. Thirteen Scots were elected to the 1640 parliament, all but one of them sitting for Ulster constituencies.

THE COMPOSITION OF
THE PARLIAMENT IN 1640

As we examine the Irish parliament, it is important to stress this diversity of Protestant interest. There were times when the Irish Commons split along Catholic-Protestant lines, occasions stressed by contemporaries who have been followed by historians. Yet sometimes the Commons could react virtually unanimously when confronted with an important issue, and on other occasions, when division occurred, religion was not at issue. So far as is possible, we must probe into the nature of these divisions despite the absence of the type of sources, such as diaries, that are available for the English parliament, and what limited documentary sources are available have to be supplemented by committee analysis. A relatively small number of MPs dominated the committees, and by looking at shifts in the membership of this group we can detect changes in the attitude of the assembly as a whole.[11]

The writs for the Irish parliament had been issued by early February and the elections, conducted under Radcliffe's supervision as Strafford remained in England, seem to have taken place without incident.[12] Sir John Clotworthy, as part of his attack on Strafford in the Long Parliament, would charge that the executive manipulated the elections. His charge had some substance in that, through *quo warranto* proceedings, seven boroughs which had previously returned Catholic MPs lost their representation.[13] Executive manipulation may also have extended beyond this measure and beyond the Commons. About the time the MPs were gathering in Dublin, Cork wrote to Strafford asking that "the like respect be given to me as unto other noblemen of my quality whose Connacht lands are fallen within the compass of plantation, as mine there are," and an undated document shows that concessions were made to other Connacht landowners.[14] The government appears, therefore, to have been trying to generate support before parliament met. It would be misleading, however, to exaggerate this type of manipulation. The government was clearly determined to ensure a Protestant majority, as it had been in 1613 and 1634, and the number of Catholic MPs dropped from over 100 in 1634 to 76 in 1640 (9 of whom were Irish) in a house of 238 members. In a majoritarian system, such a decline would have meant a considerable loss of influence, but "seventeenth century debates were designed to achieve unity and unanimity," and the parliament in Ireland, like its counterpart in England, worked to a considerable extent on the basis of consensus. During the three sessions held in 1640 not a single formal division occurred. A sizeable minority could therefore exercise an influence not directly related to its numbers.[15]

The little we know about the way this parliament was assembled suggests as much compromise and muddle as manipulation. Strafford agreed that Cork should not have to return to Ireland to sit in the Lords, but stipulated that the earl of Ormond should receive his proxy vote. This information only reached Ormond after the first session had ended. Another peer received writs to sit in both the English and the Irish parliaments, and only the late arrival of the latter writ saved him from having to choose between the two obligations.[16]

In the Commons, ten counties sent two Catholic MPs and twelve (the majority in Ulster) sent two Protestants. Ten counties (two in Ulster) sent one MP of each religion. In one case (County Offaly or King's) we know the names of most of the ninety-four freeholders who participated in the election. They included a number of New English, but a substantial majority possessed Irish names. The decision to return one Catholic, John Coghlen, and one Protestant, William Parsons, Sir William's nephew, may reflect some government influence over the sheriff; alternatively, it may reflect a compromise at the local level that would satisfy both major parties similar to those commonly found in English elections of the period.[17] As the names of the freeholders appear together on a petition to the two MPs the following year, co-operation rather than competition seems the more likely explanation of the way this county selected its members.[18] Similarly, though later a regicide, Sir Hardress Waller, the Protestant MP for Limerick, another county which divided its vote between the religions, signed a petition in April 1641, along with such leading Catholics as the earl of Clanricard, Nicholas Barnewall, and Sir Roebuck (Robert) Lynch.[19] Once again, Catholic-Protestant co-operation at the local level seems the most likely explanation. An example of muddle in the selection of the Commons is to be found at Youghal. Despite a substantial Protestant component within the electorate that could have combined to procure at least one Protestant MP, two Catholics were elected. One candidate (a Protestant at Tallow, County Waterford) expected to be elected, but hoped he would not; the electorate obligingly chose another Protestant in his place.[20]

As parliament assembled on 16 March in Dublin Castle, most political interests had some representation. As might be expected, Strafford's close allies occupied a prominent position among the 160 Protestants elected. Radcliffe, Wandesford, Sir George Wentworth, Thomas Little (Strafford's secretary), Lord Robert Dillon, and others all had seats.[21]

Cork's correspondence reveals no evidence that he concerned himself with the Irish elections, but if he "did not bother to make use of his potential electoral influence, the people whom he would have recommended were elected anyway."[22] It should also be remembered that, while the election was taking place, there was little doubt about what the parliament would do and almost certainly no expectation that any opposition would develop. Cork had reason to believe that more was to be gained by using his influence at court than by attempting to establish an anti-Strafford lobby in the Irish parliament. Indeed, co-operation in Ireland could only enhance his position in

England. His attitude was made clear to Ormond as the parliament opened. "I presume," he wrote, "after good laws are enacted a following subsidy will be demanded." The burden of past taxes would, he claimed, make this difficult to bear, yet "considering how good and gracious a king we live well and peaceably under," he would "be as forward as any man to yield him subsidies." Cork then came to the heart of the matter and stated his hope that Ormond would exercise his influence in moderating the burden that would fall on Cork personally.[23] In short, Cork clearly expected private intervention would be more productive than parliamentary opposition. Nevertheless, many of his friends sat in parliament, including Sir William Parsons and his relatives in the Commons, and Ranelagh in the Lords. He also had enemies. Sir Robert Forth, for instance, son of Sir Ambrose Forth, a judge, may well have been linked to Lord Lambert. Forth's lands lay in Cavan, but he sat for the borough of Kilbeggan, County Westmeath, where Lambert had his estate, and it is unlikely that Forth could have obtained this seat without that peer's concurrence.[24]

THE FIRST SESSION

From the government's point of view, the outcome of the first session could hardly have been more satisfactory. Strafford, who had arrived in Ireland on 18 March, appeared in state before the assembled Lords and Commons on the twentieth. The speaker, Maurice Eustace, whose speech has already been quoted, compared him to Solon and praised his administration in similar terms. By the twenty-third, the Commons had given unanimous approval to the first reading of a bill that would grant four subsidies of £45,000 each, to be collected at six-month intervals over the next eighteen months, starting 1 June. On the twenty-sixth, the bill received its second and third readings.[25] Members asserted that they would have liked to have taxed themselves more heavily had money been available: "as his majesty is the best of kings so this people should strive to be ranked amongst the best of subjects." Some went even farther and allowed that precedent permitted the king to levy taxes without parliament. Finally, a declaration was drawn up by a joint committee of both houses to be appended to the act, in which the Covenanters were exhorted to obedience and the king assured that more money would be granted if it was needed.[26] By early April, therefore, when Strafford left Ireland to attend the opening of parliament in England on the thirteenth, not only had he procured funds for a new Irish army to fight the Scots, but he had also gained a precedent for parliamentary support for the king's policy.

Table 3
Commons Committees and Leaders, First Three Sessions of Parliament, 1640

	First Session 16 Mar.–1 Apr.			Second Session 1–17 June			Third Session 1 Oct.–12 Nov.		
No. committees established	7			18			24		
Leadership criterion	on 4 or more committees (½ of total)			on 6 or more committees (⅓ of total)			on 6 or more committees (¼ of total)		

	First Session			Second Session			Third Session		
	Cath.	Prot.	Total	Cath.	Prot.	Total	Cath.	Prot.	Total
Appointed to one or more committees	21	57	78	31	52	83	46	59	105
Leaders	5	8	13	6	9	15	8	13	21
Committees with Catholic majority			1			7			9
Committees with Protestant majority			5			11			9
% of elected Caths. on committees			27			40			60
% of elected Prots. on committees			36			33			36

Strafford's evident control over the Irish parliament during this session raises the question of how the Commons, a body of 238 men, was managed. First, it has to be stressed that it is unlikely that all MPS ever attended at one time. In 1641 there were five divisions and the largest number of MPS voting in any one of these was 175.[27] Yet even this number would be difficult to direct. As in England, it was through committees that decisions were reached, and as Table 3 shows, during the first session, only seventy-eight MPS sat on committees (twenty-one Catholics, or 27 per cent of those elected, and fifty-seven Protestants, or 36 per cent of those elected).

More important than the members of the committees were the leaders in the Commons. These leaders can be identified by noting the frequency with which an MP sat on committees. The decision of where to draw the line in identifying this élite has to be arbitrary to some extent. For Table 3, those who sat on four or more of the seven committees (or over half) during the first session have been identified as leaders.[28]

Table 4
Protestant Leaders in Commons, 1640, and Number of Committees
on Which They Served

Name	1st Session of 7 committees	2nd Session of 18 committees	3rd Session of 24 committees
First Session			
1 *BYSSE*, John – P lawyer, recorder of Dublin	4	14	6
2 DILLON, Lord Robert* pro-Strafford	4	9	6
3 *FITZGERALD*, Richard – P office holder	4	pr	16 Eng.
4 RADCLIFFE, Sir George* pro-Strafford	6	Left Ireland c. 10 June	pr (5)
5 SAMBACH, Sir William* solicitor-general, pro-Strafford	5	11	pr (3)
6 TREVOR, Sir Edward* army officer	4	–	pr (1)
7 WANDESFORD, Sir Christopher* master of rolls, pro-Strafford	4	Made lord deputy, died 3 Dec. 1640	
8 WARE, Sir James member, committee of defective titles	4	pr	9
Second Session			
9 *BORLASE*, Sir John* master of ordnance, became lord justice	pr	6	–
10 *BYSSE*, Robert recorder of Drogheda	pr	7	6
11 *LOFTUS*, Sir Adam* vice-treasurer	pr	8	6
12 *MEREDITH*, Sir Robert* chancellor of exchequer	pr	6	pr (4)
13 *PARSONS*, Sir William* master court of wards, became lord justice	pr	6	pr (3)
14 *WALLER*, Sir Hardress – P	pr	6	15 Eng.
Third Session			
15 *COLE*, Sir William – P	pr	pr	6 Eng.
16 *COOTE*, Sir Charles* vice-president Connacht	pr	–	7
17 *DENNY*, Sir Edward – P	–	–	6
18 *MONTGOMERY*, Sir James	pr	pr	8 Eng.
19 *ROWLEY*, Edward	–	pr	6 Eng.
20 *TRAVERS*, Sir Robert – P	–	pr	7

Key: * = on council; P = signed November Petition; *ITALIC* = in opposition; pr (#) = present
but not leader, number of committees to which appointed in parentheses; Eng. = on committee
sent to England.

Table 5
Catholic Leaders in Commons, 1640, and Number of Committees
on Which They Served

Name	1st Session of 7 committees	2nd Session of 18 committees	3rd Session of 24 committees
First Session			
1 BOURKE, Thomas – P	6	–	13 Eng.
2 BROWN, Geoffrey – P X	6	13	10 Eng.
3 FITZHARRIS, Sir Edward – P	5	9	17
			† 3 Mar. 1641
4 LYNCH, Sir Roebuck – P X	5	7	12 Eng.
5 PLUNKETT, Nicholas – P X			
lawyer	7	13	12 Eng.
Second Session			
6 BARNEWALL, Nicholas – P			
lawyer	–	6	pr (5) Eng.
7 CUSACK, James – X			
lawyer	pr	11	10
Third Session			
8 BLAKE, Sir Richard – X	pr	pr	10
9 MacCARTHY, Sir Donough – P X	–	pr (2)	8 Eng.
10 WALSH, John – P	not a leader		pr (3)
lawyer	but appointed		
	to English		
	committee		

Key: P = signed November Petition; X = later sat on one or more of the supreme councils of the Catholic Confederation of Kilkenny (see Cregan, "Confederation of Kilkenny," 88–91); Eng. = on committee sent to England; pr (#) = present but not leader, number of committees to which appointed in parentheses.

Table 4 shows us what we might expect given the good service provided by the Commons to the executive during the first session. A high proportion of the leaders held government positions. No less than six of the eight Protestant leaders, including such men as Radcliffe, Wandesford, and Lord Robert Dillon, sat on the privy council. The remaining two were John Bysse, a lawyer and the recorder of Dublin, and Richard Fitzgerald, who held a government position. Even below this level of Protestant leadership we find such men as Dr Edward Lake, whom Laud had recommended to Strafford and who served as advocate-general. Robert Bysse, who sat on three committees, was John Bysse's brother and recorder of Drogheda.[29] Similarly, the five Catholic leaders (Table 5) were eminent men in their community, two of them being lawyers. Of the five, no less than four were chosen to represent the interests of the Irish Commons in England at the end of the year, and three subsequently served on one or more of the supreme councils of the Catholic Confederation. Sir Edward Fitzharris, who died in March 1641, had a history of defending Catholic interests.[30]

THE ENGLISH SHORT PARLIAMENT AND THE IRISH SECOND SESSION

In light of the success of the first session in securing the subsidies, it may be asked why Strafford decided to prorogue parliament to 1 June rather than to dissolve it. The answer lies in a document to be found among Cork's papers. Under Poynings's Act, all bills submitted to the Irish parliament had first to be approved by the king. As the document makes clear, the bills for this parliament were sent to England in two batches. Ten were submitted to the first session, and in the main passed into acts. There was a second batch, however, containing twenty-five bills, including the highly contentious one giving parliamentary sanction to the plantation in Connacht and the counties of Limerick and Tipperary.[31] Evidently the passing of the subsidies was not to be jeopardized by being linked to plantation, so the government needed another session of parliament to enact this and other measures. The presence of this document among Cork's papers implies a stronger concern about Irish parliamentary politics than his disinterest in the election might suggest.

Certainly the success in Ireland heartened some in the government in England: "God grant us the grace here," wrote the earl of Northumberland to the earl of Leicester, "to follow this good example."[32] Nevertheless, as Strafford returned to England to attend parliament there he can have had few illusions that the Irish example would be easy to replicate. In England the election was fought in a few constituencies in a manner that broke from the tradition of consensus or unity. More serious, however, was Charles's failure to handle the Commons in a manner that opened the door for moderate MPs to support him. Instead, he asked for backing without explaining the reasons for the war, and supply without addressing grievances. As a result, "jealousies and suspicions" arose which were easily exploited by those who opposed the war such as John Pym. Only in early May did Sir Henry Vane come forward with the sort of proposal which might have won friends earlier: that Ship Money be abolished in return for twelve subsidies. The price was considered "awesomely large," however, and the Commons rejected it, whereupon, on 5 May, what came to be called the Short Parliament was dissolved.

Division within the English council continued even as parliament sat. Strafford was too ill at the opening of the session to exert much influence, but his ultimate objective was to see Scotland governed by the English council. Vane and his friends wished to avoid war, however, and during one important vote in the Lords, Holland absented himself. The large number of subsidies demanded seems to have been Vane's idea, as was the decision to dissolve parliament, the latter gaining only reluctant agreement from the lord lieutenant.[33]

After the failure of the parliament, Strafford fell ill again, so ill indeed that Northumberland prepared Leicester to be ready to succeed him. The queen, he thought, would support such a move, Laud would not oppose it, and all would depend on Hamilton, who now "is most absolute in court."[34] Strafford recovered his health, but never his position of strong authority either in England or in Ireland where the failure of the Short Parliament made a profound impact. It is hard to accept Sir George Wentworth's allegation that one man – Vane – in league with Hamilton and Holland in England and Parsons and others in Ireland, deliberately engineered this débâcle. Yet Clarendon, no friend to Strafford, also held Vane responsible and asserted that Vane "acted the part maliciously" out of his "implacable hatred" of the lord lieutenant.[35] Certainly, what we find in Ireland shows that Parsons and his friends, with or without English allies, had also turned against Strafford.

Strafford had left Wandesford to run Irish affairs and Ormond to raise the new army of 8,000 foot and 1,000 horse for which the subsidies had been granted. Even before the Irish parliament reassembled on 1 June there were signs of impending difficulties. The spring had been late in coming and, as Bramhall had reported, there was general discontent. By this time the Scottish conflict had begun to affect Irish trade, and supplies for the new army proved difficult to collect, so that it was mid-July before it began to assemble at Carrickfergus.[36] Wandesford needed all possible support as he prepared for the second session, yet Ormond could not attend and was asked to bestow his proxies on Viscount Ranelagh and Lord Digby. "I confess," Wandesford wrote to Ormond, that "your presence would be of great countenance to the king's service, but your own particular must be attended." His "particular," let it be said, had nothing to do with raising the new army but, as a later letter makes clear, referred to his wife's "great belly."[37]

Historians have recognized that Irish MPs began their opposition to Strafford's government during the second session. They did not engage in outright defiance but caused serious embarrassment on a number of important issues. The right to return MPs was restored to the seven boroughs disfranchised by Strafford, and the bill to implement the western plantation went to a sub-committee, never to emerge. Another committee declared that the government had acted prematurely in beginning to collect the subsidies before an order had been issued by the Commons. As a result, although the collection of the first subsidy was allowed to proceed, the other three were ordered to be collected in such a way as would substantially reduce their value. The second subsidy, in fact, raised only £9,922.10.8 compared with the nearly £45,000 supplied by the first. Other indications of the new mood of the Commons were a protest against clerical fees, the acceptance of a petition alleging sodomy against Bishop Atherton, one of Strafford's agents in his dispute with Cork, and a letter from the house "requiring" the Court of High Commission to reverse two of its sentences of excommunication.[38]

In the Lords, meanwhile, Lambert, supported by the Catholics, Viscount Gormanston, Lord Kilmallock, and Lord Slane, moved to join with the Commons on the issue of subsidies. The government, led by Bramhall, with the aid of the judges, managed to beat off this attack (Ranelagh raised issues which suggest a fence-sitting position), but the fact that it had to be fended off indicated the extent to which the administration had been placed on the defensive. As part of this defence, it was moved in the Lords to prorogue parliament till October, presumably on the assumption that by that time Charles would have restored his control over Scotland and, thus, England. The Commons pressed for and received two extra days to air their grievances, but on 17 June, after just over two weeks of sitting, Wandesford prorogued both houses till 1 October.[39]

It is accepted that the large Protestant majority in the Commons meant that some Protestants had to be working with the Catholics to initiate these sorts of measures. It is unlikely that any form of opposition was contemplated till after news of the failure of the Short Parliament reached Ireland. As Wandesford did not know the final outcome of the English parliament till after 16 May, we may assume that plans for opposition, and the Catholic-Protestant link upon which it depended, only began to take shape shortly before 1 June, or even after that date. It is striking that the Commons' journals betray not a hint of resistance until 8 June, and the wording of an undated petition from the Pale counties, which seems to have initiated the move to question the method of collecting the subsidies, implies that the second session had already begun when it was written.[40] The limited nature of the opposition, moreover, suggests hasty improvisation. To probe more deeply into the composition of this opposition, and more particularly into the structure of Catholic-Protestant co-operation, we must look at the committees.

During the second session, thirty-one Catholics and fifty-two Protestants sat on one or more committees. Catholics had not, therefore, as Thomas Carte claimed, gained a majority because Protestants were serving in the new army. There is no evidence to suggest that men were appointed to committees when they were absent and some to the contrary. At least three men who were officers can be found on committees. In terms of leaders (those serving on one-third or more of the committees), the six Catholics and nine Protestants provided a more even match in this session, but if this reflects a strong Catholic influence, it was influence gained with Protestant co-operation rather than over Protestant objections.[41] Perhaps more significantly, only two of the Protestants who served as leaders during the first session were entirely absent from committees, and by implication from the house, during the second session. One of these was Wandesford. The second was Sir Edward Trevor, who does seem to have been engaged in raising the new army, but the absence of one man could not have brought about a decisive change in the power structure of the Commons. Radcliffe still qualified as a leader, but instead of sitting on more than half the committees, appeared on barely a third. This decline in participation is explained by his departure for England on 10 or 11 of June, or just as the opposition had begun. Radcliffe's departure must have seriously weakened the government's position, but the most serious threat came not from absenteeism but from defection, a defection which transformed some Protestant leaders (including some councillors) into opponents and thus diminished the influence of those who remained loyal.[42]

We may look at the Catholic leaders first because part of the evidence confirming the Protestant defection is ascribed to one of them, the Old English lawyer, Nicholas Plunkett. According to the account credited to him, it was "soon after" the 1640 parliament met that the Catholics and elements within the Irish council, including Sir William Parsons, Sir Adam Loftus, Sir Charles Coote, Sir John Borlase, and the chancellor of the exchequer, Sir Robert Meredith, began to work together. The second session is the earliest point at which such a link could have been forged.[43]

With the exception of Thomas Bourke, who seems to have been absent from the session, all those who had been Catholic leaders during the first session, including Plunkett, continued their leadership during the second. In addition, two other Old English lawyers joined the leadership group, Nicholas Barnewall, Plunkett's cousin, and James Cusack, who, like so many of the other Catholic leaders, later sat on the supreme council of the Catholic Confederation. It was this group that linked up with members of the Irish council.

By the time the rebellion broke out, the Catholics had learned to distrust Parsons and his friends more than any other Protestant faction. The assertion of an alliance could not be accepted if it rested on one source, but confirmation of some such link comes from no less an authority than Wandesford himself. On 12 June 1640, four days after the first signs of opposition in the Commons had emerged, he wrote to his cousin to report that the Commons grew "worse and worse every day." "Neither," he continued, "hath these late debates concerning the declaration [against the method of collecting the subsidies] been prosecuted by the Irish only, but those of our own party (as we call them) have joined apparently with them ... " Lord Robert Dillon and William Sambach, the solicitor-general, alone were identified as supporting the government.[44] Ten days later Wandesford wrote again to report defection, not only within parliament, but within the council itself: "would you not think it strange," he asked, "that [in] the debate which was handled at the board concerning this late declaration there was not above 3 of those gentlemen which stood to the deputy."[45] The only Protestant named by Wandesford as working with the Catholics was the "recorder," a reference to John Bysse, recorder of Dublin, but it may be assumed that his brother, Robert, recorder of Drogheda, and by this session also a leader, followed suit. We know as well that disaffection with the method of collecting the subsidies went beyond these town officials in the Protestant community.[46]

Apart from the Bysse brothers, Dillon, and Sambach, the Protestant leadership during this session included four councillors, Borlase, Loftus, Meredith, and Parsons and one Munster planter who was not on the council, Sir Hardress Waller.[47] Of the councillors alleged to have combined with the Catholics, only Coote was not among the parliamentary leaders during this session. He may have been absent from Dublin as he did not appear on any committee, but he was a leader during the following session. Parsons, as we have seen, had worked closely with Cork. H.F. Kearney has placed Sir Adam within Strafford's party. However, he had more links with Parsons, and indeed Cork, than with Strafford and was remembered in Cork's will. It is true that during his impeachment proceedings Strafford wrote two letters to Sir Adam, but that was because he possessed important information which could damage the lord lieutenant. In one of these letters, Strafford referred to Ranelagh as "your friend"; Sir Adam, therefore, clearly moved in the Parsons-Cork-Ranelagh orbit.[48] Of Meredith we know much less, but it is significant that in 1643 he was arrested, along with Parsons and Loftus, for opposing the truce between Charles and the Confederate Catholics, and there is no reason to place him among Strafford's allies.[49] Finally, although Sir Paul Davies, clerk of the council, was not among the Protestant leaders, he was active in committees, sitting on four. He too was connected to Parsons, and during Strafford's trial it emerged that it was he who had kept Cork informed about what Wentworth did on the Irish council.[50]

Sir Hardress Waller lived at Castletown, County Limerick, a seigneury inherited by his wife, Elizabeth Dowdall, whom he married in 1629. The Dowdalls were Old English but Protestant. Strafford recognized that this estate would be affected by the plantation plans for the west, which explains Sir Hardress's association with Catholic landowners in April 1641 when they petitioned for protection of land titles in the area. By October 1640 Waller had gained the reputation of making loyal speeches but "voting" against the government. He, too, was on familiar terms with Cork, serving as agent on part of his estate and living in his home, Lismore Castle, when the earl was in England.[51]

An important committee was the one which dealt with the bill to implement the plantations in the west. It was formed before any sign of opposition had developed, on 3 June, and consisted of six Catholics and ten Protestants (including loyal Strafford men such as Dillon and Radcliffe, but also Parsons and Loftus). It was this committee that, on 8 June, nominated a sub-committee to consider amendments to the bill. This sub-committee not only had a Catholic majority but was also to be advised by the two leading Old English lawyers, Patrick Darcy and Richard Martin. The bill was given second reading that day, but never surfaced again. Such a sub-committee could only have been formed with the acquiescence of numerous Protestants.[52]

Another vital committee challenged the government over the subsidies. On this committee there were nineteen Catholics and twenty Protestants, but seven of the latter can be identified with the opposition.[53] It was the same committee, with one Protestant and two Catholic additions, which drew up the grievances against the clergy. The eight-member committee which presented these to Wandesford contained only one Catholic (Sir Edward Fitzharris), but if we include him, a majority can be associated with the opposition. Finally, the standing committee on grievances and privileges established on the last day of the session to deal with Commons business during the adjournment contained at least twenty-five Protestants and only eight Catholics. Among the Protestants, most were hostile to Strafford and only three were sympathizers.[54]

These findings indicate that the disappearance of the plantation bill represented as much the wishes of Parsons and his friends as

those of the Old English. While Strafford governed Ireland, the
Parsons group stood to gain nothing from the western plantation,
but if he left the Irish post, it stood to benefit considerably from the
redistribution of the western lands. Sir George Wentworth believed
that the spoils of Connacht motivated his brother's enemies, and we
have seen that the marquis of Hamilton, as well as men like Cork
and Waller, had an interest in the project. It is hard, therefore, not
to see the Old English at this stage as being used by Parsons and his
friends as much as they were using the councillors. Moreover, there
is confirmation of this interpretation in the behaviour of such men
as Parsons during the following year. The most powerful planters
wanted not only to rid themselves of Strafford but also to enrich
themselves once he was gone.

Just as the Short Parliament's outcome affected the Irish political
atmosphere, the recalcitrance of the Commons during the second
session of the Irish parliament had political consequences in England.
Charles was desperately short of funds with which to pay his English
army. He had been led to expect at least £180,000 from Ireland, but
he could now anticipate less than half of this (and in fact he only
received a fraction of even the reduced sum). No wonder that it was
reported to the earl of Bridgwater on 26 June that Strafford became
"mightily angry" upon hearing what the Irish Commons had done
and that the news was "not well taken" by the king.[55] It is hard not
to see the earl of Cork's appointment to the English council on 28
June as a response to the news from Ireland. Bridgwater's informant,
John Castle, related that Cork had "paid both vows and obligations
at some altar or other" to gain the position. Strafford, he said,
interpreted the promotion both as "his diminution" and an indication
that Cork wished to replace him "in the government of that
kingdom." The "altars" may have included those of Laud, who had
worked for Cork before, and Hamilton, because Northumberland,
himself a member of the council, reported that the bond between
Laud and Strafford had become strained, that Hamilton kept "an
interest in them all, but deceives the world," and that Strafford had
now developed great confidence in Lord Cottington.[56] Certainly, the
news from Ireland had weakened the lord lieutenant's political position at court.

THE THIRD SESSION

While this manœuvring was taking place in England, the Scottish
parliament met in June against the king's wishes; then the assembly
sat in Aberdeen from 28 July to 5 August. By the third of that month

the Scots had decided to invade England; they entered the country on the twentieth, and ten days later, after the flight of Viscount Conway's troops at Newburn, they took Newcastle unopposed. In Ireland, Sir William St Leger had quickly brought the new army to a state of readiness. As the Scots marched into England, he was collecting the boats constructed by the earl of Antrim the previous year to launch his invasion of Scotland, but events overtook these plans. Under pressure from the English peers, some of whom sympathized with the Scots, Charles agreed to start discussions with the Covenanters and to hold elections for a new English parliament which was to meet on 3 November. Negotiations between Charles and his Scottish subjects began at Ripon the day after the Irish parliament met for its third session on 1 October.[57]

During that session, the Irish parliament passed nine bills into law, most of them about minor issues. One of these acts, however, served the interests of Cork and another those of Ranelagh. We know, moreover, that Cork's bill had been taken to Ireland by Radcliffe when he returned there in August. If this was an attempt to placate the most powerful planter interest, it not only failed but illustrates Strafford's inability to assess accurately the nature and the strength of the opposition against him, a failure underlined by his proposal in August to expel all the Scots from Ulster by force.[58] As historians have stressed, the Scottish success had weakened him to the point that his enemies could launch attacks upon him, first in the Irish parliament and, while this was still in progress, in England. The circumstantial evidence makes it clear that those who launched these assaults worked in concert.[59]

Almost as soon as it reassembled, the Irish Commons challenged the Dublin government. During the recess, the chancellor had delayed elections to the boroughs re-enfranchised by the Commons in the second session. The Commons now called him to account for his action and pressed for elections. It then renewed the demands made at the end of the second session for the reform of the church, and it took a step towards constitutional innovation.

Under Poynings's Act, Irish bills had to go to England for approval by the king before being considered by the Irish parliament. In theory there was nothing to prevent these bills having their origin in the parliament, but in practice they had always originated with the executive. On 13 October, however, the Commons set up a committee "for drawing up of Acts," and towards the end of the session it established another to meet with the council "to know, whether they have transmitted those bills into England, that were presented to them from this house; and if they have not to give their reasons."

Despite Poynings's Act, therefore, the Irish Commons had found a means of reaching for, if not attaining, the constitutional position of its English counterpart. On a more pragmatic level, while starting this tentative constitutional move, the MPS also began to implement the collection of the subsidies at the reduced rate established during the second session.[60]

Wandesford became desperate. Half the first subsidy, assessed at the high rate and due for payment on 1 June, was still owing, yet the new army was costing £1,000 per day to maintain and, to make matters worse, the harvest was poor.[61] He decided to address parliament himself, but his speech can only have encouraged the MPS opposed to the regime. After commenting on their demands for church reform, he accused them of "jealousy ... of the supreme power," then withdrew the implication of treason by saying that it was the king's ministers and not the king that they disliked. He went on to demand action on the subsidies, warned that the Scots would not be deterred by "your petulant disputations or paper declarations," and threatened that if "Caesar" did not receive his due, "he knows the way to take it himself." The Commons took no notice, proceeded to implement the lower rate of subsidy, and began to prepare its Humble and Just Remonstrance, which was ready for presentation to Wandesford on 7 November.[62]

The preparation of the Remonstrance seems to have been kept secret from men like Radcliffe, who nevertheless advised Strafford at the end of October to prorogue parliament, even at the expense of further delay in obtaining parliamentary sanction for the Connacht project. Radcliffe was at a loss what to do about the subsidies. On 5 November Strafford replied. He agreed to prorogation but insisted on the impossible condition that before this was done the Connacht bill must be passed and the Commons "kept to consider only the laws transmitted, without admitting them any new discourse of other matters." The opinion of the Commons about the size and method of collecting the subsidies was not to be accepted, and their resolutions on the matter were to be torn out of the journal.[63] Four days later the king sent instructions to the same effect, but before these arrived, on 12 November, Wandesford had, on his own initiative, prorogued parliament until 26 January to forestall further discussion on the Remonstrance. The king's instructions reached Ireland by the nineteenth, whereupon Wandesford summoned those MPS still in Dublin and in their presence tore out of the journal the pages prescribing the reduced subsidy rates.[64]

The Remonstrance had been introduced into the Commons on Saturday, 7 November. It was read twice, and challenges from the floor by Radcliffe and others were shouted down; officially, therefore, it was approved unanimously and made available to the public immediately, thus underlining its role as a public act of defiance. After its approval, the Commons appointed a select committee to present it to Wandesford. By the following Wednesday, fearing proroguement or dissolution before their grievances had been considered, the MPS took special precautions. The house, sitting as a committee of the whole, selected a committee, whose members were to be chosen "out of every province," to present their grievances to the king in England, if no redress could be obtained in Ireland before proroguement. The precaution proved wise. By the following day they had received an answer from Wandesford suggesting that a committee of the council and a committee of the Commons discuss the issue. Even as they were preparing to send a message back rejecting this proposal, they received the summons to the Lords for the prorogation.[65]

Kearney has commented that the grievances in the Remonstrance are as interesting for what they do not list as for what they do. There was no demand for religious toleration, or for stronger application of the recusancy laws. Some of the strongest desires of both poles of the religious divide were suppressed in the interests of maintaining an alliance that could benefit all. The sixteen clauses of the Remonstrance may be divided into the economic, the legal, and the constitutional. Some of the economic issues, such as the accusation that there had been a "general decay of trade" have already been discussed. Another important issue was the failure to give legal effect to the land tenure security clause of the Graces, which extended to Ireland what had been granted in England under the Concealment Act of 1624. Other economic issues included monopolies, particularly tobacco, and the "cruel usage" of the inhabitants of the city and county of Londonderry which, it was charged, reduced them to poverty and forced many of them to leave the country. The clauses concerning legal matters objected primarily to the use of the council to settle matters normally handled by the courts, a matter of some consequence to the lawyers in the house as they lost clients as a result. Finally, there were two clauses with constitutional implications: first, the claim that parliament had lost its freedom because of the powerfulness of some ministers, and, second, an objection to the restraints on access to the king.[66]

This last complaint had immediate significance. The day after proroguing parliament Wandesford called before the council the committee that was to go to England and demanded from each member an answer about whether he would go or not, and on receiving an affirmative reply in each case, he forbade the committee's departure.[67]

Yet, even before he issued the order, Strafford's opponents on both sides of the Irish Sea had been taking precautions to frustrate any attempts he might make to prevent communication between the two prongs of the attack. All parties in the struggle understood the key part that communication between the two countries was going to play in the drama that was unfolding.

In considering the communications between the two parliaments, it has to be remembered that it took at least five days for news and important government mail to pass between the capitals. As early as 4 November, the day after the Long Parliament met, Bramhall warned Laud that "some" in the Irish Commons had resolved to send agents into England.[68] Almost certainly it was the arrival of these men that sparked Pym's attack upon the lord lieutenant because it was launched on the eleventh, just when they arrived from Ireland. As the impeachment charge went up to the Lords, along with it went a resolution from the English Commons that "some fit course may be taken, that there may be free passage between Ireland and England, notwithstanding any restraint to the contrary." The Lords took the issue up with the king, and by the eighteenth a proclamation to this effect had been issued by the English council. On the same day Robert Baillie, the Scottish minister, who was in London, knew of the Irish Remonstrance and claimed that the king had received a copy of it.[69]

The Remonstrance was "annexed" to a second document, a Humble Petition, signed by eighty-four Irish MPs. The contents of this petition had little significance (it complained of the failure to deal with grievances and the restriction on access to the king), but it is helpful in that it sheds light on the way the Irish parliament was working during the third session. Twenty-eight of those who signed this document were Protestant. Because of the time it took to pass between Ireland and England, the date by which we know that this document had reached London, and the time it must have taken to draw up such a document and have it signed by eighty-four Catholics and Protestants, we can be sure that it was prepared during the third session. It can be used, therefore, in interpreting the committee membership of that session, those who signed this November petition being clearly identified with the opposition.[70]

COMMITTEE LEADERSHIP
DURING THE THIRD SESSION

Forty-six Catholics and fifty-nine Protestants sat on one or more of the twenty-four committees that met during the third session. If membership on one-quarter of these committees (six) is selected as the criterion of leadership, we are dealing with the most active twenty-one MPs (eight Catholics and thirteen Protestants). An examination of this group suggests opposition to the government in virtually every quarter of the political nation.

All but two of the eight Catholic leaders had been leaders in at least one of the two previous sessions. The new arrivals to the leadership group were Sir Richard Blake, from Galway, and Sir Donough MacCarthy, the son and heir of the influential Viscount Muskerry.[71] Six of the leaders signed the November Petition and five of them, including Sir Donough, sat on the important Commons committee of thirteen that was sent to represent Irish interests in London.[72] The two other Catholic members of this committee were Nicholas Barnewall, a leader during the second session though not the third, and John Walsh, a Waterford lawyer who had not been active during the first two sessions but sat on three committees during the third. We see, therefore, a high degree of leadership continuity from one session to another and from this to membership of the committee that went to England.

The Protestant leadership may be divided into two groups. Richard Fitzgerald sat on sixteen committees and Sir Hardress Waller on fifteen, or well over half the committees. Both signed the November Petition, both had been leaders in earlier sessions, Fitzgerald during the first and Waller during the second. Waller's role as a member of the opposition has already been noted, and both men were appointed to the committee that was sent to England. Fitzgerald sat for an Ulster constituency but lived in Dublin and in 1641 he was described as holding an unspecified office. Sir George Wentworth linked him to Ranelagh; he was also a brother-in-law to Sir Paul Davies, Cork's friend, and he served as Parsons's agent in 1642, taking dispatches to England.[73]

The second group, consisting of eleven MPs, sat on from six to nine committees. These included four councillors, Lord Robert Dillon, Sir James Ware, Sir Adam Loftus, and Sir Charles Coote. Dillon was certainly a loyal government supporter; Ware probably was because Strafford had him promoted to the council in 1639, and he had dedicated his *De Scriptoribus Hiberniae* to Wentworth that same year.[74] Loftus, as we have seen, was almost certainly part of the opposition. Coote, vice-president of Connacht and therefore a close colleague of Ranelagh, also belonged to the Parsons-Cork group. Indeed, in 1632, Coote, Parsons, and others were specifically described as "all birds of a feather and the earl of Cork's party." Possibly Coote was closer to Cork than to either Ranelagh or Parsons. He acted as Cork's messenger to England during the initial planning for the plantation of Connacht, and he was a partner with Cork in an iron works in Connacht.[75]

None of the councillors signed the November Petition; to have done so would have led to serious accusations of disloyalty though we may note that William Parsons, the nephew of the master of wards, did sign. Of the remaining seven leaders, six signed the Petition; the eight Protestant leaders who signed, including Fitzgerald and Waller, therefore formed a majority among this group. Apart from the Bysse brothers, Fitzgerald, and Waller, we find among the non-councillor leaders Sir Edward Denny, a second-generation planter from County Kerry who was not linked to the Boyle family, Sir Robert Travers, who sat for a County Cork borough and had married into the Boyle family, and three men with Ulster connections: Edward Rowley, brother-in-law to Sir John Clotworthy, Sir James Montgomery of Rosemount, and Sir William Cole. Montgomery had opposed the policy of making the Ulster Scots sign the oath against the Covenant; Cole of Enniskillen had spent some time in prison on Strafford's command. All three sat on the committee that went to England.[76] The extent of disaffection with the government is emphasized by a letter written by George Rawdon to Viscount Conway, Charles's general in England. Rawdon, who was Conway's agent in Ireland, suggested that the viscount would have identified with the Remonstrance.[77]

If we look at the composition of particular committees, we gain the same general impression of a consensus of opposition within the body of the Commons while the councillor MPs seem to have been divided. Despite the Protestant majority in the house, nine committees, including the one assigned the task of representing the Irish Commons in England, had Catholic majorities. The committee sent to Wandesford on 7 November to determine when the Remonstrance could be presented consisted of seven Protestants, including three councillors, and three Catholics. Moreover, two of these councillors can be associated with Cork. Similarly, the committee sent to obtain the answer to the Remonstrance on 11 November consisted of eight Protestants and three Catholics. The Protestants, in this case, included four councillors, three of whom, including Parsons himself, were Cork associates.[78] Table 6 shows the participation of the councillors on the committees during this session. It may be remarked that on nine committees councillors were absent.

This table takes into account those who were active in the session but who do not qualify as leaders according to the criterion used for determining leadership in this session. Thus, it shows the participa-

Table 6
Participation of Councillors on Commons Committees, Third Session, 1640

| Councillors | Dates on Which Committees Formed | | | | | | | | | | | | | |
| | October | | | | | | | | | | | November | | |
	5	10	13	13	21	23	23	24	24	24	27	7	10	11
Strafford's supporters														
Lord Robert Dillon	–	x	–	–	x	x	–	–	x	x	x	–	–	–
Sir George Radcliffe	–	x	–	–	x	x	–	–	x	x	–	–	–	–
Sir William Sambach	x	–	–	x	–	–	–	–	–	–	–	–	x	–
Sir James Ware*	x	–	–	x	x	x	x	x	x	x	–	–	–	x
Cork's associates														
Sir Charles Coote	–	–	x	x	–	x	–	–	x	x	x	x	–	–
Sir Paul Davies	x	x	–	x	–	x	–	–	–	x	–	–	–	–
Sir Adam Lotfus	–	–	–	–	x	x	–	–	x	x	–	x	–	x
Sir Robert Meredith	–	–	–	x	x	–	–	–	x	–	–	–	–	x
Sir William Parsons	–	x	–	x	–	–	–	–	–	–	–	–	–	x

Key: – = not appointed to committee; x = appointed to committee
* Ware cannot be identified definitely with either group, but was probably closer to Strafford than to Cork.

tion of men such as Radcliffe, Meredith, and Parsons. The most revealing feature of the table is the balance maintained between the two groups on the council up to 27 October, a balance which seems to have diminished to the disadvantage of Strafford's supporters after the adjournment and at the time that the Remonstrance became the primary issue. By the end of November Radcliffe, who had returned to England, had become sufficiently suspicious of his councillor colleagues to add side-notes to official correspondence that were for Wandesford's eyes only.[79]

As might be expected, the government, with the earl of Ormond's assistance, controlled the Lords much better than the Commons, though even here there was a move on 30 October to reduce the subsidies, and Ranelagh seems to have been associated with it. By the end of the session the demands of the Lords had become almost as outspoken as those of the lower house: they, too, were insisting that the Graces should be implemented, that subjects should have free access to the king, and, with pointed reference to the way they were being managed, that only peers who possessed land in Ireland should have votes in their house. Nor did the prorogation deter them from pressing their demands. Shortly after it had been imposed, "the major part of the lords" then in Dublin appointed Viscounts Gormanston, Dillon of Costello-Galen, Kilmallock, and Muskerry to take their grievances directly to the king. We know little about the activities of this committee of the Lords save that by February of the next year Gormanston, Kilmallock, and Muskerry had reached England.[80]

We know much more about the committee that the Commons sent to England. It was unique in that the house had specifically required that all four provinces be represented. Connacht sent Thomas Bourke, Sir Roebuck Lynch, and Geoffrey Brown, all Catholics; Sir Hardress Waller, John Walsh, and Sir Donough MacCarthy, a Protestant and two Catholics, represented Munster; Leinster sent two Catholics, Nicholas Plunkett and Nicholas Barnewall, and two Protestants, Simon Digby of Offaly (King's) and Richard Fitzgerald of Dublin; and Ulster's delegation consisted of three Protestants, Sir James Montgomery, Sir William Cole, and Edward Rowley. All the members of this committee signed the November Petition. Technically, the committee had a Catholic majority of one, but as Sir Donough MacCarthy returned to Ireland upon inheriting his father's title in February and was never replaced, the committee thereafter consisted of an equal number of Catholics and Protestants.[81]

By the end of November news of Strafford's impeachment and the lifting of the ban on unlicensed travel to England had reached Ireland. Wandesford fell sick and died on 3 December 1640, and by the twelfth of that month the majority of the Irish committee had reached London, Sir James Montgomery and two others remaining behind "for the gleaning of grievances." A week later Sir James and the remaining members had arrived, from which time onwards the committee acted as a lobby in England on Irish affairs and Irish politics became intertwined with those in England.[82] As a priest in Ireland remarked at the time, news of Ireland proceeded entirely from the parliament in England. In some respects he was optimistic; Strafford's government was now under examination and the plantation of Connacht had been stayed, yet he added an ominous note about the way the religious climate in England might affect Ireland: "Although we expect a reformation these times concerning the temporal state, we stand in great awe concerning matters of religion because the parliament of England is zealously bent that way."[83] He then added in a postscript that he feared the alteration of government might open a chapter of persecution and dispersion of Catholics. As landowners, the Catholic leaders found common cause with Protestant planters in asserting local interests over Strafford's centralizing government, but in adopting this cause and forging this alliance they had opened the door for the Puritan paranoia in

England to replace the tolerant if cynical ecclesiastical policy of Charles towards Catholics. To understand the repercussions of English events upon Ireland, we must now cross to England, like the Irish parliamentary committees, and observe how Irish issues often intruded into the English political process.

CHAPTER FOUR

The British Dimension: Politics and Religion, 1640–41

The early years of the 1640s are among the more memorable in British history and have evoked a vast historical memorial. Any discussion of the period owes a debt to recent contributions to this literature, but there is no intent here to duplicate it in miniature.[1] Here the concentration must be upon the decisions taken in England and Scotland that either were coloured by a perception of what was happening in Ireland or had a direct bearing upon Ireland. Very broadly, these may be enumerated as the struggle to displace Strafford, the competition to replace him, the discussions leading to the Treaty of London between England and Scotland that had implications for Ireland, and the religious debate, which also involved the Scots, in so far as it affected Ireland. These issues often overlapped, and sometimes touched on essentially Irish institutions, such as the new Irish army, but use of such themes imposes a degree of order upon a series of events of otherwise bewildering complexity. As we are looking at these issues, we have to bear in mind not only what was happening but also how those Irish who were present in England must have perceived events.

STRAFFORD'S DISPLACEMENT

We have seen that Strafford and Laud were well aware of the elements opposing them within the council. With the king's support, they could hold these at bay so long as their policies succeeded, but any failure, such as the reduction in the size of the Irish subsidies, could have quick political repercussions, in this case the promotion of the earl of Cork to the council. The military débâcle of the Scottish occupation of Newcastle had the proportional political consequence of extending the struggle from the court to the much larger arena of parliament. One of the early steps in this process was the petition of the twelve peers of 28 August 1640. Among the "evils and dangers" pressed upon Charles for remedy by the peers were the reports of the dispatch of Irish and foreign forces into England.[2] Ireland, in short, was seen as a power base from which the hated policies could be imposed. Only through parliament could the agent of these policies be separated from the means to impose them.

As we follow the trail of Irish issues in England, we have to take into account that the blend of matters of policy (even principle) with matters of person, so evident within the council, carried over into the affairs of parliament. Contemporaries assumed this blend of interest. Thus the marquis of Hamilton, Charles's principal Scottish adviser in 1640, agreed in February 1641 to a marriage between his son and the daughter of Argyll, Charles's principal Scottish antagonist. Later that year the opposition peer, Viscount Saye, could write to Hamilton that he would have no cause to regret his choice in working with the parliamentary faction. Hamilton, to preserve his position, linked up with those groups he deemed to be ascendant. In return, he received protection against attack in parliament for his past support of Charles's policies. In November 1641 Saye informed him that Pym was his "friend and servant" and ready to defend him. This last letter revealed just how deeply politics were perceived in personal terms: "men," wrote the viscount, "are the worst instruments about kings ... remove the wicked from the king and his throne shall be established with righteousness."[3] The struggle was perceived as being between men and their interests as much as about ideas, and it was in this environment that those with Irish interests had to work, both at court and in dealing with the English parliament.

The formal Irish lobbies in England were the parliamentary committees, that of the Commons becoming active by mid-December. In addition, Protestant Irish interests could operate within the English council and the English parliament. Cork's biographer has warned that his political influence can be exaggerated, yet there is circumstantial evidence to suggest that he used his position on the council to serve his interests as soon as Strafford's position weakened.[4] We have seen that he owed his position on the council to the queen and Hamilton. He also made approaches to the earls of Arundel and Holland and had established links to two opposition peers, the earls of Bedford and Bristol. As early as 1638 he had gone to Sherborne, where Bristol lived, to "present my love and service to my noble friend the earl of Bristol." Bristol returned the visit and later gave the Irish earl "daily advertisements." In January 1641, Cork's son, Roger, was married to a Howard and in July his daughter, Mary, had married Charles Rich, son and heir of one of the leading opposition peers, Robert, earl of Warwick. This marriage was his daughter's wish rather than her father's, but by this time he at least accepted the match which formerly he had opposed.[5] More significant was his activity on the council. During the last months of Strafford's ascendancy, from July to the end of October 1640, Cork attended only two of thirty council meetings. From 1 November to the beginning of August 1641 he missed only three of the thirty-one sessions, however, and his role as a hostile witness against Strafford at the trial has long been accepted.[6] Thus, although in terms of English politics his position was peripheral and he probably had little part to play in planning the downfall of the lord lieutenant, once the attack had been begun, Cork supported it with enthusiasm.

In the English parliament, the most outspoken Irish agent was Sir John Clotworthy, the Puritan planter from Antrim. Sir John, whose communication with the Covenanters has already been mentioned, had close ties with leading Irish planter politicians. He also possessed friends among the leaders of the opposition in England. He was connected by marriage to John Pym and, according to Clarendon, he was elected to the Long Parliament "by the contrivance and recommendation of some powerful persons." These almost certainly included the earl of Warwick. It has also been remarked that Cork and Ranelagh each had a son sitting in the English Commons. Neither appears to have played an active role in the proceedings; thus it would be unwise to deduce a type of Irish lobby from this sort of data, but no doubt they would have been able to feed their respective fathers with useful information.[7]

As the Long Parliament gathered, Strafford understood well that his opponents intended to use it to destroy him. As early as 5 November he wrote to Sir George Radcliffe reporting the combination of the Scots with such enemies in England as Bristol (who pretended to be friendly) and Holland. "I am," he continued, "tomorrow to London, with more dangers beset, I believe, than ever any man went with out of Yorkshire." He knew, moreover, that his enemies expected "great matters out of Ireland." In preparation, he tried to repair a position in his defences which he realized might prove an embarrassment, should an investigation be launched into his affairs. Since 1637 he had borrowed money from the crown to finance the implementation of the Irish tobacco monopoly which he possessed. He does not seem to have made any profit out of this venture, but he was well aware how the non-payment of the debt could be construed, should it become public. He therefore told

Radcliffe that "you must by any means make straight with the vice-treasurer," Sir Adam Loftus.[8]

Strafford's letter hints at the politicking taking place in private among his opponents. These included such court opponents as Holland and peers who held no office. But the attack on the lord lieutenant needed more than a combination of a few peers if it was to succeed. The parliamentary leaders of the opposition faced a major task of co-ordinating English, Scottish, and Irish grievances in a manner that would persuade many of the uncommitted in parliament to take the extreme measure needed to unseat the king's leading minister.

We cannot doubt the contemporary assertion of close co-operation between the leaders of the Lords and Commons, and the parliamentary records confirm that the tactic adopted for launching the attack was to emphasize initially grievances that aroused most anxiety; it was decided on 6 November, a Friday, that the Commons should sit every weekday as a committee of the whole to discuss specific types of grievance on particular days of the week – religion on Monday, trade on Tuesday, and so on. Thursday was to be the day set aside for discussing Irish affairs.[9] According to this schedule, the Commons should have waited till the twelfth before turning to Irish issues, yet in fact it was on the seventh that they were debated. The idea of including Ireland for discussion in these meetings was itself challenged to the point of a formal division, a select committee being deemed by some to be a more appropriate forum. Pym and his friends only won this vote by thirteen votes, an indication that for many MPs Ireland was not a priority.[10]

Pym must have wanted to have Irish affairs aired before Strafford arrived in London because, if charges were to be brought against him, they would have to deal largely with his administration of Ireland, and most in the Commons were ignorant of the details of his activities there. Accordingly, on 7 November, Sir Walter Earle, Saye's son-in-law, presented a petition from Lord Mountnorris describing the treatment he had received at the hands of the lord lieutenant and attaching a copy of the sentence of death that had been issued against him.[11] Later that day, in a committee of the whole, Clotworthy described in considerable detail the evils of Strafford's administration of Ireland. As might be expected, he harped on every feature of life in Ireland that could be calculated to arouse the most deep-seated fears among English MPs; in particular he stressed the activities of the Court of High Commission. He dwelt on the sodomy committed by Bishop Atherton, and the growing

strength of Catholicism. He concluded by warning his listeners of
the large and well-paid "popish" army, "ready to march where I
know not," while the smaller Protestant army in Ireland received no
pay.[12]

For two days other issues occupied the Commons, but on
Wednesday, the eleventh, Clotworthy again raised the threat of the
new Irish army, this time to repeat a rumour that Radcliffe had
stated that the army was intended for use against England. It was
later that day that a committee of six, including Pym and Clotworthy,
recommended to the house that Strafford should be accused of high
treason and committed while charges against him were prepared.
The house accepted the resolution, a message was taken to the Lords
by Pym, and Strafford put under arrest as he returned to the Lords
after a conference with the king. Among the reasons given to the
Commons for moving against Strafford was Clotworthy's earlier
second-hand accusation about using the Irish army against England.[13] It was on the same day that the two "gentlemen of the Parliament in Ireland" (not to be confused with the Commons'
commissioners) arrived at Westminster, and it is surely true, as the
editor of D'Ewes's journal remarks, that the speed with which the
committee's recommendation for impeachment was accepted "argues
careful organization." Knowledge of what the Irish parliament was
about to do must have proved invaluable to Pym as he launched his
attack. The very next day steps were taken to summon Radcliffe to
England and additional information harmful to Strafford reached
the Commons, part of it supplied by his arch-enemy, Viscount Loftus
of Ely, the displaced Irish chancellor.[14]

By 24 November, that is four days after a copy of the Remonstrance
from the Irish parliament had been read in the Commons, general
charges were laid against the lord lieutenant in the Lords. These
ensured Strafford's confinement in the Tower, but much more specific charges had to be drawn up if treason was to be proven during
an impeachment trial. It was to this end the Commons had taken
steps to lift the travel restrictions between Ireland and England "that
all who had grievances might come over." Come they did, and during
the rest of the month the lower house received numerous petitions
from Ireland which went to the committee responsible for preparing
the detailed charges against Strafford.[15]

However, during this period Pym and his allies had also to mobilize
Scottish complaints against the common enemy. In the negotiations
for a peace treaty with England, the Scots had included as their
fourth demand the punishment of the supposed authors of the conflict, the most obvious of the English "incendiaries" being Strafford

and Laud. As Robert Baillie reported to Scotland on 12 December, the opposition in England preferred to take no further steps against the two men until the Scottish accusations had arrived.[16]

The first steps in this process seem to have come, not from the Scottish commissioners, but from "the Irish company now at Newcastle living in exile and extreme necessity." This company, made up of Scots from Ulster who had crossed to Scotland to assist their Covenanting countrymen, submitted an "information" against the lord lieutenant on 2 December, probably to assist the commissioners to draw up their own statement. The document began by linking "the great growth of popery" with Arminianism and observing that while, on the one hand, Catholic bishops, priests, and friars went unpunished in Ulster though indicted by grand juries, the Scots, on the other hand, suffered persecution. The third and fourth clauses protested the oath introduced by Strafford to counter the Covenant among the Scots in Ulster, and the cruelties following upon its imposition, men and women being arrested and "cast into prisons amongst the vilest malefactors" and others "hastened to their graves." The remaining four clauses concentrated on secular grievances: heavy customs duties, monopolies, restrictions on the use of grain for brewing, the use of "villainous" men to prosecute the innocent, and disrespectful speech about the Scottish nation. Such complaints, while revealing much animosity and depth of feeling, hardly supplied the material needed to convict a man of treason.[17] The official Scottish complaint, submitted on 16 December, proved no more valuable though just as full of invective.[18]

It took another six weeks for the Commons to draw up twenty-eight detailed charges. When submitted on 30 January, only two of these specifically referred to Scottish concerns. Of the remainder, the majority referred to aspects of Strafford's administration of Ireland – that he had described Ireland as a conquered nation and that he had used martial law illegally, increased the power of the council and the church at the expense of the courts and parliament, interfered with trade, and prohibited appeals to England. The nature of treason in seventeenth-century England, and more specifically the treason of which Strafford was accused, is a complex question, but it is significant that when the Lords voted on the issue, the Commons won their case primarily on the basis of the fifteenth and twenty-third charges: that he levied war against the king and his people by using soldiers to collect taxes, and that he intended to use the new army to subdue England.[19]

The difficulty the Commons had in proving the treasonable nature of most of the charges emphasizes that political rather than legal processes were at work. Very shortly after the charges were laid, two protests, one from Ireland and the other from Scotland, were received almost simultaneously in London.[20] Because a common theme in these documents, as well as in the charges themselves, was objection to an overpowerful state, it is tempting to interpret this political process as a struggle between localism and centralism in which Old English and Irish Catholics could unite with Protestant planters, Covenanting Scots, and English parliamentarians in opposing the state's increasing interference and authority. This is to suggest that, once Strafford had been displaced, a decentralized government would have followed in the three realms. Not only did this not happen, but there is no evidence that Strafford's chief opponents wanted it to happen. The struggle was not to dismantle the state, but to control it, and it was, above all, a personal struggle.

After Strafford had delivered his answers to the charges on 24 February, in which he cast aspersions on Cork's reliability as a witness, Clotworthy delivered a speech in the Commons defending Cork and using such "violent speeches" against the minister that Denzil Holles, himself a member of the opposition but also related to Strafford by marriage, uttered a rebuke.[21] A few days later, a Scot writing from London to a friend, reported: "The deputy makes himself merry with his accusations, but I hope he that sits in the heavens laughs too. He would be content to go and live the rest of his wicked life at Venice. But it is presumed that the wise English know that dead dogs bark none."[22] When Strafford successfully defended himself against the charge of treason in the trial conducted in March and April, his strongest opponents resorted to an act of attainder, which avoided the judicial process by simply declaring guilt, and then forced the dithering king to kill his lord lieutenant on 12 May. On 24 April, a few days after the Commons had passed the attainder, the procedure had begun to appear to Sir John Coke's son as a "private practice for private men to work out their own ends and preferments thereupon." For all his intelligence, Strafford seems to have appreciated the nature of the struggle only slowly. After hearing the charges he wrote with relief that they contained nothing capital, as though all would be determined by due process of law. Although some of his rivals would have been content to see him retire, the hard core of his opponents would settle for nothing less than his death. In the earl of Essex's famous words: "stone dead hath no fellow."[23]

In the absence of correspondence between those who wanted to displace the lord lieutenant, there are two approaches that may shed further light on the nature of the process. First, we may look at the behaviour of the participants at the trial, particularly those alleged by Sir George Wentworth to have wanted to advance their own fortunes at the expense of his brother. Second, we may trace the competition to replace him.

The first method has to be used with great caution. The delivery of hostile evidence does not prove involvement in some plot. The very inability of the prosecution to produce convincing evidence of treason shows the reluctance of even Strafford's worst enemies to testify to anything that they doubted to be the truth. The earl of Northumberland claimed that he fell into disfavour with the king during December because he would not perjure himself on Strafford's behalf, and witnesses on both sides seem to have had similar scruples.[24] Moreover, even those who wanted to see Strafford out of office could testify in his favour without anxiety, for it became evident as early as March that, if the earl was found not guilty, he wished to retire. For some, therefore, who wanted to benefit from his fall, the trial was sufficient without a conviction. Despite these caveats, the trial does tend to reinforce rather than to undermine the picture of political faction which we have drawn from other sources.

Sir George mentioned Arundel, Hamilton, Holland, Sir Henry Vane, Saye, Clotworthy, Sir William Parsons, Sir John Borlase, Sir Adam Loftus, and Viscount Ranelagh as the principal participants in the plot. Three of these – Saye, Parsons, and Borlase – played no role in the trial although, according to Sir George, Parsons worked with Ranelagh in preparing the crucial fifteenth charge.[25] Arundel, as lord high steward, served as the presiding officer; few of his rulings favoured the accused, and during the passage of the act of attainder his attitude was reported to be hostile.[26]

Hamilton, for his part, gave evidence that sustained Strafford's claim that the new army in Ireland had been intended for use in Scotland, not England. He was absent from the Lords on 6 May because he was "sick" and he does not seem to have returned till 8 May, which suggests that he deliberately stayed away during the voting on Strafford's attainder. Strafford himself considered Hamilton an ally, for he wrote to him on 24 April asking him to encourage a sentiment that was developing that would have permitted him to leave public employment and retire.[27] Yet, as we have seen, Hamilton had been cultivating Argyll and by the summer was close to Saye; his assistance to Strafford, therefore, does not preclude a desire to use the lord lieutenant's fall to advance his own ends. Holland was among those who testified that Strafford had declared that, since the Short Parliament had denied the king money, he would have to supply himself "by other ways," a statement hardly calculated to endear the earl to his judges.[28] No more need be said of Clotworthy's attitude, which leaves Vane, Loftus, and Ranelagh.

Vane's animosity towards Strafford is notorious, as is the incident in which his son, Sir Harry, copied his father's notes of a council meeting held on 5 May 1640, when Strafford was alleged to have told the king he could use the Irish army to subdue England. As Strafford pointed out during his trial, the new Irish army did not even exist on this date (it was not due to rendezvous till the eighteenth) and everyone else present, including Hamilton, considered that Strafford's comments about the use of the army applied to Scotland, but with some hesitation, the elder Vane asserted that England was meant.[29] A contemporary account recorded that it was probable that, in taking notes, the originals of which had been destroyed by the time of the trial, Vane "designed to have something in readiness, if an occasion should be offered, that might turn to the earl of Strafford's prejudice, against whom he had a private hatred."[30]

The case of Sir Adam is less clear-cut though some of the evidence suggests that he was at least half-hearted in defending his former leader. We have seen that Strafford knew that a loan he had taken from the crown could prove an embarrassment, and as soon as he anticipated an attack he arranged with Sir Adam, through Radcliffe, for the loan to be repaid. He wrote to Sir Adam on two occasions between his arrest and his trial. In the first letter, of 15 December 1640, he thanked him "for your discreet concealing from persons very ill affected to me, how the account stood betwixt you and me." In the second, written just after he had been told of the charges, he asked Sir Adam "to befriend me ... so far as the truth will warrant you." During the trial, Loftus testified for the defence, but his testimony appears non-committal. The prosecution somehow discovered the crucial evidence about the loan, and when questioned about it Sir Adam reported that Strafford and Radcliffe had only repaid their loans to the crown within the previous three months. Pym clearly thought Loftus's testimony had been valuable in discrediting the accused.[31]

In assessing Sir Adam's ambivalence, it is worth noting that Strafford referred to Ranelagh as Loftus's "friend," and about Ranelagh's attitude at the trial there is no doubt. He did all he could to have the lord lieutenant convicted and even extended the attack to include the Irish lord chancellor, Sir Richard Bolton, and Chief Justice Sir Gerard Lowther.[32] What is interesting is that Ranelagh too came under attack. By the end of January the Irish parliamentary committee was being consulted about a petition submitted by a Henry

Dillon against Ranelagh in his capacity as president of Connacht and by early February the president had submitted a response. Despite his replies to the charges, the English council decided that some of them "were very fit to be further examined" and had to be taken seriously. Almost certainly the charges against Ranelagh did not represent a counterattack by Strafford against one of his most vociferous opponents although he knew about them as early as mid-December and Henry Dillon did testify on his behalf, but the English council's reaction to them suggests a desire to strike back even though no further conciliar action seems to have been taken. Months later, some MPs in the Irish Commons tried to move against both Ranelagh and Loftus. We do not know why, and the attempt failed, but the incident establishes yet another link between these two men.[33]

Henry Dillon's petition throws interesting light on the nature of the Irish administration at a level below that of the lord deputy and the council. The petition alleged, for instance, that Ranelagh wanted to buy Dillon's woods, but when he refused to sell, the president used his position to persecute him, putting him in jail in a "beastly smoky place." The petition also tells of a close relationship between Ranelagh and Viscount Dillon of Costello-Galen, an Old English Connacht landlord, who had declared himself a Protestant but later reverted to Catholicism, and who submitted a petition to the English House of Commons against Strafford the day after his arrest and subsequently appeared at the trial as a witness for the prosecution. The petition, therefore, not only suggests another interesting link between planter and Old English interests in Connacht, which was used to undermine Ireland's governor, but also indicates that Strafford's planter opponents faced accusations of using the same techniques of government as the man they accused. Both championed centralism of a fairly ruthless variety, sometimes with the co-operation of Old English friends, and differed only over who was to exercise power.[34]

Little purpose would be served in analysing the testimony of all eighty or so witnesses at Strafford's trial. Nevertheless, it may be noted that seven of the thirteen MPs sent to England to represent the interests of the Irish parliament testified as prosecution witnesses, including a majority of the Catholic members of the committee and Sir Hardress Waller, the ally of both Cork and Catholic landowners in Connacht.[35] Finally, perhaps the most prominent witness for the prosecution was the man who noted in his diary that Strafford's death was well deserved, the earl of Cork himself.[36] While the evidence of the trial, therefore, falls far short of confirming Sir George Wentworth's account, it does show that elements of the group of planters who held prominent positions in Ireland and were active in the challenge to Strafford in that country also played a major role in his destruction in England, and certainly some courtiers helped in the process. It is a measure of Strafford's stature that it took a combination of Catholic, planter, Puritan, Covenanter, and discontented courtier to overthrow him. Such unusual partners possessed only the common bond of a mutual hatred. Prophetically, Sir Philip Percival wrote from Ireland to his Catholic friend John Barry, who was serving in the king's army in England: "I remember I was in England when the duke of Buckingham fell, whom many men thought the only cause of all the evils, but those that were of that opinion did not find it so afterwards."[37] The unity born of deposing Strafford rapidly disintegrated when it came to replacing him.

THE REPLACEMENT OF STRAFFORD

We have seen that late in 1639 Wentworth had seriously considered making the earl of Leicester, England's ambassador to France, governor of Ireland. The king did not accept the idea, in part at least because Laud opposed it, but this did not deter Leicester's brother-in-law, the earl of Northumberland, from wishing to bring Leicester closer to the inner circle of the council. Before the Short Parliament met, Wentworth may have had similar plans because we hear in February from Sir John Temple, a man with Irish connections and Leicester's agent, that he expected Northumberland and Wentworth to work together "to bring your lordship back among us." Nevertheless, Northumberland took the precaution of cultivating the newly appointed secretary, Sir Henry Vane, who assured the earl that he would write to Leicester weekly to keep him informed of events in England.[38]

Even before the parliament had gathered, Northumberland had become uneasy about the development of court politics, in particular the rising influence of Hamilton. After the failure of the parliament and the famous meeting of the council on 5 May, when it was determined that an aggressive policy towards the Scots would be pursued, Northumberland became increasingly disenchanted with government policy. By May he could write to Leicester that "it grieves my soul to be involved in these councils; and the sense I have of the miseries that are like to ensue is held by some a disaffection in me." For a moment, when Strafford fell seriously ill in mid-May, Northumberland became more optimistic. If Strafford should "miscarry," he saw nobody more likely to succeed him than Leicester; the queen wanted it, and Laud would not be opposed to it. Hamilton, however, would have to be convinced. Lady Carlisle gave the same impression, though she added that although Strafford himself inclined towards Leicester, Laud's opposition could not be discounted and the king distrusted any friend of Northumberland.[39] Along with the rise of Hamilton's influence – "the most dangerous person in England" in Northumberland's opinion – went instructions from the king that Hamilton should receive "concealed" lands in Leinster.[40]

The rumour went the rounds at this time that Cork, who had just joined the council, had ambitions towards the governorship of Ireland, but the issue died down because Strafford recovered from his illness. We hear no more that summer about Leicester's moving to a new position, only that Vane continued to show friendliness. This is confirmed by a letter from Leicester to Vane thanking him for keeping him informed. Two days after Strafford had been arrested, however, Northumberland wrote to Leicester to tell him of "the designs of reformation" to displace not only "great ones" but also lesser officials and to advise him that, if these designs succeeded, "we shall suddenly see many changes in this court." He urged Leicester to decide which office to seek: lord treasurer, Ireland, the secretaryship (meaning Windebank's), or the mastership of the court of wards, then held by Cottington. Throughout the rest of the month both he and Leicester seem to have almost gloated on the opportunities opening up: "if in all these changes some good advantage fall not to [Leicester]'s share, I agree with your lordship that his luck is desperately ill."[41]

By 11 December, on Northumberland's advice, Leicester had decided to concentrate on securing the lord lieutenancy, but as the month passed, it became apparent that the euphoria of November had been ill founded; the issue of the governorship of Ireland grew increasingly complex. In the first place, rivals began to appear. Those mentioned in the correspondence were Henry Danvers, Lord Danby, and the earl of Holland. Neither was taken as a serious threat by Leicester's friends though in Holland's case they had more to fear than they imagined. A more serious difficulty arose from the attitude of the king. Northumberland, himself out of favour, tested the water by pretending to advance Leicester to replace Windebank, who had just fled. The king responded that Leicester "was too great for that place," whereupon Northumberland tactlessly suggested other positions would "shortly be void" to which Charles would want to appoint those he knew and not strangers. To this the king made "a very cold return."[42] Clearly Charles did not regard Leicester as a reliable alternative to Strafford although at this stage he might have been persuaded to let the lord lieutenant step down if a suitable replacement could have been found. Strafford himself wanted to be replaced, apparently because he believed the attack upon him would diminish if it were known that he would not retain office. He suggested the earl of Ormond as lord deputy, but this ran into opposition from Arundel, who had a quarrel with the Irish earl, and from the Irish MPs most of whom had arrived in London by mid-December.[43] Charles then tried to appoint lords justices on whom he could rely. Again Ormond's name seems to have come up, only to be withdrawn. An attempt to appoint Sir Richard Bolton, the Irish chancellor who had replaced Viscount Loftus of Ely in 1639, and Lord Robert Dillon, whose son had married Strafford's sister, also failed. The commissions appointing them had to be withdrawn because "that kingdom will hardly be brought to admit any to govern them that hath any kind of relation to my lord lieutenant." The king finally appointed Sir William Parsons and Sir John Borlase. We know nothing of Borlase's political connections at this time, but he was certainly suspected later of belonging to the forces opposed to the lord lieutenant.[44]

By the last day of 1640 Northumberland realized that Charles would make no move to appoint a new governor of Ireland "suddenly" and that in any case the king showed no enthusiasm for Leicester. Yet Northumberland remained confident of the final outcome because he was sure that "within a few months ... the king will be necessitated to change many of his present opinions" and because Leicester enjoyed support in parliament. Vane continued to promise to help, and Hamilton, with whom Northumberland was now reconciled and who had "sole power" with the king, seemed very willing to advance Leicester's cause. At this point the correspondence between Northumberland and Leicester ceases, but Sir John Temple's letters to Leicester have survived, and through them we can trace some of the remaining steps to Leicester's success.[45]

During January, the king continued to hope that he would be able eventually to return Strafford to authority. He arranged for him to be kept fully informed about Irish affairs. This angered the Irish committee in England and forced them, and we may guess their parliamentary allies, to conclude that unless they laid him "so much the lower," he would "prevail hereafter."[46] The queen, however, continued to favour Leicester's appointment, and it was through the queen's master of horse, Henry Jermyn, that Temple worked to advance Leicester's interest, though his immediate contact at court was Robert Long, the secretary of Prince Charles's council. Through Long and Jermyn, he discovered that, despite Vane's assurances to

Northumberland, the secretary himself coveted the Irish post. More-over, Jermyn was inclined to use his influence with the queen to promote Vane, but a promise by Long on Leicester's behalf of £4,000 persuaded Jermyn to back Leicester instead. Just as this had been accomplished, it looked as though Jermyn would lose his value as parliament showed signs of turning against him. By February it seemed as though neither Vane nor Leicester would succeed Straf-ford. To Temple's astonishment, yet another contender had entered the lists – Lord Francis Cottington.[47]

The issue of the lord lieutenancy of Ireland has to be seen in the context of the general political shift taking place in Charles's court early in 1641. In part through the influence of Hamilton and Jermyn, Charles was persuaded to add seven opposition peers to the council, including Bristol, Bedford, Essex, and Saye. Yet none of these men received a major office. Any replacement of Strafford, therefore, in January or February would have constituted a political signal that the king did not wish to issue. It can be argued that his reluctance to move decisively at this time proved a mistake as a measure of political sacrifice early in 1641 could have avoided a greater one later, and once Strafford's trial had begun in March, all decisions had to be postponed. In the interval the competition for the governorship continued.[48]

On the last day of January one Irish post was filled; Sir John Temple succeeded Sir Christopher Wandesford, who had died in December, as master of the rolls. We may guess that this appointment was achieved through Jermyn, and we know for certain that it aroused strong reaction among Leicester's rivals and their sup-porters.[49] During February the struggle for the lord lieutenancy became a three-way one between Cottington, Holland, who had again become a serious contender, and Leicester. By the middle of the month, Clarendon's brother-in-law, writing from France, had heard that Holland had won. He had strong supporters in that he was proposed by Sir John Clotworthy "and the rest." This must have been a reference to Clotworthy's Irish connections as, in another instance, Temple referred to Holland's "party of [Ireland]." Indeed, one of the reasons that this group showed bitterness towards Temple's promotion was that Holland, who had made "great promises" to secure advance-ment, had agreed to procure the rolls position for Clotworthy. Temple claimed not to be perturbed by Holland's efforts, but he took the precaution when informed by Clotworthy that Leicester was deemed insufficiently "puritan" to send Leicester's son to the family seat at Penshurst to remove some pictures from the chapel that could give substance to the charge. Charles, influenced by Laud, deemed Leicester to be too Puritan. To counter the king's opposition, Strafford was persuaded through Jermyn to write on Leicester's behalf.[50]

Temple indicated that the "Irish committee" in England had united with the Lords in Ireland to oppose his own appointment, two petitions being presented to the king in protest. This impression of unity on the Irish committee concealed disunity on another matter. By 8 March John Barry reported to Percival that the Catholics, Thomas Bourke and Nicholas Plunkett, had aroused resentment within the committee by using Cottington to persuade the king to abandon the plantation of Connacht. This division, however, cannot be perceived as a straight Catholic-Protestant split as Sir Hardress Waller signed a petition with Catholic Connacht landlords on the same subject in April. It seems likely, however, that some Catholics on the committee, possibly with the assistance of the earl of Clanricard who was still in England, had pressed the king to put Cottington in Strafford's place. Temple described Cottington as "most in the way," and although he did not specify Irish support for Cottington, it is hard to see where else it could have come from.[51]

During April Temple was able to report that Leicester no longer had a rival. Holland had been appointed general in the north and Cottington had decided to resign. This did not mean there would be a quick decision, because Strafford's trial still imposed delay, and Temple still regarded Leicester as "much mistaken on both sides," but he was fairly confident of success if Leicester came to England to look after his own interests. This the earl did, and a week after Strafford's execution Charles announced Leicester's appointment as lord lieutenant though he also decided to retain him as ambassador to France.[52]

What has been called Leicester's "sordid intrigue" is only unusual in that it is well documented. It is evident that others were similarly engaged though we have little record of their manœuvres. It reinforces the impression created by the two accounts of the background to Strafford's fall that it was as much a consequence of private greed as of public policy. Yet, important as this feature of the politics of the day was, it would be a mistake to see it as the only ingredient in the complex compound that exploded in Ireland at the end of 1641.

The prevailing system for the distribution of office led to instability in government because it was so closely linked to personality and patronage. Decisions about Irish government became intertwined with English court politics and Irish events could be used to achieve court ends. Conrad Russell has remarked that it was the relationship between the three realms and not merely its mishandling which "was the major cause of the instability in all three of them."[53] However, so far as England and Ireland were concerned, this was not a new situation. It existed before Wentworth; indeed, it had been present when Elizabeth ruled both kingdoms. There had always been intrigue surrounding the appointment to high office in Ireland; therefore, there would be no reason to link the process that surrounded Leicester's appointment to the civil unrest in Ireland five months after his promotion were it not, as will be shown, for the policies that the Irish thought this appointment represented. The situation, moreover, was aggravated by Charles's decision to send Leicester back to Paris a month after he became lord lieutenant. The period of 1640–41 in Irish history has been entitled "the breakdown of authority."[54] Had he gone to Ireland, Leicester could have restored that authority, but Charles placed English interests in Paris over the need for the stable government of Ireland, and this certainly contributed to the chain reaction that led to civil war both in Ireland and in England.

Leicester did not represent either extreme in Ireland and during the summer he began to establish a degree of balance between factions though his effectiveness was much reduced by his departure for France. Ormond seems to have supported him and, when a minor incident put Leicester under suspicion with parliament in one of the real or imaginary plots of the time, his defender was Clotworthy. By mid-July the Catholic Viscount Gormanston went out of his way to deny to Temple that the Irish committee (and he drew no distinction between Catholic and Protestant members or Lords and Commons) opposed Leicester. On the contrary, he assured Temple that when the committee returned to Ireland, it would acknowledge to the Irish parliament the new lord lieutenant's assistance. On 5 August Gormanston reiterated his support, and by 11 August Temple could report that "the animosities and distempers of some of those high spirits in Ireland" were "much calmed" and previous jealousies much reduced.[55] As we shall see, there are grounds for believing that the Old English had received important assurances from Leicester. When Temple arrived in Ireland at the end of August, his report that all was calm was an accurate description of the political situation in the Pale if, at the same time, the Irish in Ulster were plotting a rebellion.[56]

It is true that this picture of reconciliation must be tempered by the knowledge that while the Old English were negotiating with the new lord lieutenant, they too had been plotting a rebellion in case the negotiations failed. Nor did all the planters co-operate with the new administration. During July and August Ranelagh attempted to undermine Leicester's position.[57] The political equilibrium remained in balance. Had Leicester gone to Dublin immediately after his appointment, his diplomatic skills might have preserved a degree of Catholic support for the government, but the decision to send him back to Paris ensured that Irish perceptions of British attitudes developed unimpeded by any moderating interpretation, and it was these perceptions that provided the motivation for rebellion.

RELIGION AND THE TREATY OF LONDON

After the rebellion had broken out, one of the Irish explanations for the rising was the fear that "the puritans of England, Scotland and Ireland," and particularly the English Commons, intended "the utter extirpation and destruction of the catholic religion."[58] There were good grounds for this fear though it is unlikely that, in the absence of an uprising, any mid-seventeenth century English regime in Ireland would have been able to sustain any strong campaign of religious persecution as it would have required considerable military force, the cost of which would not have been tolerated in peacetime. Strafford was convinced that the crown would never be safe in Ireland "till we be brought all under one form of divine service," yet he confined his efforts in bringing this about to the persecution of dissident Protestants.[59] The laws against Catholics were not enforced for the good reason that he knew that he did not have the power to enforce them, and one of the accusations against him in England was that he had been too tolerant towards Catholicism.

Catholic fears in Ireland, of course, were unlikely to be dissipated by such careful calculation. Men of all faiths were caught up in the atmosphere of religious paranoia that suffocated most rational calculations about external threats. Englishmen suffered from precisely the same sort of fears as Irishmen. Only the objects of those fears differed: "there is a design to alter law and religion: the parties that would effect this, are papists, who are obliged by a maxim in their doctrine, that they are not only bound to maintain their religion, but also to extirpate all others."[60] Thus, John Pym used the term "extirpate" at the beginning of his first speech to the Long Parliament a good year before the Irish began to employ it, and he went on to link English bishops to his fears.

Catholic plots against English Protestantism have been well documented by Caroline Hibbard and give some superficial grounds for Pym's fears, however remote were the chances for their success, but no historian today would suggest that William Laud or any other

English bishop intended to lead England back to Rome.[61] But support for Pym's perception of the English church is to be found beyond the frenzied minds of English Puritans and Scottish Covenanters. One Catholic priest writing to another from Madrid as late as 1639 observed of England:

The protestant heretics are going on making more and more reforms every day in religious matters, admitting auricular confession, urging it in sermons and books; they praise and exalt in their pulpits the cult of the holy Virgin and of the saints; they deck out their temples with images, they adorn their altars with wax candles and other ornaments; their preachers and other ministers vest themselves as we do, and use ceremonies not very different from ours. All this is approved by the archbishop of Canterbury and other prelates.[62]

Pym might be excused for gaining the same impression. Moreover, during the first year of the war in Ireland, one of the arguments used to persuade the Roman church to use its influence to obtain material aid for the Confederate Catholics was that "on the preservation of the Catholic religion in Ireland depends every hope of England and Scotland."[63] Again, it matters not that this end was impractical. As in the case of Irish fears of the Puritans, what counted was the intent.

Fear for the security of the Protestant religion helps to explain both the distrust of the Catholic army in the north of Ireland and the hatred of Strafford who had created it. Again, we find some grounds for Protestant fears in the way this army was perceived by Catholic clerics in Ireland. The Jesuit, Robert Nugent, reported to his general that "a new opportunity for strenuous exertions has been offered to our labourers." The majority of the soldiers, he reported, were Catholics, and some of the officers "earnestly seek our ministration." Accordingly, two priests had been appointed to serve as chaplains and two more were being sought.[64] This letter was written after the prospect of the army crossing to Scotland had disappeared, and there is no hint that Nugent expected the chaplains to be used to convert the Scots, but his very enthusiasm is a measure of how the army might be regarded in Scotland, quite apart from its political purpose.

It would be pointless to record all the strums on the anti-Irish and anti-Catholic strings that Pym and his friends played throughout the first eight months of the Long Parliament. They reverberated with ominous regularity in the background as Charles's parliamentary opposition played its shrill tune against "evil councillors" and prelates. Pym's warning on 7 November that the Irish army was intended "to bring us to a better order," followed by Clotworthy's vivid account of what was happening in Ireland; Pym's reference later that month to "popery without restraint" in Ireland; the demand, when Charles spared the life of an old priest who had been sentenced to death, that he be executed; and the accompanying cries of the danger of the "increase of popery" are but a few examples of the genre found in 1640. In the new year, one rumour spread that an Irishman planned to kill the king, another alleged "the papists" in Ireland "do pull the ministers out of the pulpit." Members of parliament insisted on clearing the realm of all priests; by February Clotworthy, who at one stage seriously proposed the castration of priests who broke the law, warned that the real destination for the Irish army had been Wales; another MP reported that, at the time the Irish army was expected to land in Lancashire, the Catholics in that county provided themselves with a "greater number of attendants than formerly," and the contradiction between these two assertions was ignored.[65]

On 11 February the Commons discussed the new Irish army. Sir Walter Earle described its disorders, how the soldiers celebrated mass openly and disturbed Protestant preachers. Ulster, he pointed out, was the ancient seat of rebellion. Clotworthy remarked on the heavy cost of the army though, by this time, it was not being paid. He urged that it be sent abroad, only to encounter the opposition of Sir Simonds D'Ewes, who, in a remarkable tribute to Irish military prowess, declared that if the 7,000 Irish joined with Spain, they would tilt the balance of power in Europe in that country's favour and enable it to suppress Catalonia and Portugal, invade the Netherlands, and relieve the emperor in Germany. He agreed that Ireland should be rid of its soldiers, but he concluded: "I would have them sent to the Persian against the Turk." A few days later Pym used the presence of the Irish army as an argument to expedite Strafford's trial on the grounds that he remained its commander-in-chief.[66]

For all the farcical elements in such utterances, we have to accept that they were spoken sincerely and that they reflected the atmosphere in which the English concluded the treaty with the Scots. The attitude of the Scottish Covenanters, as revealed during the campaign against Strafford, resembled very closely that of the English parliamentary opposition to Charles. They had, after all, already abolished bishops, but if anything, the role of Ireland and the army in Ulster occupied an even more prominent position for the Covenanters in the triangular politics of the archipelago than it did for the English. There was a sense that they had not been taken seriously either by

their own episcopalians, by the English, or by the Irish. A Scottish
broadsheet of the period, after looking forward to the time

> When Englands Parliament shall end,
> And *Scots* conclud as they intend:
> When *Lad* and Wentworth love our land,
> And shall subscribe our blessed Band,

asserted that then "Jock, Jack and Irish Schane shall then Our Scottish armies worth commend."[67] It was this same sense of slight at
Wentworth's evident contempt for their religion and nation that coloured the Scottish accusations against him of 16 December. He was
the man "whose malice hath set all his wits and power on work, to
devise and do mischief against our kirk and country" and who, with
"restless rage and unsatiable cruelty," had persecuted the Scots and
Scottish ministers in Ireland.[68] There can be no denial of the emo-
tional inspiration behind the charges, but there is evidence that their
intent went beyond the death of the much hated enemy.

This is not to suggest that when the Scottish commissioners
reached London in November, they did not wish Strafford (and Laud)
dead. The fourth clause of the treaty they proposed demanded that
the authors of "this combustion" should be sentenced by either the
English or the Scottish parliament. It has also been stressed that it
was the Scots who insisted on Strafford's death.[69] Yet it will be recollected that, although Wentworth's opponents delayed procedures
until the Scots had submitted their charges, these supplied little
reinforcement to the legal process of finding him guilty of treason.

When we examine the Scottish complaints against Strafford, we
find a greater similarity between them and the issues raised in the
discussions leading to the treaty than between them and the impeachment articles presented to the Lords, a point recognized by Nalson,
who printed the complaints next to the treaty demands. The complaints against the printing of anti-Scottish pamphlets, the oath
imposed on the Scots in Ireland, the cost of defending Scotland's
west coast against the Irish army, that army itself, and the capture
of Scottish ships off the Irish coast all appeared in the Scottish
commissioners' charges and were also discussed directly or indirectly
in five of the eight proposed articles of the treaty. Moreover, underlying all the complaints lay the issue of religious persecution, an issue
covered by the first article of the treaty, by which, in effect, Charles
was required to give his approval to the measures passed by the
Scottish General Assembly.[70] In short, the Scots were interested not
only in the permanent removal of some crown officers but also in

establishing a mechanism to prevent any official being able to repeat what Laud and Strafford had attempted. Strafford had used the Irish parliament to raise money for an army to attack them and then used this as a precedent for similar action in England. Whether Ireland wished it or not, therefore, it had been dragged into the whirlpool of British politics.

To the Covenanters, of course, as to the Puritans, Catholicism represented the ultimate threat to their security, but they saw bishops, even if Protestant, to be agents of this threat. Thus, although they saw "novations in religion" as the "true cause of our present troubles," it was not long before they, in turn, began to press for "novations" in England by urging the abolition of episcopacy. Early in January a Scot wrote to Northumberland to thank him for helping with the negotiations, but at the same time pleaded for stronger opposition in parliament to prelates and papists, "our enemies and authors of all our evils."[71] It was this same linkage of bishops with Catholicism which led to the Scottish Declaration of 24 February, a document which urged the abolition of episcopacy in England as well as Scotland. The king and others saw the Declaration as Scottish interference in English affairs, and it so angered Charles that overall treaty negotiations nearly collapsed.[72]

The Scottish commissioners said they had not intended that the Declaration be published although they had wanted their views to be known within parliament as the rumour had spread that their desire for the abolition of episcopacy had waned. They pacified the king and other critics by giving assurances that, although they did not wish to conceal a desire for unity of religion according to a Scottish model, they would not press the issue. Yet the implications of the Declaration and the subsequent explanations were clear. On 10 March the commissioners drew up a document on unity in religion and uniformity of church government. This began with a genuflection in the direction of freedom of conscience, but then went on to stress "that religion" was "the base and foundation of kingdoms and estates and the strongest bond to tie the subjects to their prince in true loyalty." It followed that there should be "one confession of faith, one form of catechism, one directory for all parts ... of public worship of God ... and one form of church government in all the churches of his Majesty's dominions." Once this had been achieved, "recusants shall despair of success to have their religion set up again, and shall either conform themselves or get themselves hence."[73] In yet another document, dating from the end of March, the Scots demanded "that all good means may be used for the conversion of papists, and for the extinguishing of papistry in all his majesty's dominions."[74]

It is evident that underlying the Scottish desire for religious unity in "all" the king's dominions lay a desire for a closer degree of political unity, but with "the base and foundation" of that unity modelled upon Scottish lines. This left no room for either bishops or Catholics, the two being virtually synonymous in Scottish eyes. The Scots had, moreover, sympathizers in both England and Ireland. In England, D'Ewes, for example, remarked in the Commons at the time that this concept of unity was being discussed that "the only [way] to bring his majesty's three kingdoms into a perfect unity was to consider thoroughly of reducing Ireland to the profession of the true religion."[75] The support for this idea among Irish Protestants is in some degree less easy to document because it was less direct, but it was unquestionably there, and in terms of the Irish uprising was more significant than either the English or Scottish contributions.

It is worth noting that, according to Robert Baillie, the man who was responsible for printing the Scottish Declaration of 24 February was the earl of Holland, "our good friend, minding, as we all know, no evil to us" and also, at this time, the candidate for the lord lieutenancy supported by Clotworthy and his friends.[76] By itself, we could not give this information much prominence were it not for the effort in Ulster to reinforce the campaign in England to abolish bishops. This campaign had certainly begun in England by 11 December, the date on which London's Root and Branch Petition demanding the abolition of episcopacy was submitted to the Commons, and it continued throughout 1641, at least up to August, but it was at its most intense during June and July. The Root and Branch bill did not pass, but it gave rise to intense debates, and one of the principal tactics used by its proponents was the submission of petitions, often signed by thousands of hands. Petitions came into Westminster supporting the bill from London and some twenty English counties. What is not as well known is that two petitions were submitted from Ulster as part of this campaign.[77]

Although neither of these petitions was dated, we can establish approximately when they were circulated. Archbishop Ussher, for instance, wrote to Bishop Bramhall on 19 June reporting from London that Clotworthy had presented "a far larger petition to the house of commons here" for the abolition of episcopacy in Ireland "than that which you sent unto me, and signed with a huge number of hands," and we know Bramhall sent a copy of a petition to Ussher on 26 April.[78] This shows that the earlier one was also the shorter one and must be the one deposited among the state papers. It purported to be submitted by the British inhabitants of the counties of Down, Antrim, Tyrone, and Armagh and began by asserting that "we were a flourishing people" but now, through the "cruel tyranny of the clergy," are become "an astonishment and wonder to Angels and man." The petitioners were, they complained, deprived of their estates, "utterly beggared," and, worst of all, bereft of "our faithful ministers." These wrongs, they concluded, could have no redress "save by removal of the hierarchy."[79] We do not know the date of this petition, but there were riots among the Protestant common people in Down and Antrim in March and April, inspired by both economic and religious grievances. During the investigation into these, one deponent, on 26 March, agreed to obtain a copy of "a petition of grievances" he had seen being circulated.[80] Unless there was yet another petition making the rounds of which no subsequent trace exists, this must have been a reference to the petition sent to England at the end of April by Bramhall. The organization of the petition must, therefore, have been taking place at the latest in February, and possibly as early as December.

Ussher's letter shows that Clotworthy was connected with the much longer and better known petition, which if presented to the English parliament during the first half of June, must have been circulating in Ulster during April and May. This petition claimed to be sent by the Protestant inhabitants of some of the same counties as the first petition, though Armagh was dropped and Derry added. A long preamble explained the petitioners' British origins and their recent sufferings at the hands of bishops who, they declared, favoured Catholics. There followed thirty-one paragraphs dwelling on the same themes. As in Scottish and Puritan English documents, bishops and Catholics were linked together, leaving the clear impression that the destruction of the former would lead to the demise of the latter. The petition, moreover, concluded with a reference that suggests its author was fully aware of the wider struggle being waged in both England and Scotland: "we ... the true sons of Israel ... shall ever pray to be aiding and assistant unto you [the English parliament] in this great and glorious work of reformation."[81] This second petition was undoubtedly used by Clotworthy in June when he proposed to the Commons that the Root and Branch bill be extended to Ireland.[82] It is small wonder that the "Northern Catholics of Ireland" in their Remonstrance of 1642 objected to this petition, "framed by the puritans of this kingdom of Ireland ... for suppressing our religion and us the professors thereof."[83] Thus the Root and Branch bill, as used by Clotworthy and his friends, had a direct bearing on Irish Catholic behaviour – yet another example of the way English and Irish issues became intertwined.

The timing of the second petition needs to be stressed; it was almost certainly conceived in March, just when the first petition was circulating, and when the succession to the lord lieutenancy was still in doubt. This was also the time that a greater degree of unity between the three realms was being considered. Unity of religion lay at the foundation of this concept in the eyes of the Scots (as it had in the eyes of Laud), and such unity could only begin once bishops had been abolished (though in Laud's view only after they had been firmly established). However, this idea of unity – and possibly the term is too strong even though it is the word the Scots used – was not confined to matters of religion. The reason that it began to surface during March is that it was during this month that the commissioners began discussing the eighth article, a hold-all clause which permitted the Scots to raise issues not considered before their victory. One of the demands they broached at this time was freedom of trade among the three realms; others were the right of Scots to dwell in English colonies and the standardization of the coinage of the three kingdoms.[84] But it was in the military arrangements and the ratification process for the treaty itself that the Scottish vision of the future inter-relationship of the three realms became most evident.

The army in Ireland represented as much of a challenge during the treaty negotiations as during the armed phase of the confrontation. It was recognized in England that the Scots would be unlikely to disband their army while the Irish army remained in being. Indeed, within six weeks of the Irish army being disbanded, the Scottish parliament had approved the main elements of the treaty though without those features that would have led to greater integration of the realms.[85] But the Scots were also interested in establishing a mechanism to meet future crises between the kingdoms. They accepted that it might be necessary to move troops from one country to another although they wished to impose a limit of 10,000 on the size of such forces. At the same time they wanted some control to be exercised over the crown in using such forces and, more particularly, on the use of an Irish army against Scotland. The treaty, therefore, read that "it is agreed that an Act be passed in the Parliament of England that the kingdom of England nor Ireland shall not denounce nor make war against the kingdom of Scotland without the consent of the Parliament of England."[86] This implied that, so far as making war was concerned, Ireland lay under the jurisdiction of the English parliament, and elsewhere the Scots stated that in all the articles "we comprehend [Ireland] under the name of England."[87] Yet they also wanted the treaty to be ratified by the parliament of Ireland.[88] This apparent contradiction was explained by a statement made by D'Ewes in the Commons in May: "And for their desire to have the said articles also confirmed in Ireland it was very necessary because the Parliament there had so lately [,] either of their own accord [,] or drawn unto it by some subtle practices [,] declared their readiness to assist his Majesty with their persons and purses against the Scots."[89]

Under Strafford's leadership, the king, as king of Ireland, had raised money and levied an army for war with no external restraint. Only if the Irish parliament ratified the treaty with the clause requiring the consent of the English parliament for an army to be raised in Ireland could this power of the crown be curbed through legislation. The Scots, from an initial position of assuming Ireland to be subordinate to England, had recognized a loophole that punctured that assumption. They attempted to plug the hole by requiring the Irish parliament to agree to its own subordination. It did not do so as it did not participate in the ratification process, but the king agreed to the provision. He was thus bound to go to the English parliament before raising any army in Ireland against the Scots. Charles, therefore, had limited his sovereignty in Ireland in this respect.[90]

IRISH CATHOLIC REACTION

Although post-rebellion Irish responses to these events in England and Scotland exist, there are only scattered references to Irish reactions as they were happening. We may assume, however, that Irishmen generally were well informed. The committee of the Irish Commons arrived in England only a month after the Scottish commissioners reached London and must have been better informed than other Irishmen in London, and even those Irishmen who were not members of the committee had a good grasp of English events. During the very early days of the Long Parliament, an Irish Jesuit reported from London that "we are now tossed between hope and fear," for although parliament had not expressly dealt with religion, "yet such measures seem to be carried that from them perilous times are seriously dreaded."[91] Later that month religious issues were stated to be taking a "bad turn," and it was reported that wooden statues placed in churches by Laud were being removed by the order of parliament.[92] In Charles's northern army, John Barry and other Catholic officers heard that parliament intended to cashier them on the grounds of their faith. "Sir," he wrote to his Protestant friend, Percival, "I was never factious in religion, nor shall ever seek the ruin of any because he is not of my opinion."[93] It was three weeks later that the priest in Dublin, already quoted in a previous chapter, remarked on the danger to Catholicism posed by the English parliament.[94] A Scot writing in March asserted that the Irish, having purchased religious liberty from Strafford at a "dear rate," now feared losing both their property and religion, and by the summer Barry dared not even send news. Another Irishman in England was afraid even to go out of doors, "the persecution is so fearfully cruel and hot."[95]

The anxiety induced in the Irish by the Covenanter and Puritan campaign against bishops and Catholics is evident enough. If such attitudes appeared in the correspondence of priests and a Protestant planter living in Dublin, it may be assumed that the political leaders among the Catholics in Ireland were receiving similar if not more pessimistic information.

The impact of English and Scottish affairs upon Ireland is clear, even if the Englishmen and Scots of the time had no sense of the effect their actions would have across the Irish sea. Sir John Clotworthy's role was central. A major influence in displacing Strafford, he and "his party" wanted to put Holland into the lord lieutenancy. Just how far "his party" extended we do not know because we lack his private correspondence. That he had close ties with the Scots is not in doubt as, according to Baillie, did Holland. Almost certainly he worked in liaison with his father-in-law, Ranelagh, with Pym, and with Edward Rowley, his brother-in-law, who sat on the Irish Commons committee in England. But we can go no further than this in defining his circle. He and the earl of Cork had a common interest in wanting Strafford out of office, but there is nothing else to link the two men, though Cork must have worked with both Hamilton and Holland. What is also missing is anything but Sir George Wentworth's account to tie Clotworthy to men like Vane, Parsons, and Sir Adam Loftus. It would not have been necessary for Clotworthy to write to Sir Adam between March and June when the vice-treasurer was in England, but there is not a hint that Parsons was ever in contact with Clotworthy. Sir George, it will be recalled, accused his brother's enemies of wanting to divide Connacht between them. To test this accusation, we have to cross back to Ireland and look at the fourth and fifth sessions of the Irish parliament. In doing so, we shall see that Parsons and Loftus had frequent correspondence with Vane and that they both took a position on Connacht that conforms with Sir George's version of events.

CHAPTER FIVE

The Structure of Irish Politics in 1641

As the Irish parliament reassembled for its fourth session in late January 1641, members faced a bewildering scene. Irish issues had become tied to English ones and vice versa. As one correspondent wrote in February, "the general works of both kingdoms are so mixed that it is too hard for me to distinguish them."[1] Since November, the old hierarchical political structure of king, lord lieutenant, council, and parliament had given way to a much more complex and fractured collection of power centres. The king remained at the head although his freedom to act was much circumscribed. As the lord lieutenant, now facing trial, lost influence in determining Irish issues, that of the rest of the English privy council grew. Thus, early in the new year a committee of the English council was formed to deal with Irish affairs.[2] When this was established, it included the earls of Arundel and Bristol, and the absent earl of Leicester. The earl of Cork, initially excluded, was involved in all Irish affairs by May.

Other centres of power affecting policies pursued in Ireland were the English Lords and Commons, the lords justices and the Irish council (some members of which were in England during the early months of the year to testify at Strafford's trial), the Irish parliamentary committees in England, and, last but not least, the Irish Lords and Commons themselves. Each of these elements interacted with the others; such interaction, however, was often complicated by the time-lag in sending messages between the two realms. At the core of this complex system lay the Irish parliament and the influence brought to bear on it by those it represented. In looking at the political process in Ireland, there are three basic issues to address: first, to show what was done; second, to attempt to show who was primarily responsible for doing it; and third, to show the purpose behind the action. The course of events in the Irish parliament during 1641 has been recounted before, yet some recapitulation is necessary, in part to give a context to the other two issues, and in part because some new evidence is available.[3] The key question is the identity of those who were guiding the various measures through parliament, or opposing them.

THE FOURTH SESSION

The fourth session began on 26 January and ended on 5 March. The session began slowly because there was some doubt as to its legality, the lord lieutenant being absent and his deputy dead. This did not deter the Commons from indicating quickly the direction it intended to take. A type of steering committee was established to consider the business of the house and the enlargement of the powers of the committee in England. Within four days new instructions for this last committee had been drawn up and its powers augmented. The Commons committee in England was charged with pressing the king for six additional reforms beyond those demanded in November. The two most important of these were, first, an "explanation" of Poynings's law that would establish the right of the Commons to draw up its own bills for transmission to the king without interference from the Irish executive and, second, a remedy to the restriction on exports of certain commodities which meant, in effect, the repeal of statutes passed under Elizabeth.[4]

By 9 February the question of the legality of the sitting had been resolved. At the same time, a letter from the king dated 4 January arrived which mollified opinion by agreeing to the restoration of the pages torn out of the journal by Wandesford the previous November. Both houses nonetheless launched into a broad programme of reform.[5] In terms of time spent in the Commons, the issue that most preoccupied that house was the tobacco monopoly and the punishment of Strafford's servants, Joshua Carpenter and Thomas Little, who had been responsible for enforcing this and the linen yarn monopoly. Hardly a day passed without some comment on monopolies, and Little and Carpenter, who were MPs, were ultimately expelled from the house.[6] Yet both houses were doing far more than this to bring about what amounted to a transformation of the way in which the country was governed.

On 11 February the Lords set up a committee of grievances and by a week later it had drawn up a Schedule of Grievances to be sent to England. This contained seventeen clauses, most of which simply copied the clauses in the Commons' Remonstrance of the previous November, but the peers added a few grievances of their own. They complained in particular of the manipulation of proxy votes by the government. They also objected to men with Irish titles but no estates in the country receiving a vote in their house and to the government's failure to appoint Irish peers to Irish offices.[7]

One of the grievances specified both in the Remonstrance and this Schedule was the failure to extend to Ireland the Act of Limitations on land titles granted in England in 1624. In effect, this was a demand for enactment of the twenty-fourth to twenty-sixth clauses of the Graces, but both houses left nothing to chance and prepared separate documents to be sent to England to press for the confirmation of the more important Graces by act of parliament.[8] Both houses also issued a protest, the Commons on the seventeenth and the Lords on the twenty-second, against the preamble attached to the subsidy act which had been passed during the first session. This preamble, which praised Strafford, embarrassed those who now wished to destroy him, and it was alleged that it had been attached to the bill after its passage without the knowledge of either house.[9]

The Commons, meanwhile, began raising new grievances. Thus, the sixteen complaints listed in the November Remonstrance had multiplied to some thirty-seven issues by mid-July, many of the new ones being initiated by petitions coming in from the country to the house. No purpose would be served in tracing the course of each of these from its source, through the Commons, and on to the council in England, even if it were possible; two examples will illustrate how concerns of the country gained consideration.

On 11 January 1641, that is, two weeks before parliament reassembled, James Acheson, a second-generation Scottish settler, wrote to two of the MPs on the Commons' English committee to submit a proposal for the establishment of a mint in Ireland and the development of the mining industry. By the time he wrote, he had already submitted the proposal to the lords justices, "where it hath been cherished with their approbation and direction to prosecute this course if you will deign to give it life."[10] There is not a trace in the journals to show that the Irish Commons discussed the proposal, but they must have because the question of a mint for Ireland was being considered in Ireland by MPs and the lords justices, along with other issues, soon after the fourth session ended, and it appeared in the list of grievances being discussed by the English council in July.[11]

The second instance of a grievance that arose at this time definitely came before the Commons. When the plantations had been established, the patents of the British settlers banned the selling or leasing of their land to the native Irish. This provision was clearly intended to prevent the erosion of British settlement through land sales.

However, the Irish who received land under the settlement schemes were also prevented from selling to other Irish, and there were even similar restrictions on the leasing of land to Irishmen. By 1641 these restrictions were arousing considerable resentment, and the Irish gentry in the planted areas of Leinster petitioned against them on their own behalf and on behalf of the "the rest of the natives of the kingdom." They pointed out that these clauses in their patents had been designed for "troublesome times" and were both inappropriate and counterproductive in "better and more happy days" because they abated "the industry of the said natives being thereby accordingly discouraged" and made them "more careless of themselves and their fortunes having no hopes to gain further or great estates." They stressed, moreover, that such a "mark of separation and distinction from the rest of his highness' subjects" could not but "breed jealousy" as it denied rights to natural "freeborn subjects" that were granted to those born outside the king's dominions who were naturalized or made free denizens. The grievance, which was discussed in the Irish Commons on 23 February before being forwarded to England, indicated the strong feeling among the Irish gentry that they wished to be treated as equals in the economic system. Much would depend on the ability of the political system to respond to their desires.[12]

On the following day, the speaker wrote to the committee in England in answer to a letter sent on 31 December. This reply gives a good impression of what the house considered its priorities to be at this stage in the session. The speaker thanked the committee, and through it the king, for the conciliatory tone of the king's letter of 4 January. The concession to restore the pages torn from the journal was interpreted as tacit recognition that the lower rate would be applied in the collection of the subsidies. Accordingly, the Commons now agreed to the collection of the second and third subsidies at this reduced rate. The speaker then pressed the committee to secure the Graces, particularly those relating to the security of estates, with bills "drawn up in the House of Commons." The Commons, therefore, was already acting as though Poynings's law had been revised. Finally, the speaker enclosed copies of numerous documents, the most important being the protest against the preamble to the subsidy bill, and a copy of the so-called Queries, which had been drawn up by the Commons by 16 February and sent to the Lords for endorsement two days later. The Queries resembled a Declaration of Rights for Ireland and will be discussed later; here it is necessary to stress only that they must have been in preparation at the beginning of the session and, when presented to the Commons, evoked no opposition.[13]

The speaker's letter was sent to the committee in England on 25 February in the hands of a Catholic MP, Patrick Gough, and at the same time the Lords sent a similar letter with Lord Digby of Gaeshill (a Protestant), who was on his way to England on private business. On the same day the Commons asked the lords justices to approve bills it had drawn up. As the lords justices co-operated, a precedent was created for precisely the type of modification in Poynings's law that the Commons had asked should be passed by parliament.[14] Not content with this move towards legislative independence, on the twenty-seventh it took another major step in the same direction with the impeachment for treason of four leading men in Strafford's administration: Sir George Radcliffe, Sir Richard Bolton, Sir Gerard Lowther, and Bishop Bramhall.[15] In making this move, the Irish Commons was asserting rights over the executive similar to those exercised by the English Commons.

All of this work was accomplished without a sign of division in the Commons. It is true that, at the very end of the session, there was a hint of a split in that an effort to have the session continued was voted down.[16] But two points may be made about this incident that illustrate what was happening during the session: first, those who wanted to continue must have been associated with the campaign to assert the authority of the legislature; and, second, they were voted down by a sufficiently large majority so that no formal division had to be arranged. When, therefore, MPs wished to resist those who pressed most strongly for legislative authority, they could do so without difficulty. This confirms that the reforms demanded earlier in the session must have commanded support from the overwhelming majority of the house, Protestant and Catholic alike.

THE STRUCTURE OF POLITICS IN THE LORDS

The Lords appears to have been more divided during the fourth session than the Commons. This was partly because the bishops had no interest in pressing grievances, yet it is evident that in this house, too, the Catholics and some Protestants pressed for reform. The first issue on which there was some division concerned the legitimacy of the session. The judges were divided equally on the matter of whether parliament might continue to sit or not. We may assume that those most interested in having grievances settled in England wanted the session to continue, and we know that the chief spokesman for those urging this course was Lord Digby of Gaeshill.[17] Digby had married one of the daughters of the earl of Cork and was a nephew of the earl of Bristol, the influential opposition peer in England. Digby also had blood links with the Old English in that his mother was the granddaughter of the eleventh earl of Kildare.[18] Digby's stand in the Lords was supported by Lord Moore, an Old English Protestant, and Lord Fitzwilliam, a Catholic, and was opposed by the bishop of Meath. This issue lost its significance by 9 February, with the arrival of reassurance from the king, but not before a rumour circulated that Bolton, the chancellor, had been trying to use it to break parliament, a rumour he denied.[19]

On 11 February the Lords selected its grievance committee. This was, for the Lords, a fairly large committee, consisting of fourteen Protestants, including five bishops and the earl of Ormond, and six Catholics, including Christopher Plunkett, the earl of Fingall.[20] The Protestants, however, included Digby and Lord Lambert, who shared his views. Lambert was one of those who had lost land because crown officials had cancelled his patent without proceeding through the courts. The land in question lay in County Mayo, and the lawyers he engaged to fight his case were Patrick Darcy and Richard Martin, who had earlier fought the legal battle for the earl of Clanricard.[21] Lambert, however, cannot be regarded as within the same family orbit as Digby as it will be recalled that he also had a land feud with Cork.

There must have been other reformist Protestants because two would not have been enough, with the Catholics, to produce a majority on the committee. When we look for others, the first candidate is Thomas Roper, Viscount Baltinglass. At the end of February, when the first Viscount Muskerry died, Baltinglass replaced him on the Lords committee in England, and he would hardly have been chosen had he been opposed to reform. There were, in addition, among the Protestant peers, the Irishmen, Murrough O'Brien, Lord Inchiquin, and Miles Bourke, Lord Mayo, and the Old English peers, Lords Moore and Kerry, and it only needed two of these to produce a reformist majority on the committee.[22]

It will be evident by now that the terms Catholic and Protestant or Old English and settler are inadequate for describing the political division that was forming. The Catholics provided a solid block of reformers, but those who pressed for redress of grievances included settlers, both friends and foes of Cork, Old English Catholics, and some Irish. Indeed the majority of both proponents and opponents of reform may have been Protestant. The term "reformers" is too vague to describe those who belonged to the group that was pressing for change; it is necessary, therefore, to introduce the term "constitutionalist" to describe those who, in seeking redress of grievances, opposed the type of conciliar government instituted by Strafford and who, in resisting him, strove to increase the authority of the Irish legislature. Even the term constitutionalist may be a bit misleading because of possible connotations of an idealistic concept of balanced government. As we shall see, there was some idealism present, but there was also much self-interest. Those who were constitutionalists were conservative in both an Irish and an English sense. They harked back to an era when, to large extent, the aristocracy of Ireland controlled what went on and to an English constitution which stressed county government. The Lords, in particular, looked to a day when "nobles and peers ... may ... be preferred to ... place and office ... and trusted with the manage[ment] of the said great affairs."[23] Constitutionalists, therefore, did not seek power as a party, but worked as a loose alliance of men who knew what they disliked about the recent government, but had little sense of, or interest in, how the state was to function once they had gained the concessions they sought.

From 13 to 24 February, when Digby left for England with at least some of the grievances, the pace of reform quickened. Most proxy votes were disallowed, which reduced government influence in the house; Lord Slane, seconded by Lambert, introduced new grievances to be sent to England. The Schedule of Grievances was approved, and the Graces that the peers wanted turned into law were specified by Fingall. When the bishops attempted to withdraw from the process on the grounds that they were "against grievances," the judges told them they had no option but to be associated with the actions of the house as a whole because all was done in the name of the lords spiritual as well as temporal.[24]

After Digby had departed, attention switched from grievances to the Queries and, after the Commons laid the charges of treason against Bolton and the other officials on the twenty-seventh, to impeachment.[25] The journal does not provide a clear picture of the debates surrounding these issues, but certain features of the last days of the session stand out. It is clear that Ormond, supported by Moore and some others, led a campaign to delay consideration of the Queries and to allow the officials accused of treason to have as much liberty as possible. Ormond argued that, if Bolton, who was speaker, was removed from his position, the house could not sit until the king had chosen a new one. On the Queries, Ormond had success. He stirred up indignation against the Commons, which had already aroused animosity over another issue. When the lower house sent to know what the Lords had done with the Queries, Ormond urged the peers to respond that their house would take "a fitting course" in "due time." The matter was put to a vote and Ormond won.[26]

The absence of pressure from the Lords enabled the judges, who had been asked to comment on the Queries, to delay giving a reply until the session had ended. On impeachment, Ormond had less success, largely because he faced vigorous opposition from Lambert, who bore a personal grudge against Bolton and Lowther as they were the officials responsible for invalidating his Mayo estate. Throughout the proceedings, it was Lambert who pressed hardest for the accused to be treated according to the precedent set by Strafford's case, and when, at the end of the session, Bolton argued that Poynings's law prevented the Irish parliament from initiating impeachment proceedings, it was Lambert who retorted that, if all the Irish parliament could do was to pass bills, "that is scarce a Parliament." In the end, Bolton was removed from the speaker's chair, and the lords justices appointed a new one. Even though we cannot identify most of those supporting either Ormond or Lambert, it is evident that the constitutionalists could command a majority on occasion. The margin was narrow; a vote on whether the charges against the accused were too general divided the house equally. Ormond's success depended heavily on the votes of the bishops and on one occasion these were not enough to maintain control. We know that the bishops voted against a motion to place Lowther and Bramhall in some sort of confinement. "[N]evertheless," the two were committed by "most voices."[27] This means that a substantial majority of the temporal lords must have voted with the constitutionalists. We may now turn to the structure of the Commons in the two sessions held in 1641 before the rebellion broke out. This throws further light on the composition and, indeed, on the ideas of the constitutionalists.

THE STRUCTURE
OF THE COMMONS

It will be apparent from Table 7 that during the fourth and fifth sessions Protestants maintained the majority in the house that they held in 1640. Indeed, if we look at the MPs who participated in the committee process, we see that the Protestant majority went up from thirteen during the third session to seventeen in the fourth and forty-one in the fifth. While it is true that the Catholic participation rate was higher than the Protestant, this had been true since the second session and was probably a consequence of their smaller numbers. Nor is it particularly significant that the Protestant leaders had a

Table 7
Membership of Committees, by Religion, First to Fifth Sessions, 1640–41

	Sessions														
	First			Second			Third			Fourth			Fifth		
	Cath.	Prot.	Total	Cath.	Prot.	Total	Cath.	Prot.	Total	Cath.	Prot.	Total	Cath.	Prot.	Total
MPS															
Appointed to 1 or more committees	21	57	78	31	52	83	46	59	105	49	66	115	64	105	169
Signed November 1640 Petition							55	29	84						
Committees															
No. established in session			7			18			24			43			134
Prot. majority among those appointed to			36			21			13			17			41
Appointed to on 10 June 1641													55	66	121
% of elected MPS on	27	36	32	40	33	35	60	37	44	62*	41	48	80*	66	71
With Catholic majority**			1			7			9			17			30
With Protestant majority**			5			11			9			22			87

* By the fourth session several new elections had taken place, which added to the total Catholics in the house. Exact figures are not available.
** A few committees were evenly balanced between Catholics and Protestants. This explains why the sum of the committees with Catholic and Protestant majorities does not always equal the total number of committees in a particular session.

majority of only one during the fourth session. More significant is the number of committees where one of the religious groups constituted a majority. During every session save the third more committees had a Protestant majority than a Catholic one, and during the third there was a balance.

There is more evidence on how the house operated during the fifth session – 11 May to 7 August 1641 – than for the others because the house divided five times during that session. Some 175 MPs were present on 27 May, about 126 on 9 June, between 120 and 123 at the two divisions held on 23 June, and 100 as the session closed. There is no evidence that these divisions were on strictly religious lines because the tellers for the "yeas" and the "noes" were mixed.[28] Moreover, most of the issues on which the house divided do not suggest a religious confrontation: they were usually procedural and dealt with such matters as which petitions ought to be retained. As the division numbers indicate, attendance varied. There was also some turnover in personnel. Some MPs received permission to go to the country; others went to England; some resigned and some joined the house after new elections. The number of Catholic MPs increased as a result of this process but not, as has been suggested, decisively.[29] We gain unique insight into the composition of the house on 10 June when no less than sixteen committees were appointed to establish the fees in the various courts. Each committee was assigned a separate room in which to operate, and it looks as though every available MP had to be asked to serve as some men were appointed more than once and others were chosen who sat on no other committee either before or afterwards. On this day, 121 different men were appointed, approximately the same number that voted thirteen days later. Of these, 66 were Protestant and 55 Catholic.[30]

This is not to suggest that the house was working primarily to advance Protestant interests, but such figures challenge suggestions that Catholics were in control. Generally speaking, MPs worked together through consensus, and what they did was done by the house as a whole. It is true that there were a number of exceptions to this rule; the occurrence of five formal divisions during the fifth session is testimony to the increasing difficulty of maintaining consensus. As early as 12 May the lords justices claimed that the whole house was "swayed" by papists; in mid-June there was an attempt to impeach Sir Adam Loftus and Viscount Ranelagh which was thwarted only when the Protestants in the house "knit together" to stop the process; and four days before the session ended Sir William Parsons reported to Sir Henry Vane that "the papist votes" were "now the strongest."[31] Such evidence reveals the presence of Catholic-

Table 8
Leaders, by Religion, First to Fifth Sessions, 1640–41

	Cath.	Prot.	Total
First session: appointed to 4 or more committees	5	8	13
Second session: appointed to 6 or more committees	6	9	15
Third session: appointed to 6 or more committees	8	13	21
Fourth session: appointed to 11 or more committees	15	13	28
Fifth session: appointed to 20 or more committees	13	15	28

Protestant tensions, but it should not be used to create a picture of religious confrontation; the ideal of harmony remained and there was a great deal of co-operation between MPs of differing faiths. While each MP undoubtedly had his own particular interests, members also acted as if they understood their role to be one of advancing the interests of many groups within the community. Among the groups that petitioned the house for a redress of a grievance were the Ulster undertakers, who complained against the onerous form of *in capite* tenure imposed on them by Strafford.[32] During the adjournment between the fourth and fifth sessions, a group of Commons leaders – three Catholics and three Protestants, none with Ulster connections – wrote to the committee in England stressing the need to redress all grievances but mentioning in particular that of the Ulster undertakers.[33] The impression created, therefore, is that at this stage the leaders of the house were primarily concerned with practical considerations about how to help the population live a more prosperous life, with less intervention from the government. In contrast to their counterparts in England, references by Irish MPs to religion were noticeable by their absence.

That there was a recognized leadership in the Commons is made evident by the action of the speaker on the day after the fourth session ended. On 6 March, Sir Francis Hamilton, the Protestant MP for Jamestown, County Leitrim, arrived in Dublin with a letter from the committee in England. The speaker reacted by gathering the "leading men" of the Commons and reading them the letter "with all the proceedings that came therewith."[34]

The Protestant Leaders

When we look at the Protestant leadership, the most striking feature is the turnover in membership between 1640 and the fourth session. Of the twenty leaders identified in 1640, only two (the Bysse brothers) continued their leadership role during this session.

Wandesford had died, Radcliffe was in prison awaiting trial, Borlase and Parsons had become lords justices, and the two other councillors had had to leave for England to serve as witnesses in Strafford's trial.[35] These circumstances weakened the position of the council in the Commons, at a time when its influence was already diminished because of its internal divisions. This reduction in council partici-pation was to some extent balanced by the absence of five of the leaders who had signed the November Petition in 1640. Such men, however, continued their leadership role through membership of the committee in England, a reflection of the way in which the Irish Commons operated in two places at once.

If the departure of some MPs for service on the committee in England conceals a continuity of leadership, it remains true that those who left had to be replaced, and this directs our attention to the eleven leaders during the fourth session who had never played such a role before. Of these, the most active men were Dr Alan Cooke, Sir Robert Forth, Oliver Jones, Sir Audley Mervin, Sir Brian O'Neill, and Richard Parsons.

The most striking name within this list is O'Neill's. Understandably, given his name, Kearney included him among the Catholics, but in 1644 he took the Oath of Supremacy.[36] No sincere Catholic could take this oath as it denied papal supremacy. Nor is the delay in taking the oath difficult to explain as O'Neill went to England when the civil war broke out to fight for Charles.[37] It may be added that it was Sir Brian who was the chief mover in bringing impeachment pro-ceedings against Bishop Bramhall during the fourth session, which tends to confirm his Protestant beliefs as a Catholic would have been unlikely to launch such proceedings against a Protestant bishop.[38] Further light is shed on his attitude towards public affairs by the positions he took during the fifth session. In June 1641 he urged a protestation be drawn up against Sir Philip Mainwaring to remove him from the king's presence. As Wentworth had brought Main-waring to Ireland and appointed him Irish secretary, this marks O'Neill as one of the opposition. He also pressed for other supporters of Strafford to be brought to justice. Catholics in the house supported the same measures, but so did Simon Digby, brother to Lord Digby and a signer of the November Petition. These attacks upon Went-worth-appointed officials even after his death stemmed from general opposition to Strafford's type of administration, not from any spe-cifically Catholic, Old English, or Irish stance. In July, O'Neill accused the Protestant bishop of Raphoe, who had punished the wife of a Puritan minister, of *praemunire*, and there is an indication that he scrapped with both Protestant and Catholic lords. He was, in other

Table 9
Protestant Leaders in the Commons, 1640–41

| | Committees Appointed to in Sessions | | | | | | | |
| | | | | | | 5th | | |
	1st	2nd	3rd	4th	May	June	July/August	Total
First session (on 4 or more of 7 committees)								
1 BYSSE, John †P lawyer	4	14	6	19	13	12	18	43
2 DILLON, Lord Robert* pro-Strafford	4	9	6	Eng. witness		pr		
3 FITZGERALD, Richard †P	4	pr	16	Eng. committee				
4 RADCLIFFE, Sir George* pro-Strafford	6	pr	pr	Eng. in prison				
5 SAMBACH, Sir William* pro-Strafford	5	11	pr	pr	pr	pr	pr	(13)
6 TREVOR, Sir Edward*	4	–	pr	–	pr	left parliament		
7 WANDESFORD, Sir Chrostopher* pro-Strafford	4	made lord deputy, died 3 Dec. 1640						
8 WARE, Sir James*	4	pr	9	pr	pr	pr	pr	(9)
Second Session (on 6 or more of 18 committees)								
9 BORLASE, Sir John*	pr	6	–	became lord justice				
10 BYSSE, Robert† lawyer	pr	7	6	19	6	20	19	45
11 LOFTUS, Sir Adam C–R*	pr	8	6	Eng. witness				
12 MEREDITH, Sir Robert C–R*	pr	6	pr	–		pr	pr	(7)
13 PARSONS, Sir William C–R*	pr	6	pr	became lord justice				
14 WALLER, Sir Hardress – P	pr	8	15	Eng. committee		–	pr	(2)

Third Session (on 6 or more of 24 committees)

No. & Name						Total
15 COLE, Sir William – P	pr	6	Eng. committee	pr	pr	(13)
16 COOTE, Sir Charles C–R*	pr	7	pr	5	7	21
17 DENNY, Sir Edward – P	–	6	–			
18 MONTGOMERY, Sir James – P	pr	8	Eng. committee	9	8	
19 ROWLEY, Edward – P	–	6	Eng. committee			
20 TRAVERS, Sir Robert – P	–	7	–	15	9	22

Fourth Session (on 11 or more committees)

No. & Name						Total
21 CADOGAN, William	pr	pr	11	8	6	28
22 COOKE, Dr Alan / lawyer	pr	pr				
23 DOPPING, Anthony	pr	pr	19	pr	pr	21
24 FORTESCUE, Sir Faithful	pr	–	11	5	3	(7)
25 FORTH, Sir Robert	pr	pr	16	10	7	20
26 JONES, Oliver / lawyer	pr	pr	20	16	10	27
27 MERVIN, Sir Audley	pr (3)	pr (1)	18	9	26	32
28 O'NEILL, Brian	–	–	20	23	17	46
29 PARSONS, Richard	pr	–	26	pr	pr	50
30 REYNOLDS, Paul	pr	pr	19	pr	pr	(11)
31 STEPHENS, Stephen – P	–	–	15	pr	pr	(11)

Fifth Session (on 20 or more committees)

No. & Name						Total
32 DIGBY, Simon – P / lawyer	–	Eng.	Eng.	22	10	(4)
33 GORE, Sir Ralph	pr	(2)	–	6	9	42
34 HILL, Arthur	not yet MP		–	11	17	21
35 OSBORNE, Sir Richard – P / lawyer	pr	(3)	(9)	5	10	38
				5	10	21

Key: * = on council; † = held office though not on the council; P = signed November Petition; C–R = belonged to the Cork-Ranelagh group; pr = present during session; ( ) = not a leader during session but sat on a significant number of committees; Eng. = was in England, either on committee sent by Commons or for other reasons.

words, a man who attacked wrong wherever he thought he found it.[39] His attacks on bishops suggest not simply Protestant, but possibly Puritan, leanings. He was, above all, a constitutionalist who opposed authoritarian administration.

Of other Protestant constitutionalists, we know most about Sir Audley Mervin, and our knowledge about him throws light upon those with whom he worked. Mervin was the second son of an admiral, and through his mother a nephew to the Catholic earl of Castlehaven, after whom he was named. His estate lay in County Tyrone and he married the daughter of Sir Hugh Clotworthy. He was, therefore, brother-in-law to Sir John Clotworthy. His sister, however, married Rory Maguire, one of the leaders of the Irish rebellion and a fellow MP, and he was also related to Sir Piers Crosby.[40] Thus he possessed family ties with virtually every faction opposed to Strafford.

Mervin is particularly significant because he led the campaign in the Commons to assert the right of the Irish parliament to impeach crown officials. From statements made after the wars had broken out, it is evident that he had a touching if naive faith in the ability of parliament to resolve the problems of the country. After the cessation of hostilities between the forces in Ireland loyal to Charles and the Confederate Catholics, the earl of Ormond began negotiations for peace. Early in 1644 Mervin urged him not to agree to a peace on his own initiative, but "by a parliament," from which violent spirits had been excluded in favour of "moderate persons."[41] The prospect of the king being strengthened by Irish forces pushed the English Parliamentarians and the Covenanting Scots into an alliance which was cemented by the Solemn League and Covenant. Mervin opposed that Covenant in the Irish parliament and Ormond sent him to Ulster to resist its adoption there. Initially, Mervin did what he could, but ultimately, "second thoughts" being a privilege "that the ablest judgements will not disclaim," he swore to it himself. There was nothing half-hearted about Mervin's Protestantism. In his letter to Ormond reporting his second thoughts on the Covenant, he referred to the "perfidious catholics," yet in the same letter he expressed worry that the Covenant implied the subordination of the Irish parliament to the English one and urged that the parliament in Ireland should write to its English counterpart to refute any such interpretation.[42] For all his political and religious contortions, Mervin seems to have pressed consistently for a strong parliamentary role in the government of Ireland and for the constitutional independence of Ireland's parliament from the English one. It was here that moderate Protestants and Catholics could find a common bond.

One noticeable feature of the Commons leadership, Protestant as well as Catholic, was the strong presence of the lawyers. As Sir John Temple commented, the lawyers "made a great party in the house of commons."[43] Three of the seven Catholics who went to England were lawyers. Similarly, among the Protestant leaders during the fourth session, we find the two Bysse brothers, Dr Alan Cooke, and Oliver Jones. Jones sat for the borough of Athlone, and it has been suggested that he owed his seat to Roger Jones, Viscount Ranelagh. This is possible, but there seems to have been no close family connection and there were many families of this name living in Athlone at the time. During the Interregnum he would serve as attorney-general of Connacht and during the Restoration as a judge, when he gained the reputation of being a Catholic at heart, possibly because he declined to discriminate against Catholics in his judgments.[44] It seems likely, therefore, that his activity in the Commons during 1641 derived more from interests similar to Mervin's than to aristocratic faction. Mervin also was a lawyer, which reinforces the impression that many Protestants who worked with the Catholics during the fourth session did so because of constitutional concerns.

Sir Robert Forth, so far as we know, was not a lawyer, but he too may have had legal training as he was the eldest son of Sir Ambrose Forth, a judge. Sir Robert subsequently became an Ormondist, which distinguishes him as a moderate Protestant, but there are two other features about him that could explain his presence among the Protestant leaders when there was co-operation between them and the Catholics. First, his mother was from the Old English family of the Cusacks of County Meath, and this may have led to a sympathy for some of the positions for which the Old English stood. Second, his estate lay in County Cavan, yet he sat for the borough of Kilbeggan, County Westmeath. This is where Lambert, who was also an Ormondist, had part of his estate though he too possessed land in Cavan. It is unlikely that Forth obtained his seat without the peer's agreement and the mutual Cavan connection and Ormondist record implies some sort of link between the two men.[45] Lambert's strong, though hardly disinterested, constitutional opinions have already been described, and if Forth and he were close, this would explain Forth's prominence. Forth may also have been close to that other Protestant constitutionalist, Lord Digby, as his mother married Digby's father when Sir Ambrose died.[46]

The two remaining most active men were Sir Faithful Fortescue, governor of Carrickfergus Castle, who had quarrelled with Strafford and had married into the Old English family of Garret Moore, first Viscount Drogheda, and Richard Parsons, Sir William's son, who had married Sir Adam Loftus's daughter.[47] The presence of Parsons within the leadership is intriguing. We can only speculate that he represented an avenue of communication between the Commons and the new executive, which had been virtually chosen by the committee in England on the basis of its political distance from Strafford.

Little can be said about the remaining, less active leaders: Stephen Stephens, who sat for Athy, County Kildare, had signed the November Petition and was one of those Protestants who communicated with the Commons committee in England when parliament was prorogued. William Cadogan was an army officer who represented Monaghan. Paul Reynolds sat for Killyleagh, County Down, and Anthony Dopping sat for Bandon, the heart of Cork's settlement.[48] The distribution of the constituencies shows that Protestant leadership came from many different parts of the country.

When we turn to the fifth session, we find much continuity of leadership with that of the previous one. Seven of the eleven new Protestant leaders during the fourth session continued their leadership into the fifth. The Bysse brothers maintained their virtually unbroken record of strong participation, and two MPs who had been leaders in 1640 but absent during the fourth session, Sir Edward Denny of Kerry and Sir Robert Travers, who sat for Clonakilty, County Cork, returned. Both these men had signed the November Petition and must be regarded as constitutionalists. There were also four newcomers. By far the most important of these was Simon Digby, who sat for Philipstown, County Offaly. Digby, another lawyer, shared his elder brother's links with, first, the Old English, both his mother and stepmother coming from their ranks, and, second, the opposition in England through the earl of Bristol, his uncle, and, finally and to a lesser extent, the earl of Cork, through his brother's marriage to one of the Boyle daughters.[49] Here, among the Protestants, therefore, was a constitutionalist overlap between Commons and Lords. Simon had signed the November Petition and, no doubt in part because he had powerful relatives, had been appointed to the committee that crossed to England, where he spent the fourth session. He had returned to Ireland by the fifth session, during which he played an important role.

The remaining three new leaders included two MPs from Ulster, Sir Ralph Gore and Arthur Hill, the latter entering the house after a bye-election. Finally, there was Sir Richard Osborne, a Munster planter, a lawyer, Cork's godson, and a man who had already established a reputation for working for constitutionalist ends. He was the only Munster Protestant to have accompanied the delegation from Ireland to Charles during the campaign to secure the Graces.[50] It is not surprising, therefore, to find that he had signed the November Petition.

The analysis of the Protestant leaders indicates that nine of the thirteen MPs who led during the fourth session and twelve of the fifteen who led in the fifth can, with some degree of certainty, be regarded as constitutionalists, and this is not counting such men as Anthony Dopping and Arthur Hill, about whom too little is known to warrant an assertion about their political views. During most of the fourth session and much of the fifth, the Commons continued its practice of working by consensus. Even during the fifth session, when consensus was clearly under strain, there were only five divisions over a period of approximately three months. This means that the leaders reflected the opinion of the majority. We may suspect that men like Sir William Sambach and Sir James Ware, and Sir Adam Loftus after his return from England, did not sympathize with what was happening in the house, but they played a secondary role. Indeed, it is likely that it was impossible to become a leader during the fifth session without upholding constitutionalist views. Moreover, these leaders were substantial men. Three of those in the fourth session were knights, and in the next session the number was seven, or almost half the leadership. This solid core of Protestant constitutionalists confirms the impression derived from the behaviour of the house that it was not just a few Protestants who worked with the Old English to institute a new type of government in Ireland.

The Catholic Leaders

The analysis of the Catholic leadership in the Commons during the fourth and fifth sessions can be briefer, in part because Aidan Clarke has already provided it, and in part because there is no doubt about their political opinion. As far as we can tell, they were all constitutionalists. It will be evident from Table 10 that, because of the high proportion of the 1640 Catholic leaders who went to England (six out of nine), during the fourth session, virtually a different set of men had to provide direction. Only the lawyer, James Cusack, and Sir Richard Blake provided continuity in the leadership from 1640 to 1641. Those who took over were, on the whole, lesser men. Only three of the thirteen subsequently served on a supreme council of the Catholic Confederation. Yet such men as Patrick Barnewall, Sir Christopher Bellew, and John Bellew, the sheriff for Louth, were prominent leaders of the Pale, as was Maurice Fitzgerald.[51]

Three interesting additions to the leadership early in 1641 were Rory Maguire of Fermanagh, Dermot O'Brien of Clare, and Philip

Table 10
Catholic Leaders in the Commons, 1640–41

					5th			
								Committees Appointed to in Sessions
	1st	2nd	3rd	4th	May	June	July/August	Total
First Session (on 4 or more of 7 committees)								
1 BOURKE, Thomas – P	6	–	13	Eng.				
2 BROWN, Geoffrey – X P lawyer	6	13	10	Eng.				
3 FITZHARRIS, Sir Edward – P	5	9	17	Died 3 Mar. 1641				
4 LYNCH, Sir Roebuck – X P	5	7	12	Eng.				
5 PLUNKETT, Nicholas – X P lawyer	7	13	12	Eng.				
Second Session (on 6 or more of 18 committees)								
6 BARNEWALL, Nicholas – P lawyer	–	6	(5)	Eng.				
7 CUSACK, James – X lawyer	pr	11	10	21	–	–	pr	(2)
Third Session (on 6 or more of 24 committees)								
8 BLAKE, Sir Richard – X	pr	pr	10	21	14	21	19	54
9 MacCARTHY, Sir Donough – X P	–	(2)	8	Eng.				

Fourth Session (on 11 or more committees)

				Eng.				
10	(WALSH, John – X P lawyer)[a]	–	–	–	–	–	–	–
11	ASHE, Richard – P	–	(3)	11	pr	pr	pr	(6)
12	BARNEWALL, Patrick – P	pr	pr	17	pr	pr	pr	(15)
13	BARNEWALL, Sir Richard – X P	pr	pr	22	10	23	17	50
14	BELLEW, Sir Christopher – P	pr	pr	14	11	8	7	26
15	BELLEW, John – P	pr	pr	12	9	7	8	24
16	CHEEVERS, Garret	–	–	16	4	9	8	21
17	DUNGAN, Sir John – P	–	pr	19	9	20	14	43
18	FITZGERALD, Maurice – P	–	–	16	12	13	13	38
19	MAGUIRE, Capt. Rory – P	–	–	11	–	pr	–	
20	O'BRIEN, Dermot	–	–	13	5	10	7	22
21	O'REILLY, Philip – X	–	–	12	–	pr	–	
22	ROCHFORD, Hugh – X P	pr	pr	22	4	13	15	32
23	TAYLOR, John	pr	pr	20	7	16	13	36

Fifth Session (on 20 or more committees)

				Eng.				
24	CUSACK, Adam	–	–	–	10	16	14	40
25	DARCY, Patrick – X lawyer	not yet MP			10	17	28	55
26	MARTIN, Richard – X lawyer	not yet MP			–	–	15	15[b]

Notes

[a] Walsh has been included in this list during the fourth session because of his position on the committee in England.

[b] Martin was absent during most of the fifth session, but he was clearly a leader after he took his seat.

Key: P = signed November petition; X = attended at least one supreme council session of the Catholic Confederation (Cregan, "Confederation of Kilkenny," 88–91); pr = present during session but not a leader; ( ) = not a leader during session but sat on a significant number of committees; Eng. = was in England on committee sent by Commons.

O'Reilly of Cavan, who initially provided the Irish with a stronger presence within the Commons than in 1640. Maguire and O'Reilly, however, dropped out, apparently not attending parliament after June, and both were involved in plotting the rebellion. It may also be noted that not one of the new additions to the Catholic leadership during the fourth session was a lawyer, and as James Cusack seems to have taken leave during May and June, the absence of legal guidance would have diminished the effectiveness of the group, had it not been for the two additions to the house by bye-election of Patrick Darcy and, in July, Richard Martin. Both of these lawyers came from Connacht. Both had been involved in fighting the proposed plantation of Connacht, and both served as counsel for Lambert.

Darcy was of particular importance because, once he entered the house, he took over the campaign to have the Queries answered in a manner that would have ensured some permanent guarantees against an over-officious council. Yet, even before he took his seat, he must have been following parliamentary developments. He must also have been in close contact with his client, the earl of Clanricard, but Clanricard was in England, and it is to events in this country that we must turn to round out our picture of the fourth session of the Irish parliament and the structure of Irish politics. The two Irish committees in England, but particularly that of the Commons, worked vigorously to obtain the goal of their parent bodies, and through them, in microcosm, we see another image of the Irish parliament at work.

THE PARLIAMENTARY COMMITTEES IN ENGLAND

The composition of the parliamentary committees that were selected in November 1640 to go to England has already been described. Viscount Dillon of Costello-Galen appears to have remained in Ireland for a time before joining his colleagues, Lords Gormanston, Kilmallock, and Muskerry, in England.[52] As Muskerry had died by the middle of February 1641, initially the burden of representing the Lords' case fell on Gormanston and Kilmallock. They undoubtedly consulted Clanricard, whose knowledge of the court must have been useful.[53] Clanricard, in turn, we may assume, drew on the advice of his half-brother, the earl of Essex. The fond relationship between these two men, the one Irish Catholic and the other English Puritan, is symbolic of the developing symbiosis between the Irish and the English aristocracy before the outbreak of the war. But aside from this personal bond, Essex shared political aims with Clanricard in Ireland, where he possessed large estates, in that he too had quarrelled with Strafford and was, perhaps, among the lord lieutenant's most implacable English foes.[54]

Gormanston and Kilmallock faced a slightly awkward situation in that, unlike the Commons, which had issued its Remonstrance in November before the proroguement, the Lords had taken no official stance before it was adjourned. The two men, therefore, drew up a petition which they presented as their own opinion and that of "divers others of the nobility of Ireland." This was received by the English authorities by 19 February, or well before anyone in England could have known the contents of the Schedule of Grievances, passed in Ireland the previous day. The petition of the two lords is of interest as it contained elements not found in the Schedule, which was, as we have seen, but an elaboration upon the Commons' Remonstrance.[55]

Many of the forty clauses of this petition, such as objection to the denial of the Graces, are to be found in other lists of complaints, but this document has a vigour and force that was sometimes lacking in statements that had to command the support of an assembly, and it raised some issues that had not been mentioned before. The petition, which of course was being submitted at a strategic time in view of Strafford's impending trial, amounted to a withering indictment of his government, its unifying theme being the accusation that he had attempted to destroy a well-functioning government and had, in particular, whittled away parliamentary rights. Ireland, it began, had enjoyed a "settled government many hundred years," yet Strafford had imputed a "slavish opinion and condition upon that nation." Later it complained that, whereas "the high court of Parliament hath been anciently settled and freely practised" as the principal means for redress of grievances, Strafford had undermined its rights by influencing elections through intimidation, using proxies in the Lords, and by pressing privy council members who sat in parliament "to comply to his lordship's propositions for fear of loss of their place." It concluded with objections to the way the courts had been run and revenue collected, and an aristocratic affront at the placing of "persons of mean worth or value" in the commissions of the peace, "omitting the nobility and other prime gentlemen."[56] This affront had recently been made more galling by the appointment of Sir John Temple as master of the rolls on 31 January, a post the Irish lords had coveted for one of their own candidates.[57]

The Commons committee had originally arranged that three of its members, Montgomery, Fitzgerald, and Walsh, should remain in Ireland to organize the submission of additional grievances. These three, however, had to make a sudden and "unexpected" departure in mid-December, presumably to help their fellow committee members resist the appointment of Strafford's friends as lords justices.[58] However, new complaints and proposals continued to be collected during the fourth session. While these were being prepared in Ireland, the committee was pressing not only for the appointment of acceptable lords justices, a goal achieved by 27 December when Lord Robert Dillon of Kilkenny-West was replaced by Sir John Borlase, but also for the concessions that were contained in the king's letter of 4 January, the dispatch of which was nevertheless delayed until a favourable reference to Strafford had been deleted.[59]

Once these initial concessions had been granted, attention turned to the Remonstrance. Here again delay ensued as the king insisted on obtaining Sir George Radcliffe's answer before considering the document. The delay was a political error. The English council did not consider Radcliffe's response till 27 January, by which time the Irish parliament had resumed its sitting and had begun to proceed along its militant path.[60] When, at last, the Remonstrance was discussed, Charles initially adopted such a negative attitude towards the crucial fourth clause, which referred to the security of estates, "as the committee apprehended some doubt of the success which they expected before that time concerning the redress of all their grievances," and they were at the point of issuing a new declaration which would have undoubtedly raised the political temperature. But "by means of some," confrontation was averted. Charles summoned the committee again and adopted a more conciliatory stance towards the Graces. This still did not satisfy some on the committee, but no new declaration was issued.[61] Negotiations continued. The committee replied (rather ineffectively) to Radcliffe's answer, but progress towards a satisfactory agreement had been made by 23 February.[62] Sir Francis Hamilton was sent to Ireland to report this progress by a letter of this date, but as we have seen, he arrived on 6 March, the day after the proroguement. We do not know precisely what the news was that Hamilton brought back as we only possess the reply to it, but on reading it to those leaders of the Commons who remained in Dublin after the session was over, the speaker was able to report that it "gave them and I believe the whole kingdom much content."[63]

We must suppose that the committee's letter of the twenty-third indicated that Charles was intending to grant security of tenure and thus, in effect, to abandon the policy of plantation. Yet the matter was not settled. Opposition to the policy had developed even within the committee. By 8 March, the Catholic John Barry, who was in London, reported to Sir Philip Percival that the committee was split. Thomas Bourke and Nicholas Barnewall had obtained private access to the king through Lord Cottington, a contender at the time for the lord lieutenancy, and it was they who had persuaded Charles to call a halt to plantation in Ireland. Other members of the committee resented this private initiative, and some on the committee defended plantation though "for particular ends."[64] Nor were the members of the committee the only defenders of plantation; Radcliffe wrote a strong and well-reasoned defence of the policy.[65] However, this was also the time that the various resolutions passed by the Lords in Ireland were beginning to arrive in England.[66] Thus, when the English council returned again to consider Irish grievances on 9 March, the political argument for making concessions must have been overwhelming. A committee of the council was set up, which included Bedford, Bristol, and Cottington, to consider the Graces, the Remonstrance, the Gormanston-Kilmallock petition, and "the draft of the letter promised touching the said Graces."[67] As a result of the work of this committee, the lords justices were instructed by a king's letter dated 3 April to prepare bills granting, among other concessions, security of land tenure in general, but particularly in Connacht, Tipperary, and Limerick.[68]

Aidan Clarke has declared this to be "almost total capitulation" by Charles. It was certainly a repudiation of Strafford's policy, but the term "capitulation" implies an earlier commitment to plantation that Charles did not have. He had a commitment to his minister, but his minister's policies had failed, and it would have been the height of political folly not to reverse those policies at this stage. The king had earlier shown some political sense when he had backed Clanricard against his minister, and he was only doing in March in a general way what he had done in a particular instance earlier. His mistake was in not implementing his concessions as soon as he had decided to make them. Delay between his promise to the committee in February and the formal commitment in April, and subsequent delay in passing the necessary acts to give effect to the concessions, led to an erosion of confidence in Ireland in his ability to deliver what he promised.

The delay in implementing the concessions arose in part because of opposition to them, but it would be wrong to see the issue as one being fought out along Protestant-settler versus Old English–Catholic lines. The analysis of the structure of the politics in both houses of the Irish parliament has already undermined such a conclusion, and evidence surrounding the Commons committee reinforces the impression that Irish MPs usually worked with a sense of common interest. When Percival responded to Barry's letter relating the division on the committee over the issue of plantation, he commented that, although it was rumoured that he and others would have benefited "if things had gone on," he did not resent "the loss" if the decision was for the general good. Indeed, he went further: "If any should, out of ends of profit or honour, go contrary to their trust, which I find by you is suspected, ... it is [a] pity that they should ever return."[69]

The king's letter of 3 April containing the instructions to give effect to the concessions was taken to Ireland by Simon Digby and his Catholic colleague, Geoffrey Brown, whom he later referred to as "my brother Brown."[70] Digby's views about the political process, which must have been shared by Brown, are made clear by a letter he wrote in May from Ireland to the committee in England. He remarked on the delay in Ireland in having the bills prepared for return to England and then stated: "I have writ to divers of my friends there [England] to forward the return of bills now transmitted and have intimated to some of them the private negotiations of some that now endeavour to hinder the service only for their own benefit."[71] It may be assumed that one of those to whom he wrote was his uncle, Bristol. It is striking that he could convey these sentiments to the entire committee. Nor, as far as we can tell, was there any concern about whether this important committee had a Catholic or Protestant majority. Originally it was established with seven Catholics and six Protestants. With Muskerry's death in February, his son, Sir Donough MacCarthy, a member of the Commons committee, succeeded to the title. By the end of February he was preparing to return to Ireland, and Cork helped him out at this time by lending him money interest-free.[72] On his departure there was no attempt to replace him, and the committee thereafter was evenly balanced between the two faiths. The Lords, however, replaced his father by appointing a Protestant, Viscount Baltinglass. In May, Brown returned to England, but Digby remained in Ireland. This restored a Catholic majority to the committee in England, but we need read no subtle manœuvre into this event. Digby explained that he did not wish to return to because he was suffering from pains in his head.[73] Finally, we possess six letters from the committee to the speaker during May, June, and July. One of these was signed by more Protestants than Catholics, two by a Catholic majority, and in three cases there was a balance between the two groups.[74] Religion, in other words, did not seem to be a matter of much concern.

Perhaps as significant as this evidence is the petition of early April, which was drawn up on behalf of the landowners of Connacht and which must have been associated with the campaign to stop the plantation in that province. This was signed by Clanricard, two members of the Lords committee – Viscounts Dillon and Kilmallock – and six members of the Commons committee, including the future regicide, Sir Hardress Waller, whose interests lay in County Limerick.[75] With Digby and Waller supporting the campaign to end plantation, we may ask who on the committee wished to continue it. The most likely candidates are Fitzgerald, who was close to the Parsons-Ranelagh group, and Rowley, Clotworthy's brother-in-law.[76] In the absence of firmer evidence, no more can be said. It is even possible that the split in the committee over the issue of plantation was exaggerated. The later letters from the committee show that its members continued to work together to redress all grievances. This is not to play down the importance of the land issue; it was crucial, but to examine it properly and to see how its resolution was delayed, we must pass on to the events leading into, and through, the fifth session.

CHAPTER SIX

The Fifth Session and
the Policy of Plantation

The role of the Old English within the Irish parliament during the fifth session, which began on 11 May, has received much emphasis.[1] There is no doubt about the important part that they played in this session, but it will be argued here that the New English and Scots were at least as important as their Old English colleagues in extracting concessions from the king and in pressing for restraint upon executive power. Sir John Temple, who arrived in Ireland only weeks after the session had ended, remarked some five years later that the constitutional arguments advanced by the lawyers in the Commons "were received with great acclamation, and much applause by most Protestant members of the house."[2] The lords justices, as they reported to England, were reluctant to admit the extent of Protestant participation in the constitutionalist campaign, but the available evidence tends to confirm Temple's assessment.

BETWEEN THE SESSIONS

As the fourth session was being prorogued on 5 March, the lords justices faced an increasingly difficult situation. Charles made little attempt to consult them when shaping his Irish policies. They were asked to comment on the issue of plantation, but before they could reply, the decision had been made to discontinue it.[3] They were also asked to respond to the charges being levelled at Strafford's administration. They answered cautiously as they were themselves vulnerable to criticism, but they used the occasion to attempt to distance themselves from their former leader. To the question whether Strafford had exercised abnormal powers, they replied that he had "assumed some powers, which we remember not ... former deputies to have done."[4] This desire to separate themselves from their predecessor's record was evident in their handling of parliament. In late February, for instance, they had postponed adjournment "to avoid anything that might occasion dispute." The submission of the Queries made them change their minds, but again they delayed rather than give offence, and this respite permitted the Commons to embark on the impeachment proceedings. As parliament had reduced the size of the subsidies, and as the new army imposed an "extraordinary charge" upon the treasury, there was no money to pay either the new or the old army, "whence may arise rapine and spoil."[5]

Rapine and spoil were not long in coming in that riots broke out in late March and early April in the northeast where Protestants had settled and the new army was quartered. There was no direction from Scotland behind this unrest, but Protestant hostility towards the established church certainly played a role as the clergy often bore the brunt of the rioters' anger. The local officials, who had no difficulty in quelling the disturbances, described the participants as "the basest sort of people," being "servants without lands or families." Undoubtedly the poor were suffering hardship, in part because the last harvest had been poor, but more because the inhabitants were forced to sell food to the army at a fixed price "which gave no profit."[6] Even in areas where there were no riots there were complaints. Nor were economic complaints confined to the north. The earl of Cork's agent warned in April that he could not promise to collect the rents, "for I did never hear the like complaining of all men generally for the want of money or how to pay their rents as now."[7]

It was in this atmosphere that the Irish executive received word, on 14 April, when Geoffrey Brown and Simon Digby returned to Dublin, that the king had decided to discontinue plantation and to grant other concessions. Within a week the lords justices met representatives of the two houses, who pressed them to draft the necessary bills for dispatch to England as quickly as possible. The council discussed these bills every day until parliament resumed sitting, and Brown returned to England with the drafts.[8]

We do not know who represented the Lords at this meeting on 21 April, but the Commons delegation included Sir Richard Barnewall, Patrick Barnewall, and Sir John Dungan (all Catholics) and the Protestants, William Plunkett, Stephen Stephens, and Alan Cooke. It was this group that wrote to the Commons committee in England on the twenty-third, telling it of Brown's impending return with the draft bills and urging that everything possible be done to get these approved and returned quickly for passage through parliament in the upcoming session. They also raised a number of new issues: the cause of the undertakers in Ulster, the proposal for a mint in Ireland (which the committee had already received), and two new bills, apparently already drafted, one on free trade for certain Irish products on which restrictions had been placed during Elizabeth's reign, and another against monopolies.[9] In submitting these draft bills before declaring a grievance, they were clearly trying to speed up the legislative process which, under Poynings's law, could be frustratingly slow.

While these preparations had been taking place to implement the king's concessions, the issue of the Irish parliament's right to impeach was being discussed in England. News of parliament's actions against Sir Richard Bolton and the other three officials reached the king just as he was granting the concessions on plantation, and a legal opinion was sought at the end of March to determine if the Irish parliament had authority to exercise this power. A month later a letter was sent to Ireland which, in effect, challenged impeachment and asked for precedents. Virtually all the major issues which were discussed during the fifth session had therefore been raised in one form or another before it began.[10]

THE THREE INSTRUMENTS

As parliament met, the lords justices warned that the Lords were "swayed by papists" and that proxies should be prepared in order to give more influence to the earls of Ormond and Thomond, Lord Kerry, and Viscount Montgomery.[11] The absence of any journal for the upper house during this session makes it impossible to tell what was happening there, but the use of the word "swayed" and the list of only four lords who were to be trusted with proxies suggests that numerous Protestant peers were acting as constitutionalists. There was also a growing rift between the Commons and the lords justices, a rift in which Protestant MPs played as active a role as did Catholics. On the second day of the session (12 May) the house established a committee to draw up an answer to Sir George Radcliffe's defence of Strafford's government and to go to the Lords to hear the judges' answers to the Queries. This committee consisted of six Catholics and nine Protestants and the lawyers in the house. Five of the Protestants, including Simon Digby whose distrust of the executive is documented, had signed the November Petition, and two others have also been identified with the constitutionalists.[12]

On the following day (13 May) the lords justices summoned both houses and informed them of three royal letters: that of 28 March, relating to the legitimacy of the fourth session, the letter of 3 April declaring, in effect, the end of plantation, and that of 28 April, in which the king had challenged the Irish parliament's right to impeach and had asked for precedents.[13] There then ensued a period of debate and consultation between the two houses about how to react, the result of which was the joint submission of the Three Instruments to the king. A number of separate Commons committees took part in these discussions, two of which had Catholic majorities, but the committee that presented the Three Instruments to the Irish Lords consisted of thirty-five Protestants and seventeen Catholics.[14] Thus Catholic MPs participated actively, but it is evident that, in forming committees, the house paid little attention to the question of which faith was in a majority or what size that majority was.

The first of the Three Instruments, the Humble Supplication, thanked the king for his letters of 28 March and 3 April, pressed that the promises contained in the latter be passed into acts as soon as possible, and, taking a leaf out of the English parliament's book, asked that the Irish parliament not be prorogued or dissolved until these acts had been passed. The second instrument, the Declaration and Protestation, asserted the power of the Irish parliament to hear cases of treason and other crimes on the grounds that it was "the supreme judicatory" in the realm. The third instrument had no title, but was a petition that, again, asserted the Irish parliament's judiciary role, urged the king to be "rightly informed" on the matter, and asked him if he thought it appropriate that those who stood accused of treason should continue their role in government and the courts.[15]

The Three Instruments became a joint declaration of Lords and Commons on 24 May, and on the following day they were dispatched to the English committees with a Captain William Weldon, who was given special powers to press shipping in order to hasten delivery. Using all possible speed, Weldon delivered the instruments to the committees in the record time of four days, arriving on the evening of the twenty-ninth.[16] Along with the Three Instruments, Weldon took a covering letter to the Commons committee from the speaker in which it was advised to present the second instrument, the Declaration and Protestation, only as "occasion shall require." This letter also responded to the demand for impeachment precedents by saying that both houses believed that "common law serves for all precedents."[17] This cautious attitude towards the second instrument explains why the Commons refused to give the lords justices a copy of the Three Instruments and shows the level of distrust that had developed between the legislature and the executive.[18]

As the instruments were sped to London, a committee was established to review the membership of the Irish Commons and all committees "formerly named" and to "divide the members into several committees ... and to assign to each committee a peculiar employment in such matters, as are, or shall be depending in this House." This committee was as carefully chosen as the one sent to England in 1640 in that each province was specifically represented. Unlike the committee in England, however, Protestants outnumbered Catholics five to three. This was clearly an important committee as it amounted to a nominating committee, although it had the additional duty of reporting every Saturday "for an account to be given by the said several committees of their doings and their respective employments."[19] Given the mood at the time, it follows that all members of the committee shared constitutionalist sympathies even though only three of the eight members (two Protestants and a Catholic) had signed the November Petition.[20] Once again it is evident that Protestants from all over Ireland shared the constitutional ambitions of their Catholic colleagues.

One of the first important committees to be nominated by the new committee on committees had a Catholic majority of two (thirteen to eleven). This committee was to confer with the Lords about a reply to the judges' answers to the Queries, a matter that became more prominent as the issue of impeachment moved to England. Early in the session the Commons had pressed the Lords for the judges' answers and were promised them for 24 May, an indication that Ormond had been unable to maintain his tactic of delay. The judges' answers, when at last available, proved unsatisfactory as they failed to answer the questions directly or declared themselves incompetent to deliver an opinion. A Commons debate was arranged for 28 May, with the whole house present, at which the judges' answers were rejected, being declared no answers, and a joint Lords-Commons committee arranged, Patrick Darcy being charged "carefully to attend that particular occasion and to be prepared for it" with the assistance of Richard Beresford, Richard Martin, and other lawyers who were in town.[21]

The meeting of the joint committee was held on 9 June in the dining room of Dublin Castle. It was here that Darcy delivered his famous *Argument* in which he, in effect, supplied the answers to the Queries that the judges had failed to provide.[22] The contents of the *Argument* will be considered in a subsequent chapter, but the immediate outcome of this meeting was the Declaration and Humble Supplication (not to be confused with either the first or the second instrument), which was accepted by the Lords on the tenth.[23] The following day the Commons drew up a covering letter to the committee in England to accompany the declaration.[24] The Declaration of 10 June mentioned neither impeachment nor the Queries; its main concern was the delay in returning the bills that would give effect to the 3 April concessions. It expressed fear that this delay arose out of "misinformations" about the Irish parliament reaching the king, and in a effort to allay any royal displeasure, there was a tentative promise that additional money would be granted in return for the redress of grievances and the bills giving effect to the Graces.[25]

There is additional evidence of a concern at this time about false information reaching the king. On 8 June the Commons had set up a committee of seven Protestants and two Catholics to arrange for "severe punishment" of any MP who did anything "to withdraw his majesty's favour from this House."[26] The speaker's covering letter of 11 June is more informative. He noted that the house had received no word from the committee since Weldon had been dispatched with the Three Instruments. It was emphasized again, moreover, that the second instrument, asserting the right of judicature, was only to be shown "as occasion did offer itself and not otherwise." The committee's silence, the letter went on, "begets some doubts among us that our affairs have met with some opposition." It was these fears that led the two houses to send the Declaration of 10 June. The Commons was also puzzled by the instructions the lords justices were receiving from England about the officials responsible for collecting the tobacco monopoly. At the end of April the king had accepted that their cases should be left to the Irish parliament, but on 18 May he had issued instructions that they be released from imprisonment. This alteration the Commons also ascribed to "misinformation," which should, the speaker urged, be countered by the assurance that "if we meet not with interruption," the king would find "honourable and profitable effect of our endeavour to him."[27]

This letter had reached England by 15 June and crossed with an undated one sent by the committee to the Commons, which must have been written about the seventh and was delivered by Patrick Darcy's son. The news brought by the younger Darcy did little to reassure the house. The letter reported the arrival of Weldon and the presentation of the Three Instruments to the king. The bills giving effect to the Graces remained with the English attorney-general, Sir Edward Herbert, despite daily pleas by the committee for their dispatch. There had, the committee reported, been some discussion about grievances, but the responses so far had not been satisfactory. On the tobacco monopoly, the king declined to move before parliament had provided "a revenue for him." Moreover, "some propositions in the mean time as it seemeth hath been sent ... without our privity," and the committee had been told nothing about the king's position on impeachment until it heard about it from Weldon.[28]

The arrival of this letter from England on the seventeenth explains the sudden change in tactics on this day noted by Aidan Clarke, when the house began to consider bills and reject every one of them.[29] Members thereby registered their objections to the delay of bills in England and to the king's failure to consult their committee.

As the discussion in the previous chapter shows, this period, from 9 to 23 June, is the one during which we know most about the composition of the Commons. About 126 MPs participated in a vote on 9 June; on the following day 121 MPs were appointed to committees; and on the twenty-third we find about the same number voting in two divisions. Protestants retained a majority of eleven on 10 June.[30] This figure confirms that the proportion of Catholic membership had increased. As the justices commented at the end of the month, since January, "we find many Protestants, (and no papists at all, unless some few not able to appear) removed from the House, and new elections ordered to be made, and in some of their rooms divers papists brought in, which is a very great weakening of the Protestant party in the House."[31]

A majority of eleven was a far cry from that of eighty-two in March 1640. Nevertheless, had the Protestants wished to control the house they could still have done so, and indeed on some occasions they seem to have done just this, as when they had "knit together" to thwart an attempt to impeach Sir Adam Loftus and Viscount Ranelagh. Sir Adam reported to Sir Henry Vane that "I find the Protestant party much disgusted with the course held by the other party; in ... pressing too near upon the honour and power of the government," and he added that these Protestants had no intention of hindering the plantation of Connacht.[32] Division within the house can be detected, and sometimes this may have been on broadly Catholic versus Protestant lines, but it would be an error to see the two faiths pitted against each other in the house on a continuing basis. Sir William Parsons, Sir John Borlase, and Sir Adam had an interest in depicting for English consumption a polarity on the Irish political scene. Even they, however, had to admit that "some few" Protestants inclined towards the Catholic view on the issue of impeachment.[33] Nor should it be supposed that "some few" meant only six or seven, thus giving the Catholics a bare majority. Had this been the case, there would have been more divisions because the house would have been more or less evenly divided on numerous occasions. There were, as we have seen, sixteen Protestant leaders during this session, and we may assume that they were constitutionalists. In addition, sixteen of those who were not leaders but who were present during the session had signed the November Petition. These considerations lead to the conclusion that there were at least thirty-two Protestants in the house during the fifth session who held constitutionalist sympathies. This number amounted to about half the Protestants in the house in mid-June, and if Temple is to be believed, the number of Protestants demanding the Graces and a limitation on executive authority well exceeded those that can be identified.[34]

The Commons' rejection of all bills led to a warning from the lords justices against proceeding with impeachment in the face of the king's demand for precedents.[35] The two divisions on the twenty-third over who should chair a committee of the whole may well reflect the prevailing tension at this time and the frustration at the apparent failure to accomplish anything.[36] This tension seems to have been relieved, however, with the return of Weldon on the twenty-fifth bearing important news from the committee in England.[37] During May the English council had been so preoccupied with Strafford's fate and the revelations surrounding the first army plot that it had little time to consider Irish affairs, but by the last day of the month Ireland was again on its agenda, and it was on this day that the Irish committee presented the Three Instruments.[38] As we know, nothing satisfactory had been settled during the early part of June. Yet by the sixteenth, "after sundry debates upon several days touching the Acts transmitted hither by Mr Brown," and with the delivery of the promise in the Declaration of 10 June of "profitable effects" to the king and his posterity, Charles had agreed to the acts in full council. The committee clearly expected their early dispatch as soon as "some few mistakes" had been corrected. There remained the two acts that had been sent later – on monopolies and on the Elizabethan taxes on some commodities – which were still with the attorney-general, and the more general grievances, but the committee promised to work hard on these as well.[39]

In agreeing now to return the bills for passage into law Charles had conceded no more than he had already promised on 3 April, but his delay in implementing his promise had raised the prospect of receiving funds in return for his concessions. On the issue of impeachment, however, the English council remained adamant. The matter was debated at a meeting between the Commons committee and the privy council on the eighteenth. The councillors – who included at this meeting Cork, his son-in-law, Lord George Goring, Bristol, Vane, and Leicester but not the king – when faced with the arguments furnished through Weldon, conceded that the Irish parliament had the power of judicature in civil and criminal causes but insisted that precedents had to be supplied to warrant the inclusion of capital crimes within its jurisdiction. A sub-committee, therefore, was set up, consisting of the attorney-general and the solicitor-general and other lawyers to confer further with the Irish committee. These developments were reported back to the Irish Commons on 25 June, along with a warning that the council disliked the manner in which the Commons was withholding information from the lords justices.[40]

THE LAST WEEKS OF
THE SESSION

Early in July both Irish houses responded to the English insistence on precedents for impeachment. Such precedents were not available, but this did not deter the houses from petitioning the king on the tenth asserting such power and, at the same time, defending the concealment of information to the lords justices on the grounds that communication between parliament and king should be directly through the committees in England.[41] This petition crossed with two letters from the Commons committee in England, written on 8 and 9 of July and sent together. The first of these announced the dispatch of twelve bills to Ireland, for the most part dealing with minor matters such as the preservation of pigeon houses. The attorney-general was still delaying the dispatch of the more important bills, including that putting an end to plantation in Connacht and else-where, by trying to make insertions which the committee was using its "uttermost" endeavours to remove. Meanwhile, the discussion about general grievances had been in "agitation" and had now reached a state that permitted a set of propositions, answers, and replies to these answers, to be sent to the house. But the next day, before the first letter had been dispatched, the committee sent another note with ominous news:

we found some likelihood of alteration to be put upon us different from the former answer we had touching the council table proceedings[,] for now his majesty doth press to continue a power in that Board to proceed in plantation ... and how, and in what manner it will be settled, we yet know not, but do strive in it, to the uttermost of our endeavours, to preserve the former answer.[42]

This is the last extant letter from the committee, but we have con-firmation in a letter from Temple dated 22 July that Herbert had inserted a clause into the Act of Limitations "as will almost totally destroy the benefit they expected by it."[43]

Just after these letters had been sent, the king indicated on 15 July what it would cost to obtain the redress of grievances: customs rates were to be settled, including those on the controversial commodities of tobacco and linen yarn, and two new subsidies, at the Straffordian rates of £45,000 each, were to be granted.[44] On the following day, the official answers to the grievances were drawn up by the English council. These specified the new customs rates, which were to be approved by the Irish parliament, and included a number of important concessions by the king, such as the abolition of monopolies, the outlawing of judicial decisions by the council, and the establishment of a mint, but Poynings's law was not to be altered, and on the important issue of the right of the native Irish to purchase land from each other in plantation areas, the only concession was that the lord lieutenant would look into the matter when he went to Ireland.

The king's letter giving effect to these concessions was not issued until 31 July, by which time a completely extraneous issue had arisen which caused further delay.[45] An Ulster Scot, Henry Stewart, who had been imprisoned by Strafford during the Covenanting crisis, appealed to the English Lords for redress. As negotiations were taking place for a treaty of peace with the Scots, the matter could not be ignored. The English peers summoned the entire Irish council responsible for Stewart's imprisonment, which amounted to an assertion of English parliamentary sovereignty over Ireland. The letters from Lord Justice Parsons and the Irish Lords rejecting the summons and its implication reached Westminster on 4 August, whereupon the English Lords searched its records to prove Ireland a dependency of England. It also sent a deputation to the king urging him to punish Ireland by staying the bills that would give effect to the Graces.

The king agreed to delay the bills till the quarrel was settled, and on 5 August Temple wrote to Leicester to say that the dispute was likely to prove beneficial to Leicester's government of Ireland.[46] What he seems to have meant was that it had been brought home to the Irish committees that they needed strong representation in London to win their case. After talking to Gormanston, Temple declared that he believed the Irish committees understood how much Leicester's absence in France had hurt them. "They have been much crossed and so extremely delayed since you went, as I hear the parliament of Ireland is weary of their attendance for their Acts and resolved to adjourn ... which, if they have done it, will prove of very much advantage to his Majesty's service."[47] Intensive negotiations seem then to have taken place, for on the eleventh Temple told Leicester that "last week's work" had "much calmed the animosities and distempers of some of those high spirits in Ireland."[48] That night Cork gave a dinner to the members of the Irish committees at the Nag's Head in Cheapside – surely in celebration of a completed task – and by 25 August most of the committee members had arrived in Ireland with the much treasured bills giving effect to the Graces. As Temple recorded, on their arrival in Ireland, the committees, after conferring with the justices, retired to their homes "with great contentment and satisfaction" that they "might there refresh themselves in the mean season."[49]

None of this could be known or anticipated by the Irish parliament as it was completing the summer session. The most recent news it had received was the packet containing the information that plantation might yet be continued. This had arrived by 20 July, and on the following day the Commons went into committee of the whole to discuss the news.[50] We know nothing of their deliberations, but during the remainder of the session the house continued with the task of drawing up specific charges against those accused of treason, approved *nullo contradicente* a series of answers to the Queries which asserted various rights and sent them to the Lords for approval, drew up an eight-point statement opposing the government's intention to dispatch Irish soldiers to Spain, and, finally, pressed the upper house for a continuation of the session.[51] All of these actions reflected the growing bitterness at the delay in the implementation of the promises of 3 April, and the resolution concerning the soldiers was in all probability part of a developing plot to use the new army to win by force what could not be gained by constitutional means.

It is easier to establish what the house was doing during this period up to the prorogation on 7 August than to determine who, within the house, was responsible for what was being done. There is no doubt that there was fractiousness and dispute. On the last day of the session, before the adjournment to 9 November, there was a division that produced a tie vote.[52] The prime issue was the adjournment itself. Some members wanted the house to remain in session until further news arrived from England about the fate of the bills giving effect to the king's promises. Others wanted to adjourn, but the evidence about who was in control is obscure. Government officials wanted an adjournment, partly to give the king time to consider how to deal with some of the constitutional demands being pressed in Ireland, and "partly to give contentment to very many of both houses" that desired adjournment because of the approaching harvest and the need for the judges to go on their circuits, which they could not do while parliament was in session. But Sir William Parsons contradicted himself in describing the situation. Privately, he wrote that the "papist votes" were strongest, yet as one of the lords justices, he claimed that, in securing the adjournment, "the Protestants of both Houses gave good assistance."[53]

These statements may be compared with Catholic allegations of some eighteen months later. They recounted that Parsons, observing that the Graces were to be "passed as Acts in Parliament" and "envying the *good union long before settled, and continued between the members of the House of Commons*, and their good correspondency with the Lords," created discord and fostered national and religious divisions. When, moreover, it was known that the Irish parliamentary committees were "by the waterside in England with sundry important and beneficial bills and other graces to be passed as Acts in that Parliament," the lords justices prevailed on their own faction "in tumultuous and disorderly manner" to demand an adjournment and engineered it against the wishes of a majority of "voices of the more moderate part" by forcing the issue through the Lords using the proxy votes of those who were absent from that house.[54] Another source, also sympathetic to the Confederate Catholics, stated that a "puritan" faction prevailed upon the lords justices to have the adjournment to prevent the passing of the Graces into law.[55]

Both these versions of events contain some truth while also concealing it. At the end of August the majority of the freeholders of County Offaly petitioned their MPs, one a Catholic and the other a Protestant, to exercise every legal means to ensure that the assizes and gaol delivery were held at Birr, and the majority of the ninety-four or so petitioners had Irish names. As the lords justices claimed, there was a general desire to see the justice system back at work, and the decline in the number of MPs present to one hundred by the end of the session suggests that on the question of adjournment they were voting with their feet.[56] Yet the composition of the committees does not suggest, as Parsons claimed, that Catholics had gained control of the house or that it was divided on a strictly religious basis.

If we exclude committees that were concerned with private petitions or special issues, such as Ulster undertakers or sea sand, and examine the membership of committees with some potential significance between 20 July and 7 August, nine had a Protestant majority and six a Catholic one. One of those with a Protestant majority (ten to six) was the committee sent to the Lords on 6 August to discuss the extension of the session, and another was the committee (twenty-nine to ten) set up on the last day of the session to prepare bills during the recess. If we look at those who sat on these fifteen important committees during this period, we find that seventy-one Protestants sat on one or more committees, whereas there were only thirty-two Catholics.[57] Clearly, Catholics had nowhere near a majority. To obtain a bare majority, the constitutionalists had to command at least twenty Protestant votes, and the absence of frequent divisions suggests that they had more.

There was a high degree of continuity in leadership throughout the fifth session. On the Catholic side, men such as Sir Richard Barnewall, Adam Cusack, Sir John Dungan, and Patrick Darcy, whom we encounter as leaders at the start of the session, continued to provide leadership during the final three weeks. Similarly, among the Protestant element in the house, men like Sir Audley Mervin, the Bysse brothers, Dr Alan Cooke, Brian O'Neill, Oliver Jones, and other known constitutionalists were as much in evidence on the committees during the last three weeks or so of the session as they were in May and June. There was, however, one striking addition to the Protestant leadership during these final weeks in the person of Sir William St Leger, lord president of Munster. A month earlier Cork's agent had complained to the earl that St Leger "tides too much with the Irish."[58] He, too, therefore, may have been acting as a constitutionalist towards the end of the session.

It follows from this continuity in leadership that the ability of the lords justices to persuade the Commons to recess before the Graces arrived in Ireland was not a consequence of a shift in the leadership of the house. Government supporters, such as Sir Adam Loftus, Sir William Sambach, and Sir Robert Meredith were certainly present, but none sat on sufficient committees to be identified as a leader.[59] A tentative interpretation of this mixture of evidence is that the constitutionalists, led by lawyers of both faiths, commanded a considerable majority on such issues as the Queries and even on the disinclination to dispatch the troops to Spain, but on the issue of adjournment, the lords justices were probably able to command the support of more Protestants than on other issues and very probably a number of Catholics. Patrick Darcy was later accused by the author of the *Aphorismical Discovery* not simply of having supported the adjournment but of moving the motion to secure it.[60] For most MPs who had not already gone home, the advantages of ending the session outweighed those of waiting for the bills to arrive from England, but it is important to stress again that, contrary to the impression given by Parsons, the house was not dividing upon religious lines even at times of stress.

Two features explain the change in attitude of the lords justices towards the Commons since the fourth session when every effort had been made to avoid giving offence. First, the execution of Strafford the day after the fifth session opened removed any incentive for the Irish executive to continue to cultivate Strafford's Irish parliamentary foes. Second, the king's concessions of 3 April posed a direct threat to the policies that men like Parsons held dear. This is not to say that they opposed all reforms. In listing those they favoured, they included the abolition of the Court of High Commission and the denial of proxy votes to peers who did not live in Ireland, both of which would have been anathema to Strafford, but reforms that would satisfy the anxiety of the Irish gentry about the security of their estates were conspicuously absent from the executive's list.[61]

COUNCILLORS AND PLANTATION POLICY

The reaction of the lords justices when they received on the fourteenth the news of the king's concessions of 3 April was one of consternation. While discussing the letter with representatives of parliament, Parsons and Borlase wrote privately to Vane to stress the benefits the crown had derived from plantation, describing it as the very basis of "the peace and happiness, which of late years this kingdom hath enjoyed." Without it, they asserted, Ireland would have remained in a "tumultuary state," and Protestantism could have made no advance. To prove their point, they argued that Monaghan, the one unplanted county in Ulster, was the "most barbarous poor and despicable part of the kingdom" except where the earl of Essex and Lord Blaney had their estates. They warned that discontinuing plantation would discourage existing settlements and urged that a "trustworthy person" be sent over "to see how completely the case against plantation" could be answered.[62]

Loftus was even more outspoken in writing a few days later. His comments are of particular interest in that he was still in England. They reflect, therefore, news and opinion that were reaching him privately from Ireland – we may suspect from Parsons. There was, Sir Adam reported, nothing but bad news from Ireland. Councillors "turn tail upon us," the judges failed to support the state, Connacht had been given away, the lords of the Pale pressed for the act securing estates "and with one voice spoke against plantations in general, which is now the main work of the papists." A few days later he told his unknown correspondent that he suspected the decision to give up the Connacht plantation was part of a "fearful plot" to maintain the new army in being. This would mean that the army would be dispersed throughout the country and then fall on English settlements; indeed, he warned, the process had already begun. The king, he concluded, was strangely advised "in this and other things, particularly Connacht, and continuing the Parliament here [that is, in England] which I fear will so stir the people as will in the end much offend [the king] and certainly do him no good."[63] It has recently been suggested that the Old English forged an alliance with the king to stop plantation and that, in reaction, the lords justices made their own alliance with the English parliament to maintain it.[64] The first part of this chapter has shown that many Irish Protestants, and very possibly a substantial majority in parliament, supported the king's concessions of 3 April. Sir Adam's statement shows that those on the council who opposed them did not necessarily look to the English parliament to reinstate plantation.

It must be assumed that these expressions of exasperation stemmed as much from private disappointment as from public concern. Just when Strafford had been destroyed and a free way opened for men like Parsons and Loftus to preside over a new wave of settlement, the king abandoned the policy. Because they could not openly oppose their monarch, they resorted to as much delay as possible, as remarked by Simon Digby.[65]

On Loftus's return to Ireland in mid-June, he reported to Vane on the political situation he found in Dublin but begged the secretary to burn the letter when he had read it. He reported that the council, with the exception of Parsons, was overawed by parliament, but that he saw signs of a Protestant-Catholic split in the Commons which could be used to advantage. The Protestants, he declared, were "much disgusted with the course held by the other party" and would support the plantation of Connacht if carried out in a "moderate way" on condition that the Act of Limitations and other Graces were approved. In so saying he confirmed the Protestant support in the house for security of land tenure, but he went on to advise that, if the issue of Connacht had not been "absolutely concluded," it would be best to "make some delay in it" till he could write again on the matter.[66] Write he did, two weeks later, when he sent Vane a copy of the Irish committee's letter to the speaker dated 17 June. This he interpreted as putting an end to "all our expectations here concerning that great business of Connacht." He again urged delay in suspending plantation, at least until the Irish parliament had granted subsidies that would pay the king's Irish debts.[67] We do not know whether Sir Adam's letter had any impact, but by 9 July the king was again contemplating the resumption of plantation and on the fifteenth he specified the financial recompense he expected in return for his concessions.

It would appear that Charles was sincere about trying to bring about a settlement in Ireland, as long as there was financial compensation for concessions, and Temple's involvement suggests that Leicester was too. Charles was, at the same time, preparing to go to

Scotland to reach a settlement there. We do not know the nature of the negotiations that took place between the king and the Irish commissioners in early August, but as we have seen, most of them had returned to Dublin by the twenty-fifth, "full fraught with graces and the benefits from his majesty," despite the intervention of the English Lords to withdraw concessions.[68] During the same month the king added two constitutionalist lords, Robert Digby, Simon's brother, and Lambert, to the Irish council.[69] The king was apparently enticing some Protestant constitutionalists to his side. Parsons and Loftus, however, worked vigorously against such a settlement. As Parsons was about to procure the adjournment, he warned that no concessions on land should be made until suitable compensation had been arranged.[70]

On the return of the Irish commissioners with the bills to implement the Graces, both Parsons and Loftus immediately wrote letters to Vane pressing the, by now, familiar theme: the king had received much less than he had given. They also argued that efforts must be made during the adjournment to regain what had been lost.[71] As Loftus told Vane, he, Vane, now had time to "bethink yourself how to lay some stay" on the desires of the Irish parliament.[72] Vane, who had gone north with the king, had few ideas on the subject. All he could suggest, in answer to inquiries from that portion of the council that had remained in England about how to deal with the Queries, was that they might be suppressed "by degrees" through delays and excuses.[73]

The Irish council and Vane must have influenced the English council's discussions in London on 12 October, ten days before the rebellion broke out and a month before the Irish parliament was to hold its sixth session. On that date the council advised the king that, on the basis of dispatches from Ireland and upon reflection about the Irish parliament's past behaviour, it recommended proroguement of the Irish parliament beyond 9 November to the end of February. The public reason for this change was to be that the judges in Ireland would thereby be able to continue to deliver justice without having to return to Dublin, and assurances were to be proclaimed that the postponement did not mean any retraction of the Graces. The private reasons, however, were very different. Leicester, it was argued, had to be present at the next session of parliament, but he also had to consult with Charles before leaving for Ireland and therefore had to await the king's return from Scotland. Furthermore, the bills securing the crown's revenue in Ireland, which were clearly part of the July and August agreement for the implementation of the Graces, were not yet ready, but even more significantly, it was proposed that the issues of Poynings's law and the Queries should be taken to the English parliament, and this could be done only if the Irish parliament's session was delayed.[74] Ironically, it had been the Irish Commons which had first proposed, in March, submitting the Queries to the English parliament, with the obvious expectation that they would be approved. This initiative seems to have died in the Irish Lords, only to be revived by the English council with the equally obvious expectation that the Queries would now be opposed, thus undermining Irish claims to a high degree of constitutional autonomy under the crown. Evidently Charles agreed to delay the session because on 15 October he sent an order to Ireland requiring adjournment till February or early March 1642.[75]

In looking at the crucial period from mid-August to late October 1641, it can be accepted that on one level the constitutionalists in the Irish parliament had succeeded. Bills had reached Ireland that, once passed, would not only give security to existing estates but also diminish the sapping of Old English political power through land transfer. This had been attained through a bond between landowners of both faiths, and even men like Cork seem to have supported it. We cannot tell how long this bond would have lasted in the absence of the rebellion, but we may observe the mutual reinforcement between the gentry and the lawyers as they strove for a definition of Ireland's status as a realm on a par with Charles's other two. With hindsight, we can see that the failure to secure the passage of the acts during the summer proved fatal. Charles's decision – and he bore ultimate responsibility – to postpone the November sitting meant that, once more, the settlement over security of land tenure was delayed if not withdrawn. By accident, his order never became an open issue because, by the time it arrived in Ireland, the rebellion had broken out. Parsons and his friends were thus able to postpone a meaningful session on their own initiative, giving the rising as their justification. Undoubtedly, had the king's order for postponement been generally known before the rebellion, it would have caused bitter disappointment in Ireland. Yet, as we will see, it is just possible that Charles was not intending to renege on his promises but rather to be present himself when they were implemented.

Whatever the truth of this hypothesis, two features of the royal decision to postpone the session stand out. First, the initiative came, not from Charles nor from the English parliament, but from the Irish council and that portion of the English one which had remained in London, with an assist from Vane. Along with the attempt to make the earl of Holland Strafford's successor and Sir John Clotworthy's role in that move, Simon Digby's remark about private interests in

Ireland delaying settlement, John Barry's earlier and similar remark, and the obsessive concern by Parsons and Loftus during the summer to preserve the policy of plantation, this manœuvre tends to confirm the credibility of the two contemporary accounts which stressed that Connacht land and other Irish perquisites were the prizes for which certain councillors strove. The second point about the decision to postpone the session is that the reasons advanced for it involved not land or the king's revenue, arguments which had been advanced earlier but which had failed to stop the concessions, but were connected with the constitution (Poynings's law and the Queries). Ironically, the Irish lawyers, by raising such matters, had given those who wished to thwart the land settlement the means to do so.[76] Land and crown revenue were not the only sources of the tension between Charles and his Irish subjects. There were some genuine constitutional principles as stake which touched on the crown's prerogative, a matter always close to Charles's heart. It is to this aspect of the picture that we must now turn.

CHAPTER SEVEN

The Constitution

The frequent rebellions during Elizabeth's reign tended to thrust constitutional issues to the background, and even with the coming of more settled times after 1603 such matters remained in abeyance for a generation.[1] Ireland was administered without reference to the legal basis for that administration. Yet underlying government in Ireland, and the constitutional links between the two realms inherited by James of Scotland, lay the application of common law in both realms and two statutes: Poynings's Act, passed under Henry VII, and the Act of 1541 which had transformed Ireland from a lordship into a realm. Both acts, it has to be stressed, were passed without reference to the English parliament. In law at least Ireland entered the seventeenth century with a considerable amount of autonomy, but with one important qualification. The monarch's Irish subjects could appeal to their monarch for justice, who might receive advice from his English council or courts, including parliament, in giving it. Thus, as Aidan Clarke has remarked, "the English and Irish legislative systems were co-ordinate, while their judicial systems interlocked."[2]

STRAFFORD AND THE CONSTITUTION

With the appointment of Sir Thomas Wentworth as lord deputy of Ireland, a new phase in Ireland's constitutional history began. Wentworth made it clear when he took office in 1633 that he would not tolerate appeal beyond the Irish executive while he was governor, and in 1635 he issued a proclamation forbidding travel from Ireland to England without licence.[3] He thus effectively cut Ireland off from the English judicial system, which in theory widened the gap between the Irish state and the English one, though not from the crown. Under the pressure of the Scottish challenge, Charles resumed the practice of hearing some Irish causes in England, most notably that of Viscount Loftus of Ely.[4] While attending one of these cases, Wentworth was reported to have burst out, in response to a remark that he disliked made by the counsel of one of the defendants, that the counsel had "traduced his person, and in him, his Majesty's himself whose character and image he was." This not only displeased the lawyers and the court but revealed the extent to which the deputy had come to see himself as governing a separate kingdom.[5] In 1640, as the Scottish crisis became acute, Wentworth took another step with constitutional implications when he raised an army in Ireland with the intention of invading Scotland. He did so only after consulting the English council, and the army was initially supported with English money, but by going to the Irish parliament to raise funds for its future support, the impression was given to the Scots that the kingdom of Ireland was preparing to make war against them.[6]

The link between the fear of the Irish army and the religious and political aims of the Scots has been noted. The Scots desired not only that Laud and Strafford be removed but that a repetition of their policies be prevented. They therefore insisted that the Treaty of London, which the parliaments of England and Scotland ratified in August 1641, should include a clause which required English parliamentary sanction before Irish forces could be launched against Scotland. But the treaty involved its signatories in a constitutional contradiction because it required Irish ratification, thus recognizing Ireland's legislative autonomy.[7] Nevertheless, the Scots wanted Ireland to be a dependency of England because then, through England, they could ensure that the monarch could not use his authority in Ireland against them without consulting his English subjects.

The Scots may be excused for assuming Ireland's subordination to England, for, with as much logic as irony, those in Ireland in 1640 who wished to destroy Strafford had to adopt a similar constitutional stance. Strafford's invulnerability in Ireland depended on his separation of Ireland from England in all respects save the crown. In England his position was more open to attack, yet most of the actions he had taken which could be used against him had occurred in Ireland. Only if Ireland came under English jurisdiction could he be held responsible in England for what he had done in Ireland as lord deputy. The co-operation between the two parliaments in November 1640 as the attack on Strafford was launched was based on this assumption. Nor did the Irish MPs have any compunction about using the power of the English parliament to ensure their free passage to England even though, strictly speaking, this was a matter that concerned only the king and his Irish subjects.[8] More striking still was the reference at the beginning of the November Remonstrance to the "happy subjection" of Ireland "to the imperial crown of England" as the Irish Commons laid claim to the same rights as those enjoyed by the king's English subjects.[9] This looked back to the days before the creation of an imperial crown of Ireland and implied that Ireland was, as Sir William Parsons had argued in the 1620s, part of an English empire. As late as 3 March 1641 the Irish Commons had planned to order its committee in England to submit the Queries to the English Commons to "lay down a course ... for declaration of the law in the particulars of the said questions."[10] Underlying the proposal lay a tacit acceptance that the English Commons had a stronger declaratory power than the Irish parliament, and it was probably because the Irish Lords saw the danger of such a position that the idea got no farther than their house.[11]

Strafford's trial forced the issue of Anglo-Irish constitutional arrangements upon men's minds. When the trial opened, the earl of Arundel, the presiding peer, called upon the lord lieutenant to answer the impeachment of high treason directed against him "by the Commons of England and Ireland."[12] Later, when the prosecution addressed the charge that Strafford had used the Irish army as a police force without a warrant, it based its case on the assertion that "Ireland was a portion of the English crown" and that therefore the governor's actions had to be judged according to English law.[13] During the trial, the issue of whether the English parliament had the right to judge the actions of Ireland's lord lieutenant while in Ireland was never addressed directly though there was an implied assertion that it did. However, when the Commons had decided to abandon the impeachment route and pass instead an act of attainder, the issue was discussed at a joint Lords and Commons conference on 29 April. Those who wished to kill Strafford argued that, as he was an English peer, any decision concerning him had to be taken by the English House of Lords. They pointed out that another lord deputy, Sir John Perrot, had been tried in England for what he had done in Ireland. But in the pursuit of their prey, they went even further in enunciating the constitutional relationship between the two realms. Ireland, they agreed, was "united to England, and the Parliament of England had always had cognizance of the original suits in Ireland," and, like their Irish allies, they maintained that the "common law of England and Ireland are the same" because the parliament of England had introduced that law into Ireland in the reign of John. Ireland's status, they asserted, could be compared with that of Jersey and Guernsey.[14] Bad history was joined to bad law to destroy the hated enemy.

The confusion in English minds about where Ireland fitted in the constitutional picture is illustrated by the approach of English MPs to Irish issues not linked to Strafford's fate. It was on 5 March 1641, after Sir Simonds D'Ewes made his comment that the only way to bring the three kingdoms "into perfect unity" was to reduce Ireland "to the profession of the true religion," that a committee was set up to look into the operation of the Catholic hierarchy. Ireland was certainly included in its mandate.[15] Yet, ten days later, when debating a proposal from the Lords to increase the size of the old Irish army, D'Ewes remarked that Ireland was "as free a kingdom as England itself." Therefore, England should not impose an army upon Ireland but leave it to the Irish parliament "to debate and resolve thereon."[16] The Commons, in explaining its position to the Lords, stated that it wished to see the new army disbanded as soon as possible because that army concerned "the safety of this kingdom"; it also insisted that no Catholics be employed in the old army, but on the question of the size of that army MPs considered themselves "not fit to interest or engage themselves therein."[17] The English Commons, therefore, asserted itself on Irish affairs only when it perceived English interests to be threatened. This was definitely a limitation on the autonomy of the Irish parliament, but one exercised with some discretion. When, the following June, English MPs were given the opportunity of compelling an Irish peer to appear before them, it was decided to remit the matter to the Irish parliament in recognition that the issue "might breed long dispute." That they were right was confirmed by the dispute that developed between the English and the Irish Lords in August.

The English parliament's primary concern related to the crown's policies in England and the limitations on the power of the executive there. English-Irish constitutional matters lay on the periphery of its interests and arose only occasionally after Strafford's death. Similarly, the Irish parliament was primarily concerned not with Ireland's place in the system of the three kingdoms but with the behaviour of the Irish executive. As Aidan Clarke has put the matter: "the campaign for legislative independence which historians have supposed to have been conducted in this parliament rests upon a false emphasis. It was not the relationship of the Irish and English parliaments which was at issue, but the relationship of the executive to the law."[18] It is even possible that, if the bills giving effect to the king's letter of 3 April 1641 had been processed quickly, interest in constitutional issues, first raised substantively in the fourth session, would have declined; but once discussion about them developed, it became impossible to confine them to a strictly Irish context.

POYNINGS'S ACT

The three constitutional issues raised in Ireland were Poynings's Act, impeachment, and the Queries. Poynings's law, although not mentioned by name, had become a concern of the Commons as early as October 1640 when that house had set up a committee to draft bills and, subsequently, set up another to find out what the council had done with those it had drafted.[19] During the recess there must have been more discussion of the issue because, within four days of the opening of the fourth session, the committee in England was asked to obtain an "explanation" of Poynings's law that was to leave no doubt about the right of the Commons to draft legislation. In practice, parliament continued to exercise this right and the lords justices co-operated by forwarding such bills to England.[20] By May the Irish parliamentary committees had prepared a paper on the subject for discussion in England. It stressed that the law had not been intended to be used as Strafford had done – to prevent the initiation of bills by the Irish legislature – but to stop the Irish executive from passing laws without the knowledge, and against the interests, of the crown. The committees proposed new legislation providing for consultation on draft bills before parliament met and the right to initiate new legislation in either house once it had commenced. The executive was to be permitted to comment on such bills but not to prevent them passing to England.[21] This was a conservative proposal which attempted to return to the Irish parliament some of the initiative that it had lost under Wentworth. The English council rejected the idea, and the move by that body in October to refer Poynings's law and the Queries to the English parliament suggests that it wanted some support in insisting upon the preservation of the law in its existing form. This, in turn, leads to the suspicion that part of the reason for not changing the law was that it was perceived as an important instrument for English control over Irish affairs.[22]

IMPEACHMENT

The question of the use of impeachment in Ireland had much greater constitutional implications than did Poynings's law.[23] As early as 1634 the Irish parliament had shown interest in exercising its judicial function, and although Wentworth managed to prevent this right being asserted, he admitted privately that it would have been hard to justify its denial had the matter been pressed.[24] By 27 February

1641 this is precisely what the Commons had decided to do. On this date it set up two committees: a large one, led by Sir Audley Mervin, of twenty Catholics and twenty-four Protestants, to present the impeachments of Sir Richard Bolton, Bishop Bramhall, Sir Gerard Lowther, and Sir George Radcliffe to the Lords; and a second one of seventeen Protestants and fourteen Catholics to draw up charges. We have already seen that in the Lords, Lord Lambert argued most vigorously for impeachment and the earl of Ormond sought ways to obstruct it. If we look at these two committees of the Commons, we find a similar Protestant commitment.[25]

The charges – the intended destruction of the realm, the assumption of regal power, and the intention to subvert the rights of parliament – were laid on 4 March, their vagueness betraying the haste in their preparation.[26] This was mirrored in Mervin's long-winded speech to the Lords as he presented the charges. Magna Carta, thanks to the accused, lay "prostrated, besmeared and rolling in her own gore." Statute law lay upon its death bed "stabbed by proclamations" and "strangled by monopolies." Charles's advisers were likened to those of Edward II and accused of provoking rebellion, and the call was for the restoration of a government that operated within the law.[27] Mervin, in other words, appealed to the past with standard conservative arguments.

As soon as the recess began, the accused prepared answers to the charges. Bramhall, for instance, drew up a draft of his defence on 6 March. Because of the vagueness of the charges, all he and his co-accused could do was to deny them, although he also made the telling point that, as everyone else on the council had acted as he had done in settling disputes in an extrajudicial way, they were as guilty as he. Bolton could hardly conceal his contempt for what he evidently regarded as an act of political vengeance. It would, he asserted, have been "worse than madness" to settle with his family in a country whose laws he was trying to subvert, and as he went on to point out, the charges did not specify in "what causes" regal power had been assumed.[28] But even as the answers were being penned, the debate was shifting from the particular accusations to the legality of the procedure. By the end of March the English council had appointed a committee of lawyers, chaired by the attorney-general, to determine under what statutes, if any, or by what precedents the Irish parliament had the right to displace or try (for his life) an officer of the crown. This was followed a month later by the letter from the king to the lords justices requiring precedents.[29]

As the fifth session opened, on 11 May, and what has been described as the "increasingly well-defined struggle for control between the executive and the legislature" began, we must recollect that it was during April that Parsons and his friends had had to adjust both to their failure to secure the lord lieutenancy for their party and to the royal embargo on future plantations.[30] The Irish executive faced a struggle, therefore, not only with the legislature in Ireland but also with the executive in England. Constitutional questions, however, while they served to increase the friction between the executive and the Irish assembly, also provided a basis of mutual interest between Charles and the Irish executive, and to some extent between Charles and his English parliament. The king and the English parliament needed to control Ireland, and ultimately they could only do so if the executive there depended on England and not upon the legislature in Ireland.

When the lords justices informed parliament of the king's demands for precedents as the summer session began, "some guiding men" in parliament declared that they intended to "have judicature in such cases by common right of Parliament," even though they could supply no precedents.[31] A week later, on 24 May, both houses drew up the Three Instruments, the last two of which were devoted to the assertion of the right of judicature. Sir Audley Mervin led the Commons committee that helped to draw up these instruments and it was at this time that he addressed the Lords on the subject.[32]

Mervin's speech is of considerable interest because it is the only detailed statement from a Protestant constitutionalist that has survived.[33] He began by expressing appreciation for the granting of the Graces but added that they would be valueless without parliament to confirm them. He then challenged directly the king's argument that impeachment required a precedent by outlining "a rough-drawn map of the jurisdiction of this high court of Parliament." The judicial right, he claimed, was the soul of parliament because the basis of parliament was speech with judgment and reason, "but I think we speak with none of these, if we cannot maintain our jurisdiction." He appealed to the practice of a succession of pre-Norman kings, including Alfred and Canute, to prove that "time out of mind, this high court and its judicature hath flourished before the conquest ... and ever since the conquest, until this present hour." Those who denied these rights and "instilled this jealousy of judicature into his majesty's thoughts, did *ipso facto* subvert Parliaments."

Having analysed the nature of parliament and established its antiquity to his own satisfaction, Mervin's next task was to "prove our claim to judicature by the title of co-heir with the Parliament in England." Parliament, he argued, was "a structure founded upon the common laws of England." King John had ordained that Ireland be governed by the laws of England, and Richard II had granted to the

Irish parliament and its members the rights "held by the subjects of *England*." It was, therefore, no more sensible to demand of the Irish parliament precedents for impeachment than to insist that the Irish Court of King's Bench find an instance of trial by battle in Ireland before delivering judgment, "nay inquire of the petty constable by what precedent in Ireland he executes his office." If, he pointed out, the first person found guilty of treason had claimed immunity on the grounds that there was no precedent, treason would have flourished.

In his conclusion Mervin made two additional points. First, he directed a well-aimed appeal to the interests of his audience: "The high-prized tincture of your lordships' robes begins to fade, the ermines lose their complexion if they lose their judicature. That well-becoming title to a nation, peerage, begins to hang down its head, and blush, and curses the influences in its nativity, if it should come to such an untimely end." His second point touched on a fundamental aspect of the relations between England and Ireland. He recognized that some might argue that the granting of the right of judicature to the Irish parliament was a step towards the separation of Ireland from English jurisdiction. In parrying this anticipated thrust, he half admitted its truth. England, he said, would not envy the Irish "an equal interest in their laws," for a union of laws was the "best unity of kingdoms."

Sir Audley was preaching very largely to the converted. Lambert supported impeachment, and the co-operation of the Lords in approving the Three Instruments and sending them to England as a joint statement with the Commons shows that Lambert's opinion was general in the upper house. The Commons sent Mervin's speech to their committee in England to provide its members with the material to argue the case for judicature with the English council.[34] Despite English resistance, the Irish parliament persevered. The Commons sought to draw up more specific charges against the four accused, and as late as 10 July the two houses repeated the assertion that they possessed the same rights to try crown officials in Ireland as the English legislature exercised in England.[35]

What Mervin said sounded, on the surface, conventional. His words resembled statements delivered by Englishmen in defence of parliamentary rights. Yet the impeachment procedure and Mervin's defence of it had very far reaching implications for relations between Ireland and England. In England, major parliamentary disputes usually reflected a contest between rival court factions, and impeachment had been used as a tool by one faction against another. Ireland too had its political factions, yet because it had no resident court, victory or defeat for a faction ultimately depended upon its political strength in England, usually at court, but, as the case of Strafford illustrated, the English parliament could be the determining arena for settlement of the struggle.[36] If the Irish parliament had the right to impeach, it would move judicially as well as legislatively towards independence from English jurisdiction. It would follow that Irish factions would use impeachment in Ireland as English factions used it in England. The king's officers in Ireland would thereby become answerable to the Irish parliament and would as a consequence have to cultivate a local faction in order to secure support. In theory, the king could keep control by preventing the completion of the impeachment process, but the case of Strafford had shown that this theoretical power was not a reliable impediment to the process. The effect of impeachment, if allowed, would be to grant Ireland a measure of political autonomy it had never before possessed as the executive in extreme situations would become responsible to its legislature and the king's authority proportionately compromised.

By mid-July Parsons was resisting the claims for the right to impeach despite his apparently co-operative attitude in February and early March when Strafford had stood on trial. Now he warned that if the Irish parliament acquired the right of judicature, it would be "very dangerous for the king's servants and the English." In opposing it, he argued that Poynings's Act "had taken from them all immediate judicature."[37] This was to argue that the Irish parliament had no judicial function, a position as radical in its way as Mervin's and in keeping with Parsons's opinion in the 1620s that Ireland had to be incorporated into an English empire. Even the English council did not deny all judicial functions to the Irish parliament but drew the line at treason and capital matters.[38] They preferred, moreover, to rely on the absence of precedent – surely the weak point in the Irish case – in resisting impeachment rather than to depend on Poynings's law, a stance which would only have increased the pressure to have the law revised or repealed.

The last point in Mervin's speech indicates that he, like Parsons, understood where the claimed right of the Irish to impeach was leading, though it is probable that the level of understanding of the complexities involved remained rudimentary in both men. Impeachment in Ireland touched on one of the most fundamental dilemmas of a system that claimed to be imperial yet adhered to a tradition of *dominium politicum et regale* and therefore maintained a monarchy that was supposed to work in concert with representative institutions.[39]

An imperial system implies strong direction from one source. Ireland had been incorporated into a new type of state that was being formed at the time of the Reformation by being transformed into an imperial realm of its own. During most of the sixteenth century there was little danger of the two realms being separated as the *politicum* part of the duality played a secondary role to the *regale*, and only the monarch of England could wear the two imperial crowns. Once the parliament of England began to play a stronger role in the governance of England, however, and in practice to share sovereignty with the king or at least to make claims in this direction, it followed that the parliament in Ireland, which was constitutionally modelled on that of England, would do the same. But the interests of the king in parliament in England were not identical to his interests in parliament in Ireland. The fully sovereign monarch could wear two crowns and balance the interests of both realms, in theory at least, but the concept of the sovereignty of the king in parliament in the presence of two parliaments with a single king led naturally to the question of which parliament was sovereign on which issue. Thus, however desirable it was in the eyes of English MPs to limit the power of the crown in England, any limitation on the crown's authority in Ireland was likely, as Parsons realized, to affect English authority and interests adversely.

This inherent contradiction in the concept of the sovereignty of the king in parliament in the presence of two legislatures could only be resolved in one of four ways: a form of federalism, significantly tried first in the English-speaking world by the Confederate Catholics, the recognition of the superiority of one legislature over another (the system in Ireland in the eighteenth century), the absorption of one legislature by the other (as tried in the nineteenth century), or the complete autonomy of both states. Mervin placed his faith in the unity of law to maintain the bonds that linked Ireland to England, but unity of law, which in any case did not exist entirely, did not lead to unity of interest between the two states. With hindsight, we may observe that such a tie was no more likely to keep Ireland and England in one political unit in the seventeenth century than it was to maintain England and the American colonies together in the eighteenth. Here, too, the existence of separate legislatures formed on the English model challenged the imperial system. The claim to be able to impeach royal officials was only one of a number of moves taken to reduce the executive's authority in Ireland to what it was perceived to have been in the 1620s, but because this campaign enhanced not simply the rights of Irish subjects but the authority of the institution of parliament, Mervin's statement was a stronger expression of Irish autonomy than the more elaborate and better known pronouncement of Irish rights delivered two weeks later by the Old English lawyer, Patrick Darcy, in his response to the judges' answers to the Queries.

THE QUERIES

The Commons had drawn up the Queries by 13 February, and three days later they were ready to be sent to the Lords to procure answers from the judges. They have to be read in the light of the November Remonstrance and Irish grievances as expressed both to the English council and through the charges against Strafford. While the grievances sought to remedy particular situations, such as the abolition of monopolies, the Queries raised in principle the legitimacy of the introduction of the measures that led to the grievances. They also asked how those who governed with measures not sanctioned by law ought to be punished. The Queries have been compared to the Petition of Right, but like that document, most of the points raised referred to specific incidents in the recent past.[40] The eighth query (out of twenty-one), for instance, asked if Irish subjects could be tried by martial law in time of peace, a direct reference to the Mountnorris case. The ninth was clearly aimed at the measures taken against the Scots in Ulster who took the Covenant, and the thirteenth asked whether Irish subjects were "censurable" for repairing to England.[41]

The nature of many of the Queries, along with the timing of their presentation to parliament, points to an intention to use them against Strafford at his trial. Ormond, in delaying any response from the Lords, helped his friend. This also explains why the Commons planned to send them to the English parliament when no answers were immediately forthcoming from the Irish judges. The plan was not implemented, possibly because of opposition from the Lords, and the lower house had to wait till the fifth session for a response.[42] Almost as soon as this session began, the Lords promised that the judges would respond quickly and the replies were ready by 25 May. When the Commons considered them, they rejected them as not fit to be called answers.[43] The judges protested in their preamble at having to make any answers, and those they provided were evasive. The first query, for instance, asked whether the inhabitants of Ireland were a free people "to be governed only by the common laws of *England* and statutes of force in this kingdom." If the answer was affirmative, Strafford and his executive had clearly acted outside the law, but the judges argued that the law had been applied differently in Ireland than in England and that therefore Ireland had, in a sense, its own common law.[44] Other questions they preferred not to answer at all, on the grounds that they impinged upon the crown's prerogative and thus lay beyond their competence.[45]

The Queries and Darcy's response to the judges' answers are the most prominent Irish constitutional statement of the period. They have rightly attracted the attention of historians on this account. It has been observed, for instance, that, by being phrased as questions, the Queries avoided the possible challenge that Poynings's law did not permit them to become official.[46] Eventually, with Darcy's assistance, the Irish parliament moved towards issuing a declaration by giving answers to the questions it had raised, although these did not have time to emerge from the Lords before the proroguement of 7 August.[47] The purpose of the Queries had gradually changed from being yet another arrow aimed at the lord lieutenant to a statement of principle about the rights of Irish subjects.

The historian, in attempting to show what the Queries meant to those who drew them up, has to bear in mind not only what was said but the context in which it was said. As Aidan Clarke has observed, it was not Darcy's intention in answering the judges to assert the legislative independence of Ireland from England, but when he delivered his *Argument*, the consciousness of the equality of Ireland's parliament with that of England was never far from the surface, particularly in the Irish Lords.[48] In February, the judges had aroused the ire of the nobles when they attempted to avoid having to answer the Queries by asserting that Ireland's parliament was subordinate to England's.[49] Mervin understood that an impeachment procedure reinforced the equality of the two parliaments, and the quarrel between the Irish upper house and the English one in July and early August not only emphasized the continuation of the attitude held in February but also revealed the depth of feeling upon which that attitude rested.[50] Darcy made an implicit assertion of Irish legislative independence when he argued that ever since the passage of Poynings's law Irish subjects were bound only by Irish statutes.[51] Almost certainly those who heard or read him overlooked his sometimes technical legal arguments and drew from his words a message that placed Ireland on a par with England as a realm. It is hard to see why the Confederate Catholics would publish his speech in 1643 if they did not see it in this light, yet when Darcy spoke in the dining room of the castle, his prime purpose was to set limits upon the Irish council so that there could never be a repetition of Strafford's government. The redress of grievances was intended to set right that which had gone wrong; the Queries were intended to serve Ireland as the Treaty of London was to serve the Scots – to ensure that the wrongs never happened again. The judges' answers had essentially denied the principles contained in the Queries, and Darcy set out to reinstate them.

The *Argument* begins by defending the submission of the Queries and attacks the preamble to the judges' answers in which the very concept of the Queries had been challenged. Darcy then provided the answers the judges had failed to supply. One theme recurred again and again: the abuses of Strafford's type of conciliar government. Had Darcy wished to dwell on the constitutional relationship between Ireland and England, his opportunity lay in the first query, which asked if the subjects of Ireland were a "free people." But he justified the query simply on the grounds of "the late introduction of an arbitrary government." He complained of the imprisonment of large numbers of persons and the seizure of their goods "by the colour of proclamations" and acts of state. He accused the judges of accepting in one of their answers the idea that the "chief governor" could suspend the ordinary course of law by means of an act of state. Proclamation did not alter common law; all proclamations against the law were void; the "kings of England did never make use of their prerogative to the destruction of the subject." This theme was hammered home. Even the section about Irish statutes being the only ones applying to Ireland after the passage of Poynings's Act was intended primarily as an argument to ensure that the council introduced no new law without the approval of the Irish parliament. Another famous passage of the *Argument* – that "no man can affirm that England is *pars extra* as to us, Ireland is annexed to the crown of England, and governed by the laws of England" – was directed against the power of proclamations. Darcy understood that a proclamation could legitimately stop people going to foreign countries, but if England was not a foreign country, such proclamations could not apply to Irishmen going to England to seek redress of grievances.[52]

Yet another well-known passage is that which described parliament as a supreme court with authority for "making, altering or regulating of laws and the correction of all courts and ministers." This could be interpreted as a reference to impeachment, but Darcy seems only to have made the remark in preparation for an attack on the judges' failure to give more satisfactory answers. The king, he said, had four courts, headed by the Commons and the Lords. Below these came the privy council, and at the base were the "judges of his law."[53] This somewhat novel view of a hierarchical court structure was designed to establish that the judges could not challenge the actions of a superior court – the Commons. It also prepared the way for the Commons to issue declarations in answer to its own questions, which it did on 26 July.[54] Darcy, like Mervin, referred to a unity of law between England

and Ireland, but if the Irish parliament exercised judicature in cases of treason and other capital crimes, that body became the supreme court. In Aidan Clarke's words, Darcy made a two-way assumption about the English parliament: "as the supreme lawmaking body in England, in which respect it was simply equivalent to the Irish parliament in Ireland, and as the pinnacle of the English judicial system, in which respect it was to some extent authoritative."[55] When, therefore, we compare Darcy's position with Mervin's in defending the Irish parliament's right to judicature, Mervin appears to have been more willing to assert Irish legislative independence than was Darcy.

To draw this distinction is perhaps to create a polarity which neither Mervin nor Darcy would have accepted. There must have been a considerable measure of agreement between the two men.[56] Yet the distinction is valuable nevertheless because it emphasizes the consensus that lay behind the constitutional concerns within the Irish parliament during the fourth and fifth sessions. Darcy only took his seat in May yet the Queries had been drawn up by 13 February, very possibly after some discussion during the recess in December and January. Almost certainly Darcy acted behind the scenes – the presence of his son in England suggests that he was involved in the negotiations there – and it would appear that the Old English set particular store by the Queries. The five committees that dealt with them from March to August all had Catholic majorities (by contrast with the impeachment committees).[57] There was sound reason for this too. The Queries attempted to provide protection from arbitrary government through the law, which would have supplied protection independently of parliament, where the Catholics were likely to be a permanent minority. Impeachment could only be exercised through parliament, which in any case met infrequently, and the limits to its value had been demonstrated when the Protestant majority united to prevent the impeachment of Loftus and Ranelagh. This, however, does not mean that Protestant constitutionalists were lukewarm towards the Queries, some of which addressed issues of particular interest to Protestant groups, such as the Scots who had taken the Covenant. Confirmation of the close to unanimous support for the Queries came on 26 July, when the Commons approved their answers *nullo contradicente*, beginning with the declaration that the king's Irish subjects were a "free people."[58] This was a house, as we have seen, in which about one hundred MPs were in attendance, sixty-five to seventy of whom were Protestant.

There was one further difference between the Queries and impeachment: the former were harder to overrule in England. The English council had avoided using Poynings's law as a means to stop impeachment and thus avoided direct confrontation on the issue. The king, after all, was hoping that by remedying most of the grievances he could persuade the Irish parliament to make substantial financial concessions and wished to avoid conflict in so far as he could. Instead, he and his English council stalled impeachment by asking for precedents which they knew could not be supplied. No such avenue of escape was available in dealing with the Queries and the parliamentary responses to them. Even the lords justices did not suggest using Poynings's law against them. All that could be done was to adjourn the Irish parliament in the hope that Sir Henry Vane and the rest of the English council could use the time gained to think of some way to frustrate its constitutional ambitions. Vane advocated "delay," and the English council's plan of 12 October was certainly designed to accomplish this. By a curious twist of history, the Ulster Irish came to the rescue of the English officials by starting the rebellion. From then on the debate was continued, but by other means.

The constitutional ideas of Darcy and Mervin should not be endowed with unwarranted originality. Like most such ideas in the seventeenth century, they were directed towards specific issues. Nonetheless, the two men did, if unconsciously, touch upon some of the more fundamental questions concerning relations between the state and those who lived within it, and on how diverse groups are to be governed by a single sovereign. It is striking that, whereas before the rebellion Ireland spoke on these issues with virtually one voice, after October 1641 not only was the country bitterly divided between those who wanted more autonomy and those who wanted less, but the two sides were split upon religious lines. Possibly such a division would have occurred eventually even without the rebellion, but that there was an alternative is suggested by the available evidence on one other participant in the drama: the earl of Leicester, the new lord lieutenant.

LEICESTER AND
THE IRISH CONSTITUTION

There is one intriguing inconsistency in the privy council's records of 12 October. Those listed as present at that meeting were: Edward Littleton, the lord keeper, Henry Montagu, earl of Manchester and lord privy seal, his son and successor, Viscount Mandeville, the earls of Northumberland and Dorset, Henry Wilmot, Lord George Goring, and, last but not least, Leicester (Cork had left for Ireland). Those who signed the letter recommending adjournment of the Irish parliament included all these men, with one exception – Leicester.[59]

We also know that special efforts were made to get the letter "full signed."[60]

The absence of Leicester's signature would be hard to explain were it not for the existence of another letter, from Leicester himself, dated Holyrood House, 14 October, in which he stated that he had arrived in Edinburgh on the eleventh, or one day before the privy council record listed his presence at the meeting in London.[61] Clearly, the council decided to advise the king to postpone the meeting of the Irish parliament in Leicester's absence. It will also be recalled that one of the reasons advanced for extending the Irish adjournment was to permit Leicester to consult Charles before departing for Dublin, yet we find that, as the letter saying this was being written, Leicester was in the king's Scottish residence. It follows that Leicester was not only absent when the letter was drawn up but was not consulted (possibly because he was thought to be sick, which he was on the seventh), and the rest of the council did not know of his departure for Scotland.[62]

The exclusion of Leicester from the decision becomes particularly significant when we take into account that his private views on the Irish constitution did not conform with the advice that the council was giving. In an undated and marginal entry in his commonplace book, he remarked: "It may be observed that in Poynings' law for —— calling of parliaments, there is no mention at all made of the parliament of England, but only the king and his council which shows the —— dependence of Ireland upon the king and not upon parliament." He went on to outline Poynings's Act, after which he commented that "it seems to me very clear, that an Act of parliament made in England neither is nor ever was in force in Ireland until it be resolved and confirmed by the parliament in Ireland."[63] Leicester does not seem to have understood fully the intricacies of Poynings's law. He had read the 1494 text, but he does not seem to have been aware of the 1557 revision, which excluded the English council from the approval procedure for an Irish bill (though not England's great seal), but in essentials Leicester's interpretation of Ireland's constitution agreed with Darcy's. Had he been consulted about the council's proposal, therefore, he might well have opposed it. Indeed, he may have known what advice was about to be given and decided to go to Scotland himself to argue against it because there is another puzzle connected with the order to postpone the Irish parliament's sitting. The king wrote to the lords justices on 15 October giving effect to the advice he had received from London, but the letter did not reach Dublin till mid-November.[64] Communications were slow, but not that slow, and we may speculate that the letter was not sent until after the rebellion had broken out on 22 October and that the delay in sending it was connected with the lord lieutenant's presence in Scotland.

Leicester never went to Ireland so we cannot tell how he would have handled the Irish parliament, but his constitutional ideas are important because they almost certainly had a direct bearing upon the attitudes of the Old English leaders, which in turn affected the way in which the plots to start the rebellion developed. It is to this very complex topic that we must now turn, and because of this complexity, the first feature that we must examine is Charles's plans for the new Irish army in 1641.

CHAPTER EIGHT

Charles and
the New Irish Army

There have been numerous references in earlier chapters to the new army formed by Strafford to threaten the Scots from the west as Charles confronted them from the south. Sir John Clotworthy used its existence and its largely Catholic rank and file to arouse fear in the hearts of English MPs as he and John Pym prepared their onslaught against Strafford. As that attack developed, the alleged role that this army was to play in English affairs became a crucial issue at Strafford's trial. The existence of the army also affected Scottish thinking during the negotiations for their withdrawal from England. Quite apart from the constitutional issue the formation of the army had raised, the Scots were reluctant to disband their army while some 9,000 well-trained Irish soldiers remained ready to descend on their western shore as soon as shipping could be supplied. Yet, important though the existence of the new army was in these respects, its continuing presence in Ireland played an even more significant role in contributing to the outbreak of the rebellion. As Edmund Borlase remarked many years later, if the new army had gone abroad to serve France and Spain, "it is very clear that there would have been no rebellion," and the Spanish ambassador made the same comment to Charles himself one month after the rebellion had broken out.[1] Even before this, Viscount Montgomery had reported from Ulster just after the Irish rose that they were "chiefly supported by those who, under colour of going to serve the king of Spain, had commissions to levy forces."[2] It was because those forces, which were being recruited for foreign service, did not depart, and because some of the colonels who had been sent to Ireland to do the recruiting became involved in the pre-rebellion plots that some have suspected from that day to this that Charles had a hand in fomenting the rebellion.

An assessment of the charges against Charles must await the next chapter when the plots are considered, but it is pertinent here to summarize the most cogent defence of the hypothesis that Charles deliberately worked in secret to prevent the new army from being disbanded. This is supplied by Aidan Clarke. Clarke argues that the king's "main concern" was "to keep the army on foot, preferably in Ireland, but elsewhere if necessary."[3] Initially, he licensed nine colonels to recruit troops, ostensibly for Spanish service, but eventually, over the summer of 1641 some sixteen regiments were raised, with the earl of Ormond acting as the chief organizer in Ireland. The English Commons wished to defeat these intentions, but the Irish parliament, including its agents in England (or at least the Catholics among them), "shared his wish that the soldiers should be kept at home" and pressed at the end of July to prevent their departure. The colonels in conjunction with some of the gentry of the Pale devised a plan for seizing Dublin Castle, but this scheme was abandoned when it became clear that Charles was able to reach an accommodation with his Scottish subjects. The Ulster Irish, however, who had learned of the colonels' plot, "determined to present him with a preemptive coup" that would force him to redress their long-standing grievances.[4] If we are to test this hypothesis, or indeed if we are to consider any other that helps to explain the outbreak of the rebellion, we must look in some detail at the events that surrounded the new army in 1641.

THE NEW ARMY, 1640 TO JUNE 1641

The new army had been well trained during the summer of 1640 and, until September, reasonably financed as Charles transferred some £50,000 to Ireland from England to cover the initial costs of raising and equipping it.[5] The reduction in the size of the Irish subsidy and the delay in collecting it – the second, reduced subsidy had not been collected by December – meant that from November onwards there was virtually no money to support the army which Sir Christopher Wandesford claimed was costing £1,000 per day. Strafford reacted by sending the men into winter quarters, mainly located in such planted centres as Belfast, Derry, Moneymore, and Armagh, and placing them on half-pay. Despite this cost-cutting measure, and by the following year the cost of maintaining the army had been reduced to £6,000 a month, the presence of the army in the north amounted to a financial and political time bomb; with every passing month, the soldiers grew more discontented and the money necessary to meet their demands more difficult to find.[6]

By January 1641 the question of the continued existence of the new army was beginning to arouse reaction outside Ireland in two entirely separate institutions: the English parliament and the Spanish diplomatic service. On 4 January Sir Walter Earle told his fellow MPS that the army aroused great fear in Ulster and he elaborated on his theme with a tale of the seizure of Londonderry and the use of a church there to say mass. Sir Simonds D'Ewes gave credibility to these stories by declaring that he had heard from Ireland that the Irish were guided by priests, Jesuits, and titular bishops and that, "being fallen from their late hopes, they would speedily break into some desperate action and set all on fire."[7] A few days later Earle repeated his warning and called for a conference with the Lords to discuss the need to disband the army, but Sir Henry Vane, who must have been speaking for the king, opposed such action on the grounds that the Irish army should be kept together until the Scots had disbanded theirs.[8] The issue of the Irish army continued to concern parliament during the spring and on one occasion the city of London petitioned the Commons on the subject.[9] During these debates Clotworthy urged that the army should not be disbanded but shipped abroad, and it was in this context that D'Ewes opposed him on the grounds that the Irish troops serving Spain might tip the balance of power in Europe in Spain's favour. No action followed these debates, in part no doubt because the Commons had difficulty in reaching consensus on the matter and in part because a dispute arose with the Lords over whether the old Irish army should be increased in size as the new one was abolished, but also because Charles at this time wanted to keep the new army as a potential fighting force.[10]

Charles had pressed the lords justices in January to persuade the Irish parliament to raise the necessary money to keep the army in being. Despite warnings from his Irish officials that no such funds were available, that it was increasingly difficult to supply them, and that general disorder was ensuing as the unpaid troops took out their frustrations on the local population, the king did nothing to change this policy during the early months of the year. Indeed, as late as 28 March, he had written to the lords justices telling them to use their "best care and industry" to support the new army while remarking that under Falkland, it had been possible to keep an army together without paying it.[11] Only at the end of April had the king decided to alter his policy, by which time the first army plot was being revealed.

During April the two houses of the English parliament had at last worked out a common policy regarding the new Irish army, and on the twenty-fourth the Commons presented the king with a petition which demanded that it be disbanded and that Catholics be excluded from court and disarmed throughout England.[12] Four days later Charles replied. On the issues relating to Catholics, his responses were obviously intended to be accommodating, since Strafford's life still hung in the balance, but they were also evasive. On the issue of Catholics at court, for instance, he gave assurances only that there would be no cause for scandal. There are various versions of his response to the demand about the Irish army, in itself an indication of some ambiguity, but they agree that it was negative. According to one source, he said that the army could not be disbanded for reasons "best known to himself"; according to another, he was "already upon consultation how to disband it" but was facing many difficulties and those who pressed him to disband the army should "show the way how it may be conveniently done." Yet another version indicated that he thought the English and Scottish armies should be disbanded first. Whichever version or combination of versions of this speech is correct, MPs reacted coolly.[13]

Charles may be credited with wishing to resist the vicious intolerance against Catholics of some of his subjects, and he faced the genuine difficulty of raising the necessary £10,000 without which the army could not be disbanded.[14] Moreover there is evidence that on 26 April, or before he had delivered his response to the Commons' petition, measures had actually been taken to begin disbanding the new army.[15] By 4 May a commission had been granted to Colonel John Barry to lead 1,000 men into Spanish service, and by 7 May the decision to disband the army was given formal effect.[16] Nevertheless, it is tempting to see Charles as being involved in a plot in which the Irish army would be used in England to support him. The measures to disband the army coincided with Pym's revelations of what has become known as the first army plot, which had been hatched during March, but which was, in fact, two plots. One of these, known as the king's plot, included the idea of keeping the Irish army in readiness, and the other, the queen's plot, seems to have incorporated a scheme to move Irish and French troops to England to exert pressure on parliament. We have the coincidence of the formation of these plots just at the time that Charles was doing his best to keep the new Irish army in being against the advice of his Irish officials. We also have to remember that at the same time he was negotiating with his Irish subjects about the security of their estates and other matters, and they, in turn, were pressing for Lord

Cottington to succeed Strafford in order to ensure that their interests would be protected.[17] Moreover, on 4 April the king had promised Daniel O'Neill, an officer in his army in the north of England, an annual pension of £500 on completion of his service to the crown. Daniel was the Protestant nephew of Owen Roe O'Neill, the Irish champion in exile, and was undoubtedly involved both in the army plot of the spring and, later that summer, in what is known as the second army plot.[18]

Despite these suspicious circumstances, Conrad Russell has shown that the expectation of help from France was misplaced, and we may remark that not only was assistance from Ireland equally unlikely, but that Henry Percy, one of those involved in the plotting, reported that when the idea of moving troops from France and Ireland was mentioned to Charles, he dismissed it as "vain and foolish." Charles had no plan to use the Irish army in England, though he threatened "through rumours spread by the earl of Holland, to use the Irish army against the Scottish if the Scots should fight to secure the death of Strafford."[19] Both the existence of suspicions about Charles's plans and the ultimate rejection of these suspicions by the opposition are confirmed by Pym. "I do verily believe," he declared in mid-May as he was revealing the details of the first army plot, "the king never had any intention to subvert the laws, or to bring in the Irish army, but yet he had counsel given him that he was loose from all rules of government."[20]

The crucial element that emerges out of this complex situation is that by the end of April Charles had changed his policy of trying to keep the Irish army together and had decided to ship most of it abroad. On 8 May orders were sent to Ormond to disband the army, and nine days later the lords justices indicated that the men's arms had been collected and that 7,000 of them would be sent abroad to serve foreign princes.[21] By 9 June Ormond could report that, so far as the men were concerned, the operation had been completed "with reasonable contentment" and that only the officers remained to be satisfied.[22] Initially, the king had tried to borrow from the earl of Cork and others to pay off the men on the personal security of Sir Adam Loftus, the vice-treasurer, who was still in England, but when Sir Adam declined to bear the risk, Cork cancelled the loan. Thus £8,000 had to be borrowed in Ireland "with great difficulty" in expectation of the future payment of the outstanding subsidies.[23] Nevertheless, by mid-June all that remained to be done was to ship the men out of Ireland, and this leads to a look at the second institution that had taken an interest in the new army since January, the Spanish diplomatic service.

SPAIN AND THE COLONELS

During the 1630s Spain developed two interests in Ireland. The first was to strengthen Catholicism. Thus, in 1634 when the college at Louvain ran short of funds, which jeopardized the Franciscan mission to Ireland, Philip IV personally insisted on its financial support. Spain's second interest in Ireland, possibly not unconnected with the first, was to use the island as a recruiting ground for its armies in Europe and South America. So strong a tradition had this become that when in 1636 Sir Thomas Wentworth showed signs of undermining it, Spanish authorities restored his enthusiasm with the gift of a tapestry.[24] There was even discussion between the lord lieutenant and the Spanish authorities in 1640 about solving Charles's financial problems by selling the right to recruit between 3,000 and 10,000 Irishmen in return for a loan of £100,000.[25] The negotiations failed, in part because of the difficulty of sending Irishmen abroad at the same time as Charles was raising an Irish army himself, but the project underscores the reasons for the Spanish ambassador's interest in the new army once it became apparent that Charles might not use it. Here were some 8,000 well-trained Catholic troops, already assembled and available for the cost of recruiting and shipping them, without large additional sums having to be directed to the English king as loans.

An English official suggested sending the new army to serve Spain as early as October 1640, but it was not till January of the new year that the matter was considered seriously.[26] On 18 January, Alonso de Cárdenas, the Spanish ambassador in London, informed Philip IV's governor of the Netherlands, Don Ferdinand, that he had been told by Cottington that if colonels were sent over to arrange transport, Irishmen could be levied from the new army, which Cárdenas was under the impression had already been disbanded. He believed that this might be accomplished at a cost of 50,000 crowns, but he urged quick action in case the French heard about the operation and tried to prevent it. Philip himself pressed his officials early in February to do what they could to take advantage of the opportunity.[27]

After Cottington's initial encouragement of Spanish recruitment, the government seems to have turned against the idea. A few Irishmen were permitted to go to Flanders between February and April, but the numbers were small and they went from England and not Ireland. Con O'Neill, for instance, Daniel's brother, who served under his uncle in the Netherlands, left for England in January on a two-month leave as he had heard that Daniel had died. On discovering his mistake, he used his brother's influence at court to get permission to return to his regiment with 150 to 300 Irishmen who were then in England. However, another Irishman, Colonel Hugh O'Brien, reported in mid-April that Charles had denied him permission to take 2,000 men out of Ireland, and it was the opinion in Brussels later that month that it would be impossible to get men from either England or Ireland.[28] This period of resistance to recruiting coincided with Charles's desire to keep the Irish army together and with the army plots of the spring.

After the discovery of the plots and Charles's simultaneous decision to disband the army, his attitude towards Spanish recruitment in Ireland changed. Thus, on 4 May John Barry received the commission to transport 1,000 men into Spanish service. Three days later eight officers, including Barry, were each given permission to transport 1,000 disbanded men.[29] By the thirteenth, two of these officers had been dropped from the roster, but had been replaced by two other colonels, Richard Plunkett and George Porter.[30] One of the colonels, Christopher Belling, proceeded immediately to Ireland, and with the co-operation of officials there had left the country with 1,000 men of the new army by the end of June despite the attempt by priests to persuade the soldiers not to board ship.[31] At least one of the others, John Barry, wanted to leave England immediately but could not because of a lack of money. This deficiency was rectified by Cárdenas, who had reached an agreement with the officers by mid-June that he would pay their costs, and who had, by this time, begun to secure the necessary shipping.[32]

On 5 July Cárdenas wrote optimistically that he had made progress with the levies. He had established contact with an Irish merchant – who was not named but must have been Geoffrey Brown – whom he could trust because he possessed property in Spain and who, as an agent of the Irish Commons in England, wielded considerable influence. It was with Brown's help that he was able to contract the ships to transport the troops.[33] Although he remarked in his next letter that the "enemy" left no stone unturned to thwart his efforts, by 9 July four more colonels, John Butler, Richard Plunkett, George Porter, and John Bermingham, had arrived in Ireland, and all save one of the remainder had reached Dublin by the twentieth.[34] Porter stated that he expected to be ready to embark his men at Waterford between the tenth and the fifteenth of August, and Plunkett, on 19 July, gave 20 August as the date for his rendezvous although he boasted that he could assemble 1,500 men within eight days, such had been the co-operation of the lords justices and the members of the Irish parliament "who for the most part are relatives of mine."[35]

It was from the third week in July that matters began to go awry for Spain in both Ireland and England, and in both countries it was parliament that provided the focus for those who wished to prevent

Spain from acquiring the soldiers. In Ireland, on 27 July, Sir Audley Mervin led a Commons committee with a Catholic majority to discuss with the Lords the shipment of the men. By the end of the month the two houses had drawn up a joint nine-point statement opposing their departure.[36] It was argued that the embarkation of such a large body of men would cause a shortage of labour, that Spain was an ancient enemy, and that the men might be used against Holland or Portugal, which would not serve English interests.[37] Two independent sources tell us that it was the Catholics in the house who opposed the embarkation most vigorously, but the reasons given for the opposition appealed to Protestant prejudices and must have garnered some planter support as the presence of Mervin on the committee to discuss the matter with the Lords bears witness.[38]

Sir William Parsons suspected a political purpose behind the move to keep the troops at home. He recalled the attempts in June by priests to prevent Belling's men from departing and argued that the king's orders to export the men should be obeyed over parliament's objections, though he delayed any action until further instructions were received.[39] The eight officers quickly petitioned the king against parliament's action which, they complained, caused them "great damage." The petition was undated, but had arrived at court by 8 August, just as Charles was about to set off for Scotland. He referred it to the Lords and asked them to discuss it with the Commons but stated his own preference for the transportation of the troops to proceed.[40] In Ireland, one of the colonels, Garret Barry, was reported to be "in disorder" over the delay, and others crossed to Scotland, John Barry by 18 August and Butler and Bermingham by the end of the month.[41]

Almost certainly these visits to the king were intended, like the petition, to regain the right to export recruits. John Butler, who was Lord Mountgarret's brother, took with him a letter from the justices recommending that his right to ship 1,000 men be restored. John Barry subsequently went to London where he entered into a formal agreement with the Spanish ambassador to have 1,000 men ready at Waterford or Kinsale by 25 September and posted bonds to guarantee fulfilment of his promise on condition that Cárdenas provided the necessary vessels.[42] It was also expected in Spain that Irish soldiers would be arriving at Coruña at the end of September.[43] Barry met his side of the bargain, as Cárdenas acknowledged on 27 November, but the ships failed to turn up "by reason of the stay put upon shipping by the parliament of England."[44] Barry ultimately defied an order from the president of Munster to disband the levy, and he joined forces with the Irish Confederates, but there is no reason to believe that he would not have embarked in September had the ships arrived.[45] At least one ship did reach Dublin by October and troops of the new army embarked on it, but it was not permitted to sail.[46] Another ship or ships turned up at Galway in November to pick up the regiments levied by Theobald Taafe and Sir James Dillon. By 17 November Taafe had reached that city but was refused permission to embark. As a result, his men joined the Irish forces, but as the earl of Clanricard explained to his Puritan half-brother, they were forced to do so for "want of means and employment, being stopped from foreign service, and no use made of them here."[47]

The arrival of the ships after the rebellion had begun indicates that the plan to export the troops was not a royal ruse to fool the English parliament. It is true that the shipping arrived at Galway after Charles's accommodation with the Scots, and this might be used to support a theory that Charles was prepared to let the Irish army leave once this had been accomplished. However, if the ships had sailed for Ireland when Cárdenas intended, many of the troops would have embarked in mid-August, and even after the initial delay, a new departure date of mid-September was set for some of them. Nor is it possible to explain, if it was Charles's intention to delay the departure of the Irish army until he had a settlement with the Scots, why he permitted Belling to leave with his regiment in June. Nor can it be accepted that Charles would have continued to exercise authority over the troops once they had set sail for Spanish service.[48] Charles agreed that up to three of the regiments might serve in Flanders; the rest seem to have been destined to fight in Portugal.[49] It is as inconceivable that Charles expected to use an army that was scattered about Europe against the English parliament as it is to believe that Philip, who needed the soldiers badly and had spent considerable sums to collect them, would have allowed them to return. Only if Charles can be shown to have deliberately delayed the arrival of the ships in Ireland, and thereby the departure of the army, can there be any grounds for suspecting that, after May, he planned to use the Irish army for political purposes. This takes us back to England to look at why the ships were delayed.

From the beginning the Spanish officials had worried that their opponents might try to use the English parliament to undermine plans to procure Irish troops. Cárdenas was particularly anxious about French intervention, and we know that the Portuguese were also working against the Spaniards in June. It is not surprising, therefore, to find parliament becoming involved in the issue soon after the French ambassador, who had been absent, returned to England in the middle of July.[50] On the twentieth the Commons, which was under the impression that 14,000 men were to leave Ireland, told the Lords that care should be taken that these troops did not end up in the hands of those hostile to England, and this message was delivered as the Commons learned that the French ambassador, M. de La Ferté Imbault, had asked for and received the king's permission to recruit forces for France.[51] Some days later the king asked both houses to endorse the departure of the Irishmen for Spain. After some discussion and after some of the Lords had met with Cárdenas, they agreed that 3,000 men might leave, and by 6 August this figure was raised to 4,000.[52]

The Commons' records for late July and early August are silent on the matter, but when the issue rose again on the twenty-fourth, D'Ewes explained what had happened and, incidentally, why nothing had been recorded earlier. In late July, Sir Henry Vane had informed the house that, for "the more speedy dispersing" of the Irish army, the king had decided to allow its soldiers to serve any king in amity with him and that certain regiments would enter the service of Spain. After the officers involved had been identified, there "followed a great silence in the House," whereupon Vane remarked that, since nobody had raised any objection to the king's message, he took it "for the allowance and consent of this House."[53] D'Ewes admitted that he too initially considered that consent had been granted though later he changed his mind.[54] Under the circumstances, Charles cannot be blamed for thinking that parliament had agreed to the departure of 4,000 men. When, therefore, Cárdenas saw the king just before his departure for Scotland, Charles indicated that he was sure that 4,000 men would be permitted to go and that "he would give a secret order for Ireland for them to permit me [Cárdenas] to have a further 2,000 men."[55]

Despite, therefore, the news from Ireland that the Irish parliament wished to stop all the troops from leaving, Sir Philip Mainwaring was sent to Ireland with orders to permit 4,000 men to depart, and soon after Charles arrived in Scotland a similar order was sent to Ormond.[56] No sooner had this been done, however, than La Ferté made representations to the Lords that he too had the king's permission to levy troops but that he had desisted from raising them until parliament had approved. Now, however, since parliament had apparently approved the Spanish levy, he asked that his master might be treated equally and be allowed to raise the same number. In response, both Lords and Commons grew increasingly cautious about permitting any foreign prince to receive Irish soldiers, and by 14 August asserted that consent could still be withheld.[57] No wonder Cárdenas exclaimed on 9 August that "life is hardly worth living" after he had explained that the business had changed "altogether" over "the last two days."[58] To him, the hand of the French ambassador lay behind the destruction of his plans and behind La Ferté lay the queen.

When the king heard that parliament was likely to withhold agreement for the departure of the troops, he wrote to Sir Edward Nicholas:

I am so far now engaged to the Spanish ambassador for four regiment [sic], that I cannot now go back, for it was assured me before I came from London that both Houses were content, only it wanted the formality of voting: whereupon I gave an absolute order for the leaving and transporting of those men, but also reiterated my promises to the ambassador: wherefore ... the Houses [must be told] from me that these levies must not be stopped.[59]

This message was conveyed to parliament, but to no avail; the Commons decided on 28 August that the ships hired to transport the soldiers should be prevented from sailing and that the French should also be denied levies.

The motives for this stance undoubtedly included distrust of what was being arranged in Ireland. The lords justices had to refute a rumour, which they ascribed to Jesuits, that 12,000 soldiers had been levied and were standing "ready" in Ireland.[60] Pym and other MPs examined an Irish gentleman concerning the forces raised in Ireland and the ships provided for their transportation.[61] In view of the association of the new army with the plots of March and April, such distrust was understandable. But not all MPs voted to stop the ships for the same reason. The plots of the spring persuaded D'Ewes to reverse his position of February, when he had opposed the departure of the troops, to one of support for their dispatch to the continent, where it appeared they would be less of a danger than in Ireland.[62] For other MPs, however, the plots at home were less important than the diplomatic situation among the European powers. During the final debate leading to the resolution to stop the ships from sailing, Sir Richard Cave, the agent for Elizabeth, the queen of Bohemia and Charles's sister, pleaded against giving any help to Spain against Portugal. It would, he argued, send a signal to the German princes that England had veered towards Spain and against the elector palatine.[63] That day Sir John Penington, admiral of the narrow seas, received orders to prevent the ships from sailing to Ireland, a decision which led Giovanni Giustinian, the Venetian ambassador, to remark "how little trust can be placed in the promises of this government."[64] The Commons had placed their concern about the Protestant position on the continent above considerations of security at home and the international reputation of their king.

The opposition of the Commons to the departure of the troops from Ireland continued into September, when Cave pressed his diplomatic argument even more strongly. On 9 September, just before parliament went into recess, the Commons instructed its speaker to write to the lords justices banning the transport of troops from Ireland.[65] Even though the Spaniards seem to have found a way by November to circumvent the shipping ban, at least so far as Galway was concerned, it was then too late to prevent the levies from providing a blind behind which the preparations for the rebellion might go forward. The failure to send the troops away when Charles wished to do so also ensured that the Irish had well-trained forces at their disposal when they needed them.

If we accept that the presence of the new army in Ireland, albeit disarmed, provided crucial support to the Irish once the rebellion had begun, we must accept that those who were responsible for it being there made a considerable contribution to the outbreak and initial success of the rebellion. The interaction of the king, the English parliament, the Spaniards, the French, the Portuguese, and, on the sidelines, the Irish parliament led to the delay in getting the army out of Ireland during the summer. Undoubtedly the distrust between the king and the majority in the English Commons provided a catalyst in this process and here Charles bears a heavy responsibility. Even if he did not intend to use the Irish army against parliament during the early months of 1641, he wanted to keep the army in being as a threat against the Scots and he was involved in the army plots to a degree that was bound to arouse distrust. His queen, moreover, does seem to have considered the use of the Irish army in England, and contemporaries may be forgiven for not drawing the fine distinctions between the aims of the king and those of the queen available to historians who can survey the evidence at leisure and with a measure of detachment. At the same time, it must be stated that, once the king had abandoned the idea of keeping the Irish army together, all the English and Spanish official correspondence points to his genuine desire to get the army out of Ireland as quickly as possible. He tried to ship virtually the entire army out of Ireland; he allowed Christopher Belling to leave; and when his policy encountered opposition, he tried to ensure the dispatch of at least 4,000 men openly and another 2,000 surreptitiously. It was the Irish parliament which initially delayed the process, but the English parliament, independently and for very different reasons, moved in the same direction, urged on by the French and Portuguese.

After Charles heard of the outbreak of the rebellion, he wrote in the margin of a letter sent to him by Sir Edward Nicholas, his secretary of state: "I hope this ill news of Ireland may hinder some of these follies in England." This note has been used by historians to demonstrate Charles's relief at the "Irish distraction," but this interpretation is hard to understand.[66] It seems more likely that it reflected his exasperation at the English parliament's interference in his Irish policy which had led to disaster, and the hope that this would now stop. His hope was but one more example of the way he misunderstood his parliament. The Commons could not or would not see its own contribution to the event and preferred to believe, as many historians subsequently have, the assertions from the Irish that Charles had a hand in instigating the rising. How that belief has become so prevalent leads us to examine how the rebellion was, and was not, plotted.

CHAPTER NINE

Plotting the Rebellion

We may never know all the details of how the Irish rebellion of 1641 was planned, but the question has been unnecessarily complicated by the assumption that Charles himself lay at the centre of the rebellion plots. Since 1887 it has been accepted that Charles did not issue a commission to his Irish subjects, as they said he did, to rise up in arms in the autumn of 1641. Nevertheless, it has been accepted that Charles plotted with the Old English to use the new Irish army to instal a government in Ireland sympathetic to royalist policy and, subsequently, to overthrow his opponents in the English parliament. Historians who have shared this view include S.R. Gardiner, J.C. Beckett, Aidan Clarke, Patrick Corish, David Stevenson, Jerrold Casway, Caroline Hibbard, and Jane Ohlmeyer, to name only some of the more prominent ones.[1] After finding new evidence, Conrad Russell has challenged this view, and, as I have suggested earlier, there is nothing in the events surrounding the efforts to export the new army that implicates Charles in a plan to use it for political purposes in either Ireland or England after April 1641.[2] Yet, because the opinion that Charles was engaged in such plotting has become ingrained in the historical literature, it is necessary to look very carefully at the evidence on which this view is based before advancing any alternative version of the plots leading to the rising.

The belief that Charles was involved in the Irish plotting rests on four primary supports. First, there is the account of Randal Mac-Donnell, the earl of Antrim, given in 1650 to Commonwealth officials, which specifically, and in some detail, implicated Charles.[3] Second, there is the failure of the new Irish army to leave the country, for which Charles cannot be held responsible although some of the colonels sent to Ireland were involved in the pre-rebellion plotting. Third, there is the evidence supplied by Count Carlo Rossetti, papal agent to the queen; and, finally, there are the activities of Viscount Dillon of Costello-Galen, both before and after the outbreak of the rebellion, which make it look as though he was an intermediary between Charles and his Catholic subjects. There are a few other sources that can be pressed into service to support the allegation of Charles's involvement. One of these is the deposition of Robert Maxwell of August 1642.[4] Maxwell was a Protestant cleric who lived in Armagh and spent most of the first year of the rebellion as a captive of the Irish. He reported information Irish leaders gave him which can sometimes be used in assessing Irish motives, but his information was derived from those who had no knowledge of events at court and who are known to have fabricated evidence when it suited them.

ANTRIM'S TESTIMONY

The testimony of the earl of Antrim is crucial, because his alone is direct. Other sources report only circumstantial evidence. If Antrim's story can be believed, the rest of the evidence reinforces the idea of Charles's complicity, but if Antrim's account of events after May 1641 is not credible, the rest of the evidence must be examined very critically and an alternative explanation of what happened must be entertained.

In summary, what Antrim said was as follows: some time during the fifth session of the Irish parliament (11 May to 7 August 1641), Charles sent a relative of the earl of Clanricard to Ireland to tell the earl of Ormond and himself that the new army should not be disbanded. After some delay, the two earls met to discuss the king's message. The meeting led to no action. Thus a second meeting was arranged, at which Ormond indicated that he did not wish to reply to the king while in Dublin but stated that he would repair to the country "for preparing of the said dispatches." A further meeting with Antrim was to take place in County Kildare at a later date. Instead of meeting Antrim, however, Ormond sent a messenger – none other than the Colonel John Barry who had arrived in Ireland in mid-July – to tell Antrim to go to the king in person "rather than so great an affair should be trusted by any other." Antrim declined the mission, but sent instead a Captain Digby to the king "signifying the already disbanding those 8,000 men [sic]." This dispatch reached the king when he was at York en route to Scotland, that is on 11 or 12 of August. On receiving Antrim's information, the king allegedly sent a message back "that all possible endeavours should be used for getting again together those 8,000 men so disbanded; and that an army should immediately be raised in Ireland, that should declare for him against the parliament in England ..." On receiving this message, Antrim imparted the plan to Viscount Gormanston and Lord Slane and others in Leinster and Ulster (though he did not mention Ormond), "but the fools" in Ulster did not wait to work with Antrim, rose prematurely, and so spoiled the plan.[5]

It is important to note the detail in Antrim's account which is much more extensive in the original than in this summary. The main thrust of the account must either be accepted in full or not at all. If parts of the story are incredible, there is no reason to accept other parts selectively. Russell has challenged Antrim's reliability on two grounds. First, Charles had no interest in fomenting a rebellion in Ireland in August because he had every expectation of settling Scottish discontent and because his opponents in England were beginning to lose their grip on parliament. More damaging to Antrim's credibility, however, has been the discovery of a plea in July to his friend, the marquis of Hamilton, to secure a commission for one of his kinsmen to transport men to Spain. As Russell has remarked, if Antrim was engaged in one of the king's most delicate and dangerous missions of the time, it is odd that he had to beg for a commission for one of his dependents, and to do so through an intermediary.[6]

There is much additional information which throws more doubt on Antrim's word. After the Restoration, when his behaviour under the Commonwealth was being investigated in 1661, he denied categorically that he had ever made a statement involving the king in the conspiracy. He had never heard, nor had he ever claimed, that the "late king was privy to the insurrection in Ireland," and he remembered nothing about letters being sent by Charles to Ormond about raising forces in Ireland.[7] Therefore, either Antrim lied to the Commonwealth officials, or to those of Charles II, or to both (the original statement was untrue as was the denial that he had ever made it), or, what Antrim said after the Restoration was the truth and the 1650 statement was the fabrication of those who wished to deprive him of his estates. One way or another, Antrim's word, or that ascribed to him, is highly unreliable.

What we know of Ormond's behaviour during the summer of 1641 further undermines any theory that he was involved in a conspiracy with Charles to re-assemble Strafford's army. It is true that, as Antrim claimed, Ormond does not seem to have gone to the country. He signed every outgoing letter from the Irish council during May to 31 July, but during this period he seems to have opposed the constitutionalist position of the majority in parliament.[8] We may assume this because, the following year, when he was accused of complicity with those in rebellion – by others besides Antrim – he was able to appeal to the clerk of the Irish Lords, Sir Philip Percival, to remember how during that summer in the Irish parliament "(when doubtless this mischief was hatching) I was as far at least from complying with them in any of their designs as any man that is now most vehement against them." If, he protested, he had not joined with them in "less essential things," he was unlikely to join in "barbarism and murder."[9]

Two more points may be added that undermine Antrim's account. He sent three letters to Hamilton during the summer though one of these was intended for the king. The first, dated 3 June, was sent to Hamilton from Dublin. In this, the Irish earl asked his friend to intervene on his behalf so that he might serve as "housekeeper" of the palatial new house built by Strafford, at Naas, on which Antrim's wife had set her heart.[10] He also asked Hamilton to intervene on another matter. This concerned a reduction in his taxes on the grounds that he was "sinking under my great debts," and his letter to the king was on the same subject. As his letter to the king remains within the Hamilton collection, the request does not seem to have been delivered, let alone considered.[11] The third letter to Hamilton, dated from Dublin on 19 July, repeated this request while asking for the commission which has been noted by Russell and which was also not granted.[12] From the point of view of Antrim's story, however, the most striking feature of this last letter was its revelation that Antrim had been away in the country for a month and that because of his absence, he "could not learn the conditions for the Irish colonels which were allowed to carry men into Spain."[13] Far, therefore, from being trusted with the king's most secret plans, he did not know what was going on.

We can also catch Antrim out in another inconsistency. It will be recalled that he declared that it was John Barry who delivered the message from Ormond to him in the country. That message would have had to arrive in late July or early August for Antrim's dispatch to reach the king on 11 or 12 August. Barry was a friend of Ormond and was subsequently identified as one of the conspirators (incorrectly, in my view). However, we know that he arrived in Dublin from England between 10 and 20 July, or just as Antrim arrived back in Dublin. Thus, there was no need for Ormond to use Barry as a messenger as all three men were in the same place. We may also observe that Barry himself went to Scotland, but instead of going back immediately to Ireland as a person involved in a conspiracy as described by Antrim could be expected to do, he went to London and signed an agreement with the Spanish ambassador to take the soldiers out of Ireland and then made every effort to do so even though, according to Antrim, these troops were to be used in a rising in November.[14]

Antrim was of little consequence in the summer of 1641 and there can be little doubt that, if the 1650 statement is authentic, he implicated his king in the rebellion after parliament's victory in order to survive, just as he denied having made such a statement to save his position after the Restoration. To be able to claim knowledge of what was going on in Ireland before the rebellion, he wove himself into his story. He was rewarded with a pension a few months after delivering his account, which was among very few such pensions granted by Cromwell to Catholic noblemen in Ireland.[15] It is just possible that Antrim used the first army plot or one discussed in Old English circles during the summer as a basis for his story, but this does not begin to prove that Charles was plotting in the manner that Antrim said he was during the summer and autumn of 1641.

ROSSETTI'S EVIDENCE

If Antrim had some basis on which to build his fabrication, it has been, nevertheless, deeply misleading. Equally misleading has been the interpretation of the correspondence of Count Carlo Rossetti, the papal agent to the queen, who had to leave England at the end of June 1641 in order to evade a summons to appear before the English House of Commons.[16] On 4 June by the English calendar, Rossetti reported that he had often had the opportunity to tell the queen that her husband's problems would continue until he became reconciled with the Roman Catholic church. He then went on to describe how the queen had summoned him to her presence on 2 June to make a proposal to him. She told him that, although the king declined to become a Catholic, he would promise to grant freedom of worship to the Catholics in Ireland and a greater degree of freedom to those in England if the pope would give him money. Once he had gained the upper hand in England, the queen continued, Charles promised to grant the same concession to Catholics in England as that already described for Ireland. It was, she continued, the king's intention to allow only the Catholic and Protestant religions in his kingdoms and to "extirpate" ["estirpare"] the others, particularly the Puritan one. At this stage in the conversation, Rossetti asked how much money would be needed and the reply was £150,000, though he had the impression that two-thirds of this sum would be sufficient. The count understood that there might be some scepticism in papal circles about Charles's ability to honour such promises, which he anticipated by declaring that he considered that an alliance of Irish and English Catholics, English Protestants (as opposed to Puritans), the French, and the United Provinces of the Netherlands might ensure Charles's success.[17]

To list the members of such an alliance is to point to the futility of such expectations, and Charles seems to have been extremely cautious about his wife's proposal. A second interview was arranged, and during this one the king was present for part of the time. The meeting almost certainly took place on 26 June, just after Rossetti had been summoned to appear before the Commons.[18] The part of the conversation in which the king participated lasted about forty-five minutes. Charles began by praising both Rossetti and the pope, but he made no offer to extend religious freedom to the Irish Catholics as an initial step, nor was there any reference to money. After the king left the room, the queen repeated her earlier suggestion of liberty of worship for Catholics in Ireland in return for papal assistance and similar provisions for Catholics in England once Charles had restored his authority. Rossetti indicated that the price of papal support would be open conversion by Charles, a condition which the queen declared she had discussed with her husband, but which he had rejected as he considered that such action would cost him his throne and his life.[19]

Gardiner used Rossetti's later correspondence with Barberini to link Charles and his wife with the Catholic lords in Ireland, but from the time Rossetti left England, he was not in a position to know first hand about what was happening there, let alone in Ireland.[20] After he had left England, he conveyed the impression that Archbishop Ussher, the Protestant primate of Ireland, was seriously considering conversion to Catholicism![21] It must be stressed, therefore, that Rossetti's accounts of his interviews in June are the last dependable information that he supplied about Charles's activities. The later evidence used by Gardiner is a letter written by Rossetti a month after the rebellion had broken out, but there is no evidence in this that the count had any more information to implicate Charles in the conspiracy than he possessed the previous June.

Rossetti's discussions of June coincided with the second army plot, which, like its predecessor, failed. As Daniel O'Neill was mixed up in this plot as well as the first one, it has been suggested that the coincidence in timing points to Charles's interest in bringing the Irish army over to his side while the second plot was taking place.[22] However, it was clearly the queen who provided the driving force in the discussions with the count. Charles was extremely cautious. Nor can it be argued that the correspondence is but a part of a larger conspiracy the evidence for which has subsequently disappeared.

Rossetti himself remarked that his sudden departure from England precluded any further action in the matter.[23] There is nothing in Rossetti's June letters to point to an alliance between the king and his Old English subjects in Ireland during the summer.

DILLON OF COSTELLO-GALEN

Those who argue for Charles's complicity in the Irish plotting point to one other person: Viscount Dillon of Costello-Galen. This Old English noble is supposed to have acted during the autumn of 1641 as the intermediary between Charles and the Irish Catholics in planning to bring the Irish army to his assistance. Any such claim rests primarily on an anonymous propaganda pamphlet published in 1643, first in Edinburgh and then in England, the title of which was: *The Mysterie of Iniquitie, Yet Working* in the Kingdomes of *England, Scotland, and Ireland,* for the destruction of Religion truly Protestant. *Discovered, As by other grounds apparent and probable so especially by the late Cessation in Ireland, no way so likely to be ballanced, as by a firme Union of England and Scotland, in the late solemne Covenant, and a religious pursuance of it.* As its title and contents make clear, its purpose was to discredit Charles and to promote the alliance between the English parliament and the Scots.[24] If read in full, it cannot be taken seriously. It said, for instance, that the king's armies were made up of "papists, prelates, courtiers, superstitious clergymen, dissolute gentry and a herd of profane, ignorant people."[25] It alleged that Charles had arranged in July and August of 1641 with Viscounts Gormanston, Muskerry, and Dillon, and Nicholas Plunkett, Geoffrey Brown, and Thomas Bourke, as members of the Irish parliamentary committees, to remove the English parliament and "the puritans." When, the pamphlet continued, most of the members of the Irish parliamentary committees had returned to Ireland, Dillon stayed behind, accompanied the king to Scotland, was made an Irish councillor, and served as a link between the monarch and the colonels who had been sent to Ireland.[26]

It is true that Dillon's activities did provide some substance upon which the author of *The Mysterie of Iniquitie* could construct his tale, but only by twisting the evidence to suit his purpose and by making unwarranted assumptions. In this he was assisted by Dillon's actions in the months immediately following the rebellion when he did, indeed, try to serve as an intermediary between the Irish in arms and their king.[27]

It is true that Dillon did not return to Ireland with the other members of the parliamentary committees. He was also the brother of Sir James Dillon, one of the colonels who became involved in the plot to seize Dublin Castle. Moreover, Dillon did go to Scotland, and after his arrival, it was reported to Ormond that "there was never a noble man" with the king "of English or Irish but Dillon." He was appointed to the Irish council in October, and we also know that he carried letters from the king to Ormond, which he delivered a few days before the rebellion broke out. However, these letters cannot have been connected with an urgent plot in which Dillon and Ormond were involved because he left them at a friend's house and did not remember to forward them for three days![28]

Dillon also had grounds for remaining in England which had nothing to do with an army plot. He had a suit pending in the English Commons, which was only resolved at the beginning of the second week in September.[29] We do not know why he followed the king to Scotland, though it could have been in connection with the suit, but we do know that Ormond's agent in Edinburgh, Sir Patrick Wemys, who was trying to persuade Ormond to go to Scotland, regarded Dillon's presence at court as dangerous to Ormond's interests. Indeed, he referred to the viscount as "a great traitor."[30] This remark could have a number of meanings, but it shows that, if plot there was, Dillon and Ormond were not in it together.

A second letter from Ormond's agent indicates what the king and Dillon were discussing: that "he [Charles] will after the next spring or summer after come into Ireland and has commanded Dillon to speak it from his majesty."[31] This is the first reference to Charles's intention to go to Ireland himself. Because of the plan to postpone the passing of the Graces once again, it is conceivable that the king wanted to be present when the long-sought promises finally became law. Whatever the truth of this supposition, the private information reaching Ormond lends no weight to a conspiracy theory involving the use of Strafford's army in November with Ormond at its head. On the contrary, it looks as though Charles, seeing the effect of his own presence in Scotland in bringing about a settlement, planned to repeat the experiment the following year in dealing with the grievances of his Irish subjects.

THE PALESMEN'S PLOT

Once it has been established what was not plotted, it becomes easier, if not easy, to discern what was plotted and why. There were, in all probability, two major plots, one devised by the Old English and the second by a combination of Irish leaders, including Rory O'More, most of whose estate lay in Armagh, Connor, Lord Maguire, of

County Fermanagh, and the O'Neills of County Armagh. This second conspiracy was assisted by some elements of the Catholic church. In addition, there was a third plot, almost certainly inspired by Owen Roe O'Neill from the Netherlands. This included a plan to seize Dublin Castle and involved some of the colonels who were recruiting troops for Spain. Owen Roe also tried to persuade some of his relatives in Ulster to join a rising. By the end of August O'More's plot and that involving the colonels had become intertwined.

It has to be admitted that there is no direct evidence on the Palesmen's plot, and Thomas Carte denied its existence.[32] Yet Ormond, soon after the rebellion had broken out, indicated to the king that he suspected that the rising had other "fomenters" besides the northern Irish, and there is sufficient indirect evidence to believe that during the summer some Old English leaders considered using the men from Strafford's disbanded army to obtain by force that which seemed to be beyond their constitutional means to secure.[33] Sir Phelim O'Neill, the Irish leader, remarked to one of the British in his keeping during the early days of the rebellion that the men of the Pale "should not draw their heads out of the collar because they were as deeply engaged as he was," and he made a similar remark to Robert Maxwell.[34] But it will be noted that Ormond only suspected other "fomenters" for the very good reason that, initially, the Ulster Irish acted on their own without the support of the Old English. This, in turn, raises the important question of why the two groups of conspirators, assuming there were two, did not act in concert. In other words, any analysis of the outbreak of the rising must explain, not only why the Old English contemplated rebellion but also what made them pull back from such action so that they did not initially co-operate with their fellow Catholics to the north. It was not, as Antrim claimed, that they were planning to rise in November but were anticipated by the Ulstermen. There is not a shred of evidence to support that story. In recent discussions of the behaviour of the Old English, their decision has again been linked to Charles, and it has been suggested that the Palesmen's plans were dropped because Charles had reached an accommodation with the Scots.[35] This is not, of course, what Antrim said, nor is there any other evidence to support the idea save Dillon's passage from Scotland to Ireland in October, but this by itself proves nothing, particularly as the Old English decision not to rise seems to have preceded Dillon's return. If, therefore, an explanation with a stronger basis can be found, it should be adopted.

In seeking an explanation, we note Clarendon's remark in his history that the Catholics on the Irish committees in England were upset at the appointment of the earl of Leicester as Strafford's successor because he was thought to be a Puritan.[36] This induced the Old English to conspire to keep the new army in Ireland and plan a rebellion. That it was Leicester's appointment that sparked the idea of rebellion among the Old English is confirmed by a Catholic source. There was at least one other man, besides Rossetti, who sent reports from London about Charles's affairs to Rome. He cannot be identified, but he received much information and, more significantly, he remained in England after Rossetti made his hurried departure. He was also capable of acute political analysis.[37] On 16 July by the English calendar, this informant sent word that he had received news from Ireland of great importance. He was informed, he reported, that the Irish parliament had reconstituted the Irish army, which had begun to disband, and had appointed Ormond as its general. Moreover, the Irish parliament did not want to accept Leicester as viceroy as it believed his appointment was a decision of the English parliament, and while the Irish parliament recognized the authority of the king, it denied the authority of the English parliament in Ireland.[38]

The inaccuracies in this report are almost as informative as the elements that we may believe. Ormond made no move to reconstitute the Irish army during the summer. As we know, he was in Dublin and attended council meetings, and he would remind Percival the next year that he had opposed the Catholic Lords in parliament in the summer of 1641. Nor was the Irish parliament as a whole making such a move at this time, though there certainly were attempts to prevent the disbanded men from leaving the country, first by priests as the soldiers recruited by Belling were embarking in June, and ultimately by Catholic MPs in late July, when they took the initiative in passing the Commons' resolution to stop the disbanded soldiers from being transported abroad.[39] The mention of Ormond's name suggests a desire among Catholics for a compromise governor, Protestant but Old English. Ormond had been unacceptable as governor to both Catholics and Protestants at the end of 1640 on the grounds that he was too close to Strafford.[40] Now, after Strafford's death, and the failure to get the sympathetic Lord Cottington into the position, the Palesmen were faced with the prospect of Leicester, who had a reputation as a Puritan and was perceived as the creature of the rabidly anti-Catholic English parliament. Under these circumstances, it is understandable if there was talk in Ireland about resisting the English parliament with the help of the disbanding army, if possible with Ormond as its leader.

Despite its inaccuracies, this report cannot be dismissed as a product of the imagination. It is one of the first surviving contem-

porary references to the preparations for what became the Irish
rebellion. It is important to note that, although our informant was
in England, the report came from Ireland. It was not, in other words,
the product of court gossip and cannot, therefore, be used to implicate the king, or even the queen. The origin of the document also
tells us something about when the plot to use the re-constituted Irish
army was beginning to form. Even official correspondence from
Ireland took five days to reach London and sometimes longer. There
would also have been some delay between the formulation of the
plans in Ireland and the dispatch of the information about them to
England. It is likely, therefore, that the use of the Irish army was
first being considered by the Catholics in Ireland in June, or well
before the colonels arrived from England to recruit men for Spanish
service. This timing also fits with what we know of Leicester's
appointment, which was announced in mid-May.[41] If we allow a week
for the news of the appointment to reach Ireland, it would have been
in June that reaction to the appointment began there.

Those who believe that Charles was involved in the conspiracy
could remark that this dates the Irish plotting at precisely the time
of the royal discussions with Rossetti. It is, however, inconceivable
that a Catholic source would not have reported an intention to link
the regrouping of the army with the granting of toleration to Catholicism, had that been part of the plan. The report made no reference
to expectations of religious concessions. What it revealed was a fear
of the English parliament, which undoubtedly included a fear of
religious persecution, with Leicester acting as its agent. This could
be held at bay only if Ireland remained constitutionally independent
of the English legislature. The Old English, in other words, were
primarily concerned with their constitutional position because they
saw it as the mechanism for the preservation of their interests, which
included religious interests but not to the exclusion of all else.

The scraps of evidence that are available to us from English sources
about events in the summer tend to bear out this interpretation and
tell us more about the development of the conspiracy as well. We
know, for instance, that despite earlier concerns among the Irish
Catholics in England about the appointment of Leicester, by mid-
July the Catholic Irish leader in England, Gormanston, went out of
his way to deny that the Irish committee in England objected to
Leicester.[42] On 5 August, he reiterated his support, and by the eleventh of that month, Sir John Temple, Leicester's agent, could report
that "the animosities and distempers of some of those high spirits in
Ireland" were "much calmed" and jealousies previously held much

reduced.[43] The calming of "animosities," therefore, coincided with an acceptance of Leicester's appointment.

The most obvious reason for Irish sentiments to be "much calmed" was that the long negotiations over the security of Irish estates, which had encountered a last-minute hitch early in August arising from the quarrel between the two houses of Lords, had reached a satisfactory conclusion. An acceptable outcome to these negotiations could hardly have been achieved against the wishes of the new lord lieutenant. Yet, as we have seen, Leicester had probably made an even more fundamental concession. The papal source recorded the fear in Ireland of English parliamentary authority there. It must also be noted that Gormanston had first expressed his appreciation of Leicester by 22 July, at a time when Leicester was returning to France as ambassador and before the problems arose in early August that temporarily delayed the dispatch of the bills for the Graces. It is likely that the comment about Poynings's law found in Leicester's commonplace book, in which he recognized that the Ireland was dependent on the king but not on the English parliament, was penned at about the same time. In short, Leicester had been persuaded on precisely the point that had been of concern to the Old English in June, and his acceptance of the constitutionalist position, which must have helped to gain Gormanston's confidence, would seem to have occurred before his return to France. This interpretation is supported by one further communication. When Temple had been appointed the Irish master of the rolls early in the year, the reaction in Ireland had been extremely hostile. Yet, when he crossed to Ireland late in August, after having been involved in the negotiations of the summer, he was able to report back to Nicholas that he was not encountering any resistance, but only "extraordinary civilities." The change in the attitude towards Leicester's agent mirrored that which the new lord lieutenant enjoyed.[44]

It would appear, therefore, that the initial alarm among the Old English at Leicester's appointment, and their concerns that he would subject them to the bigots in the English parliament, had been set at rest by the end of the summer. It was no longer necessary to harness the Irish army to the preservation of Ireland's independence from the English parliament because the lord lieutenant had been persuaded to accept the constitutionalist position on what that relationship should be. The plan to use the Irish army, to seek another governor, and to assert independence from the English parliament could be set aside. The plot, which had never included the king, could be discontinued. Or it could have been discontinued but for the conjunction of the northern Irish, whose demands had not been met, with elements of the Catholic clergy in forming a plot of their own.

THE IRISH PLOTS

There are three contemporary documents that provide us with fairly reliable evidence about the opinions of Irish leaders at this time. First there is the account of the plot provided by Lord Maguire of County Fermanagh, one of the leading conspirators. His relation, although given while in captivity, is usually regarded as an attempt to explain accurately what happened, though at times the information he supplied was second hand.[45] We have also the information given in February 1642 by Henry Cartan, Owen Roe O'Neill's quartermaster.[46] Finally, we possess the text of a letter by Owen Roe O'Neill dated 8 July 1641 to Luke Wadding, the Franciscan founder of St Isidore's College.[47] There is supplementary material, but it has to be treated very cautiously, either because of its late vintage, such as Sir Phelim O'Neill's statement before his execution in 1653, or because the information about Irish intentions has been filtered though British spokesmen.[48] Many of the statements of British refugees contained in the depositions that were collected after the rebellion had begun fall into this last category. Some of the information in them is demonstrably false, but if handled cautiously, it can provide insight into what was happening in Ulster and it can also sometimes reinforce Maguire's account.[49] We have, finally, the circumstantial material, such as the movements of the colonels, which can be related to events described by Maguire and others.

The initial moves in the plotting are well known. There had been continuing correspondence long before 1641 between the Gaelic Irish in Ireland and their fellow countrymen serving as priests and soldiers abroad. The O'Neills, in particular, had maintained close contact with each other.[50] Sir Phelim, a gentleman and MP with an estate at Kinnard in Armagh, had been conducting an encoded correspondence since the summer of 1640 with Owen Roe, his cousin, and there was similar communication between the O'Neills in Ireland and John O'Neill in Spain, the claimant to the earldom of Tyrone and commander of a regiment for Spain. These communications laid the foundation for continental involvement as the tenuous plans of the O'Neills to regain their estates in Ireland, which had been lost at the time of the plantation, became intermingled with more concrete plans for a rising during 1641.[51]

The first plan to take shape in 1641 seems to have been that of Rory O'More, who came from Longford, even though his diminished estate lay primarily in Armagh. In February, he met with Maguire, who was attending parliament, and stressed the sufferings caused the Irish by the plantations. The conflict with Scotland, he argued, presented those who had lost estates with an opportunity to regain them which was unlikely to be repeated, and this perception of the Anglo-Scottish conflict is echoed by Maxwell's account of attitudes in Ulster.[52] O'More drew attention to Maguire's own debts and claimed, probably inaccurately, to have support for his plan in Leinster and Connacht. Another meeting followed, attended by leaders of the Ulster Irish including: Philip O'Reilly, of Ballynacargy Castle, County Cavan, also an MP, Turlough O'Neill, Sir Phelim's brother, and Colonel Brian MacMahon of County Monaghan, the leader of the MacMahons.[53] It was at this meeting that reference was first made to the opportunity presented by the existence of the new army, "all Irishmen, and well armed," but it was decided that nothing should be done until the overseas Irish had been consulted. Nevertheless, a tentative date was set for the rising early in the winter, a time when it would be difficult for forces to cross from England to suppress it.[54]

There does not, at this stage, appear to have been any contact between O'More and Owen Roe O'Neill. Instead, help was sought from John O'Neill. He, however, had died by 26 January although it took months for news of his death to reach O'More. During April O'More visited O'Reilly in Cavan but seems to have made no further move to involve the O'Neills in central Ulster. Maguire stated that Sir Phelim was only told what was happening in September, and Sir Phelim's claim to Maxwell soon after the outbreak of the rising that he was "one of the last men" to whom the plot was communicated bears this out.[55] When parliament resumed sitting in May, O'More had another meeting, this time with Maguire and O'Reilly, and Maguire's brother, Rory. At this stage the date for the rising was set for 14 November, but some confusion was caused by the arrival of the news of John O'Neill's death.[56]

Just before this May meeting, O'More and Maguire seem to have tried to send a message to Owen Roe about what they were planning to do, but this either did not arrive at all or failed to reach him till after 8 July. Owen Roe, meanwhile, had apparently been making his own plans. According to Cartan, he sent Captain Con O'Neill, his nephew and brother of the Daniel O'Neill serving in the king's forces, to England to get permission to raise men in Ireland, ostensibly for service in Flanders, but in reality to make preparations for a rebellion.

As we have seen, this visit is confirmed by Con's visit to Cárdenas, reported on 20 April.[57] Con did not go on to Ireland but returned to Flanders after about six weeks in England. He was, therefore, almost certainly in London when the colonels received their commissions to transport men to Spain, and it was probably from his nephew that Owen Roe first heard of Charles's plan to dispatch the new army into Spanish service.

Some time after Con had returned to Flanders, almost certainly in May, Owen Roe was visited by a Colonel Hugh Byrne, who had formerly served in John O'Neill's regiment in Spain. He stayed with Owen Roe for about twenty-four hours, during which time the two men discussed how they could help Ireland. Byrne then crossed to England, and by 9 July, that is at the time that the other colonels were beginning to arrive in Ireland, he had obtained a licence from Charles to transport 1,000 men from Ireland, over and above those contracted to Cárdenas.[58] Just as Byrne was receiving his licence, that is on 7 and 8 July, Owen Roe and Luke Wadding of St Isidore's were writing to each other in preparation for an ultrasecret meeting.

Owen Roe's letter of 8 July to Wadding reveals how much (and how little) he knew about what was happening in Ireland. He knew that the new army had been disarmed and feared "extirpation" would follow. The Catholics in Ireland, he wrote, would have to unite or face "the great tempest that will surely burst upon them, to deprive them of their property, and reduce the survivors to perpetual slavery." He agreed, therefore, with Wadding's desire to help "remedy these things" and offered to finance a journey to Ireland by Wadding though he warned him that such a venture might alert the English to what was being planned.[59] In concluding his letter, he relayed a rumour brought by a priest that the Irish had refused to disarm, a rumour which, although false, may well have reflected the growing concern in June, as demonstrated in the report from Ireland reaching Barberini's informant in England, about the implications of Leicester's appointment. June was also the month that priests had tried to stop the men recruited by Christopher Belling from boarding ship.[60] According to Maguire, as the colonels arrived in Ireland in July to take more men away, "a great fear of the suppressing of our religion was conceived and especially by the gentry of the Pale, and it was very common amongst them that it would be very inconvenient to suffer so many men to be conveyed out of the kingdom, it being as was said very confidently reported, that the Scottish army did threaten never to lay down arms until an uniformity of religion were in the three kingdoms and the Catholic religion suppressed."[61]

This view ties in with the rest of the evidence about the mood in Catholic circles in Ireland in June and July. Moreover, Wadding's involvement, the report of the intervention of the priests with the embarkation of the troops, and the frequent references to priests in Maguire's relation leave no doubt about the involvement of the clergy in the plotting – the counterpoint, as it were, to the involvement of the ministers in the Covenanting movement. The Irish challenge to the dominant government of the three kingdoms, therefore, was based on the same alliance between clergy and nobility as had succeeded in Scotland. In the case of Ireland, the international nature of the church gave it an advantage not possessed by the Scottish clerics, yet it was this international feature which aroused nationalist fears in England that the Scottish movement did not invoke to the same extent.

Chronology becomes very important in tracing what happened next. Maguire tells us that he left Dublin after Colonel Richard Plunkett had arrived (about 9 July) and before parliament adjourned (7 August) and also before Colonel Byrne had arrived. He also says that, before he left Dublin, John Barnewall, a friar, had told him that the gentry of the Pale and some MPs had been discussing the possibility of keeping the disbanded soldiers in Ireland. This must have been well before the resolution to this effect was introduced into the Commons on 27 July because otherwise the information would have been common knowledge in parliamentary circles and Maguire would not have needed Barnewall to tell him what was going on.[62] This suggests that Maguire left Dublin about 20 July, a conclusion which is supported by what we know of Byrne's own movements. As Byrne only received his licence from the king on 9 July, it is unlikely that he was in Ireland much before 20 July. It will also be recalled that the information that the Catholics were planning to regroup the Irish army had reached Barberini's informant in England by 16 July. Thus it is likely that Maguire received similar information early in this month.

It must also be remembered that it was at the end of July that the colonels discovered that they would not be able to transport men out of Ireland as they had planned, causing considerable consternation, the departure of three of them for Scotland, and John Barry's subsequent trip to London to renegotiate with the Spanish ambassador. Some of the colonels, however, remained in Dublin, and about the middle of August Maguire and O'Reilly heard, again through Friar Barnewall, that the colonels were willing, once they had raised their levies as though for Spanish service, to seize Dublin Castle and arm their men from its stores. They were, however, desisting from making any definite plans as they were not sure about what support they would receive from Ulster. It was decided, therefore, by the northern conspirators, who at this stage still did not include Sir Phelim, that Maguire should return to Dublin to make contact with the colonels. He arrived in the capital towards the end of August, met one of them, Sir James Dillon, by accident, and found himself being persuaded to join a plot for the overthrow of the government in Ireland, which included the seizure of Dublin Castle, in a manner which showed that Sir James and the colonels knew less about the northern conspiracy than Maguire and his friends knew about theirs. In this way the two separate groups of conspirators came together.[63]

It is important to note that in July Barnewall had said nothing to Maguire about a plan to seize Dublin Castle or about the colonels. The plan to take the castle first surfaced only after Colonel Byrne arrived in the capital and after Maguire had left it. It is tempting to think that when Byrne reached Dublin and found the discontented colonels, he directed their energies towards the ends he and Owen Roe had discussed earlier in Flanders and drew them into a plot to surprise Dublin Castle. Although speculative, this interpretation fits with the chronology up to August and is also supported by what Maguire tells us of the plot as it developed. Soon after Dillon and Maguire had met, other colonels were brought into the discussion, and the feasibility of a rebellion was assessed at a series of meetings.

Maguire's account of the planning at these gatherings reveals a number of features of the colonels' plot. First, only some of the colonels were "privy to the action." Maguire named Dillon, Byrne, and Plunkett. It is almost certain that John Barry, John Butler, and John Bermingham were not among them; all had left for Scotland before or just as Maguire was arriving in Dublin.[64] Second, Maguire related that Byrne indicated that he had recently been in contact with Owen Roe O'Neill; thus Maguire's and Cartan's accounts are confirmed in this detail by each other. Third, Maguire reported that the colonels were "the first motioners and contrivers" of the scheme to take Dublin Castle. Finally, Maguire stated that one of the topics discussed with the colonels was "how to draw in the Pale gentlemen."

In attempting to reassure the group on this last point, Richard Plunkett could only say that he was as "morally certain as he could be of anything" that the gentry of the Pale would assist them. He had, he said, spoken in London with Lord Gormanston and others, and they had approved "his resolution."[65] This is second-hand information, and we know that Plunkett was given to exaggeration in that he told Cárdenas that he was related to most members of parliament in Ireland.[66] Nevertheless, it is just possible that in late June or early July, when discontent in Old English circles, even in England, was at its height and there were in all probability plans to use the new army to protect Catholic interests, Plunkett and Gormanston may have discussed such a scheme, but certainly by mid-August these worries had been largely set at rest. Moreover, the very fact that the conspirators were seeking Pale support but obviously not receiving it indicates that either Plunkett was again exaggerating, even lying, or that he had been involved in the scheme of the early summer which the Palesmen had since abandoned. As we shall see, most of the colonels later withdrew from the plan precisely because they could not gain assurances from the Pale – another reason, let it be said, for dismissing Antrim's claims.

By the time Maguire had concluded his discussions with the colonels in late August, the date for the rising had been set for 5 October, but another meeting had been scheduled for 20 September to settle final arrangements. Maguire returned to Ulster, visited O'Reilly, and the two of them went to Sir Phelim's house on 5 September to attend the funeral of Sir Phelim's wife. It was then that Sir Phelim was drawn into the O'More-Maguire scheme for the first time. Sir Phelim had, however, been in contact with Owen Roe. In July, according to Cartan, Owen Roe had sent a friar and two captains, Edward Byrne and Brian O'Neill, to Ireland via England, and when O'Reilly and Maguire arrived at Sir Phelim's, they found Captain Brian, "lately come out of the Low Countries, sent over by Colonel O'Neill to speak to and provoke those of Ulster to rise in arms."[67] The two independent accounts once again bear each other out. Through this visit to Sir Phelim at Kinnard, the three skeins of the conspiracy, O'More's, the colonels', and the O'Neills', had come together even though the last two both drew inspiration from the same source in Flanders.

Maguire again visited Sir Phelim on his way to attend the 20 September rendezvous with the colonels in Dublin, at which time the O'Neill leader urged Maguire to advance the date for the rising. This delay became imperative once Maguire discovered what had been happening in Dublin. Owen Roe by this time was in direct contact with O'More and had urged him to take quick action to seize Dublin Castle "by any means" (a possible indicator as to who had had the idea in the first place), but Maguire also found that all but two of the colonels, Byrne and Plunkett, had lost their enthusiasm for the scheme because the latter had proved unable to engage Pale support.[68] Even Plunkett seems to have played a secondary role from that time on, but his place in the leadership was filled by Sir Phelim who, with Captain Brian O'Neill, followed Maguire to Dublin. Yet another meeting was held on 26 or 27 September between O'More, Sir Phelim, Captain Brian, and Colonel Byrne. After considerable debate, it was resolved that "all those that were of our faction" should proceed with the rising, but that another meeting be held in County Monaghan to fix the final details.[69] This meeting took place on 5 October, when it was agreed that O'More, Maguire, and Colonel Byrne were to surprise the castle on 23 October. Meanwhile, Sir Phelim or one of his subordinates was to take Londonderry on the same day, and other objectives were similarly assigned. It was also agreed at this meeting that the Scots in the north should be left alone unless they proved hostile.[70]

There is one additional witness, in the person of Owen O'Connolly, who can throw further light on the conspiracy. O'Connolly lived at Moneymore in County Derry and was the foster brother of one of the conspirators, but he was also a Protestant and a servant of Sir John Clotworthy. Around May he had been informed by his foster brother, Colonel Hugh MacMahon, who lived in Monaghan, that the Irish were about to take a national oath against their English governors, a report allegedly passed on to various magistrates but dismissed as of no consequence. He heard nothing more till 18 October, when he received a letter from the colonel telling him, "as you tender your own good and my love," to be at his house in Monaghan on the twenty-first at the latest. O'Connolly, who was on his way to Dublin at the time, rode to Monaghan, found the colonel had left for the capital, but found him there late the following evening. The story of how the plot was revealed to him as he and his foster brother were drinking is well known. He was informed that Maguire was in the city and was intending with "great numbers of noblemen and gentlemen of the Irish papists" from "all parts of the kingdom" to take Dublin Castle by surprise, and "to cut off all the Protestants that would not join them." The Irish, as he reported, "had prepared men in all parts of the kingdom" to "destroy all the English inhabitants there" and "all the Protestants should be killed this night." In doing this, he was informed, the Irish were imitating Scotland, "who got a privilege by that course."[71]

It was this story that O'Connolly broke to the astonished lords justices just before the Irish struck and which permitted the authorities to thwart the plan and arrest Lord Maguire. O'Connolly may have embellished what he was told (by the time he reached Sir William Parsons he had had a lot to drink), or his foster brother may have exaggerated the extent of the conspiracy, but what is important is that it was in this inflated form that the plot first reached the ears of the lords justices.[72] Whatever the true intent of the Irish may have been, the English only knew of their intent through O'Connolly's account. Somewhat later O'Connolly gave a fuller account of his discovery of the plot and in this he threw light on the motives of the conspirators. His foster brother originally joined the plot out of fury at being slighted at the assizes by a New English justice of the peace, who had only recently risen from being a "vintner or tapster." To Hugh MacMahon the aim of the rebellion was to deliver the Irish "from bondage and slavery" under which they "groaned."[73] This comment about the resentment at the New English as social upstarts is as revealing as the details of how the plot took shape and the concern about the safety of the Catholic religion in explaining why the rebellion broke out. Once again we see that it was as much their exclusion from the administration as the nature of that administration that gave the Irish a motive to rise in arms.

On the whole, the pieces of the jigsaw puzzle fit together. Where Maguire's account overlaps with Cartan's they reinforce each other, and on the crucial point of Sir Phelim's late involvement in O'More's plot, Maguire's testimony is supported by Maxwell's. There are gaps. It would be fascinating to know who, if anyone, in the Pale was approached by the colonels. If we do not know this, at least the information from Maguire of the Palesmen's refusal to get involved confirms the impression that, whatever plans may have been in existence earlier to use the new army, by September the Old English regarded the political situation that had arisen out of the negotiations in the late summer as satisfactory.

One piece of the puzzle alone does not fit: Antrim's story. If Charles wanted to use the new army during the summer and if he had sent the colonels to Ireland to gather it together for him, why did the colonels split up, some remaining in Ireland and some going to Scotland, just as, according to Antrim, Charles was sending a message back to Ireland to keep the army together? Moreover, if it was the royal purpose to use the army, why did the colonels get no co-operation from the Old English when they asked for it? All the evidence points to the satisfaction of the Old English from August to October. They did not, of course, know of the campaign by Parsons and others to undermine their agreement with the king, nor did they know that the king had agreed to postpone parliament and therefore delay, yet again, the confirmation of the Graces. It was only after the rebellion had broken out and they were able to observe how the authorities intended to deal with it that they began to realize that their original fears of the early summer were warranted. Those who had captured control of the Irish government in late 1640, ironically with Old English backing, used the rebellion to forge a link with the extreme group in the English parliament to ensure the continuation of plantation and the expansion of Protestantism. Their attempt to use the court to this end during the summer had failed. Now, in the new situation provided to them by the Ulster Irish, they could turn to the court's enemies.

CHAPTER TEN

The Outbreak
of the Rebellion

The fighting that broke out in Ireland in October 1641 did not cease till 1653. Once the war had begun, it took on a momentum of its own as the various parties in England, Ireland, and Scotland struggled for dominance. This long-range contest is not our concern, but the actions and pronouncements of the protagonists during the early stages of the rebellion throw light upon attitudes that contributed to the outbreak of the conflict. In the environment of war, ideas were voiced that had previously been harboured only in secret. Moreover, the very nature of the war during its initial months revealed features of the political struggle that had had no mechanism for expression during the pre-war negotiations. The discussion up to October 1641 had been conducted among élites. The war itself involved a cross-section of Irish society and produced, even if only at second hand from the statements from British refugees (themselves from all strata of society), some insight into the attitudes and convictions of the rank and file Irish and Old English.

As we look at the outbreak of the rebellion, we must first trace the military engagements because it was these that set the context for all else. Yet the relative military strength of the contestants was in part determined by the political decisions made after the conflict had begun. Not until early December was it clear that the rebellion would extend substantially beyond the borders of Ulster. Thus the reaction in Ireland to the rebellion played a crucial role in determining the extent of the military theatre. As the military and political events interacted, a succession of statements was issued, often in the form of demands, which revealed the motives of those in arms as circumstances changed.

THE FIRST PHASE
OF THE REBELLION

Sir Phelim O'Neill struck in Ulster on the evening of Friday, 22 October, "the last day of the moon." He took Dungannon first, and two hours later he was in possession of the strong castle of Charlemont to which he gained access by pretending to search for some stolen cattle. By the Saturday evening, the Irish controlled Moneymore to the north, and to the south, Portadown, Tanderagee, and Newry.[1] In a matter of some thirty-six hours, therefore, Sir Phelim had established a chain of positions which effectively prevented any possible conjunction of the British in the north with any that might survive the actions of the conspirators in Dublin.

Sir Phelim, of course, acted in the belief that Dublin Castle itself would be in Irish hands by Saturday, and it is clear that he did not hear of the failure of the Dublin prong of the rising till after the Tuesday.[2] The proclamation he issued from Dungannon on the Sunday must therefore have been written on the assumption that the initial phase of the rising had succeeded. Thus it reflected Irish goals as established before the rising began and before British reaction or the prospect of failure could affect them. The proclamation gave assurance that the Irish remained loyal to the king and that they "in no way" intended harm to either "the English or Scottish nation," but that they sought "only for the defence and liberty of ourselves and the natives of the Irish nation." It then gave instructions that all persons should return to their homes under pain of death and promised that "any hurt done to any person or persons shall be at once repaired."[3]

Even had Dublin Castle fallen, Sir Phelim's task would not have ended here. Considerable British strength remained in Antrim and northern Down, and to the west and north in a line of centres from Augher, through Omagh, Newtownstewart, and Strabane, to Londonderry. Word of the rising reached British leaders in Antrim and Down late in the evening of Saturday, 23 October. Viscount Chichester at Belfast and Viscount Montgomery in the Ards quickly sent word to the king in Scotland and began to organize resistance.[4] During the remaining days of October Sir Phelim continued to score successes to the south. Armagh had surrendered by the twenty-eighth and Dundalk by the thirty-first, but the momentum of the Irish push to the east was gradually halted.[5] Lurgan was captured on 1 November and Dromore was burned, but by the beginning of this month some 1,000 British soldiers had been moved to Lisburn (Lisnegarvey), and despite repeated attacks on 8, 22, and 28 November, Sir Phelim was unable to dislodge the defenders and,

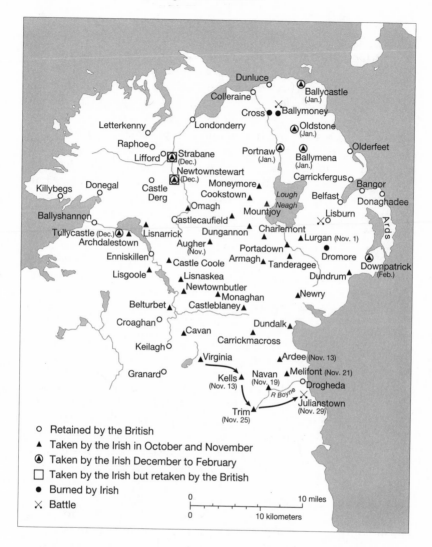

Map 3 The Ulster Forces and the Rebellion, October 1641–February 1642

indeed, suffered severe losses in the last attempt. This check at Lisburn pointed to the limits of Sir Phelim's military capabilities, for, as a British source remarked, he could have bypassed this town and marched on to Belfast and even Carrickfergus, which lay virtually undefended and "full of men, women and children fled thither."[6]

One of the most striking features of the initial days of the rebellion was the Irish ability to take action in several directions at once. While engaged in eastern Ulster, they were simultaneously challenging

British forces led by Sir William Stewart and Sir Audley Mervin in western Tyrone and preparing for an assault on Drogheda. The Irish army which attacked Lisburn numbered some 8 to 10 thousand men, and the size of this force, leavened as it was by the well-trained men from Strafford's disbanded army, undoubtedly gave the Irish a decisive advantage initially. Their central location and their mobility assisted this rapid deployment of forces. Nevertheless, in the west of Ulster, as in the east, the Irish found it impossible to overwhelm the British once they had lost the advantage of surprise and resistance had been organized. Augher seems to have been in Irish hands by the end of November after an initial attack in the middle of the month had failed, and by 16 December, Sir Phelim had occupied Newtonstewart and Strabane. This, however, was the limit of his advance in this direction, and indeed the British recovered these towns during the first half of 1642.[7]

Another reason for Sir Phelim's ability to move in a number of directions at once was the assistance he received from other Irish leaders in Ulster who had, in accordance with the plan, taken up arms simultaneously. The first assistance he received was from Fermanagh. Here, under the leadership of Rory Maguire, Lord Maguire's brother, most of the areas settled by the British in this county, from Newtownbutler in the south to Lisnarrick and Archdalestown (on opposite sides of lower Lough Erne) to the north had fallen to the Irish within two days of the start of the rebellion. The two major exceptions were the towns of Enniskillen and Ballyshannon, the former being saved by a warning to Sir William Cole, its governor, who had time to prepare to resist. One smaller British settlement, Tullycastle, also in the north, held out till Christmas, and there may have been other such pockets of resistance, but quickly a great many British began moving south, out of Fermanagh into Cavan, and Rory Maguire was sufficiently confident about the situation in his own county that, by 4 November, he was able to join Sir Phelim in Newry for a meeting and, later that month, to assist him with 4,000 men in the thrust to secure the western part of Tyrone.[8]

One reason for Rory Maguire's success in Fermanagh seems to have arisen from his ability to separate many of the Scots from the English. It will be recalled that during the planning of the rebellion it had been decided to leave the Scots alone. Owen Roe had recommended the same approach, and this policy was put into effect by the Ulster Irish once the rising began.[9] Sir Phelim wrote to Sir William Stewart to emphasize that the "intention of these troubles is nothing against your nation" and told him to "give notice to your countrymen of our good will," and other sources confirm the Irish insistence that the Scots were not to be touched.[10] As a consequence, Scottish settlers sometimes attempted to remain aloof from the conflict, but in Fermanagh a few seem to have gone a step farther and joined with the Irish. One of these was identified as Lieutenant William Graham of Lisnaskea and another as Lieutenant Grymes, the county muster-master, indicating that this co-operation was taking place at a social rank above that of an ordinary tenant.[11] Richard Parsons, a clergyman in County Cavan, reported that such was the hatred of the English by the Scots in Fermanagh that when "any of the English fled unto them for refuge or succour from those that pursued them that those Scots delivered them up into the hands of the Irish again."[12]

This division between Scots and the English was certainly encouraged by stories disseminated by the Irish in Tyrone and Fermanagh that pictured the rising as a combined operation of Ireland and Scotland against England. Two Fermanagh deponents who came from separate parishes declared that they had been told that the Scots, including the earl of Argyll and the majority of the Scottish nobility, had joined in a covenant with the Irish "for the extirpation of the English," and we also find a reference to Argyll's alleged support for the rising in a deposition given by a Protestant minister in the barony of Dungannon.[13]

We may suspect that the purpose of the policy that lay behind these pronouncements and stories was short term and tactical. An Armagh deponent commented that the Irish told the Scots that they intended to share Ulster with them but told the English that "together they would banish the Scots."[14] The earl of Castlehaven, one of the Catholic Confederation generals, commented that the Irish hated "no nation upon earth" more than the Scots, and the depositions suggest that after a few weeks the actions of the Irish towards the Scots were not as friendly as their words. In Glaslough, Monaghan, all the Scots had been put into prison by 16 November, in Fermanagh it was reported that by about 4 December the Scots had begun to be robbed, and in Tyrone there were also reports that the Irish "fell upon the Scots" after having dealt with the English.[15] Yet what we may be detecting here is the difference in attitude between those who planned the rebellion and the common people or second level leaders. One of the most devastating incidents involving Scots occurred about mid-November after the Irish had failed in an assault upon Augher. Numerous Scots were killed, apparently after being taken into protection. After this incident, Turlough O'Neill wrote to one Sir Robert Knight to emphasize that the Irish leaders still bore no ill will towards the Scots: "But for that ill favoured massacre near

Augher, of those that were first taken to mercy, which did since cost much blood, and it were better that [the relations of] both the nations [Scots and Irish] being formerly on should still so continue, and like brethren than to be at variance together." He then went on to propose to Knight that a conference should be held between influential Scots and Irishmen, presumably to avoid any recurrences.[16]

If there was some sincerity in seeking Scottish neutrality, another claim by Irish leaders – royal support for their actions – was definitely meant to confuse and deceive their opponents and to reinforce the morale of their followers. According to deponents who lived far from each other and who could not have co-ordinated their testimony, both Rory Maguire and Sir Phelim O'Neill claimed the king's authority for their actions during the first days of the rebellion.[17] It was not surprising, therefore, that when these two men met in Newry early in November to plan strategy in the light of the situation they faced after the failure to take Dublin, they devised a scheme to publish more broadly an assertion that had already proved its worth.

The meeting led to a joint declaration, dated 4 November, addressed to "all Catholics of the Romish party both English and Irish" to which they wished "freedom of conscience and victory over the English heretics who have for a long time tyrannised over our bodies and usurped by extortion our estates." They went on to declare that the king had given them a commission under the great seal of Scotland, dated 1 October from Edinburgh, along with instructions of the same date to publish the commission. The alleged commission complained that the English parliament had forced the king to reside in Scotland and had usurped his authority. Since, it continued, "the vehemency of the Protestant party" in Ireland was likely to endanger royal power there too, the holders of the commission were empowered to "meet together" and consult with neighbours to effect the "great work mentioned and directed unto you in our letters" and to "possess yourselves" of all the forts and castles in Ireland "except the places, persons and estates of our loyal and loving subjects the Scots." The commission then gave power to "seize the goods, estates and persons of all the English Protestants."[18]

No historian today accepts the validity of the commission, but it is of interest because it reveals the thinking of the Irish leaders at a time when they realized that the rising had fallen short of its original objectives. They had begun to appeal to their co-religionists in Ireland, and, to reassure potential allies and confuse their enemies, they claimed royal authority while continuing to try to neutralize the Scots, whose strength in the northeast and northwest of Ulster, quite apart from their recently victorious army at home, was well appreciated.[19] The forged commission also represents a statement of war aims in that it united a reversal of the Protestant domination of the government of Ireland with a statement of intention to reclaim land that the English settlers had occupied.

While Maguire and Sir Phelim had been so engaged, County Monaghan had risen under the leadership of the MacMahons. The town of Monaghan, Castleblaney, Carrickmacross, which belonged to the earl of Essex, and all other major centres in the county were in Irish hands by the end of the first day of the rebellion.[20] Thus, by the time the forged commission was published, the Irish controlled a band of territory which included most of Fermanagh, Monaghan, Armagh, the southern and western shores of Lough Neagh, and much of Tyrone. Had the rising received as much support in Donegal as elsewhere, Sir Phelim might have been able to push on to Derry. The O'Donnells did, in fact, send some men to assist him, and one of the Gallaghers who had served in the Netherlands attempted to organize his compatriots, but he arrived back in Ireland only three weeks before the rising began, leaving little time to make the necessary preparations. What we know about events in Donegal during October comes to us from Everden MacSween, the Irish justice of the peace for the county, who seems to have been surprised by the events and anxious to do what he could to stop them. Certainly, from Sir Audley Mervin's account of the following year, it would appear that, although the Irish could raise as many as thirteen companies in the county, the British retained control of most of the major centres in Donegal and prevented any disturbance in Inishowen.[21]

CAVAN AND THE ENCIRCLEMENT OF DROGHEDA

As a stalemate developed in the north, it was in the south that the momentum of the rebellion was maintained. The advance south, and the encirclement of Drogheda, seems to have been organized by the MacMahons, particularly Colonel Brian MacMahon, with the assistance of Captain Con O'Neill, Owen Roe's nephew. MacMahon began to penetrate Louth as early as 1 November.[22] His forces, however, received important assistance at the end of that month from the O'Reillies of Cavan, a county which had also risen at the appointed time and which was, like Fermanagh, very largely in Irish hands by early November though slower than Fermanagh to link up with another body of Irish.

In Cavan, the Irish leaders were Philip O'Reilly, who combined the authority of the old and the new worlds by being both the O'Reilly and MP for the county, and Miles O'Reilly, the high sheriff of the

county, who is referred to in documents as Mulmore MacEdmond
O'Reilly as he shed his English name once the rebellion had begun.
Word reached the British in Cavan from Sir William Cole at Enniskillen and from Monaghan about what they could expect just as the
rising began. Mulmore O'Reilly, taking advantage of this information, collected weapons from the British under the pretence of ful-
filling his duties as the sheriff in resisting the rebellion. However, it
quickly became apparent to the inhabitants of Belturbet, where the
British were most numerous, that, far from opposing the movement,
he was one of its prime leaders. Some attempts at defence were made,
but the town had no walls, and despite the presence of a few soldiers
of the king's army under the command of a Captain Ryves, resistance
was ultimately deemed impractical, and Ryves retreated south to
Ardbracken, near Navan.[23] Thus, by the end of October the king's
forces had retreated to Meath and the Irish controlled all major
centres in Cavan save Keilagh, occupied by Sir Francis Hamilton,
and Sir James Craig's castle at Croaghan, both in the barony of
Tullyhunco. In this county there was again an effort to persuade the
Scots to side with the Irish. A Scottish minister, George Creighton,
who lived at Virginia, was told by the Irish that the Scots "had not
oppressed them in the government, and that if the Scots would be
honest and take their parts, they would share the kingdom amongst
them: And they believed the Scots would not forget the great troubles
that the English lately procured unto Scotland: now it was their case
with the English."[24]

Creighton, like deponents elsewhere, suspected that this solicitude
stemmed from a recognition that the task of ridding Ireland of the
planters would be easier if the Scots were attacked after the English
had been expelled.[25] Such an interpretation may be difficult to reconcile with the letters written by Philip O'Reilly as late as 27
December to Irish leaders in Longford and Leitrim to remind them
that they were "not to meddle with any of the Scottish nation except
they give cause." Particular respect was to be shown to Sir Francis
Hamilton of Keilagh, who had sided with the constitutionalists in
parliament, and Lady Forbes, his mother, who lived at Granard,
County Longford, and "whose fair carriage in all her lifetime
amongst us doth deserve all favour."[26] Such letters may be touching
reminders of the days when Irish and Scots gentry lived together in
harmony and sought common goals. Yet they were written in English
and copies were sent to the Scots. Moreover, they were sent at a time
when Sir Francis had begun to harass the Irish in Cavan while their
main forces were helping to besiege Drogheda. So threatening did
the Scots become that one of the O'Reillies had to be sent back to

Cavan to organize opposition to the Scottish pressure.[27] This suggests that the apparently friendly letters were again intended to induce Scottish neutrality. By the following year the Irish were clearly determined to eliminate such British centres from their midst. Sir Francis surrendered in June and Castle Forbes on 2 August.[28]

The O'Reillies, like the northern leaders, had to adjust to the situation created by the survival of the Dublin government. News of the failure of the Dublin plot reached Cavan on Monday, 25 October, and three days later (Thursday) one of the colonels involved in the plot, Richard Plunkett, turned up at Virginia.[29] In response to this news, the O'Reillies, while continuing with their military preparations, also debated "how to put a fair gloss ... upon all that had been done."[30] The fruit of this discussion was their Remonstrance, which had been drawn up by 3 November, and which they sent to Dublin in the hands of Henry Jones, the Protestant dean of Kilmore.[31]

The Cavan Remonstrance warrants careful scrutiny as it reflects Irish thought just after the discovery of the failure of the Dublin coup and before the Catholics of the Pale made common cause with the Ulstermen. The O'Reillies claimed to speak only for the Irish in Cavan, a reflection of the decentralized nature of the rebellion. While they expressed fears for their religious liberty and "utter expulsion" from their estates, their greatest cause of fear lay "in the proceedings of our neighbour nations" and the threat posed "by certain petitioners, for the like course to be taken in this kingdom." Here was a clear reference to the Scottish demands of the previous spring and to the petitions circulated in Ulster in connection with the Root and Branch bill passed by the English Commons. Rumours, the Remonstrance continued, circulated about invasion from "other parts," which would dissolve the "bond of mutual agreement" whereby all the king's "dominions have been till now linked in one." It was argued that it was only to preserve these liberties that the forts and strong places had been taken, but assurances were given that no hurt was intended to anyone. As for "the mischiefs and inconveniences that have already happened" to the English, which they blamed on "the disorder of the common sort," they agreed to make every effort to ensure restitution. They asked that their grievances be submitted to the king and that the measures taken to redress them be confirmed by the Irish parliament. Finally, they urged speed of action "for avoiding the continuance of the barbarity and uncivility of the commonality, who have committed many outrages and insolencies without any order, consent or privity of ours."[32]

What the O'Reillies were evidently seeking was a reaffirmation of the Graces and the concessions granted by Charles the previous summer, though now with the added assurance that "the liberties of our consciences" would also be guaranteed. It is impossible to judge what its authors expected from this document. They were in a difficult position because the failure to take Dublin meant the state's ability to respond militarily exceeded their expectations. They may only have hoped to gain time, but they knew that parliament was scheduled to resume sitting on the ninth, and the timing of the dispatch of the Remonstrance suggests a hope that it could be considered when the session resumed and that their stance would win some support among MPs. In fact, on the ninth the resumption of the session was further postponed until the sixteenth because of poor attendance.[33] Thus, when the council replied, which it did on the tenth, it did so before parliament could hear of the document.

The council's response insisted that their grievances would only be forwarded to the king if the Irish returned to their homes immediately, but by the time Jones had returned (on the twentieth) with this response, the Remonstrance had become irrelevant.[34] The O'Reillies had assembled 3,000 men at Virginia, and by the twenty-fourth this force had advanced beyond the borders of Cavan to take Kells and Ardbracken (near Navan). By Sunday, 21 November, Colonel MacMahon's Monaghan forces had begun to gather outside Drogheda; indeed, Melifont, Viscount Moore's home, which lay only three miles to the north of the town, fell to the Irish on that date. By this time the Old English in Louth had decided to join with the Irish. MacMahon had called a meeting of the gentry of the county soon after he had entered it early in November and had persuaded many of the leading families, such as the Barnewalls, Dowdalls, and Bellews, to join him. When the O'Reillies marched southeast, therefore, they knew that they would be well supported, and by the twenty-seventh they had crossed the Boyne at Trim.[35] Clearly it was intended to complete the encirclement of Drogheda from the south.

The O'Reillies' force now included 300 horse, who were armed with pistols, carbines, and demi-lances. As they began taking up their position on the southern bank of the Boyne, they must have heard of the approach of a force of some 600 English foot and half a troop of horse that the lords justices had dispatched from Dublin on the twenty-seventh to reinforce the garrison at Drogheda. This contingent had reached Julianstown by the morning of the twenty-ninth, when a detachment of the O'Reillies, taking advantage of an early morning mist, ambushed it. The Irish were well led, one of their commanders having spent three years commanding a regiment in France. By contrast, the English officers had failed to get their men, many of whom were recent recruits drawn from those who had fled the plantations, to meet up with a force that had been sent out of Drogheda to support the final stage of the march. They ignored a warning from Lord Gormanston, whose residence was in the vicinity, of the likelihood of an ambush. Finally, when the Irish attacked, one of the English officers, instead of giving the order to fire, gave the order to countermarch by mistake, and the cavalry, when they charged, did not fire their pistols. Not surprisingly, the Irish put the English horse to flight, killed virtually all the foot, and captured a much needed supply of weapons.[36] The Irish victory not only sealed off Drogheda from Dublin but enhanced Irish morale. Creighton, who was still living in Virginia, remarked: "the O'Reillies did much extol themselves for being the destroyers of those 600 English, for by their valour all the Pale and the rest of Ireland were brought to be joined together in this war."[37]

THE NORTHERN PALE, LEITRIM, AND LONGFORD

Undoubtedly the Julianstown victory reinforced the alliance that was beginning to bind the Old English to the Irish, but as we have seen, the Louth gentry had associated themselves with the rebellion before this action. Moreover, if we look at Meath, we find the Old English acting against the Protestant inhabitants of the county almost as soon as the Irish struck in Ulster though in a less organized way. The lords justices reported on 25 November that north of the Boyne the common people and the younger sons of the gentry had joined the rebellion, but the depositions make it clear that well before this the Old English gentry had begun to move against New English settlers. Some fifty instances of robbery were reported by the deponents for this county as occurring between 23 October and 4 December.[38] The rate at which these incidents occurred increased after 23 November as the O'Reillies entered the county, some deponents specifically identifying the Cavan men as the robbers, but half of the robberies occurred before 16 November (twelve of them in October) and in many cases those named as responsible were gentry of the Pale.[39]

Old English and British sources confirm this picture. The inhabitants of Navan greeted the news of the rebellion in the north with enthusiasm as soon as it occurred.[40] Moreover, we have James Dowdall's statement that as early as 8 November Protestants were being robbed at Longwood, near Trim, and that a few days later, about the twelfth, "which was before any northern Irish came into those borders," many Meath gentry met at Longwood and armed their servants, who then proceeded to rob Protestants living in the area. On talking to those so engaged, Dowdall was told that "it was agreed on amongst all the Catholics in Ireland to root out and pillage all the Protestants."[41] Those doing the robbing obviously had a sense of a religious cause, which suggests clerical involvement in what was happening.

We gain the same general impression of the situation in Meath from Captain William Cadogan's deposition. Some Old English gentry lent their support to the attacks on Protestant property from an early stage. About 29 October, for instance, Cadogan was told by the English settlers around Ardbracken that they had been pillaged and warned not to go to Dublin as the government there had fallen and that if they did their throats would be cut. He asked who was doing the pillaging and was told that it was Sir William Hill and his son, Francis, who was married to the earl of Fingall's sister. Three days later, Cadogan and some others in the county, including fellow justices of the peace, arrested the sovereign of Kells and some sixty or eighty others who had been engaged in the robbing. "Divers" of these confessed under questioning "that they had received command to rob and destroy the English, and some of them did confess that they were commanded so to do, by one Mr Arthur Fox who lived in those parts."[42] Cadogan's ability to call on the assistance of JPs suggests a division within the gentry, some joining and some resisting the rising. It would have been odd if such a division had not existed, as knowledge of such a conspiracy had to be restricted to reduce the danger of detection and the last to be told would probably be those, such as JPs, who had some record of co-operation with the government.

The evidence for Westmeath is sparser. We have to bear in mind that, because information about what was happening locally is heavily dependent upon the depositions, our perception is shaped by the geographical distribution of New English settlement. Robbery, so far as we know, did not occur when such settlement was absent, and it was the robberies that produced the refugees who have supplied us with the little information that we possess about local events. New English settlement in Westmeath seems to have been much rarer than in the area around Navan. Nevertheless, eight of the eleven cases of robbery reported for this county occurred in October or early November.[43] This would indicate advance knowledge in the county of the intent to rise. Not one of these early actions seems to have been instigated by a member of the leading gentry of the county, however, though accusations against men with names such as Taite, Nugent, and Expall suggest some Old English involvement.[44] This raises the possibility of some division on social lines. One deponent reported a conversation between some of the gentry of Westmeath and some friars in which the laymen bitterly attacked the clergy for having instigated "this mischievous rebellion," arguing that there had been a high measure of religious freedom before the rebellion and that generally the priests enjoyed the "best horses, meat and drink"; they "therefore most bitterly cursed them to their teeth, saying that they hoped that God would bring that vengeance home to them, that they by their cursed plot laboured so wickedly to bring upon others."[45] Significantly, those reported to have spoken in this way were the JPs of the county, and we have confirmation that the next year one important member of the Old English gentry of this county was still holding out against joining the rebellion. When Antrim made his way north in 1642, he stayed with Sir Thomas Nugent of Dariston "who would admit none to his house but those who were loyal to the king."[46]

Apart from Meath, Louth, and the Ulster counties, English officials had reported rebellion before Julianstown in Tipperary, Wicklow, Wexford, Longford, and Leitrim.[47] The last four of these counties had undergone formal British settlement schemes and many English had gone to live in Tipperary to work the silver mines there.[48] Wicklow's proximity to Dublin gave it a strategic importance, but Leitrim and Longford command more attention because, although outside Ulster, their inhabitants clearly acted in concert with the Irish in the northern province. When the lords justices described the extent of the rebellion on 5 November, these were the only two counties listed apart from those in Ulster.[49] The depositions list twenty-three robberies for Leitrim, all but three occurring during October, and the O'Rourkes, who constituted the principal Irish family in this county, seem to have had close ties with the O'Reillies.[50] Similarly, all sixteen of those who complained of being robbed in Longford indicated that they were first attacked in this month, and, as in Ulster, those who acted against the British claimed to do so on the basis of a commission of the king.[51]

The O'Farrells were the leading family in Longford, and it is this name that turns up in the depositions most often, but the presence of names such as Nugent, Stafford, Pettit, and others of English origin among those accused by the deponents indicates the way in which the Catholics in the county operated in concert. For this county, however, we are not entirely dependent on British sources to determine attitudes among the Irish. On 10 November twenty-six of the O'Farrells, though not including the two leaders of the name, sent a letter to Viscount Dillon of Costello-Galen, governor of County Roscommon and recently appointed to the Irish council after returning from Edinburgh. Both the timing and the content of the letter suggest that the O'Farrells, like the O'Reillies, had some concern to put their case, in view of the failure to take Dublin, and to indicate their terms, should the government wish to negotiate. "We and other papists" were, they asserted, as loyal to the king as any of his other subjects. They then pointed to the exclusion of Catholics from office, the appointment of "strangers and foreigners" to such offices instead of the Old English and "meer Irish" who had "swum in blood" to serve the crown of England in the past. They objected to the anti-recusant legislation passed in Elizabeth's first parliament in Ireland, to the use by officials of "quirks and quiddities of law" to find flaws in their land titles which defeated the king's purpose of confirming their estates, and finally they complained of "the restraint of purchase in the meer Irish of lands in the escheated counties, and the taint and blemish of them and their posterities doth more discontent them than that plantation rule; for they are brought to that exigent of poverty in these late times, that they must be sellers and not buyers of land."[52] Here was a direct reference to the Irish petitions submitted early in the year for equal rights in the purchase and sale of land in the planted areas. This petition, it will be recalled, in contrast to many other grievances, had been left for Leicester to discuss further.[53]

The letter concluded by asking Dillon to intercede for them "and the rest of the papists" to the king. They asked for an act of oblivion and a general pardon "without restitution or account of goods taken in the time of this commotion," liberty of religion, the repeal of all anti-Catholic legislation – all to be confirmed, not by proclamation, but in a "parliamentary way" – and, finally, for a "charter free denizen in ample manner for meer Irish." All of this, they asserted, if granted, "will prove an union in all his Majesties dominions instead of division, a comfort in desolation, and [bring] a happiness in perpetuity" instead of calamity.[54]

This document serves to emphasize the lack of central direction in the Irish operation. The O'Farrells were proposing an act of oblivion without restitution, whereas only a week earlier the O'Reillies had offered to pay compensation for damage done. Both seem to have been concerned about the outcome of the rising once it became evident that one of the key objectives had not been attained, but the reaction to this situation, even in counties that lay next to each other, differed markedly. Moreover, not all the O'Farrells who signed the petition ultimately joined the rebellion. One, indeed, was fighting with the royal forces by December 1641.[55]

The decentralized nature of the Irish organization of the rebellion had provided some distinct advantages. It had permitted a simultaneous attack over a wide geographical area which had achieved almost complete surprise, and it had enabled each county to respond to particular military situations quickly. Furthermore, it had not prevented military co-operation such as that between Maguire and O'Neill and the O'Reillies and the MacMahons. Nevertheless, it meant a lack of political co-ordination, the institutions for which only became available as those in the north linked up with their co-religionists in the south.

THE POPULAR REBELLION

This account of the early weeks of the rebellion has concentrated on the actions of the leaders and the movements of the main bodies of Irish troops. However, events took place at this time that were not controlled by those responsible for starting the rising. There were, in a sense, two rebellions taking place simultaneously: the first led by the most eminent gentry, and the second an essentially popular rebellion, unleashed by the first and to some extent directed by it, but also with its own purpose, momentum, and mode of operation, which was sometimes used by the gentry but was often beyond their control. The lords justices understood that the rebellion was unlike any other that had occurred in the past. This was, they reported at the end of November, "another kind of rebellion, and proceeding from another original [sic] than any former rebellions here" because "the meaner sort of people of the natives rise up unanimously, men women and children, and joining together in multitudes in imitation of the rebels fall on their near neighbours that are English or Protestants and rob and spoil them."[56] Some of the early statements of the Irish leaders also referred to this popular movement. Sir Phelim must have been aware of some excesses of the common people as early as 24 October, when he issued his first proclamation. Otherwise, he would hardly have referred to reparation for hurt done. His brother, as we have seen, described the event near Augher as a "massacre." Similarly, the Cavan Remonstrance, issued early in November, made explicit reference to "the barbarity and uncivility of the commonality."

Historians have recently devoted considerable attention to this aspect of the rebellion. By using the depositions, they have been able to show that some of the "barbarity and uncivility" was motivated by local conditions and stemmed from economic and social pressures.

Nicholas Canny, for instance, has argued that popular Irish responses to the uprising were linked to the stake that each of several groups had in the existing social order. Animosity towards the settlers depended on the extent of contact with English culture before the rebellion; where contact had been close, behaviour was generally restrained. The plans of the leaders went astray because they lacked the resources to maintain discipline and failed to take into account the discontent of some of their subordinates whose contact with the English had been less close than their own. Nevertheless, some of the excesses arose precisely because contact had been all too close, for many Irish had become indebted to English, frequently Protestant, clergymen, who were particularly resented. Those Irish, Canny concludes, who showed "barbaric ferocity" were those "who enjoyed no place in the land settlement," and it was they who wished to "cancel the plantation of Ulster," and such persons had no interest in constitutional politics. This type of analysis must be incorporated into any general description of the rebellion as it supplies the context of many of the specific instances of violence associated with the popular reaction to the rising. Yet such an analysis tends to obscure the changes in attitude that occurred as the situation itself changed, and the information in the depositions must be integrated with other sources. Even if the leaders never intended any general or systematic massacre of the settlers, some of their actions tended to encourage the latent tendencies towards violence at the popular level.[57]

Initially, the Irish seem to have limited their actions against the settlers to pillage. Often this meant that the British were deprived of everything they possessed, including the clothes they wore. Many, particularly in Fermanagh, seem to have fled towards British-held centres at once, but as some of them were virtually naked and the weather was bitterly cold, numbers of them died of exposure.[58] Again in Fermanagh, some settlers seem to have been killed almost immediately and Donogh Maguire, Lord Maguire's uncle, was identified as being particularly harsh.[59] However, elsewhere it would appear that little deliberate murder took place for the first few days. The Cavan Remonstrance suggests that killing had begun by early November, and one of the deponents remarked that it was only after the first two weeks that such incidents began to occur.[60] By this time a large number of settlers in the counties initially involved had already been robbed, and frustration had begun to build up among those who sought their property when no more was to be had. One deponent reported being tortured to extract information from him about the location of money, and there are other instances where brutality seems to have been associated with robbery. In another case, some Irish in Cavan, who were supposed to be escorting a group of British who had already been robbed, were alleged to have turned on their charges and, when additional payment for protection was not made, killed some of the refugees.[61]

If some settlers were forced to flee, others were compelled to remain in Irish-held territory, where they too felt the effects of Irish hostility. In many instances where British people were persecuted while under Irish jurisdiction, the incidents appear to have been personal and sometimes related to the war. There were, for instance, a few (remarkably few it has been observed) reports of rape or attempted rape; one Scottish woman was accused of being a witch; another was stoned to death as she was suspected of having taken messages to the British forces; and a blacksmith had his hands cut off and face mutilated as he was thought to have made pike-heads for the British.[62] Other incidents were on a different scale, such as those at Augher, Portadown, and Belturbet, when approximately 100 or more British were killed at once.[63] Two such large-scale killings occurred during the early months of the rising, and it is striking that both took place after an Irish military setback. The massacre near Augher followed a failure to take the town, and another incident in which men women and children were deliberately burned to death in a house in which they were confined was associated with one of the Irish failures at Lisburn. Similarly, during the following year, mass killing in Armagh seems to have been a reaction to the British recovery of Newry.[64]

The precise extent of the Irish leadership's involvement in such incidents is not easy to determine. In so far as they were in power when atrocities occurred they were involved, but it was extremely difficult to maintain order in the seventeenth century during periods of unstable government. Lapses into "barbarism and cruelty" when men were "released from the restraints of protected society" were not confined to Ireland. The horrors of the Thirty Years' War are notorious, but in England, too, the parties to the civil war accused each other of massacres, plundering, and other atrocities. In England, however, a conscious attempt was made by the leadership on both sides to follow a code of conduct that would keep the consequences of popular passions to a minimum.[65]

The evidence on the degree to which the Irish leadership did the same is mixed. In some instances they were directly responsible for inhuman conditions. Some British, for instance, complained of having been confined in a room in such close quarters that they could not lie down. Conditions of this nature must have had some official sanction.[66] There are also many instances in the depositions where Irish leaders were accused either of doing nothing to stop the popular violence or of giving orders that certain British should be killed. When Owen Roe O'Neill arrived in 1642, he was shocked at the behaviour of both sides and managed to stop the killing of British persons where he was in command, an achievement remarked by more than one deponent.[67] A code, therefore, could be imposed, but was clearly not in place before Owen Roe arrived. At the same time, we have the testimony of an Irish deponent that, at the start of the rebellion, he found Sir Phelim vainly trying to stop the plundering of the British settlers. He also executed some Irish for killing English settlers, and British deponents remarked from time to time that they were saved by the intervention of Irish leaders.[68] Moreover, it is evident that neither Turlough O'Neill nor the O'Reillies liked what was happening. Irish leaders like Sir Phelim seldom had much military experience, and the command structure (in so far as there was one) depended on kinship links. This often gave local men an opportunity to pursue their own ends without reference to those responsible for starting the rising. We may note that the British commanders found it just as difficult to restrain their forces from atrocity. "Such," remarked an officer serving with the British forces, "was the fury of both Scots and Irish for blood and revenge, that they thought it a service to God, to destroy one another," and discipline on the British side was only established when the Scottish army arrived in Ulster in the spring of 1642. The professional soldiers behaved much better than the irregulars.[69]

Nevertheless, one action taken by the Irish gentry leaders substantially contributed to the maltreatment of non-combatant British. This was the proclamation issued by Sir Phelim O'Neill and Rory Maguire early in November in which they cited the forged commission. The intent was to maintain a following when the failure to take Dublin created the prospect of a long-term struggle. Yet the proclamation also declared the king's approval of the seizure of English Protestant property and persons. Even if we discount an English claim that the Catholic bishop of Raphoe, after capture, pointed to the proclamation as the explanation of the popular violence, the abundant references to Irish assertions that they had the king's permission for what they did leave no doubt about the influence of such statements in encouraging actions against the settlers.[70]

It was, of course, one thing to issue a proclamation and quite another to have its contents disseminated widely within the population, and here we come to another level of leadership: the clergy. As in most early modern rebellions, not excluding that of the Scottish Covenanters, the clergy served as communicators at the various levels within such movements. The Old English gentry who opposed the rising in Westmeath held the clergy responsible, and there can be no doubt of their role as animators of the rebellion. One Irish source declared that before Julianstown the Irish troops were addressed by their clergy in the following terms: "Dear sons of St Patrick strike hard the enemies of the holy faith."[71] More striking still is an undated letter, but one almost certainly written after 1641, to Luke Wadding, which declared: "There is not an army or a regiment, not a province or a county, not an angle of land, not a camp or a meeting, not a single expedition or a battle, that the friars are not in the midst of it ... Such zeal for the promotion of the Catholic cause do I find in my subject friars that they need reins rather than the spur."[72] Such Irish sources reinforce the evidence in the depositions about the role of priests as promoters of the popular rebellion.

When we look at the deponents' comments about priests, however, some ambivalence again emerges. Many priests were reported to have encouraged the ferocity of the populace against the settlers, yet some were depicted as a moderating influence. Priests promised their compatriots help from France and Spain after military setbacks; in Monaghan three priests were accused of instigating murder; another priest told a deponent that it was "no sin to kill all the Protestants for they were all damned already"; friars, it was reported, preached that "it was as lawful to kill Englishmen as a dog"; and in another case a friar was said to have told the people that all who died for the cause should become saints.[73] These and many other such comments may be placed beside fewer reports of priests intervening to protect settlers. Priests, let it be said, were not alone among the Irish in helping the British. On numerous occasions the deponents reported the assistance they had received from Irish who, by supplying it, often ran considerable risk themselves, even of excommunication.[74]

This is not to say that the gentry or priests by themselves created the animosity towards the newcomers. The link between Irish indebtedness to the settlers and robbery has already been mentioned. It is also evident that the British frequently possessed more material goods than their Irish neighbours and this distinction led to demands for cash as well as the seizure of items such as clothing.[75] Nevertheless, such motivation, widespread though it may have been, does not adequately explain the deep and abiding hatred that is evident from British reports of what was said to them by the ordinary people. The Irish, as one deponent put it, cursed "the time that any of the English protestants either came upon their land or into the kingdom."[76] Or, as another remarked, he had often heard the Irish say that they would not leave any Englishman or Scot alive in the kingdom save some artificers "who would be kept as slaves," and a similar sentiment lay behind the remark that "we have been your slaves all this time now you shall be ours."[77]

The Protestant clergy were particularly resented. Some of this feeling may, indeed, have arisen because of their moneylending function, but they provided a similar service in England, as Ralph Josselin's diary tells us, without arousing similar animosity. Tithes, however, aroused much complaint in England, and it is not surprising to find such attitudes replicated in Ireland, particularly because they supported a rival faith. As the matter was once put, Owen Roe would come, who "would thrust out the black devils and then tithes should be their own."[78] It must also be observed that Irish hostility was not confined to the New English. The Old English in the Pale were described as "stinking English churls with great breaches [sic]," and even after the Pale had joined the rebellion, it was common to hear the Irish say that the "Old English of the Pale though they joined with them ... deserved to be hanged as well as the other English."[79] It is observable, wrote the lords justices to Sir Henry Vane, "the most inveterate and virulent hatred they bear to the English nation."[80]

One manifestation of this hatred was the reported behaviour of the Irish women. In at least seven different counties it was remarked that the women took a strong role in hurting the British (in Kilkenny a jury which imposed punishment on settlers was made up completely of women).[81] Sometimes this seems to have occurred in the absence of Irish male leaders. Thus the wife of Rory MacMahon went before an English woman who was to be executed for communicating with the enemy "with a white rod in her hand and a skene by her side saying she would be sheriff for that turn: and so stood by, till the poor woman was hanged accordingly."[82] In another instance, an Irish child was observed to batter an English child to death.[83]

But the deep-seated nature of the resentment at English intrusion was revealed in its most bizarre form in the deliberate defacement of English buildings and the slaughter of English cattle. The lords justices reported on this phenomenon, and in the Mayo depositions, not only was it recorded that the "the name of English was so hateful to the Irish that they would not only kill all they met with ... but would kill all the English breed of cattle," but in one instance, they had the animals tried by a jury.[84] This last story could be used to illustrate the lengths to which the English would go to discredit the Irish and make them appear absurd, were it not that such trials of animals have been documented in many parts of Europe from the Middle Ages to the nineteenth century. The references in the depositions to these procedures are too brief to allow for much commentary, but two points may be made. First, it has been remarked that such trials may illustrate the "interaction of various legal levels and cultural influences." The reference here to the jury reveals the penetration at the popular level of Irish society of an English institution which is being used to deal with a social problem – in this case the presence of the English. It is, therefore, a manifestation of the process that was taking place as one culture came into contact with the other, however deep the cleavage between the two may have been. Second, when animals were tried, it was usually because a specific animal had committed a crime, such as killing a person, or because of the "harmful character of the animals in question" such as locusts. Ecclesiastical trials of animals, and subsequent exorcism, were justified on the grounds that the devil used animals to cause harm. However, in this case, so far as we know, it was not the animals that were perceived as doing harm but their owners. Thus, this appears to be a unique case of an attempt to exorcise the agents of the devil, not directly but by the use of the animals as symbols of the diabolical presence. This in itself is a measure of the strength of Irish popular hatred of the English.[85]

THE EVOLUTION OF THE AIMS OF THE REBELLION

The decentralized command structure and the differing treatment of settlers – some being expelled, some being killed, and still others being retained and protected – have a bearing on any interpretation of Irish objectives. The very confusion is a warning against the expectation of a neatly packaged, unified, and unchanging strategy. Robert Maxwell observed that Irish war aims changed according to their military success, and Nicholas Canny has warned against assuming non-existent constitutional ambitions.[86] Nevertheless, the Irish had goals that may be classified under the separate headings of the immediate, the pragmatic, and the long term, though the three were inter-related.

The immediate Irish goals were derived from the conditions that preceded the war. We have seen how the Scots and the English parliament during the previous spring and summer had aroused deep-seated fears in Irish minds that a campaign was about to begin to persecute and even "extirpate" them. Their very awareness of Scottish and Puritan rhetoric was a reflection of the way in which the élites of the two major islands of the archipelago had come closer together culturally, but this nearness bred friction not mutual understanding. Sir John Temple reported in December 1642 that the

Jesuits and other priests had spread the story before the rebellion that all the Catholics in Ireland were about to be massacred. To Temple this allegation appeared a deliberate act of deceit, but the Jesuits seem to have been convinced of this impending massacre as we find a Jesuit in January 1642 explaining the outbreak of the rebellion to compatriots abroad, a context in which there was little need to deceive, in terms of a pre-emptive strike to forestall this English plot. It is not strange, therefore, to find the same Irish motive surfacing in the depositions. As one Cavan deponent was told, it was the English parliament which had caused all the trouble because it had planned to imprison all Irish Catholic MPs when the Irish parliament next met "and the Protestants were to murder all the papists throughout the kingdom," which caused the Irish to strike first. Thus we may say that the most primary aim of the Irish was to prevent this Scottish-Puritan plot, which, if imaginary, was the harvest of the anti-Catholic rhetoric of the Scots and Sir John Clotworthy and others in England earlier in the year.[87]

In view of these fears, it is not surprising to find a similar motivation in the official pronouncements of the Irish leaders. From the first public declaration by Sir Phelim O'Neill to the dispatch of the O'Farrells' letter to Viscount Dillon, the Irish leadership consistently stressed religious liberty as the motive for their actions, and the reference in the Cavan Remonstrance to the "fear in the proceedings of our neighbour nations" indicates the way in which the demand for toleration was tied to the fear of an assault upon Catholicism. As the *Aphorismical Discovery* remarked, religion was the primary motive of the Irish.[88]

There can be little doubt that the Irish rising weakened Charles's position in England and therefore served to advance the cause that the Irish most feared, but from their perspective this irony was not to be perceived because it was apparent that the Scots had achieved toleration for their religion by force of arms. This brings us to another feature of Irish planning which emerges out of the depositions although it is absent from the early public statements of the Irish, namely, the extent that the Scottish Covenanting movement served as a model for Irish resistance. A clear expression of this link emerges from the deposition of a Peter Mainsell of Limerick, which purported to describe the conversation of a former mayor of Limerick, Domnick Fanning. According to Mainsell, who was a wealthy citizen, he had heard Fanning say words to the effect "that the Scots ... have mightily abused his majesty and that they in this kingdom would see him righted," for as the Scots "took up arms for the maintenance of their religion or rather the profanation [of one] so we have done for the main because of ours being the true religion."[89] In the north, Creighton, the Scottish minister, was assured by Colonel Plunkett that the Scots had taught them their "ABC," and similar statements can be found elsewhere in the depositions. This, of course, was a major misperception of the political relationships among the three kingdoms – the Scots could call upon some popular feeling in England – yet it is understandable why the Irish thought they could replicate the Scottish model.

The concern about religion and the interest in the Scottish example suggests that the Irish intended to negotiate from strength, as the Scots had done after their occupation of Newcastle, and to insist upon at least the toleration of Catholicism or possibly its establishment as the official religion in Ireland. Yet the presence of the British settlers living among them faced the Irish leaders with a unique problem which cannot be compared with the episcopalian presence among the Covenanters. The Irish statements about, and the early treatment of, the Scots in Ulster suggest that the Irish had given some thought to this issue before the rising began. Indeed, initially some Irish leaders may not have intended to disturb either English or Scottish settlers below the level of those who commanded places of strength. This would explain the tenor of the proclamation issued by Sir Phelim from Dungannon on 24 October, in which he assured the English as well as the Scots that they would come to no harm and be recompensed for damage done.

The same sentiment is to be found in the letter from four O'Neills (excluding Sir Phelim) to Sir William Stewart. The "true meaning" of their actions, they assured the Scot, was "not to hurt any of his majesty's subjects either of the English or the Scottish nation either in body or goods." What they did intend to do was "speedily to show their grievances by their humble petition to his majesty." In the meantime, they would hold the forts and strong places of the English. This impression of the intentions of some of the conspirators is reinforced by Creighton's description of Colonel Plunkett's reaction to the miserable spectacle of the British refugees, many of whom came from Fermanagh, as they passed the Scottish minister's door in Virginia. According to Creighton, Plunkett:

wept and said Rory Maguire had undone them all: their plot was not to kill or rob any man, but to seize upon the persons and estate [sic] of the British, and when they had all in their hands then to present their petition to the House of Commons in England, if their petition were granted, then to restore every man as he was, if their petition were not granted, then to do as seemed good unto them.[90]

Similarly, the O'Reillies' denial of responsibility for the treatment the British were receiving points in the same direction.

Yet another source of information on Irish war aims is a report of a meeting that took place at Multyfarnham, a Franciscan abbey in Westmeath, attended by both lay and clerical leaders of the Irish early in October. Our knowledge of what was said here comes to us second hand, through Dean Henry Jones. Although Jones was hostile to the Irish cause, there is confirmation that such a meeting did take place, and Jones's account of what he was told can be compared with what happened.[91]

The treatment of the settlers posed a major problem because, as Protestants, they did not fit into the picture of a Catholic Ireland. Yet, as hostages while negotiations took place to create such a state, they afforded a substantial bargaining chip. Their numbers, moreover, posed a moral dilemma as it was difficult to know what to do with them. What Jones claimed to have been told about the discussion at Multyfarnham was that there were three positions taken with regard to the settlers. There were those who wished to kill them, those who wished to expel them as the Spaniards had expelled the Moors, and those who wanted "neither to dismiss nor kill."[92] In short, there was considerable disagreement among the leaders of the rising about how to deal with this major problem. Jones remarked that, to judge by events, all three options were followed at once. Certainly, as a consequence of the decentralized nature of the Irish organization, considerable variation in policy ensued, and it is evident that, from the start, the Maguires adopted a harsher attitude towards the English than the O'Neills – hence Plunkett's comment about Rory Maguire.

The unexpected survival of the Dublin government meant that the harsher policies towards the settlers favoured by the Maguires were more attractive to the O'Neills than when they considered the next step was to open negotiations with the king, and this change in direction is reflected in the O'Neill-Maguire proclamation of 4 November. The harsh policies became a means to persuade large numbers of men to serve during what was likely to become a long campaign in opposition to the English power in Ireland. Concessions had to made to popular feeling if there was to be popular support for the necessary military measures. As Sir Phelim seems to have encountered difficulty in restraining the common people even when he wished to protect all the settlers, it is not surprising that an official policy of plundering the English, but not the Scots, degenerated into indiscriminate plundering and such incidents as that at Augher.

If the sources have to be examined minutely to determine the immediate aims of the Irish and their approach towards the practical problems presented by the settlers, the determination of their long-term objectives presents an even greater challenge. Once the Pale became officially involved in the movement, we have a number of statements about Irish objectives, but at this early stage of the rebellion, information is sparse, particularly on what the private intentions of the Irish leaders were, as opposed to the aims that they broadcast to their followers. Nevertheless, it is evident that, if the immediate and primary aim of the rebellion was the security of Catholicism in Ireland, a change in the arrangements for the government of Ireland would have to follow. New English dominance on the council, for instance, which was so firmly wedded to the extension of both Protestantism and plantation, would have to be modified. Nor would it be possible to accept any English legislative control over Ireland. We may recollect that Charles had already agreed, in the face of sustained opposition from men like Parsons and Loftus, to end plantation, and the appointment of Viscount Dillon to the council, Protestant though he was, indicated a willingness to accommodate Old English interests. In these circumstances, it is not inconceivable that Charles, unhampered by the English parliament, could have reached an agreement with the majority of his Irish subjects if their terms had been moderate. He could, for instance, have given legal definition to the pluralistic society that Ireland had become. He had, after all, reached an agreement with his Scottish subjects whose religion was probably less palatable to him personally than that followed by his Irish subjects.

There is a hint in a Catholic – if not an Irish – source that the Irish leaders were, in fact, initially prepared to accept moderate terms, but that the popular dimension of the rebellion pushed the demands to a point that Charles could not consider them. The papal informant in London admitted in November that he was puzzled by what he found to be the contradictory messages coming out of Ireland. It was unclear, the papacy was told, whether the Irish hoped simply to remedy past abuses, or whether they intended to establish a state entirely separate from England. On the one hand, the agent reported, the Irish had written letters to the king in Scotland full of respect and with assurances that it was their intention to live and die as Charles's faithful vassals. On the other hand, it appeared that the conditions that were carried, as he put it, on the ends of the Irish swords and pikes were very high – "assai alte." These insisted, first, that Ireland should cease to be considered a conquered nation and that its crown should be accepted as independent from the crown of England; second, that the laws of Ireland should be revised in accordance with the wishes of those in arms; and, third, that there should be free exercise of the Catholic religion.[93] These terms closely resembled those reported by the lords justices on 5 November, although they included the additional demand for the restoration of the planted lands to the descendants of the original owners.[94]

We have one further source on the initial demands; Jones's account of the Multyfarnham meeting. His informant, he related, told him that the Irish intended to maintain their recognition of Charles as their king, but that his revenue and "government must be reduced to certain bounds." Crown rent was to be reduced to pre-plantation levels and customs revenue, though still to be levied, established as "thought fitting." The executive was to consist of two lords justices, one of Irish origin and the other of "ancient British" descent, but both would have to be Roman Catholics. Parliament was to sit, but MPS were to be limited to those the Irish "shall think fit to be admitted." Poynings's Act was to be repealed, as were all acts against Catholicism, which was to become the only religion practised. Ireland was to be declared a kingdom independent of England; the Irish peerage was to be purged of those with recently created titles and of Protestants; plantation lands were to be restored to the descendants of those who had originally held them; and a standing army and navy were to be created, the latter to be financed by revenue from certain abbey lands. Finally, Jones reported that it was proposed that an army from Ireland was to cross into England, and thence into Scotland, and ultimately this force would help Spain against Holland "giving their rebellion (as they term it) its due correction."[95]

These proposals may have been embellished in the telling; but there is nothing inherently incredible in them. They were in line with a plan drawn up the following year for a "National Confederation in Ireland" which included the concept that Ireland should have "all which Scotland hath, and commonly all kingdoms subject to any monarch."[96] It was no more unreasonable to demand a political monopoly for Catholicism than for the Covenant. Yet such terms clearly belong within the category of extreme demands, in that Charles's position in England would have been threatened had he accepted them and he would have had to accept the dissolution of the Church of Ireland.

We, therefore, like the papal informant, are faced with two sets of signals: one from the *Aphorismical Discovery*, from the initial and moderate statements of the O'Neills, from Plunkett's statement to Creighton about Maguire, and from the information that private assurances of loyalty had been sent to Charles, and a second set from the slogans attached to the pikes, the information reaching the lords justices, and Jones's report on Multyfarnham. One explanation of this inconsistency is that the Irish leadership was itself divided and subscribed to differing aims. This seems to be borne out by the division of opinion about how to deal with the settlers. We must remember that, even according to Jones's account, the Multyfarnham meeting resembled more a debate than an assembly which laid down policy. Another explanation, and one that complements rather than refutes the first, is that there were initially some moderate long-term aims which it was thought could be obtained, as the Scots had obtained theirs, through negotiation. As with the policy for dealing with the settlers, the failure to secure Dublin forced the moderate leaders to adjust their long-term aims to satisfy a populace that was going to have to support an extended military campaign. These adjusted aims veered heavily towards the extreme. Irish war aims turn up in this form in the depositions because the deponents would have heard only those demands that were part of the process of developing popular support. Once again, the leadership seems to have been swept along by their followers. The English in Ireland and in England, for their part, heard about the aims of the rebellion first from Owen O'Connolly, and his version was alarming, and thereafter in the form of public aims that were designed to deal with the situation which had emerged after the Irish had learned of their failure to secure Dublin. Such demands only confirmed attitudes which the authorities already held and created a counter-extremism. It is to these British authorities that we must now turn to trace their reaction to the rebellion.

CHAPTER ELEVEN

Reaction to the Rising in Ireland

On 11 October Sir William Cole had written to the lords justices from Enniskillen to warn them of unusual activity and meetings among the Irish leaders in Ulster, "tending to no good ends," and of levies, ostensibly for Spanish service, by men who held no commissions.[1] The lords justices failed to take precautions in response to this warning and only understood its import when Owen O'Connolly revealed the plot to them on the evening of 22 October, by which time the rising had already begun in Ulster. Another consequence of the way in which the English authorities learned of the rising was that their first impression of Irish intentions came not from any statement of the Irish but from O'Connolly's account of a plan to "cut off" all Protestants, an account rendered more credible by the stories of what was happening in the north. It was at this early stage of the rising that the myth of the intended massacre was born.[2] In response, on 23 October, Sir William Parsons and Sir John Borlase issued a proclamation blaming the rising on "some evil affected Irish papists." The proclamation gave considerable offence to loyal Catholics, and after the lords of the Pale sent a deputation of four, including Viscount Gormanston, to dissociate themselves from the conspiracy and protest their loyalty, a disclaimer was issued to correct the impression created by the original wording.[3] Nevertheless, although the attitude of the Pale was recorded when the council sent its first report to England on the twenty-fifth, it was O'Connolly's words that were used in describing the aims of the Irish to the English authorities, and we cannot doubt that this first report sank deep into the English psyche.[4]

The lords justices and the council quickly arranged for the defence of Dublin. The earl of Ormond, who was at his home in Tipperary, was asked to return to the capital with his troop of horse to take command of the army, and this decision coincided with the king's who sent a commission to the same end on 31 October. The old army now consisted of no more than 2,297 foot and about 1,000 horse, and these were scattered about the country in garrisons.[5] Units from the country were summoned to assist in the defence of the capital, which, as Sir William St Leger, the lord president of Munster, complained, had the effect of making it more difficult for commanders in the provinces to maintain control over their districts. To these regular forces were added recruits from among the refugees who were beginning to enter the city.[6]

While these defensive measures were being taken, the Dublin government and some of the Old English leaders were developing separate and opposite perceptions of events, each equally wrong but equally understandable given the circumstances in which they were formed. The Irish council in its dispatches to England repeated the reports of British refugees about Irish cruelty, and as early as 5 November relayed Irish war aims as they were hearing of them, which was in their extreme populist form, including the intent to "extirpate the English and Protestants" and recover planted land. They depicted the rebellion as a vindication of their position of the summer when they had opposed the concessions being made on the issue of plantation, looked forward to the day when plantation would be resumed, and warned that forces would have to be sent quickly from England if a costly re-conquest of the kingdom was to be avoided.[7]

On the Old English side, some interpreted the misguided initial proclamation as a sign that "an army of Scottish reformers" was about to impose Protestantism by force.[8] As we shall see, it had occurred immediately to some in Britain, including Charles, that the Scottish soldiers should be sent to Ireland to deal with the crisis, but it was not till late November that the idea was discussed in Dublin. Parsons, like many of the New English, distrusted the Scots only a shade less than the Irish. The next year, after Scottish troops had landed in Ulster, he declared to the earl of Cork that "I desire this war should be totally carried by the English without mixing any fresh helpers."[9]

The concrete manifestation of the Old English perception was the conjuncture between elements in the Pale and the Ulstermen. We have seen that robberies of New English occurred in the counties bordering Ulster almost simultaneously with the outbreak of the rising, and many of the gentry of Louth had joined Colonel Brian MacMahon of Monaghan in an organized way by early November. Even where there was no formal commitment, Pale attitudes were ambivalent. Attempts have been made to blame the ultimate defection of the Pale on the failure of Dublin to distribute arms for

defence, but the evidence does not support that accusation.[10] Some
1,700 arms were initially distributed to the gentry in the Pale, and
over 700 of these were still in their keeping when they made a formal
alliance with the Irish of Ulster early in December. It was also
reported that when MacMahon entered Louth he found arms in the
houses of the gentry, but there was no attempt to use them against
him. The Louth gentry quickly formed a military organization once
they had decided to join the Irish, and, finally, in statements made
by Louth gentry in 1642 describing the link with the Irish, there is
no mention that it was forged out of fear or threat.[11]

We may conclude that by the time parliament reconvened in mid-
November, a substantial number of Pale gentry, particularly those
with close ties to Ulster and in the middle and lower social ranks,
had already committed themselves the cause of the Ulstermen. The
leading men held back. Neither Lord Louth nor Sir Christopher
Bellew accepted the offer to become the military commander in
Louth, but even they acted more as neutrals than as opponents of
the insurgency. The "greater lords," remarked Hugh Bourke, the
commissary of Irish friars minors in Germany and Belgium, began
"the fighting by their cousins or brothers, who have little to lose if
the main enterprise should miscarry."[12] This same push from the
middle rank of Irish society was observed a little later by the Catholic
but pro-government earl of Clanricard. "The disturbance grows," he
reported, "from turbulent people of the middle rank, encouraged
and set on by ambition of some I fear to name."[13] Those he would
not name included bishops and clergy. The "greater lords," even had
they wished, would have had difficulty in resisting this alliance
between the middling gentry and the Catholic hierarchy. There
remained but one avenue of escape – parliament, but communication
between the Protestants who controlled the council and the Catholic
nobility, never good, had now virtually ceased, and the sixth session of parliament became not an avenue to peace but a highway to
war.

THE SIXTH SESSION

As has already been related, part of the English council, under
pressure from Irish officials, had advised the king to postpone the
meeting of the sixth session till early in 1642 to give time for a
resolution of the constitutional questions surrounding Poynings's law
and the Queries. By 15 October, Charles had accepted this advice,
but his instructions giving it effect did not reach Ireland till a month
later.[14] On the outbreak of the rebellion, Parsons and Borlase, on

their own initiative, postponed the session till the following February on the grounds that a gathering of men in the capital could jeopardize security. The postponement angered the Old English as it reflected a distrust of them and further delayed the legislation confirming the Graces. Moreover, it was argued, with support from some of the council and all the judges, that a session could not legally be prorogued until it had met. The Commons, therefore, met briefly on 9 November, but as the house was "but thin" adjourned till the sixteenth, the very day that the king's instructions for a postponement of the session arrived.[15]

The broad outlines of the sixth parliamentary session of two days are well known, though some of the details are obscure. There were two primary issues: first, the question of how long the session was to be allowed to continue, which despite the pre-session discussion remained a matter of contention; and, second, the question of the response that parliament should make to the rebellion. There was one division in the Commons in which about seventy MPs voted. We have the names of thirty-five of these participants, eighteen Catholics (ten from the Pale) and seventeen Protestants. The Catholics almost certainly commanded a small majority in the house. Many of the Protestant MPs came from Ulster and could not attend because they were either captives or engaged in the fighting. This must have affected Protestant numbers, and we find two of the three committees formed during this brief session had Catholic majorities. It appears, however, that a few of the Catholics, led by Patrick Darcy, sided with the Protestants.

The session began inauspiciously as the lords justices had required the MPs to walk between files of armed soldiers to enter the chamber, and this none-too-subtle threat added to the atmosphere of distrust.[16] Darcy tried to guide the house to a consideration of "our common calamity," but this did not prevent an altercation over the prorogation. John Taylor, the MP for Swords, argued that the house could not conduct business because the threat of prorogation had kept some MPs away. This elicited a response from Captain William Cadogan, fresh from his experience in Meath, to the effect that many who had not come were traitors "and whether they come or not is not material." Thomas Bourke, while also protesting the prorogation, nevertheless urged the house to issue a statement about the rebellion in order to answer "divers calumnies" that had spread in England. But when the house moved into committee, with Taylor in the chair, it began to consider only the "safety of our lives," the preservation "of our estates," and loyalty to the king. In short, there was no inclination to condemn the rebellion.[17]

Pressure was maintained in both houses to extend the session. The lower house even set up a committee to draw up a protestation against the prorogation, but at the same time a statement was drafted concerning the Ulster situation which avoided referring to it as a rebellion. Even John Bysse, the constitutionalist Protestant, thought that the draft implied that "we do connive at their wicked actions," and the Lords insisted on stronger wording.[18] The lords justices allowed the session to continue into the next day, whereupon a revised Protestation and Declaration concerning the rebellion was drawn up and approved by both houses. This was a compromise, using the term "sundry persons ill affected to the peace" instead of "rebels" but the words "traitorously and rebelliously" in describing the actions of such persons.[19]

Even after this compromise, the Protestation and Declaration still aroused much dispute because it led to one of the rare formal divisions in the Commons. The question put was whether it "should be entered." What this means is not clear. As the document had already been approved by both houses, the vote cannot have been about its acceptance. It seems instead to have been about the inclusion of the Protestation and Declaration as part of the process of negotiating with the Irish because the vote was taken just after the selection of a committee for this purpose. In any case, the vote went against "entering" the document, twenty-eight voting for it, with two Old English serving as tellers for the yeas, and forty voting against it, with Sir Paul Davies and Patrick Darcy serving as tellers for the nays.[20] If I am correct in assuming a Catholic majority in the house, Darcy must have drawn some Catholics with him. This is entirely possible in that he and two other Old English MPs had written to Clanricard in October indicating their detestation of the rebellion.[21]

The committee with which this vote seems to have been associated and which was authorized to negotiate with the Irish consisted of nine lords, including the earls of Antrim and Fingall and Viscount Gormanston, and eighteen MPs, the large majority of whom were Catholic.[22] This committee sent a letter to the Irish, who "finding their own strength, and our [English] succours not come," tore it in pieces and rejected the offer of negotiations.[23] At the same time, the Catholic lords in parliament sent Viscount Dillon on a secret mission to Charles in Scotland to offer to suppress the rebellion on their own without assistance from England. This action, when the lords justices heard of it, only served to increase their distrust, which now extended to some members of their own council.[24]

When the lords justices reported the events of parliament to the lord lieutenant — and their messenger was none other than Sir

William Parsons's son – they depicted the debate as between the "popish" party working hard to avoid having the Irish called rebels "under pretence of danger to themselves and their estates" and the "Protestant party."[25] Yet the evidence in the depositions on the situation in the counties, as well as the parliamentary record itself, points to a division among the Catholics. There were those like John Bellew who were sympathetic to the Irish cause and looked to parliament to redress grievances and bring peace. When it was obvious that parliament would not be allowed to deal with the issues, they quickly adopted the Irish cause as their own. A minority, however, led in the Commons by Patrick Darcy but including the lords of the Pale, saw the primary objective to be the prevention of English or, worse still, Scottish, military intervention. Their position was to negotiate a peace with the Irish before forces arrived from Britain or, failing that, to obtain permission and the necessary resources to defeat the Irish themselves, again with the intent of keeping external intervention to a minimum.

Events, however, moved too quickly. By early December Julianstown had demonstrated English weakness in Ireland, and a successful expedition by Sir Charles Coote against the Irish in Wicklow revealed a ruthlessness which boded ill for recognition of Catholic interests in any settlement dictated by the Dublin government, which was perceived to be in alliance with the parliamentary Puritans in England. It became imperative to strike down that government before it could be assisted. Julianstown suggested that this was possible, but only if the Old English joined as a body with the Irish and did so without delay. Twice the lords of the Pale met with Rory O'More, the most skilful politician among the Irish leaders, who stressed the extent to which Catholics had been excluded from office over the past decades and the loyalty of the Irish to the king.[26] Reassured on this last point at a meeting held on the hill of Crofty, by 7 December the lords of the Pale had agreed to join with the Irish and those Old English who had already taken up arms, and by 12 December Darcy had intimated to Clanricard that he too would go into opposition.[27]

The division among the Old English was mirrored on the Irish council though the nature of the division is less easy to describe. The lords justices, Sir Adam Loftus, Sir John Temple, Lord Lambert, James Ware, and Robert Meredith, most of them former enemies of Wentworth, wrote to the earl of Leicester privately on 26 November. They complained that they could not trust some other members of the council and referred in particular to the difficulty of persuading parliament to issue a condemnation of the rebellion.[28] This supports Thomas Carte's contention that there was a moderate group in the council that wanted to keep parliament in session. Just who belonged to this group is open to question, but is certain that its most important member was Ormond.[29] It becomes important, therefore, to trace as far as possible his reaction to events.

Before Ormond returned to Dublin, he had begun to organize the gentry in his own county of Kilkenny, where 240 foot and 50 horse were raised.[30] It is likely, therefore, that when parliament met he considered that the Old English, if offered sufficient incentive, would resist the rebellion. The other faction in the council was not averse to drawing on the Old English for support, but as they explained in their secret letter to Leicester, they wished to await the formation of a strong army before doing so.[31] Ormond wanted to move more quickly, without waiting for an army to arrive from England. He was not unaware of the difficulties. He had begun to hear of the disaffection of Louth as early as 16 November, and in his letter to the king in which he reported the division among government leaders, he remarked: "I fear this infection is too general and that religion has engaged many that do not yet appear so that it is hard to say who are enemies [and] who are friends." Yet he was convinced that some of those who fought against the king "aim not at shaking your majesty's government."[32]

Ormond's entanglement "in many intrigues and distractions" continued into December, when he still hoped for some Old English cooperation. Even as he was having to confirm to the king that his fears about the general Catholic disaffection had been justified, he was writing to St Leger of the impossibility of doing any service "without a party of the natives." St Leger, who had nothing but contempt for the lords justices and the timid way they had responded to the military situation, agreed with him. At the same time he considered that the only way to ensure the good faith of such a party would be to procure hostages, but by now Connacht and Munster were being sucked into the storm. Such was the distrust that had grown up on both sides that Ormond's moderate policy had no hope of success.[33] As Ormond himself told the king, to many the issue was becoming one of "no Protestant or no papist."[34] There was no middle ground.

CONNACHT

Of the five counties in Connacht, Leitrim, under the leadership of the O'Rourkes, had risen almost simultaneously with the Ulster. Most of the depositions for that county that specify a date when the rising began give 24 or 25 October. Sir Charles Coote's iron works, for instance, was pillaged on the twenty-fourth, and the eighty or so workers fled to Jamestown, on the border with Roscommon.[35] At the other extreme, Galway remained relatively quiet into 1642 because of the influence of Clanricard. The earl had recently arrived from England to take up residence at his castle at Portumna, and it was here that he heard the first rumours of the rising on the twenty-sixth and confirmation from Coote, vice-president of the province, three days later.[36] By chance, just before he heard the news of the rising, information came in of the progress of the two regiments raised for Spanish service by Theobald Taafe and Sir James Dillon as they marched though the county to board the ships waiting for them at Galway. The earl, who had few forces to spare in any case, had therefore to explain to Coote that he could send no assistance "especially at this time when troops are to pass through."[37]

Elsewhere, preparations for the rising often took place under cover of the recruitment of men for Spanish service. Yet in this case there seems to have been nothing sinister about the presence of Taafe and Dillon with their regiments. If Charles's initial plan for disposing of them had not been thwarted by the English parliament, they would have been out of Ireland when the rising began. Clanricard did what he could to get them on board ship, only to face opposition from the customs authorities in Galway, who refused to allow them to embark.[38] It is not certain what happened to these regiments, but from a remark made by the earl in December to Leicester, it would appear that they ultimately joined the rebellion because there was nothing else for them to do.[39] Quite apart from these two regiments, several men in Connacht who had served as officers in Strafford's new army provided military leadership to the insurgent forces.[40] Once again, therefore, we see the way the Scottish crisis, and the way that both Charles and his opponents in England reacted to it, served to enhance the possibilities for a successful rebellion in Ireland.

It might have been expected that Leitrim's southern neighbour, Sligo, would be the next county to rise, but if we are guided by the depositions, it was in Mayo that English authority declined most rapidly, although this occurred with the participation of some Sligo men. That degeneration, however, seems to have been gradual and the result of popular action with clerical rather than gentry leadership. The economic conditions in this county seem to have been particularly bad. Mayo, it was said, "abounds with many loose desperate men," and the actions taken were not those of an organized force but of "small bands of local men" who, contrary to the idea that only those who had little contact with the settlers attacked them, were well known to the deponents.[41]

Although Clanricard reported as late as 14 November that Mayo was quiet and was himself able to march to Shrule at the end of the month, Shrule lay on the county's southern border with Galway, where the earl's influence kept the country quiet.[42] Information about what was happening in the north of the province reached him only slowly. Several of the deponents described the rebellion as beginning in this county between 1 and 20 November.[43] There seem to have been some preparations for the rising during the summer as there was a report as early as July that the Irish smiths were making weapons though the authorities took little notice. When word reached the county from Dublin of what was happening in the north, many of the Protestant ministers fled immediately.[44] This departure may well have helped to precipitate disorder as it left a number of dwellings unoccupied and a vacuum in local Protestant leadership.

It appears that it was the Catholic clergy who supplied the leadership in bringing Mayo into conjunction with the northern movement. By 1641 every Catholic church in the archdiocese of Tuam had a priest, and its archbishop, Malachy O'Queely, was particularly able. It was reported that he urged the population to rise on the grounds that Catholics were about to massacred. He, too, allegedly claimed that there was royal sanction for the rising, and later he raised a company of troops at his own expense, as much to keep order as to fight the royal forces.[45] O'Queely's actions at the start of the rebellion, if accurately reported, must have preceded the meeting of the Irish parliament as it was upon its meeting that the Catholics were supposed to be slaughtered. This story, therefore, both reinforces the picture of some planning for the rising before November and shows that it was independent of any action taken by the lords of the Pale.

Another feature of the situation in Mayo was the inability of gentry to unite to resist the rebellion. Viscount Mayo, who at this point was a Protestant, attempted to obtain the co-operation of the New English landowner at Castlebar, Sir Henry Bingham. Bingham, however, suspected a plot and refused to join forces; he was later surrounded and forced to surrender his garrison. Mayo, lacking support from the government in Dublin and distrusted by other Protestants, did what he could to protect the British settlers, but soon converted to Catholicism (an example many of the British settlers apparently followed) and ultimately participated in the Catholic Confederation.[46]

More is known about what led up to the rebellion in Sligo than in most other Irish counties because of the research of Mary O'Dowd.[47] She perceives several preconditions to the rebellion, many of which have been remarked elsewhere. There was, she points out, animosity between the lower Irish social strata and the Protestant clergy as both bishops and ministers attempted to increase their income. Often this was accompanied by British settlement, which increased the competition for land, but it was the collection of tithes by the Protestant clergy which was particularly resented as a tax levied by one faith upon another. It may be remarked here that when ministers declared what they had lost in the rebellion, they claimed considerable wealth, which must have looked to the local inhabitants as though it had been acquired at their expense.[48] Moreover, the efficient organization of the Catholic clergy under O'Queely meant that as in Mayo, clerical leadership in inspiring both anti-English and anti-Protestant sentiment encouraged popular support for rebellion.

At the level of the gentry, there was also resentment against attempts by the Protestant bishops to regain land they claimed had once belonged to the church. Strafford's government, and more specifically the plantation scheme for Connacht, added to the tension in the area. In 1634 Donogh O'Connor Sligo, one of the major landowners in the county, had died deeply in debt. In the settlement of the estate, Sir Philip Percival, one of the plantation commissioners, had arranged that Wentworth and Sir George Radcliffe should acquire the land in return for paying off the debts. This denied the estate to Patrick French, an Old English leader in the county and the major creditor. As O'Dowd points out, there is no simple equation between financial problems and participation in the rebellion; some of those who rose in arms had benefited from the land transactions of the 1630s. Yet such arrangements, coupled as they were with the acquisition of land by New English administrators, aroused resentment and added to instability. This instability was, moreover, increased by the distribution within the county of unemployed soldiers, the consequence of the failure to ship the new army abroad. It was these ex-soldiers, frustrated by the denial of permission to seek employment abroad and often short of food, who engaged in some of the early pillaging, and former officers in this army provided military leadership in the organization of the sieges of Sligo and Templehouse.

O'Dowd explains the decision of the Sligo gentry to join the rebellion by linking it to the defection of the Old English in the east. Viscount Ranelagh certainly held this opinion, but there is some reason to believe that the motivation for joining the rebellion lay closer to home.[49] By early December, two meetings of the gentry had been held at Ballysadare under the auspices of Andrew Crean. At the second one it had been decided to march on the towns of Sligo and Templehouse, the siege of the former beginning on 10 December and of the latter on the fifteenth.[50] It will be recollected that Gormanston and other lords of the Pale did not decide to join the Irish till the meeting at Crofty on 7 December. While the gentry in the west, therefore, may have known the way matters were moving in the east, particularly in view of the decision of the gentry in Louth, they seem to have acted before the final defection of the lords of the Pale. Furthermore, it is hard to conceive that the two sieges, both of which were ultimately successful, could have been organized in the matter of a week. Some preparation must have taken place in November.

Clanricard did what he could to prevent the rebellion from spreading. By the end of October the lords justices had made him governor of County Galway, and he immediately prepared his company, stationed at Loughrea, to resist any disorder that developed. At the same time he was beginning to hear reports of unrest elsewhere, particularly in Roscommon.[51] He asked for some of the arms stored in Dublin Castle but was told by the lords justices that he could expect no assistance until reinforcements arrived from England.[52] His bitterness at this lack of support was reflected in his letter to Lord Cottington of 7 December. The rebellion, he said, was spreading, and he could have kept the whole province quiet with arms for 1,000 men. All was likely to be lost because the old army was called from outlying areas and "shut up" in Dublin.[53] Two days later he complained to Ormond: "I have frequently applied myself to the state without comfort or relief from them and know not what more to do."[54] Nevertheless, he managed to raise 800 foot and two troops of horse and armed half of them from the store at Galway. With some of these he made a circuit of the county between 20 and 27 November.[55]

Yet Clanricard attempted to do more than keep the peace. He understood the political implications of the rebellion with its potential to ruin the arrangements that had been worked out between Charles and the Old English the previous summer. It is significant that, in addition to his half-brother, the earl of Essex, he corresponded at this time with three other persons in England: the earl of Bristol, the earl's nephew, Lord Digby, and Cottington, all of whom had been involved in the negotiations to secure the summer settlement with the Old English.

In writing to England, Clanricard tried to do two things. The first was to emphasize the loyalty of the Old English gentry as he was anxious that no action be taken in England that would alienate potential support in Ireland. In mid-November he mentioned to both Essex and Bristol rumours of defection and conspiracy "throughout the kingdom" but then went on to stress the "general distaste and hatred of the rebellion" among the gentry. Those in rebellion were "loose people," he reported; Munster and Leinster were quiet, and isolated incidents should not be interpreted as a sign of general disloyalty.[56] This image of what was happening, though no doubt sincere, was overly optimistic because information reached him slowly, and his perception was possibly tinged with wishful thinking. We have seen that his view of the situation in Mayo does not coincide with most of the information in the depositions. Nor could his assertion to Essex on 6 December that no gentry of quality in Sligo had joined the rebellion have been accurate. Similarly, Clanricard did not begin to refer to the situation in Offaly, only some fifteen miles to the east of Portumna, till December, yet we have considerable evidence that there had been unrest in this county from the middle of November. There were thirteen instances of robbery which occurred before the middle of the month, and forty-one between the sixteenth and the thirty-first. One of the deponents dated the start of the rebellion in that county as from 20 November, an assessment supported by the word of William Parsons, nephew of the lord justice, who lived at Birr.[57]

Clanricard's second point confirms that, for all his assurances, he was worried that Old English loyalty might not continue. The implementation of the Graces that had been reaffirmed over the summer was essential. "I give them [the gentry]," he told Bristol, "all the comfort and assurance I can possible, that whosoever stands firm and dischargeth his duty in this time of danger, may be confident, not only of obtaining those Graces, but to receive them with addition."[58] What worried him, and the events of the summer when he was in England surely gave him reason, was that the Catholic gentry of the province might once again be denied the benefit of the Graces because of misinformation fed to the government in England by some in Ireland "either through too much ... distrust ... zeal, or some private ends."[59] Bristol would have known that this was a veiled reference to men like Sir William Parsons and Sir Adam Loftus.

Clanricard's achievement in keeping Galway quiet despite the government's lack of support shows what could be done to resist the rising when the will to resist was present, and it is evident that he wanted the rest of the Catholic gentry to behave like him. But Clanricard's case points to the reasons that this will was absent in the Pale and elsewhere among the Old English. Clanricard, though Irish and Catholic and among those who had formulated the accommodation of the summer, was much more closely linked to the English élite than any other Irish noble with the possible exception of the earl of Antrim. As the half-brother of Essex and the husband of Northampton's daughter, he was more a member of the English aristocracy than of the Irish – indeed, he held an English title. Moreover, because of his unique influence in the English court, he did not depend on parliamentary ratification of the Graces because his estates enjoyed the security of a new patent issued by the king, and his attitude towards the hierarchy of the church was tinctured with an aristocratic aloofness. He regarded many of the bishops as social upstarts.[60] Thus, for a number of reasons, including the security of his estates, but more importantly the retention of influence at the centre of power, Clanricard provides an exception with which others may be compared. How exceptional his case was becomes apparent when we look at Leinster and Munster.

LEINSTER AND MUNSTER

Munster and Leinster have to be considered together because the rebellion spread in a haphazard way in these provinces. Map 4 shows the spread of the rebellion by county as reflected by the dates given by deponents of when they were robbed. In the majority of counties to the north and east of Tipperary, robberies took place throughout November. However, what is most useful about these data is that they show when robbery reached a significant rate. Thus, although there was considerable variation among counties bordering on Ulster in terms of the peak rate of robbery (virtually all occurring in Longford during October and 76 per cent in Meath during November), only in these counties were robberies recorded for October at a significant rate (24 per cent or more).[61]

The southeastern counties of Wicklow, Wexford, Carlow, and Laois were the next to be affected. Here, virtually no robberies were recorded for October, but 20 per cent or more of those reported took place between 1 November and 15 November, and they had almost ceased by the end of that month. In the next group of counties (Offaly, Kildare, and Kilkenny), few incidents were reported for the first half of November, but a substantial number (over 40 per cent) occurred in the second half of the month and they continued during December.[62] By contrast, Limerick, Tipperary, Clare, and Waterford were relatively quiet throughout November, but the rate of robbery picked up in December (50 per cent or more of reported incidents in the first three counties and 28 per cent of those in Waterford) and continued into the new year. Finally, in the three remaining counties, incidents became frequent in January, but many were dated as happening in February or even later in 1642. (County Dublin was

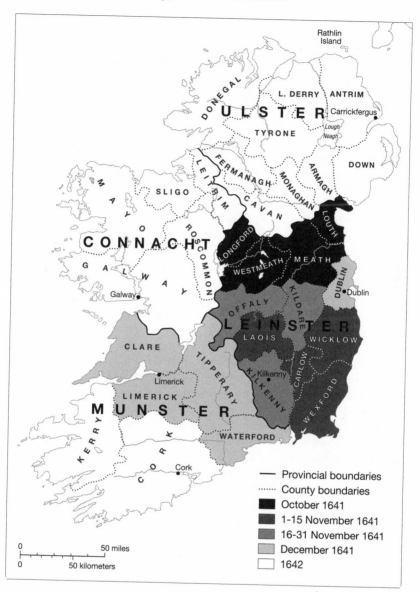

Map 4 The Earliest Reports of Numerous Robberies in Leinster and Munster.
The sources for compilation of this map are the post-Rebellion depositions for the counties concerned which are in the archives of Trinity College, Dublin. There is much variation in the number of reported robberies from county to county. All cases have been counted in counties where there are under fifty instances and the first fifty listed in the relevant volume have been used as a sample where there are more than fifty. In one county, Waterford, where there were over 100 robberies reported, all were counted and a high correlation was found between the percentages for the various periods derived from the first fifty and those obtained when all instances were counted.

a special case because of the continued control of the capital by the government).[63]

Map 4 depicts the way in which the rebellion spread south and west from Ulster and the southeast like a bush fire. That the southeast became a combustion point so soon after the Ulster phase of the rising points to pre-rebellion planning that extended beyond the northern province. Such generalization, however, tends to conceal local variations, and a clearer picture of the processes at work may be gained by looking some particular areas in more detail.

One of the more interesting accounts recorded in the depositions was that of William Tymes, who lived in the vicinity of the royal silver mines in the Tipperary barony of Owney, which lay next to County Clare. Tymes, who styled himself "gent.," first heard about the rebellion on 29 October from a Mr Woodhouse of Birr. As Tymes feared the rebellion would spread, he went to John O'Mulryan, "chief lord" of the barony, John Kennedy of Downalley, and other Irish gentry, "never thinking nor so much as suspecting that those gentlemen or any in those parts would rise out in rebellion also." He suggested to the other gentry of the area, Irish and English, that they should arm themselves, and it was agreed that "all and everyone of them" should remain loyal "and partake together for the defence and good of the country." By general consent, Tymes was sent to Limerick to obtain supplies of gunpowder, and he set out for that town about 13 November. He bought the powder, primarily from ships in Limerick harbour, but he was also allowed a little from the king's store, and he began his return journey on the seventeenth. Two miles outside Limerick he encountered men who had been employed at the silver mines coming in the opposite direction. They reported that they had been robbed and that when they had sought protection from Tymes's supposed friend, John Kennedy, he had denied it. Subsequently, Tymes met some of his own tenants, also fleeing, who told him that the rising in Tipperary was now general and advised him to return to Limerick. He nevertheless pressed on as he wished to return to his wife and children, but the next group he met on the road were a "great rowt" of Irish, armed with staves, darts, and other such weapons, who had come out of County Clare. He managed to escape from them, but this encounter convinced him to return to Limerick, from where he sent a message to his wife. A message came back from one of the Irish gentry that he would be given protection if he returned with the powder, but when the protection arrived in the shape of two priests who tried to convert him in return for an assurance of the security of his estate, he decided to remain where he was. His wife and children, it may be added, were ultimately allowed to join him.[64]

There is no reason to doubt the general accuracy of Tymes's account, and although the statistics indicate that in Tipperary as a whole the rising did not begin till December, disorder was beginning to break out by the middle of November in the northern part of the county and men from Clare were participating in it although the depositions for this county also indicate that disorder there was not general till December.[65] An interesting feature of Tymes's account is that it tells us about an area that was not part of any formal settlement scheme. Tymes was a landlord, but he lived in the area because of an association with the silver mines, and most of the other important gentry seem to have been Irish, with whom Tymes thought he was on good terms. Indeed, the return of his wife and children seems to show that his assumption about his relations with his neighbours was not entirely misplaced. It could be argued that, initially, the Irish gentry did nothing but deny protection, and we have to take into account cases that can be found in England when the gentry, faced with riot they could not control, tried to remain uninvolved.[66] Yet the terms offered to Tymes, the emissaries sent to offer them, and the obvious desire to acquire the powder suggest a gentry-church alliance that went well beyond a desire to remain aloof from a difficult situation.

Evidently, in Tipperary at least, the Irish gentry below the level of the peerage had joined the movement to ensure a Catholic establishment in Ireland without any armed threat from Ulster and before it could have become evident that the Graces would, once more, be denied parliamentary ratification. It is, moreover, extremely unlikely that this church-gentry linkage and the political aims that evidently inspired it were the result of spontaneous decisions reached upon the news of what was happening in Ulster. It follows that there had been some pre-rebellion discussion and that some of the Tipperary gentry knew what was intended even if they had no plans for an October strike themselves. In Carlow, too, there was evidently some knowledge of what was planned because a deponent was told that the intention had been "to go on in a fair way which they had done if their design of taking of the castle of Dublin had taken effect."[67]

Evidence of this sort at the barony level is rare, but it is useful to bear in mind as we look at the broader picture. The lords justices knew that the rising had started in Wicklow by 13 November (which is confirmed by the depositions), but they did not mention Carlow, even though English settlers were fleeing to Carlow Castle early in

November and fifteen of the thirty-one robberies reported for this county were dated before the sixteenth.[68] Here there is no doubt about the gentry's leadership though it may have developed for local rather than national reasons. During the first week of November, the two men appointed jointly as governors of the county quarrelled. (The joint appointment was itself an indication of some division.) Walter Bagenal, of New English descent but related to the Butlers by marriage, switched sides to take over command of the rebel forces, armed the county with weapons that were already in the hands of the gentry, and sent to Galway for powder. His rival, Sir Thomas Butler, seems to have lost all influence and become one of a number of Old English neutrals.[69]

In Kildare, out of the twenty-two reported robberies, two occurred before the middle of November, ten in the rest of November, and the remainder during December. Against this must be balanced the statement of Erasmus Burrows, high sheriff of Kildare, that the rebellion began in his county "on or about" the first day of November and that the rebels grew in strength daily after that.[70] A resident of Athy, however, dated the start of the rising at 16 November.[71] At Naas the rebellion started later, largely because as early as October the earl of Kildare, a Protestant, raised three companies of troops, which were armed from the store in Dublin. This force was led by the local gentry, including men like Maurice Fitzgerald of Allen, the MP for the county and one of the Catholic leaders in parliament, but it had defected and deserted the earl by 3 December, and most of the gentry joined the rebellion as soon as the lords of the Pale declared their unity with the northern Irish.[72] Kildare himself went to Dublin and thence to England, and his newly built house at Maynooth was burned down.[73]

In Kilkenny, where the statistics are very similar to those for Kildare, there is again evidence of rebellion breaking out at different times according to local conditions. The north of the county seems to have been affected first, partly on account of Carlow men moving west. English settlers were attacked and sought refuge in the city of Kilkenny, where the countess of Ormond was living.[74] On 18 November Ormond's cousin, Edmund Butler, Viscount Mountgarret's son, wrote to assure the earl that a force of 240 foot and 50 horse had been organized.[75] Nevertheless, St Leger reported early in December that the county had been overrun, and by the middle of that month the English refugees in Kilkenny town were being pillaged and having to seek the protection of the countess of Ormond, who was left unharmed but was not permitted to join her husband.[76] Mountgarret was present while this plundering was taking place and does not seem to have been able to prevent it initially, but he intervened to protect the English later.[77] Almost certainly, by the time of the action taken against the English in Kilkenny, Mountgarret and his son had decided to join the rising, persuaded, according to one deponent, by Walter Bagenal, the erstwhile governor of Carlow, and other gentry. Very shortly afterwards the Irish in Tipperary asked the viscount to be their commander.[78]

We have seen that parts of Munster, particularly northern Tipperary, were already involved in the rebellion by the middle of November, and a report to Ormond confirms this. According to this report, both the Irish gentry and the Catholic clergy attempted to prevent the pillaging of the English settlers in Tipperary, but Philip O'Dwyer of Dundrum, near Cashel, "alleging that he could not keep those of the country in peace" and "pretending" that the local population "could not sleep safely in their houses while Cashel was a receptacle to the president's troops to come thither and rush among them," marched on Cashel and took control of the town on the last day of December.[79] This is confirmed by the depositions, though they also indicate that other centres in Tipperary, like Clonmel and Fethard, were under Irish control a week before O'Dwyer took Cashel.[80]

Undoubtedly the countermeasures taken by St Leger in Munster to restore order aroused an aggressive response among those who, at first, hesitated to go into rebellion. He too faced orders from Dublin to send some of the troops under his command to help defend the capital, an indication that the policy of denying protection to outlying areas in order to save Dublin was not applied to the Old English alone. He could hardly contain his fury at being weakened in this manner as he was convinced that Dublin had nothing to fear so long as the Irish lacked weapons. The authorities in Dublin, he confided to Sir Philip Percival, were "frightened out of their wits" and by depriving him of his troop of horse would be responsible for any deterioration of the situation in the province.[81] Despite this reduction in strength, or perhaps because he was conscious of his weakness, St Leger responded to outbreaks of the rebellion in Waterford and Tipperary with ferocity. On scattering a force of 300 Irish in the former county, he took fifty prisoners and executed them all by martial law. "How this may hand with Magna Carta," he remarked to Ormond, "I know not," but he urged that similar action be taken elsewhere which would ensure that the rebels would "melt like snow before the sun."[82] Such tactics had been used in the past, and in the case of Mountjoy in Elizabeth's time, it can be argued that they produced the desired results, but St Leger's action only increased the hostility towards the regime he represented.

The last stage in the outbreak of the rebellion was in the counties of Cork and Kerry. Here the depositions show that incidents were rare before December and most occurred in 1642.[83] The relative stability of the area is all the more striking in that Colonel John Barry had kept together in Kinsale the 1,000 men that the English parliament had prevented from sailing to Spain despite efforts by the authorities to make him disband them.[84] This stability in the region must be ascribed to the initial reluctance of the young Viscount Muskerry to have anything to do with the rising. Yet by December or early 1642 he too had begun to have reservations about supporting the government. Fortunately, we do not have to guess at the process that led him into rebellion because he explained it himself to his fellow peer, Viscount Barrymore, Cork's Old English son-in-law. Even after Leinster and Connacht had joined the Irish cause, he wrote, he abhorred the "desperate attempt (as I took it)." Yet he sought an explanation of the rising and was told that it was because the Catholic religion was threatened. This he "did not altogether believe" to be the true cause until he realized that all of Munster was about to join the rising too and that the general fear "of persecution, ruin and destruction" was genuine. What ultimately convinced him that these fears were justified was the reaction of the authorities to the rising. As he put the matter: "And though I were resolved not to stir nor join the country, as I have done, I have [seen] such burning and killing of men and women and children, without regard of age or quality, that I expected no safety for myself, having observed as innocent men and well deservers as myself so used."[85] We may allow for some self-justification, but Muskerry's arguments had to be well based to be convincing since his correspondent knew what the situation was as well as he did.

Muskerry took up arms only after considerable thought, after it became apparent that the country would, in any case, rise whatever he did and after the ruthlessness of English countermeasures demonstrated that there was no interest in a negotiated settlement. The desertion of the earl of Kildare by the gentry, along with Muskerry's explanation for his own behaviour, lends credence to the claim that Mountgarret's decision also followed gentry pressure. The rebellion, therefore, seems to have moved up the social hierarchy in stages, often beginning as popular riot with, as often as not, some clerical encouragement, to be joined thereafter by the gentry and, ultimately, by elements of the peerage. The abundant references to English settlers being persuaded to attend mass and indeed to the conversion of once-Protestant ministers indicates the desires of the insurgents and the active participation of the clergy.[86] In the process, the syndrome of atrocity and counter-atrocity, with each side blaming the other and denying responsibility itself, created almost identical stereotypes of barbarity that were reinforced by the conviction on both sides that one ideology or the other must win outright. There were moderates, such as the "neutrals" who turn up in the depositions, and leaders like Ormond, Clanricard, Muskerry, and Mountgarret who, left to themselves, could have reached an accommodation, but the aristocracy, for all their involvement, had become politically powerless in the face of two ideological juggernauts, English nationalist expansionism and Catholic religious supra-nationalism.[87]

What is perhaps striking about the southern counties, in contrast to those of the Pale and Connacht, is that the inflexibility of the government in parliament and the land issue seem to have played a less important role in making up men's minds than the issue of religion and the reaction of the government to the initial incidents. Had parliament, and the non-ratification of the Graces been of crucial importance, men like Bagenal would have waited longer to join the rebellion, and men like Mountgarret and Muskerry would not have waited as long as they did. This serves to remind us that motives varied from place to place and were far from monolithic. Whereas in northern Tipperary and Carlow and, we may suspect, Laois, Wicklow, and even Kilkenny, there seems to have been some intimation of what was to happen before the rebellion broke out, there is no evidence of this in counties such as Cork or Kerry.[88]

Educated Catholic opinion was appalled at the slaughter and destruction that followed the outbreak of the rebellion. Father Robert Nugent, writing to the Jesuit vicar-general in March 1642, commented:

Nothing is here to be seen, nothing to be heard, especially in the eastern parts but rapines, butcheries of little children and of women, just as much as of men, flames devouring the household goods and all the substance of a blameless family, in fine such is the fury of each party, namely of the English and our countrymen, that it seems impossible to appease it without the extinction of one or other nation or its expulsion from the kingdom.[89]

Consistent with this position was the desire within the Catholic hierarchy to re-endow the church with land and buildings. Thus, when one of the Butlers asked the Catholic bishop of Ossory for assistance in prosecuting the war, the condition of assistance was that the church lands and tithes "should be first invested in the possession of himself and the rest of the clergy and the churches hallowed and masses said

in them."[90] Moreover, in seeking help from overseas, the clergy
stressed that only by controlling Ireland could there be any hope of
recovering England and Scotland.[91]

The similarity of the analysis of the situation by the Protestant
planters to that of the Jesuits might have surprised both parties.
"Every man," wrote Cork to the earl of Warwick in February, "hath
laid aside all compassion and is as bloody in his desires against the
papists, as they have been in their execution against the Protestants,"
though he stressed that the other side had started the cruelty. He
too considered that it was impossible for the adherents of the two
religions to live "intermingled together" in peace. It followed that
the king and parliament should "root the popish party of the natives
out of this kingdom" and plant English Protestants in their stead.
Furthermore, the planters, like the Catholics, insisted that they had
to have assistance if they were to survive. The Irish had started the
rebellion, Cork stated, only after assurances had been obtained that
neither the king nor parliament "would supply us with men or muni-
tion."[92] The planters, therefore, had to stress the advantages of
sending assistance. The lords justices had early emphasized the need
to secure an army from England to crush the rebellion, and in
December they remarked on the way the land confiscations that
would follow the suppression would enhance crown revenue. It was,
in part, to ensure such confiscation that the depositions were collected, so that evidence would exist against landowners who had
participated in the rebellion after it had been suppressed, and Cork
also harped on the value of future confiscation in his letter to Warwick.[93]

Both sides procured assistance in 1642, but not in sufficient
strength to make a decisive difference to the outcome of the struggle.
The nature of this struggle takes us beyond the outbreak of the
rebellion, and therefore beyond the confines of this book, but just as
English and Scottish events influenced those in Ireland, so the situation in Ireland had repercussions in those two kingdoms. If the
Irish did receive advice that neither the king nor parliament would
be able to intervene, it was not entirely misleading. The question of
sending a force – either Scottish or English – to Ireland raised some
fundamental political issues in Britain which delayed any immediate
response. It is with the discussion about this response and the issues
so raised that I conclude this book.

CHAPTER TWELVE

The Reaction in Britain to the Rebellion

Any account of the reaction in Britain to the outbreak of rebellion in Ireland becomes linked to the divisions within Britain which led to the English civil war. Because historians have examined these divisions often and minutely, and in so doing have recognized the impact of the rebellion upon both England and Scotland, the task of tracing the reaction becomes, to some extent, one of integrating the work of others, from Clarendon onwards.[1] Yet my primary objective is not to retread the well-worn historical paths that lead to the conflict in England, but to explain why the British response to the outbreak of the rebellion, from October 1641 to March 1642, was, in Karl Bottigheimer's words, "disjointed, halting and thoroughly Lilliputian," and to show how events in Ireland created attitudes in Britain which affected policy.[2]

By the spring of 1642, the impending conflict in England ensured a disinclination to intervene decisively in Ireland, at least until 1649. As England went to war with itself, the Irish established the Catholic Confederation with Kilkenny as its capital, but it was the absence of strong intervention from Britain at the outbreak of the rebellion, when Irish leadership remained embryonic, which permitted the rising not only to spread but to take root. The plant was fragile, and even as late as April 1642, when the first contingent of Scottish forces began to embark for Ulster, it looked as though it might be destroyed.[3] However, by this time the Irish had sought assistance abroad and this help, combined with England's internal divisions, enabled them to establish the Confederation. Yet the very fragility of the Irish cause in April serves to highlight the consequences of the inability of the various political elements in Britain to unite effectively to oppose a rising that challenged them all. To explain why so little was done, the behaviour of each of these elements has to be assessed in turn.

THE KING

The king was among the first to hear of the rebellion as Viscount Chichester had written directly to him in Edinburgh. On 28 October Charles reported the matter to the Scottish parliament. He explained that he did not yet have sufficient information to assess the situation. If the revolt was a minor one, he thought that no Scottish aid would be needed in putting it down, but he warned that if it "proved a great one," assistance would be required. He judged correctly that Spain was too occupied elsewhere to be involved and that France had no hand in the rising either. What did concern him was a possible link with English Catholics. While he sought more information, therefore, he urged that the English parliament be informed and that the Scottish parliament consider the matter.[4] It was at this time that he confided to Sir Edward Nicholas that he hoped that this "ill news from Ireland" would diminish the "follies" in England, presumably with parliament's interference with his plans for the Irish army in mind.[5]

By 1 November the king knew that the revolt was general in the north. He consulted with the English parliamentary commissioners who were in Edinburgh, and he urged the Scottish parliament to be ready to act, and particularly to be ready to reinforce Carrickfergus and Londonderry as soon as the English parliament agreed to Scottish intervention.[6] He purchased arms and powder and had them sent to Ireland from Dumbarton at his own expense, and he claimed later that he and the duke of Lennox assisted in sending 1,500 volunteers to Ulster before 18 November.[7] Some soldiers did indeed cross to Ireland from Scotland at this time, and they were the only substantial body of troops to reach Ireland from Britain before the end of the year. In short, as has been recognized, Charles played a leading part in sending help to the British in Ulster and contributed substantially to the military survival of that province.[8]

The rebellion hastened Charles's departure from Edinburgh, and he had returned to London by 25 November. Here the decisions about sending aid to Ireland were largely out of his hands. He had no money to finance an expedition on his own, and had he tried to raise funds by non-parliamentary means the Commons would have protested vigorously. Nonetheless, most of the surviving evidence points to a continuation of his desire to send forces to Ireland. On the day after his arrival in London he indicated to the council that he would order all officers to Ireland as soon as he had the money to do so, and on 28 December he declared his intention to raise 10,000 volunteers for Ireland – with the impressment bill stalled in the Lords compulsion was not, as yet, deemed legal – even though again any action was dependent on the supply of funds.[9] Indeed, if Charles was responsible in any way for the delay in sending assistance to Ireland it was in showing an insensitivity to parliament's suspicions of him by trying to do too much. In a speech delivered to parliament within ten days of his return, he pointedly stressed that its preparations for assisting the Irish government "go but slowly on."[10] In a subsequent speech, on 14 December, he remarked that the Commons had passed a bill for raising forces but that bill "sticketh with you my lords, for which I give you no thanks."[11] This remark led to the accusation that he was interfering with the deliberations of the upper house, and he was charged with breach of privilege.[12] Certainly the remark was disingenuous, for it looks as though he had let it be known that he would pass the bill only if it did not infringe upon his prerogative, but he cannot be saddled with the responsibility of mixing the separate issues – help for Ireland and the crown's prerogative – and the bill certainly did try to curb crown powers.[13] Charles's stance on the latter is not evidence of a half-hearted attitude towards the former.

Charles began the new year by issuing a proclamation denouncing those in arms in Ireland as rebels.[14] This was an unusual step in that proclamations dealing with Irish affairs were usually (though not always) issued by the authorities in Ireland. Indeed, several such documents regarding the rebellion had already been proclaimed in Ireland. There was some sentiment in England that the king should have issued such a proclamation much sooner, but there was no reason to do so.[15] When he acted, he acted in response to a request from the lords justices written on 14 December. They asked for twenty copies of a proclamation issued directly by the king, on the grounds that the Irish would only accept the authenticity of such a document if "they see his [the king's] own hand and privy signet" on it.[16] Evidently this request was made to counter the Irish claim that they acted with the king's approval. Because of the time that was required for the lords justices' request to reach England, the king seems to have acted promptly. There was, it is true, a delay in getting the copies of the proclamation to Ireland, but there is no reason to believe that this was deliberate.

On 8 January Charles initiated the Fast Sermons, which were preached before parliament and were initially intended to generate public support for action in Ireland, although they later became a form of parliamentary propaganda. Despite reservations, he agreed by the end of that month to hand over Carrickfergus to the Scots as a base for their army in order to expedite its dispatch.[17] By 10 February the Scots had received a letter from Charles in which he tried to accelerate their departure for Ireland, and by the middle of the month he had signed into law the impressment bill even though he recognized that it undermined his prerogative.[18] By the end of the month he had agreed to the Adventurers Act, whereby money was to be raised to fight the war in Ireland in return for a promise of forfeited land. Finally, in April, he indicated his intention of going to Ireland in person, as he had discussed with Viscount Dillon before the rebellion, and was only dissuaded by the united opposition of his English and Scottish parliaments.[19]

It has been suggested that as soon as the Covenanters heard about the rebellion they suspected Charles of being implicated in it, and certainly his English opponents shared these suspicions.[20] There were good reasons for such suspicions. Earlier in October, the earl of Argyll and the marquis of Hamilton had only narrowly escaped being kidnapped by those close to the king in Edinburgh during the so-called Incident, and in England, just before the news of the rebellion reached London, some of the details of the second army plot of the previous summer had been revealed.[21] Moreover, by 6 November the Irish claim of royal approval was known in England, and a few days later it was rumoured that the Irish claimed Charles himself was going to land in Ireland at Dunluce.[22] Because Charles undoubtedly did plot against his opponents, it is easy to assume participation in plots in which he was not involved. In this context, the actions he took in response to the rebellion can acquire unwarranted innuendo. Thus S.R. Gardiner concludes that Charles requested help from the Scottish parliament because he was startled by "the wild shape which his intrigue with the Irish Lords had taken."[23]

I have argued that there is no reliable evidence to connect Charles to the plotting of the Irish rebellion, but it would be unwise to use his behaviour after the rebellion broke out to clinch the argument for his non-involvement. It is notoriously difficult to prove a negative, and in this case everything he did that appeared to press for the suppression of the rebellion could be asserted to be a cover for past folly, or a device for obtaining an army to use against his enemies in England. At the same time, there is nothing in his behaviour from October to April which in any way points directly or indirectly to his implication in Irish plotting. Had Charles had his way, a substantial army would have crossed from Scotland to Ireland almost immediately, and the help that the authorities and planters in Ireland were requesting would have been dispatched from England more promptly and in greater quantity than it was. This army would not, moreover, have been available to him to turn against the English parliament.

Charles's aim was to restore Ireland to its pre-war state as quickly as possible. What frustrated his policies was not his secret sympathy for the rebellion but a suspicion among his English and Scottish subjects that he did not identify fully with what they perceived to be their interests. Ireland, even partly in the hands of a Catholic aristocracy, posed a threat to the English and Scottish religions and thus, in the context of the seventeenth century, to national identity. Ireland in the hands of a Protestant aristocracy not only eliminated this threat but opened up the opportunity for English (and Scottish) expansion and its accompanying enrichment.

THE SCOTS

Throughout the negotiations leading to the Treaty of London, the Scots had maintained that Ireland was a dependency of England and not a kingdom in its own right. They may, indeed, have recollected that before their king became king of England their status in Ireland by act of the Irish parliament was that of outlaw.[24] The position of the Scots in Ireland, therefore, was itself dependent upon the union of the Scottish and English crowns which dictated caution before intervention in Ireland. In any case the Scots had no desire to alienate their allies in England by acting without consultation. When Charles asked the Scottish parliament to assist in suppressing the rebellion, it agreed to set up a committee to look into the matter, and on 29 October it agreed to offer assistance, subject to the agreement of the English parliament. As news began to reach the Scots about what was happening in Ulster, they became increasingly concerned. Lord Balmerino, for instance, declared to parliament that the Irish were intent on "the utter demolition of the Christian religion."[25] After a renewed appeal from the king, therefore, they expressed willingness to send an army of 10,000 men to crush the rebellion, but only with English parliamentary approval and, by implication, financing. The size of the force the Scots offered is a measure of their concern. The English Commons initially discussed a force of only 1,000 men.[26]

The negotiations relating to the Scottish army fall into two phases. The first, which concerned the size of the army, took almost two months. The second phase dealt with the terms under which the Scots would serve. Most of the major issues connected with this phase had been resolved by February 1642, but matters such as baggage horses were still being discussed as late as July, and the treaty giving effect to the expeditionary force was not ratified by the Scottish parliament till 1644.[27] The issues that remained outstanding after February did not, however, delay the departure of the army; 2,500 troops landed in Ireland in early April and the remainder over the summer. It was the delay between November 1641 and February 1642 which proved most advantageous to the Irish.

During the first stage of the negotiations, the position of the Scots was clear: they offered 10,000 troops and the question was whether the English parliament would accept this assistance or not. In England, matters were not as simple, and there was considerable division of opinion in both Commons and Lords. The decision to ask for 1,000 Scots was reached only after much debate. Indeed, after agreeing on 4 November to seek assistance, the Commons almost reversed its decision the following day, causing Sir Simonds D'Ewes to remark: "I did much wonder that we having debated this matter at large yesterday ... should now fall into dispute of it again; but it seemed that we had much leisure time."[28] Subsequently, only step by step and after much debate was it agreed to send an army of the size that the Scots proposed. There is no need to chronicle the changes of mind in the Commons, but one example of the sort of discussion that took place will illustrate the confusion that reigned.

John Hampden, who served on the parliamentary committee in Edinburgh, arrived in Westminster on 11 November with the information that the Scots wanted to send 10,000 men. The next day a debate took place about whether to limit the force to the size originally contemplated, or to expand it. After much disagreement, the Commons voted to stick with its original decision of 1,000 men, by a formal division of 112 to 77.[29] On the same day, however, it also agreed without a vote that if the Scots thought more men were needed, it could be left to the Scottish parliament "to send such further forces as the necessity of the occasion should require."[30] Then the following day, again without a division but "after long debate," it was agreed that the Scottish force should be increased to 5,000.

Through the Holland diary, we gain some insight into the opinions on both sides of what was obviously a volatile discussion. Those in favour of sending a large force, who included D'Ewes and John Pym, pointed to the Irish fear of the Scots, the saving to English resources if Scots were employed, the devastating effect on the Irish of Mountjoy's winter campaign at the end of Elizabeth's reign, and the consequent shortening of the war and saving of money. Those who opposed increasing the size of the Scottish force believed that the Scots would have great difficulty in raising such an army and that a winter war could not be fought, particularly because it would be impossible to supply a large force.[31]

These differences of opinion in the Commons reveal that the debate was not, as has been suggested, confined to one between Commons and Lords.[32] Obviously, many MPs had misgivings about a large Scottish contingent crossing to Ireland, an opinion shared by Nicholas, who feared the Irish would become more desperate in reaction to the threat from Scotland.[33] Nevertheless, it is true that after two Scottish commissioners arrived in London on 3 December to negotiate directly with the two houses, it was in the Lords that the most vociferous opposition to strong Scottish participation was maintained.

The Lords first tried to limit the army to 5,000 men, and only on 21 December, after a protest from the Scottish commissioners, pressure from various groups including the Commons, and intense debate, did the upper house finally agree to the 10,000 figure.[34] We know little about the details of the debate in the Lords, only that there was "great opposition at first" though ultimately there were only six negative voices.[35] We may assume that many of the arguments made earlier in the Commons surfaced again in the upper house. More significantly, at the time of the debate the Venetian ambassador reported a fear within the English council that the Scots might take over Ireland and a little later indicated that similar fears were prevalent in the Lords.[36] Charles's repeated efforts to get the Scots to cross to Ireland and his ill-advised criticism of the peers on 14 December would indicate that he did not share this fear. The issue cannot, therefore, be painted as one which putted royalist versus parliamentarian. It was much more a manifestation of Anglo-Scottish national rivalry, of which the Irish were well aware and had tried to exploit. On this issue, Charles and Pym agreed with each other perhaps more than either would have been willing to admit.

Once the Lords had accepted the dispatch of 10,000 Scots, the conditions under which they were to serve had to be agreed. The initial Scottish terms revealed that the fears about a Scottish territorial imperative were not entirely misplaced. In the face of this apparent Scottish ambition, opposition to the Scots surfaced once again in the Commons as well as the Lords. The Scots insisted that they should control the three major ports of Ulster: Carrickfergus, Coleraine, and Londonderry.[37] In addition, they demanded "reward [for] our service with like honours, recompense and plantations" as deserving English and Irish would receive "in this business"; in other words, Irish land was expected in return for service.[38] These and other demands, such as virtual military autonomy for the Scottish army commander in Ireland, were deemed by the earl of Leicester as of a "hard digestion," and there was also resistance to them in the Commons.[39]

The negotiations continued into February, often interrupted by the growing friction between king and parliament.[40] Yet the situation in Ireland was deteriorating to the point that both the English and the Scots realized that something had to be done. Alexander Montgomery, earl of Eglinton, had been receiving numerous dispatches from Ireland, and on 27 January he reported to the Scottish council the "pitiful condition" of the British in Ulster and showed that without "speedy assistance there will be no place left for landing of any forces" and "no hope of safety for the British there."[41] Thus, in mid-February the council told its commissioners in London that if Londonderry "cannot be granted do not hinder the service for it."[42] Similarly, the demand for forfeited land was dropped though Scots were permitted to subscribe to the Adventurers scheme introduced by the English parliament in February whereby land owned by those in rebellion was promised in return for money. As it turned out, only two Scots subscribed, and the Scottish council noted this lack of interest.[43]

Among the English, there was a similar recognition that Ireland would be lost by protracted councils.[44] Thus, on 24 January, a committee of Commons and Lords, including Sir John Clotworthy, the marquis of Hamilton, the earl of Bedford, and Viscount Saye, approached the Scottish commissioners with a proposal. This group argued that the negotiations for a treaty would require a "longer time nor the present necessity of any supply might spare" and therefore proposed that the Scots send 2,500 men to Ireland immediately.[45] The commissioners replied that they had no mandate to discuss such a force, but at the same time, they urged the Scottish council to give them such a mandate and to agree to the proposal to prevent both "the ruin of [the] Protestant religion" in Ireland and "the erection of a popish kingdom in so near a neighbourhood as may continually disturb our peace and privity."[46] The Scottish council was in a receptive mood for such a proposal, and as the English were willing to advance money, the two sides were able to overlook the issues that still divided them and to arrange limited assistance to the British in Ireland. By mid-March 1642 the Scottish troops were boarding ship though it was another two weeks before the force stepped ashore in Ulster.[47]

One feature of this force deserves special mention. One element of it was Argyll's regiment, and on 22 February Argyll was given a commission by the king to land in Ireland and the right to occupy Rathlin Island. This was clearly a response to the decision of most of the Irish MacDonnells to make common cause with the Irish. The motives behind the Scottish decision to reach the interim agreement with the English, therefore, included traditional clan rivalry as much as the stated concerns for religion and the strategic interest of Scotland.[48]

If this limited agreement ensured that the British in Ulster were not overwhelmed, it also relieved the pressure on the English to conclude the negotiations for a treaty with the Scots. As Charles and his English parliament advanced towards armed conflict, Ireland became less of a priority. At one point in March the Anglo-Scottish negotiations stalled because the English commissioners simply failed to turn up at a scheduled meeting as they had "some great business in Parliament," and when the Scots eventually landed in Ulster, the English failed to pay or supply them adequately.[49] A means had been found for preserving the British presence in Ulster and that was enough. The Scots assisted the Irish by putting their terms for service too high and thus contributing to delay. Yet, initially, their reaction had been prompt. As Robert Baillie remarked in self-defence: "this rebellion made both the king and us to haste all affairs."[50] The primary explanation for the absence of a decisive response to the rebellion in Ireland, therefore, lies not with the king or with the Scots, but in England and particularly within parliament.

ENGLAND: PUBLIC OPINION AND PAMPHLETS

During the weeks following Charles's departure for Scotland in August and up to the outbreak of the rebellion in Ireland, it looked to his advisers as though he was, at last, coming out of the crisis which had preoccupied him for so long. Settlement in Scotland seemed within reach even if gained at considerable political cost. In London, plague had broken out during parliament's adjournment and some MPs wished it to adjourn as soon as it re-assembled. Others wanted it to reconvene, but safely at Salisbury, which would also have meant away from London influence. Only Pym and "his junto" insisted that it should sit and sit at Westminster, even at the risk that MPs should "die together." Ireland was far from most men's minds, the only Irish issue concerning officials being how to react to the Queries.[51]

As Conrad Russell has remarked: "It was the outbreak of the Irish rebellion which brought this brief period of euphoria to an abrupt end."[52] As a sort of prelude to the main performance, albeit played in innocence of what was to come, on 30 October Pym revealed some of the details of the second army plot of the previous summer. Those behind the plot were described as "papists and others, and those most near the queen," and one of the two key witnesses was Daniel O'Neill, the Protestant relative of some of those in rebellion. It was the next day, Sunday, that Leicester received news of the rebellion and the person who brought it was Owen O'Connolly. On 1 November, Leicester, in turn, informed the Commons.[53]

In this case the messenger was, in effect, the message, for, just as the lords justices received their first impression of Irish intentions from O'Connolly, so too did the English parliament. Like the Irish officials, the English were given the impression from the first that a wholesale massacre was intended. This undoubtedly coloured opinions, particularly as O'Connolly did not confine himself to formal statements. One letter writer mentioned having talked to him, and no doubt the account of what was happening in Ireland became more lurid with each telling.[54] Only three days after Leicester had informed parliament, Thomas Smith, the earl of Northumberland's secretary, wrote to a friend repeating the story that the Protestants were to have their throats cut and adding that the Irish, whom he described as "those popish hellhounds," were "murdering, ravishing, burning and taking what they could."[55] Another correspondent declared on the same day that, had the plot taken effect as intended, not a Protestant would have been left alive in Ireland. This man also repeated O'Connolly's view that the Irish used the Scots as their model as they hoped "to purchase ... privileges in their religion as otherwise they never expected to have granted."[56]

As might be expected from the source and nature of the information about the rebellion, there was a sense of betrayal mixed with much anti-Catholic feeling. "Thus are we used and this we get for our discretion and moderation" was one reaction, and it was common to blame Strafford for his toleration of Catholicism in Ireland. Nicholas held this view, as did Smith, though Smith went further and used the rebellion to vindicate "God's servants." He argued that Irish events ought to stop those who "rail on the poor puritans," and he drew the understandable, if wrong, conclusion that the rising was linked to plots at home.[57] This is not to suggest that everyone reacted in the same way. Clarendon, indeed, who was an MP at the time, remarked in his *History* on the diversity of opinion. Some recalled the "blood and treasure" that past wars in Ireland had cost. Others hoped that "all ill humours and indispositions would be allayed" and that all parties would be united in suppressing the rebellion. This group included Sir Henry Vane, who hoped the rising would "unite men's minds." Still others, if Clarendon is to be believed, met the news with "smooth brows" on the grounds that secretly they rejoiced that now parliament would have to continue to sit. Among them were those who "whispered" that the king had encouraged the rebellion in order "to form an army of papists that should be at his devotion to invade this kingdom and oppress the Parliament."[58] Finally, if the Spanish ambassador's view can be considered a part of public opinion, there was at least one person who blamed parliament for the rising. If parliament had not hindered the export of the disbanded army, he claimed, the rising would not have taken place.[59]

These opinions were those of persons close to the centre of affairs. It is much harder to assess public opinion outside such circles, but the spate of pamphlets published following the outbreak of the rising makes it clear that interest in what was happening in Ireland was by no means confined to the élite. This pamphlet literature, however, raises more questions than it answers. The only published study of English reaction to the rebellion argues that, once parliament knew of the rising, "little time was lost in communicating the news, sensationalised with lurid tales of atrocities, to the nation at large."[60] This association of parliament with a pamphlet campaign is based on the number of pamphlets about the rebellion published between October 1641 and the following May which are listed, month by month, in the catalogue of the Thomason Tracts. Thus 10 such pamphlets are listed as having been produced in October, 17 in November, 25 in December, and 153 over the next four months. It has subsequently been shown, however, that this catalogue and, indeed, often the stated months of publication in the pamphlets themselves are an unreliable guide for this sort of information. There could, of course, be no such pamphlets published in England during October as nobody there knew the rebellion had broken out till the thirty-first. Furthermore, the contents of pamphlets listed for November and December often refer to events that took place later. An analysis of the pamphlets listed for November suggests that eight only can be verified for this month though a few of the October ones should possibly be added.[61]

As Steven Greenberg has argued, the pamphlets are a tricky source to use. Apart from those reproducing speeches or official statements, few appear to be authentic in the sense of being in fact what they purport to be. A great many describe events in Ireland that never happened. Some undoubtedly were published for propaganda purposes, but the motive is sometimes concealed. Two examples of the 200 or so pamphlets that relate to Ireland from October 1641 to the following April must suffice to show how easy it is to be misled.

The first pamphlet is entitled *The true Demands of the Rebells in Ireland. Declaring The Causes of their taking up Armes. Sent into* England *by Sir* Phelom O-Neale, *their Generall: To the Honorable and High Court* of Parliament and is dated "Ulster, February 10 1641," that is, 1642. It goes on to explain that it is published "for preventing false copies already extant, or that may be hereafter printed." However, it lets down its guard as to its true purpose with its first heading which is: "The Irish Rebels Unreasonable Demands." These demands are listed, and some are similar to those made in Ireland. However, the list includes a demand that all legislation passed "against us and our religion" in Ireland and England be repealed.[62] No authenticated Irish demands insisted that English anti-Catholic legislation be repealed. In other words, the pamphlet does not provide us with "true demands" but was intended to arouse hostility to the Irish cause.

This pamphlet may be regarded as a rather crude example and not likely to fool anyone. The second is worded with more subtlety. Its title is: *The Petition of Sir* Philomy Oneale *Knight, Generall of the Rebels, in* Ireland, *and the Lords, Nobility and Commanders of the Army of the Catholiques in that Kingdome Presented to ... the Lords and Commons ... in Ireland.*[63] Fortescue's catalogue lists this pamphlet with a note that in it Sir Phelim denied "charges of cruelty."[64] This is what the pamphlet purports to do, and it does it very well. It alleged that the stories of "inhumane and savage cruelties, and most bloody massacres" were the fabrication of "divers false papers and pamphlets" and that the casualties that had occurred took place in "skirmishes" with those who sought to destroy "not only our religion, but lives and fortunes." It has been accepted as an authentic denial by Sir Phelim of atrocity accusations.[65] Yet its authenticity may be doubted because it purports to be signed not only by Sir Phelim, but by "Osmond," Antrim, Mountgarret, "Nettersfield," and Dillon. There was at this time an attempt to implicate Ormond with the Irish and indeed with Dillon's mission to the king.[66] Almost certainly, therefore, this pamphlet was part of that attempt to undermine Ormond's position while trying to prove that Dillon was not an intermediary but a leader of the rebels. By implication, the king was also associated with the Irish because Ormond was known to be close to him and Dillon had been sent to him.

Another interesting feature of this pamphlet is that it was reprinted in Edinburgh.[67] In contrast to England, few pamphlets about Ireland were published in Scotland. Why should this one be an exception? The inclusion of Antrim as one of the supposed signatories suggests that it suited Argyll (who was about to dispatch his clansmen into MacDonnell territory) to have Antrim appear as a leader of the rebellion, even though there is virtually no evidence to substantiate any link between Antrim and the Irish at this time (barring his own later statement under the Commonwealth which I have earlier argued was untrue).[68] In short, it would appear that the pamphlet was part of a propaganda campaign conducted not by the Irish but by various English and Scottish factions against each other.

Members of parliament and the Irish planter gentry who were in London were aware of the way this spate of pamphlets was spreading false information. In mid-November the Commons committee charged with the supervision of the press was required to find "some means to restrain this licentious printing."[69] In January, John Greensmith, who was responsible for printing many of the pamphlets, admitted to the Commons that he had arranged for "sundry pamphlets" with titles like "Good News from Ireland" to be written by two Cambridge students and sold for 2s. 6d. per copy.[70] So concerned were the Irish Protestant gentry in London about the matter that they petitioned the Lords "against the common abuse of printing false and feigned news from Ireland."[71] As Richard Cust has shown for the pamphlet literature of the period as a whole, some was produced in response to genuine news hunger, which might be satisfied even if the news had to be invented, while some was deliberately manipulative.[72]

We may presume that one of the reasons for concern among Irish Protestants was that the spate of publication was not serving their interests. It was reported to Admiral Penington in mid-November that "we have much more printed than is true," and the reporter ascribed this printing to the Puritans who were trying to diminish the already low reputation of Catholics in England still more.[73] Some of the early pamphlets which dealt with Ireland seem to have been associated with such aims. Thus *Bloody Newes from Norwich: Or, A True Relation of a bloody attempt of the Papists in* Norwich, *to consume the whole City by fire … Likewise here is added the last bloody Newes from* Ireland appears to be using the Irish situation more to warn about what Catholics might do in England than to address what they were doing in Ireland.[74] As refugees from Ireland began to flow into England, concern for the plight of Protestants in Ireland grew at the popular level. This interest has been well documented, and demands from the counties for the "speedy relief of distressed and gasping Ireland" were common in 1642.[75] During the initial weeks of the rebellion, however, there seems to have been more concern expressed in the pamphlets about popish plots at home than about finding the means to suppress them in Ireland.

The Protestant planters in London, not content with complaining about pamphlets that did not serve their ends, seem to have arranged for the printing of others that did. The most striking example is *Worse and Worse Newes from Ireland being The Coppy Of A Letter read in the House of Parliament, the 14 ... December Wherein is contained such unheard of Cruelties, committed by the Papists against the Protestants, not sparing Age nor* Sex, that would make a Christians heart to bleede. This was, indeed, read to the Commons on 14 December by Sir John Clotworthy and purported to be a letter from a Thomas Partington, who was supposedly still in Ireland.[76] It described some Irish atrocities in terms similar to those found in the depositions (which had not, at this time, been recorded), yet it also stressed rape, which suggests that it was made up for the occasion because rape was very seldom reported by the deponents. It played upon popular dislike of bishops and Catholics by reporting that a Protestant bishop in Ulster had joined the Irish and by urging that seven condemned priests in England should be executed, but it must be recollected that this was the time that the debate was becoming intense about how much Scottish and English assistance was to be sent to Ireland. It is hard not to see the pamphlet as a planter-inspired effort to influence parliament during this crucial debate. Moreover, in this case the propaganda seems to have been effective because two days after Clotworthy had read the letter we find a private newsletter describing what was going on in Ireland in terms that were derived directly from Clotworthy's statement. Such was the shock effect of the information that the newsletter was able to add: "this I am assured, that the party of Lords and Commons for the popish and delinquent party are not so many as they were."[77] This pamphlet (and there may have been others of a similar genre) raises the question of the aims of the planter lobby and its relationship to parliament, and particularly to John Pym.

ENGLAND: PLANTERS, PARLIAMENT, AND PYM

Some of the letters from Ireland that were read to the Commons were authentic. Most of these were from members of the Irish council, and they reinforced the impression that the rebellion posed as great a threat to Protestants in England as to those in Ireland. Indeed, hardly a week passed without a letter being read to the Commons from an Irish official describing the treatment of Protestants, the need for help, or the links between the Irish and Catholics in England. Clotworthy, for instance, citing a letter from Sir William Parsons, asserted in mid-November that "this design of Ireland" was "hatched" in England.[78] Again, Sir John Temple, one of whose letters was read to the Commons on 24 December, warned that the Irish had begun to plan "the invading of England."[79] Very clearly, the reading of such letters was intended to heighten the sense of fear and encourage the dispatch of troops.

Fifteen English MPs had substantial Irish interests. These included Clotworthy, William Jephson, who had an estate in Cork and was related to Pym, and Lord Lisle, Leicester's son.[80] These men may not have worked as a group, but there was much sympathy in the house for the planters' fate because, as D'Ewes remarked, "I conceive most of this House have friends and kindred" in Ireland.[81] In addition, another group of planters united to press home their interests. Their efforts to suppress spurious pamphlets have already been noted. More striking was their petition to the Commons on 21 December to urge the king and the Lords to accept the 10,000 men proffered by the Scots and to send a similar army from England. This group consisted of twenty-three men who for various reasons had come to England since the outbreak of the rebellion or had been there in October, Clotworthy being the only English MP among them. The others included such familiar Irish Protestant figures as Viscount Loftus of Ely, Sir Faithful Fortescue, Lord Digby, Arthur Jones (Ranelagh's son), Lord Mountnorris, and Richard Fitzgerald, who was associated with the Clotworthy-Ranelagh group of planters.[82] The day after they had petitioned the Commons the same group, except for Clotworthy, were summoned before the Lords committee on Ireland and asked to explain why they wished the Irish parliament to be adjourned beyond 11 January.[83] There are no other signs of this group at work, but this appearance is enough to show that it must have been active on other occasions and that from time to time it may have drawn on the support of allies in the Commons.

The planters had two primary interests which were interconnected. First, they had to encourage the dispatch of troops to Ireland. Second, they wished to preserve, regain, or expand their Irish estates, a goal which could only be achieved if the rebellion was suppressed without substantial concessions. Their support of the dispatch of the Scots was virtually automatic and in this their aims were at one with those of the king and Pym. Pym had few qualms about a Scottish army going to Ireland as Charles would not control it, but the formation of an English army for Irish service raised much more difficult issues. The king would be the commander-in-chief of any English army, and this would give him the potential to destroy his English opponents, a policy which the army plots indicated he might be willing to adopt. The planters were placed in a predicament. On the one hand, they inclined towards Pym because of his influence in the Commons, without which no military expedition could be financed. On the other, Pym's concerns about Charles's use of the army could and did delay the dispatch of this expedition and thus jeopardized their prime objective. The interests of Clotworthy and Pym were not identical. Like the Scots, Pym had no desire to see an independent and Catholic state created in the west, but he had to balance this threat against the greater one of giving Charles a free hand to run England as he wished.

Pym's attitude towards Ireland is revealed best by looking closely at the activities in the Commons during the first two weeks after O'Connolly's revelations. During this period, virtually all the causes for delay in sending men, money, and supplies to Ireland were voiced. Parliament lacked the administrative capacity to run a military campaign. The confusion in the Commons following the Scottish offer of assistance shows how inept the house was in responding to an emergency. Parliament sensed the danger of the rebellion but, as Northumberland observed, "if they intend to keep the ordering of those forces within themselves, I much fear the slowness of the motions of that great body will beget inconveniences which will not appear to them till too late."[84] But if there was one person who did intend to "order those forces" within parliament it was Pym. It has been said that, assuming the seriousness of the rebellion, he was "prepared to sacrifice the Protestants of Ireland to his own interests in England."[85] In a general sense this is correct, though it has also been remarked that in December his preoccupation with raising forces for Ireland caused him to neglect English affairs.[86] He was not disinterested in Ireland, but he was determined to fight the war on his own terms and in so doing he began to create institutions that permitted parliament to "order forces," and we can see the conception of these institutions during the first two weeks after O'Connolly's arrival. Ultimately, because of the way the struggle developed in England, these institutions were directed against the king in England as much as against the Irish, but it must be emphasized that this was not Pym's original intention.

Upon hearing about the rising on 1 November, one member set the tone of the debate by demanding quick action, including the dispatch of Leicester with men and money. The house as a whole agreed to raise £50,000 to meet the emergency and to consult with the Lords in order to borrow money from the city. It was also agreed to reward O'Connolly, to examine him further, and to form a select committee with the Lords for Irish affairs. But at this point the direction of the debate was diverted for an hour and a half by questioning whether the earl of Portland, whose father had died a Catholic, was a reliable governor of the strategic Isle of Wight, and it is clear that it was Pym who wanted him removed.[87] The Lords, for their part, agreed to borrow the money and to form a select committee to deal with Irish affairs but insisted that this consist of seventy-eight men (twenty-six lords and fifty-two MPs), hardly the body to run an effective war effort. The issue of Portland "lost us two or three hours" when it was first discussed with the Lords as they refused to dismiss him, and it caused further delay the next day.[88] Pym's intention to use the rebellion to exclude those he distrusted from office, even if it delayed the dispatch of help to Ireland, had already become apparent. Similarly, it transpired that his intent behind having O'Connolly examined was to find "correspondencies" between Irish events and plots in England, but on this matter O'Connolly failed to provide any hard evidence.[89]

It was Pym who reported back to the Commons about the first meeting of the select committee on 3 November, and it was in this context that the Commons agreed to raise an army in England of 6,000 foot and 2,000 horse to fight in Ireland and to establish means to supply British forces there. Yet it was also Pym who once again raised an issue that diverted the house from Ireland, this time on the question of the number of persons who were visiting a priest who had been put in the Tower of London.[90] Only through the intervention of Sir John Culpepper, a future royalist and chancellor of the exchequer, was the house brought back to the Irish question and, in this case, to an issue of considerable constitutional importance.

What Culpepper asked was "how [and] in what manner" the army was to be raised?[91] Either it had to be made up of volunteers or it had to be recruited by pressing, and the hidden agenda was the prerogative power to enforce military service. D'Ewes, always ready with a precedent to suit his opinion, overlooked Elizabethan practice and went back to Henry II who, he related, had conquered Ireland without resorting to compulsory military service. If impressment was necessary in the present instance, then new legislation would have to be introduced to give it the force of law, and the majority in the house obviously agreed with him because a lawyer was assigned to draw up the necessary bill. The bill was introduced the next day, 4 November, whereupon a debate ensued about whether such an act would itself be an intrusion upon the liberties of the subject.[92] Had volunteers been easy to raise, the bill would have had little significance, but there was little enthusiasm for Irish service, an indication of a basic lack of interest in Ireland at the popular level despite the numerous public statements of horror at what was happening there.[93]

The lack of volunteers meant that help for Ireland was tied to the impressment bill and this raised the constitutional question of the crown's control over military power. The crown's counsel argued that the king had the right to impress under the prerogative.[94] Charles nonetheless agreed to act instead under statute, but he was reluctant to accept a clause in the bill which prohibited him from moving soldiers from one English county to another except when faced by a foreign threat. This clause had implications for England and not Ireland and is another instance in which the Irish crisis was used as a weapon in the political struggle in England. Even here Charles ultimately gave in, and the bill he signed in February contained the offensive clause.[95] It is impossible to pin the responsibility for its inclusion upon Pym, but in view of his known stance on the linkage of assistance to Ireland with English constitutional questions, the clause must clearly have received his approval.

On the same day that the impressment bill first came before the Commons (4 November), Pym introduced a motion to empower the lord lieutenant to appoint officers to take volunteers to Ireland. The house confirmed this authority the following day by ordinance and passed another ordinance giving, in the king's absence, the master of ordnance the power to move arms from one depot to another, and the Lords confirmed these ordinances on the sixth.[96] Leicester saved the king from another constitutional squabble with parliament by declining to accept the validity of a warrant that lacked the king's approval, an indication of his constitutional scruples and a recognition that parliament was moving into an area normally preserved for the king.[97] Here, whatever delay ensued cannot be pinned on Pym, but his attempt to supply military authority of questionable legality is an indication of his desire to acquire as much control over the war effort as possible. The establishment on 9 November of a council of war composed of army officers to give military advice to parliament in prosecuting the war, and an order to control the dispatch of arms to Ireland were clearly steps in the same direction.[98]

It will be evident that there was from the start an element of ambiguity in Pym's position on Ireland. On the one hand, he tended to contribute to the delay in sending assistance by raising tangential issues. On the other, he tried to fashion a mechanism for fighting the war. The thinking behind these cross-purposes emerged most clearly during his intervention in the debate of 6 November, when the Commons was discussing its response to the original offer of Scottish aid. At the end of the debate, Pym stood up and said that although no man should be more ready than himself to venture his estate and life to suppress the rebellion, he feared that as long as the king "gave ear to those evil councillors about him all that we did would prove in vain, and therefore he desired that we might add some declaration in the end of these instructions that howsoever we had engaged ourselves for the assistance of Ireland yet unless the king would remove his evil councillors and take such councillors as might be approved by Parliament we should account ourselves absolved from this engagement."[99]

The comment was almost out of context, in that the debate was about whether the Scots would be paid for their assistance or not, but it shows how strongly Pym believed that nothing could be done until power was wrested from Charles's hands. Subsequently, in the face of opposition, he had to modify his position to gain majority support (151 to 110) and the declaration was changed. If the king would not take parliamentary advice on who he appointed to his council, it said, although due obedience should be shown to him, "yet we should take such a course for the securing of Ireland as might likewise secure ourselves."[100] Despite a vigorous presentation of his position to the Lords, that house rejected it, but what is important is not that Pym failed to secure this wording but that he revealed his priorities so openly at this very early stage of the rebellion. At this time, no course could be taken to secure Ireland without the co-operation of the king, but Pym was not prepared to allow the king the means to act on his own.

The effect of the delays for which Pym was at least partly responsible are best illustrated by contrasting the assistance that was intended with that which actually arrived. Instead of £50,000 only £16,500 reached Ireland by the year's end, and instead of an English army of 6,000 foot (increased to 10,000 on 11 November) and 2,000 horse, only 1,400 men reached Ireland in 1641. These men, commanded by Sir Simon Harcourt, landed on 30 December. They brought no money for their pay or supply, and 300 of them arrived without arms.[101]

It was recognized as early as 11 November that even the figure of £50,000 fell short of what was needed, and after considerable debate it was agreed that £200,000 would have to be raised for Ireland.[102] The city, on its part, agreed to the loan but indicated a number of concerns, including the need to have its money secured by act of parliament and the desire to see bishops denied votes in parliament.[103] These were not conditions, and by 18 November £16,000 of the loan had been collected, but they reflected the uneasiness in the city about both financial and political affairs.[104] The financial situation certainly justified this concern because on 9 December it was reported to the Commons that £454,044 was still owed for costs incurred by the Scottish and English armies, and on 14 December, spurred on by Clotworthy's tales of horror in Ireland, the Commons agreed to increase the sum assigned to the suppression of the rebellion to £400,000.[105]

It was also evident that the Commons did not know how it was going to raise the money. Various proposals were mooted, such as fining bishops, recusants, and monopolists, but such measures could not be expected to raise the large sums required.[106] Moreover, just as the need for money for Ireland was being stressed, deep concerns arose about the possibility that the Irish might be granted religious toleration. As early as 20 November Pym informed the house of the Cavan Remonstrance demanding liberty of conscience, and by 8 December MPS knew of Dillon's mission to the king.[107] D'Ewes and others beat back an attempt to make grants of money for Ireland conditional upon a declaration by the king that he would not tolerate Catholicism, only for Dillon himself to be discovered on his way to the king with instructions from the Irish to make toleration one of the conditions for peace.[108] It is not surprising, therefore, to find the city declining to grant a further loan of £100,000 at the end of January. It complained of the "slow proceedings of the Irish wars," that past loans had not been repaid, and that "ill affected persons" remained in positions of trust "by the votes of bishops and popish lords."[109]

It is in this financial context that the question of Irish land has to be considered, an issue which, in turn, had vital implications for the constitutional relationship between England and Ireland. The lords justices believed that the spread of the rebellion opened land to the king's "free disposal and the general settlement of peace and religion by introducing English."[110] They may have been in touch with planters in England about such a scheme, but they did not originate it. They commented on the new opportunities for plantation on 14 December, but well before this the idea had already been broached in England. The first mention of Irish land being used as a means of financing the war occurred in the declaration of parliament sent to the lords justices on 4 November assuring them of assistance.[111] Those who raised forces to suppress the rebellion would be rewarded with "lands of inheritance in Ireland." The idea surfaced again a few days later in the preamble to the Grand Remonstrance, which was in its complete form by 11 November.[112] Thus, within days of the news of the rising reaching England, the Irish claims of the preceding summer for parliamentary sovereignty had been swept aside, and the English Commons had taken unto itself the authority to redistribute Irish property through English legislation.

The king, in responding to the Remonstrance on 2 December, avoided committing himself to a policy of using Irish lands to finance the war by saying that it was unwise to dispose of the bear's skin before it was dead, but this was not a complete rejection of the idea.[113] Nobody in December could be sure that Pym would hang on to the slim majority with which he had pushed through the Remonstrance, and there is a hint that Clotworthy may have been preparing for a royalist comeback by cultivating the king. At the end of the month a Scot recorded that someone might be feeding information from the two houses to the king and that suspicion fell on Clotworthy.[114] The exclusion of the bishops from the Lords, the ill-fated attempt to arrest the five members, and the king's subsequent withdrawal from Whitehall ensured Pym's renewed influence, making it incumbent for the planters to work with him, but if he was to do anything in Ireland, he had to have money, which meant that the idea of using Irish land to finance the war had to be given substance.

We know very little about what led to the proposal for the Adventurers Act or, more accurately, "an Act for the speedy and effectual reducing of the rebels in his majesty's kingdom of Ireland." The idea made its first appearance on 11 February when Denzil Holles delivered a petition from "certain Londoners" in which they offered resources for the "speedy relief" of Ireland in return for rebel estates.[115] This private enterprise scheme for financing the war was referred to a sub-committee of the Irish affairs committee, where it grew from a plan to forfeit 800,000 acres of Irish land to one in which 10 million acres were promised at some time in the future in the expectation of raising £1 million quickly. It was in this form that the king, who had apparently overcome his scruples about selling the bear's skin before it was dead, agreed to it on 24 February, and it passed into law on 19 March.[116]

Closely connected with this scheme for raising the funds to prosecute the war went administrative changes which both streamlined military management and gave Pym greater control over it. As early as 17 December Sir Philip Stapleton, one of Pym's associates, had proposed that a small number of MPs should be responsible for the day-to-day decisions about Ireland, but there was no progress in changing the administrative structure till February. On the third Pym reported on "certain instructions" that were to be given "to such as should be made commissioners for Irish affairs concerning the means to manage the war and to establish peace and true religion" in Ireland. During the ensuing days there was considerable discussion about the mandate of the proposed commissioners, but a proposal finally went to the Lords on 7 February.[117] Here, just three days before the Londoners presented their petition, Leicester told the Lords that Irish affairs would be conducted with greater dispatch "if they were managed by some few members of both Houses, to be chosen as commissioners, authorised by Parliament ... and the great seal of England."[118] What emerged from this proposal, which was obviously sponsored by Pym and backed by Leicester, was a commission composed of seven lords and fourteen MPs. The MPs selected as commissioners included Pym, Holles, Henry Marten, Oliver Cromwell, Henry Vane Junior, John Hampden, Sir John Evelyn, and Robert Reynolds, all of whom were among Charles's leading opponents, along with other less well known men of similar sympathies.[119] On 4 April, after some hesitation, Charles signed the commission, though with the proviso that the soldiers raised for service in Ireland should serve only in that country.[120]

Charles's signature on the commission coincided with the landing of Scottish troops in Ulster, both events marking an end to the first phase of British reaction to the rebellion. As the proviso suggests, Charles suspected his parliamentary opponents of planning what they suspected him of wishing to do; namely, using an army intended for Ireland in England. This, indeed, is how Pym and those who thought like him used some of the resources assigned for Ireland. In July £100,000 was borrowed from the Adventurers fund for parliamentary objectives in England; officers intended for Munster were ordered to serve in England and at least one brigade originally recruited to operate in Ireland fought for parliament at Edgehill. This is not to say that Pym struggled to gain control of the army going to Ireland in order to fight Charles in England. During April every effort seems to have been made to ensure that both men and money went to Ireland.[121] Pym was willing to delay aid reaching Ireland in order to win control of the Irish war effort, and later he was willing to divert resources from that theatre to the conflict in England, but so far as we know his actions were determined by immediate circumstances, not by any long-range plan save that of remaining in control.

We cannot tell what Charles would have done had he been able to control an army destined for Ireland. On the evidence available, he wanted to act quickly to defeat the Catholics, and the impediments to Scottish and English forces crossing to Ireland were not of his making. Indeed, he seems to have been sufficiently anxious to quell the rebellion to concede control – if reluctantly – over the army that was to do the deed. Pym's concern about the Irish situation did not stretch this far. Yet what counted politically in England was not what Charles actually wished to do, but the perceptions of his intentions, and here he had several strikes against him. First, his past behaviour indicated a willingness to use force against his opponents in England,

and these men had neither the interest nor resources of modern historians to determine when he was plotting and when he was not. They could not risk placing another army in his hands, given the experience of the recent past. Second, not only his defects but also his more admirable characteristics counted against him. However devious and untrustworthy he may have been, he was tolerant and judicious in dealing with Catholics and did not share the crude fanaticism of men like Pym and Clotworthy. But in the eyes of many of his English subjects, this rendered him unfit to deal with the situation as they saw it, coloured as their image was by a belief in a wholesale massacre of Protestants. Nor did it help Charles that the Irish claimed his sanction for what they did and that their deeds were often sufficiently gruesome to be open to exaggeration. Even those who understood that Charles had not encouraged the rebellion nevertheless considered him ill fitted to deal with it. Richard Baxter, in explaining why many turned to parliament, illustrated the way misinformation about what had happened in Ireland was mixed with a sense that Charles could not be depended on to end the rebellion. In summing up what turned men into parliamentarians, Baxter concluded:

But above all, the two hundred thousand killed in Ireland, affrighted the Parliament and all the land. And where as it is said the king hated that, as well as they: they answered, "that though he did, his hating it would neither make all alive again, nor preserve England from their threatened assault, as long as men of the like malignity were protected, and could not be kept out of arms."[122]

This misinformation arose in part from a press feeding the demand for sensationalism during a period of strong public anxiety, in part from the Irish excesses that did not diminish in the telling as large numbers of Protestant refugees arrived in England, and in part from a deliberate campaign by Protestant planters to ensure military assistance by depicting Irish behaviour in the most lurid colours and emphasizing the type of threat to England which we can detect in Baxter's analysis. With the planters, Charles was also at a disadvantage. During the previous summer he had shown a willingness to make a land settlement with Catholic landowners, to the horror of the more extreme – and more powerful – planters. Much as they deplored the parliamentary delays in sending aid to Ireland, this did not turn them into supporters of the king. Pym, moreover, by including the clause in the Grand Remonstrance for the forfeiture of estates of those in rebellion, identified his cause with a grandiose plantation scheme that made Strafford's ambitions in Connacht look moderate. In the short term, the Irish gained advantage by the divisions in Britain as they won crucial time while they consolidated their position and while they, too, sought assistance. But just as actions in Britain led to unforeseen reactions in Ireland inimical to British interests, so too did events in Ireland create reactions in Britain which, in the long run, proved disastrous for the majority of the population of Ireland. The Irish, instead of having to deal with Charles Stuart, had to face Oliver Cromwell. It was a game in which nobody saw more than one move ahead.

Conclusion

The Ireland that emerged in the 1650s out of the civil war was fundamentally different from that which had been taking shape in the 1630s. It was argued at the beginning of this book that, until the Anglo-Scottish conflict began, Ireland under Charles I had enjoyed a period of relative prosperity: postwar opinion seems to have been unanimous on this. It has also been shown that the various political components of the island had begun to work together. This is not an original perception. In 1990 Conrad Russell cited Aidan Clarke's comment of 1970 that the rebellion amounted to "a startling interruption of a mood of peaceful cooperation."[1] In other words, the trend up to 1638 was towards accommodation and away from conflict. What has been attempted in this book is to show how this co-operation turned into a ferocious war.

Economic conditions in Ireland undoubtedly worsened at the end of the 1630s. Such conditions served to aggravate existing social tensions such as indebtedness and may have reinforced an inclination to challenge the existing authority, but the Irish conflict cannot be explained in predominantly economic terms. A direct causal link between the poorer economic conditions in the late 1630s and the decision to attempt to change the government in Dublin cannot be demonstrated. Significantly, although poor harvests and other essentially Irish influences contributed to the dip in economic activity, an equally important factor was the shock delivered to Irish commerce by the Anglo-Scottish conflict. As Ireland's favourable trade balance depended to a very large degree upon the economies of England and Scotland, the quarrel between these two realms produced an immediate and depressing impact upon Irish commerce in general and led in Ulster to a decline in the labour force as Scottish settlers fled Strafford's measures to counter Covenanter influence. Thus, at the root of some of the more important negative economic pressures affecting Ireland lay the political and religious dispute between Charles and his Scottish subjects.

The harsh regime of Thomas Wentworth also undoubtedly contributed to the climate that nurtured rebellion. When Robert Maxwell asked his captors what made them rise, they included among their complaints the lord deputy's "intolerable government." However, as Maxwell remarked, this lay "no heavier on them than on him and the rest of the British Protestants."[2] The common dislike of Wentworth had, indeed, served to unite the realm rather than to divide it. There was also religious tension, and particularly much resentment among the Irish at having to pay tithes to the clergy of a church to which they had no wish to belong. To cite what Maxwell was told again, if the Scots could fight for ceremonies "which are but shadows," the Irish had every reason to rise on grounds of religion, "which is the substance."[3] Such sentiments certainly fed the flames of rebellion once it had broken out, but the religious differences within the population were not the sparks that set off the blaze. On the whole, where Protestants and Catholics lived close to each other, both groups adopted an attitude of live-and-let-live before the rebellion. Similarly, although we find the abolition of plantation to be one of the Irish demands, and this demand undoubtedly reflected a pre-war attitude, the dislike of the Jacobean plantations by itself never became so acute within the country as to produce a concerted effort to overthrow the government. Indeed, some of the leaders of the rebellion had benefited from the plantations.

It may be observed that Maxwell ignored an important difference between Protestant settlers like himself and his captors. Whereas he and his associates may have hated Wentworth as much as the Irish, he could look to a day when Wentworth would be replaced and to institutions which would be responsive to his views as change was wrought. The Irish gentry, though part of the political élite and participating in the political process, were also marginal in that they held no office and wielded little influence except in combination with their Old English co-religionists. Their complaint was not so much against the new order as against their exclusion from it. However, even this sense of exclusion could have been remedied over time. That the time was not available can be ascribed to a series of decisions taken primarily in England and Scotland.

Any list of such decisions must begin with those that led to the Scottish rebellion, for this supplied the opportunity, the model, and, to some extent, the motive for the Irish rising. The Scottish Covenanters weakened and divided Charles's England and thus rendered rebellion in Ireland a practical possibility. The Scots also furnished the Irish with an example of how their grievances might be redressed, and as J.C. Beckett has pointed out, the success of the Scots "seemed to justify others in following their example."[4] As important, however, was the anti-papal and anti-episcopal rhetoric that accompanied the Scottish success because it appeared to presage a fundamental shift in policy towards Catholicism in Ireland from tacit toleration to annihilation. Such a threat, if believed, meant that rebellion became the better of two evils, for it gave at least a fighting chance of religious survival.

Nevertheless, the Scottish rebellion did not make an Irish one inevitable. Of equal importance was the instability within Charles's council which led to the appointment of second-rate men to official positions. At the beginning of this book I tried to show the way Ireland played a particularly important role in this conciliar rivalry. It is no accident that such enemies of Wentworth as the earls of Arundel, Essex, and Holland, the marquis of Hamilton, and Sir Henry Vane held, or wished to hold, Irish land, or Irish office, or both. An opportunity was thereby created for a type of fifth column within the Irish government as represented by Sir William Parsons and Viscount Ranelagh which was happy to work with the lord deputy's English enemies. It was this rivalry which created a government in Ireland which was unable to control the impact of the Scottish upheaval. In particular, it gave men like Parsons and Ranelagh the opportunity to delay the settlement of the crucial issue of the security of land titles. Had Charles been able to appoint the earl of Ormond as lord deputy in December 1640, as was his wish, it is likely that there would have been a different outcome. Instead, he was pushed into selecting Parsons and Sir John Borlase as lords justices. Such men, including Vane, who espoused a policy of continued plantation, could, nevertheless, only delay the agreement in England to confirm Irish land titles despite their possession of office; they were unable to stop it. A considerable body of Protestant MPs continued to support this land reform into the summer, and they had the support of such men in England as the earl of Bristol. Had Ormond been in charge in Ireland, he, along with his fellow Old English and the planters associated with Bristol, could have settled the land issue before the Irish parliament was prorogued in the summer of 1641. Instead, the bills that were to achieve this, although approved in England, could not be introduced into the Irish parliament before the outbreak of the rebellion, which transformed the situation.

The debate during the sixth session in November about how long the session might continue, although overshadowed by the rebellion, was a continuation of the campaign to confirm the Graces. Only if the session continued for a reasonable length of time could the bills confirming estates, which all knew to be ready to be introduced, be presented to parliament. The failure to pass the bills, which had been promised since 1628, gave the signal that those who ran the government were determined not to introduce them and that the only way of changing the government appeared to be by force, a conclusion that had been reached by many, even beyond the borders of Ulster, before parliament met.

To this interpretation it may be objected that Charles had, unbeknownst to all in Ireland, and before the rebellion broke out, already issued an order to postpone the parliamentary session. He had done so at the urging of what remained of his council in England, which, in turn, had been persuaded to this course by officials in Ireland. The desire of these officials for a postponement of the session may have been inspired by a wish to postpone, yet again, the confirmation of the Graces, but the argument they advanced concerned the constitutional issue, and on this they had more allies, including, we may assume, the king, than on maintaining the process of plantation.

In retrospect, the decision by MPs to raise the constitutional issue before the Graces had been confirmed proved a tactical mistake. The desire to avoid a repetition of Wentworth's government makes the error understandable, but both impeachment and the Queries, although only intended to deal with the situation in Ireland, raised questions about royal authority and the relationship of Charles's kingdoms to each other, and gave Parsons and Vane an opportunity in their campaign to thwart the land settlement which would otherwise not have been available. There is no reason to believe that even Ormond supported Sir Audley Mervin or Patrick Darcy on the constitutional question. His remark in 1642 that he had opposed those then in arms in parliament the previous summer suggests that he shared the misgivings of the lords justices about the constitutional direction being taken by the lawyers. It may be that Charles's discussion with Viscount Dillon in September about going to Ireland in 1642 was an attempt to grapple with this tricky question, but the issue would not have become acute had the land question been settled quickly. Once the Graces had been confirmed, the Irish parliament could have been prorogued for a long time, or even dissolved, without much complaint, and there would have been no forum in which to discuss the constitution. Vane correctly understood that the issue had to be postponed, but by working against the confirmation of estates, he, in combination with Parsons, had denied Charles the means to implement delay without causing exasperation.

Even in the delicate area of religion, Ormond's appointment as a lord justice could have made a difference. Most of his relatives were

Catholics, and he shared none of the religious prejudice of men like Parsons and Pym, as is borne out by his evident moderation after the rebellion had begun. With the land issue out of the way, the strength of the moderates in both religious groups, led by Ormond and the earl of Clanricard respectively, would almost certainly have increased, which would have served to keep the intensity of religious feelings under control and denied the men like Clotworthy on one side and some of the priests we hear about in the depositions on the other the opportunity to wreak their havoc.

Charles cannot be blamed for the failure to appoint Ormond as interim governor. The divisions in the English council and Ormond's closeness to Wentworth made such an appointment politically impossible. Thus the Old English, blinded by suspicion and shortsightedness, permitted the government of Ireland to fall into the hands of those who pursued interests opposite to their own. Yet even the sidelining of Ormond did not lead inevitably to rebellion. The failure to secure Lord Cottington as governor and the appointment of the earl of Leicester probably led the Old English to contemplate rebellion during the summer. However, had Leicester gone to Ireland soon after his appointment as lord lieutenant in May, he too would have had a good chance of resolving the principal grievances of the realm. It is even possible that the native Irish would have seen their complaints addressed because it will be recalled that these were referred to Leicester, and the little evidence that exists about him suggests that he approached problems with an open mind. Instead of going to Ireland he returned to France. This was Charles's decision, and in retrospect it can be seen to have been a mistake, but the king was not to know that the time for resolving Irish problems had run out.

It is hard to say categorically whether the rising would have been forestalled had the new Irish army been shipped out of the country as originally planned. Contemporaries believed that the presence of the unemployed but well-trained troops was crucial, even though they do not appear to have played much of a military role in the rising during the early weeks save at Lisburn. They did, however, provide a blind behind which the Ulstermen could make their preparations. It is also hard to imagine the formation of a colonels' plot, had they all left Ireland at the same time as Colonel Belling or soon after. Moreover, it is doubtful that the Ulstermen would have risen without the conviction that, as they did so, the government in Dublin was being rendered powerless. They followed the Scottish model, and it has been remarked that what gave the Covenanters their political strength was the possession of the capital and the control of the government.[5] The presence of some of the colonels certainly helped to convince the Ulstermen that they too would enjoy this advantage. If the failure to get the army out of Ireland was crucial, this was not Charles's fault. During the summer he did all he could to have it shipped abroad. He was thwarted by the English MPS, with assistance from their Catholic confrères in Ireland. The latter knew what they were doing, but the English Commons knew little of Irish affairs and allowed prejudice and extraneous issues to undermine the sensible policy of the king.

An exhaustive list of significant decisions which, if different, might have avoided the rebellion would be tedious, but one more may be highlighted because it illustrates the way in which the absence of communication between the extremes on both sides created the climate of desperation that led to the rebellion. The circulation of petitions in Ulster in connection with the Root and Branch bill in the spring and summer of 1641 had a very profound impact upon Irish attitudes. Like the rhetoric that flowed from the Covenanters, these petitions and their supporters, led by Clotworthy in Ireland and Pym in England, appeared to threaten the very existence of Catholicism. Pym and his followers believed that Catholicism was about to try to destroy Protestantism in England, but in resisting this supposed threat, he created a similar, if reversed, fear in Ireland. The Irish, in turn, in countering what they believed to be Puritan intentions, appeared to confirm every suspicion the militant Protestants in England possessed. The Root and Branch petition was an English document which was supposed to address English issues, but once again we see how an English or "British" issue had a very profound impact upon Ireland.

Despite Charles's efforts to take the right action on several occasions, he must bear ultimate responsibility for the conflict. He gave neither the Scottish nor the Irish nobility a sufficient sense of participation in the administration of their respective realms, and he presided while extremists in all three kingdoms reinforced each other's worst fears. There were times, as in the case of the confirmation of Irish land titles, when he allowed his officials to delay action when he should have intervened decisively. At other times he had a clear idea of what he wished to do, as when he wanted to save Strafford, only to discover that he was powerless. He also became involved in plots, which cast a shadow over all he did. Because of these failings, he helped to create a situation in which the majority of the population in Ireland saw, on the one hand, the prospect of an administration in England dominated by Pym and his friends that would pursue policies inimical to their interests, and, on the other, an opportunity to diminish English dominance as the English disputed among themselves along with a model in Scotland of how to do it.

This, it is true, turned out to be a double miscalculation. The rebellion helped to strengthen those elements in England that the Catholics in Ireland feared most. Once Oliver Cromwell had refashioned as well as restored English unity, English authority returned to Ireland with a severity which Charles, whatever the composition of his council, had neither the means nor the desire to impose. It was a measure of the change in the English state wrought by Cromwell and his colleagues that, whereas the Tudors had taken decades to subdue Ireland, Cromwell did the job in three years, while accomplishing that other Tudor goal of uniting Scotland to England. The Scots, whatever their feelings about the process, survived it with their land and most of their institutions intact, but the result for Ireland was devastating. The land was destroyed, much of the ancient aristocracy was lost, estates were confiscated on a scale that perhaps not even Parsons imagined was possible, and by the end of the century the Catholic majority was excluded from the political process. The divide that separated Irish Catholics from Protestants may not have reached its fullest extent until the 1690s, but we cannot doubt that the initial blow which created this split was delivered in 1641. Well into the second half of the eighteenth century Irish Protestants marked the anniversaries of the rising with a sense of deliverance as well as warning, and Catholics lived in fear that the memories of it would be used to reinforce the penalties imposed upon them.[6] Even as the twentieth century closes, the animosities that were unleashed in Ireland in 1641 still linger under the surface. It is to be hoped that an exposition of the complex mixture of prejudice, personal ambition, lack of communication, misunderstanding, and miscalculation in Charles's three kingdoms that gave rise to these animosities may help to diminish their vestigial remains.

Notes

ACLS	American Council of Learned Societies
Add. MSS	Additional Manuscripts
BL	British Library
Bodl.	Bodleian Library
Cal. SP	*Calendar of State Papers*
Commons' journ. England	*Journals of the House of Commons* [England]
Commons' journ. Ireland	*Journals of the House of Commons of Ireland*
DNB	*Dictionary of National Biography*
HMC	Historical Manuscripts Commission
Lords' journ. England	*Journals of the House of Lords* [England]
Lords' journ. Ireland	*Journals of the House of Lords of Ireland*
NLI MSS	National Library of Ireland Manuscripts
NLS	National Library of Scotland
PRO	Public Record Office (England)
PROI	Public Record Office of Ireland
PRONI	Public Record Office of Northern Ireland
SCL	Sheffield City Library
SRO	Scottish Record Office
TCD MSS	Trinity College, Dublin, Manuscripts

INTRODUCTION

1 *Commons' journ. Ireland*, 1: 134–5.

2 Bottigheimer, "The Reformation in Ireland," 140–9; Bradshaw, "Sword, Word and Strategy," 475–502; Canny, "Why the Reformation Failed," 423–50; Bottigheimer, "The Failure of the Reformation," 196–207.

3 Bush, *Government Policy of Protector Somerset*, 7–39.

4 Bradshaw, *Irish Constitutional Revolution*, 195–212, 217–21, 238–9; Bradshaw, "Sword, Word and Strategy," 477–83; Ellis, *Tudor Ireland*, 139–41.

5 Ellis, *Tudor Ireland*, 221, 230–1, 234, 237, 279, 309–10; Hayes-McCoy, "Conciliation, Coercion and the Protestant Reformation," 85.

6 Throughout this book I refer to those descended from the mediaeval settlers as Old English. Historians have sometimes reserved that term for families of this origin who were Roman Catholic by faith, as most of them were. I include within the term those few such descendants who became Protestants, but those Old English who acted together as a political group were all Catholics. Similarly, to all those English who arrived in Ireland after the Reformation and their descendants, I apply the term New English, regardless of their religion. The term "Anglo-Irish" has deliberately been avoided as it does not seem to have been in common use until the eighteenth century (see Beckett, *Making of Modern Ireland*, 15n). The broader application of the term Old English ensures that such men as James Butler, twelfth earl of Ormond, who was a Protestant, but whose family had lived in Ireland for generations, is not designated in a manner that implies that he or his family were recent arrivals.

7 Ellis, *Tudor Ireland*, 257–8.

8 Bradshaw, "Sword, Word and Strategy," 479–80; Ellis, *Tudor Ireland*, 257–8.

9 Ellis, *Tudor Ireland*, 256–9, 268; Andrews, *Trade, Plunder and Settlement*, 12, 148, 184, 186; MacCarthy-Morrogh, *Munster Plantation*, 118.

10 MacCarthy-Morrogh, *Munster Plantation*, 295; Perceval-Maxwell, *Scottish Migration*, 289; Clarke and Edwards, "Pacification, Plantation, and the Catholic Question," 220–1.

11 Ellis, *Tudor Ireland*, 257, 260, 264.

12 *Statutes Ireland*, 1: 176; Perceval-Maxwell, "Ireland and the Monarchy," 279–95.

13 Edwards and Moody, "Poynings' Law, part I," 415–16.

14 *Statutes Ireland*, 1: 44.

15 Ibid., 246–7; Edwards and Moody, "Poynings' Law, part I," 419.

16 Bradshaw, "Beginnings of Modern Ireland," 85–6.

17 Casway, *Owen Roe O'Neill*, 32–3; Clarke, *Old English*, 216n.

18 *Cal. SP Ireland, 1625–32*, 190.

19 Gillespie, "End of an Era," 193–4; Casway, "Two Phelim O'Neills," 338–9; Bodl., Carte MSS 118: 32.

20 Gillespie, "End of an Era," 194; McGrath, "Membership of the Irish House of Commons," 41.

21 Clarke, "Genesis of the Ulster Rising," 35.

22 Clarke, *Old English*, 45–6.

23 *Acts Privy Council England, 1628*, 398–401.

24 Clarke, "Genesis of the Ulster Rising," 33.

25 Clarke, *Old English*, 15; Clarke, "Irish Economy," 170.

26 Clarke, *Old English*, 86.

27 Ibid., 245; Russell, "British Background to the Irish Rebellion," 171.

28 Clarke, *Old English*, 36.

29 The Graces are most accessible in the appendix to Clarke, *Old English*, 238–54.

30 Clarke, "Selling Royal Favours," 239–40.

31 Kearney, *Strafford in Ireland*, 58–9.

32 Bossy, "Counter-Reformation and the People of Ireland," 158–9, 169.

33 Corish, *Catholic Community*, 25–6.

34 Ibid., 19; Mooney, "Golden Age of the Irish Franciscans," 22.

35 Mooney, "Golden Age of the Irish Franciscans," 24.

36 Kearney, "Ecclesiastical Politics and the Counter-Reformation," 203–4; Cregan, "Social and Cultural Background of a Counter-Reformation Episcopate," 89; Corish, *Catholic Community*, 21.

37 O'Sullivan, "Franciscans in Dundalk," 47.

38 Mooney, "Golden Age of the Irish Franciscans," 30.

39 "Brief Discourse Concerning the Promotion of Catholic Bishops in Ireland," 3 Sept. 1639, Bodl., Clarendon MSS 17: 82–3.

40 Canny, *The Upstart Earl*, 5.

41 Lodge, *Peerage of Ireland*, 4: 16; Jackson, *Intermarriage*, 78.

42 Cooper, "Fortune of Wentworth," 168–72; Watts, "Wentworth," 106.

43 Falkland to Conway, 23 Aug. 1625, *Cal. SP Ireland, 1625–32*, 31.

44 Ibid., 362.

45 Ibid., xxvii, 193, 441–2.

46 Ibid., 239.

47 Ibid., 441; Hickson, ed., *Ireland in the Seventeenth Century*, 2: 77. I thank Rolf Loeber for directing me to this last reference.

48 Clarke, "Selling Royal Favours," 241.

49 Ranger, "Richard Boyle," 250; Kearney, *Strafford in Ireland*, 11; Perceval-Maxwell, "Protestant Faction," 235–6, 245–6, 252. There were two Sir Charles Cootes, the elder and his son. The records seldom distinguish between the two. In this case as in most others, the reference is almost certainly to the elder.

50 Clarke, "Selling Royal Favours," 239.

51 *Cal. SP Ireland, 1625–32*, 56–8.

52 Ibid., 589–90.

53 Clarke, *Old English*, 53.

54 Ibid., 64–5; Kearney, *Strafford in Ireland*, 86–8.

55 Ellis, "Parliament and Community in Yorkist and Tudor Ireland," 43–5.

56 Ranger, "Richard Boyle," xiv.

57 Knowler, ed., *Strafforde's Letters*, 1: 199; Clarke, "Selling Royal Favours," 247.

58 Ussher's answers to questions, 28 Mar. 1641, BL, Add. MSS 34253: 3; Kearney, *Strafford in Ireland*, 60.

59 Kearney, *Strafford in Ireland*, 89–90, 98.

60 Ibid., 98.

61 Ibid., 97–9, 172–4.

62 Ford, *Protestant Reformation in Ireland*, 193.

63 TCD MSS 812: 33v., 73v., 116–17, 205, 327. These references are to the counties of Carlow and Kilkenny and record Protestants turning Catholic after the rebellion had broken out, neutrals, and Irish working with the English. Similar references for many other counties could be supplied.

64 Gonzalez to Peregra, 15 Jan. 1639, Irish Jesuit Archives, MSS A: no. 66; translation: 224–6.

65 Wentworth to Wandesford, 25 July, 1636, in Knowler, ed., *Strafforde's Letters*, 2: 18.

66 Laud to Bramhall, 4 Mar. 1635, HMC, *Hastings MSS*, 4: 65–6; ibid., xix.

67 Naylor to [Cork], 18 July 1639, NLI MSS 13237: 24; Watts, "Wentworth," 100; Kearney, *Strafford in Ireland*, 126.

68 Perceval-Maxwell, *Scottish Migration*, 269–73.

69 Ibid., 270; Adair, *True Narrative*, 34, 42; Perceval-Maxwell, "Strafford and the Covenanters," 528.

70 Adair, *True Narrative*, 40, 42–9.

71 Perceval-Maxwell, *Scottish Migration*, 114, 156–7; O'Dowd, "Rebellion and War," 6–7; TCD MSS 829: 302; TCD MSS 823: 169; TCD MSS 830: 1v., 4. I am grateful to Mary O'Dowd for permitting me to consult her typescript before publication.

72 This information is partly derived from chapter 2 of Jane Ohlmeyer's thesis, "A Seventeenth Century Survivor: the Political Career of Randal MacDonnell, First Marquis and Second Earl of Antrim (1609–83)." I thank her for permitting me to see this before it was submitted. For correspondence between Hamilton and Antrim during this period, see: SRO, GD 406/1/283, 333, 652–3, 1155–8, 1171.

73 Stevenson, *Scottish Covenanters*, 92; Perceval-Maxwell, "Ulster Rising of 1641," 158.

74 Perceval-Maxwell, "Strafford and the Covenanters," 530.

75 Ibid., 531; Bramhall to Laud, 23 Feb. 1638, *Cal. SP Ireland, 1633–47*, 182.

76 Perceval-Maxwell, "Strafford and the Covenanters," 535–40.

CHAPTER ONE

1 BL, Sloan MSS 1008: 355.
2 BL, Sloan MSS 3838: 3. Sir John Temple in his *Irish Rebellion*, published in 1646, made a similar comment (p. 12), but the wording of the passage quoted is very different from Temple's and must have been written independently.
3 Gilbert, ed., *Irish Confederation*, 1: 2.
4 Gilbert, ed., *Contemporary History*, 1, i: 11.
5 TCD MSS 836: 171.
6 Bodl., Carte MSS 64: 314–314v.; BL, Add. MSS 41844A: 12–12v., 15v.
7 *Lords' journ. Ireland*, 1: 152–3.
8 Kearney, *Strafford in Ireland*, 130–70.
9 Clarke, "Irish Economy," 168–86.
10 Canny, "Irish Background to Penn's Experiment," 139–56, and *Kingdom and Colony*, 69–102; MacCarthy-Morrogh, *Munster Plantation*.
11 Robinson, *Plantation of Ulster*.
12 Gillespie, "Migration and Opportunity: A Comment," 90–5, and "End of an Era," 191–209.
13 Cullen, "Economic Trends, 1660–91," 389; Gillespie, *Transformation of the Irish Economy*, 13.
14 Bodl., Carte MSS 63: 126v. Petty estimated that there were 850,000 people in Ireland in 1652, of whom 160,000 were Protestants (see Corish, "Cromwellian Regime," 357). It must be admitted that neither Petty nor Ormond knew the size of Ireland's population in 1641, nor will anyone because we lack the evidence to provide a precise figure.
15 MacCarthy-Morrogh, *Munster Plantation*, 253–60, and "English Presence in Early Seventeenth Century Munster," 172.
16 Perceval-Maxwell, *Scottish Migration*, 228, 311, and "Strafford and the Covenanters," 549.
17 Robinson, *Plantation of Ulster*, 105–6. Robinson calculates the British population of seven Ulster counties, excluding Cavan, Donegal, and Tyrone, to be 20,000 adult males circa 1659. If we double this figure to reach an approximate number for all adults, and bear in mind the excluded counties and the decline in population during the 1640s, the figure of 40 to 45 thousand British adults in 1641 which I use looks on the conservative side.
18 Canny, "Migration and Opportunity," 11.
19 For the presence of Scots outside Ulster, see above, 25.
20 MacCarthy-Morrogh, *Munster Plantation*, 256; Moody, *Londonderry Plantation*, 278; Sheehan, "Irish Towns in a Period of Change," 175;

Clarke, "Irish Economy," 175; Cullen, "Economic Trends, 1660–91," 390. Cullen calculates that Dublin's major period of expansion was the first half of the seventeenth century and that there was a fivefold increase in population between 1600 and 1660.

21 Robinson, *Plantation of Ulster*, 155–6. Many of these boroughs were created to provide additional seats for Protestants in parliament where the population did not justify the creation of a borough, and some were established on sites where there was some existing development, but there is no question that urban development in Ulster increased substantially after 1603.

22 Dietz, *English Public Finance*, 2: 434, 436; Russell, "British Background to the Irish Rebellion," 173; lords justices to king, 2 Apr. 1641, BL, Egerton MSS 2533: 114v.; lords justices to Vane, [7 June] 1641, *Cal. SP Ireland, 1633–47*, 299; BL, Harleian MSS 162: 351; PRO, E 405/285: 299.

23 The Chester-Ireland trade confirms a rapid rise in trade volume from 1635: see Clarke, "Irish Economy," 185.

24 Radcliffe's deposition regarding the customs revenue of 1634, 13 July 1636, SCL, Wentworth Woodhouse MSS 24–5: no. 196.

25 Radcliffe to [Ingram], 28 Oct. 1634, HMC, *Various Collections*, 8: 44; PRO, SP 63/258: 145v.; *Cal. SP Ireland, 1633–47*, 252.

26 BL, Harleian MSS 2138: 164; PRO, SP 63/259: 217v.–18, 220–21v.; SCL, Wentworth Woodhouse MSS 24–5: no. 199; Huntingdon Record Office, Manchester MSS dd. M 70/30; Dunlop, "A Note on the Export Trade of Ireland," 754–5.

27 Canny, "Irish Background to Penn's Experiment," 142–8, and "Migration and Opportunity," 11.

28 MacCarthy-Morrogh, "English Presence in Early Seventeenth Century Munster," 187–9.

29 Robinson, *Plantation of Ulster*, 145–9, 178–9; PRONI, D 3632/1: 4v., 15v., 17v., 34v.; PRONI, D 282/2.

30 McCracken, *Irish Woods*, 165–8; TCD MSS 821: 188.

31 Note on Walley to Cork, 28 Jan. 1639, NLI MSS 13237: no. 21.

32 Walley to Cork, 28 Sept. 1639, ibid., no. 24; Henry Smethwick to Cork, 9 Sept. 1640, Chatsworth, Lismore MSS 21: no. 46; Walley to Cork, 14 April 1641, Lismore MSS 22: no. 6. See also Walley to Cork, 25 June 1641, Lismore MSS 22: no. 31.

33 Wandesford's speech, 15 Oct. 1640, SCL, Wentworth Woodhouse MSS 24–5: no. 138, 9; Clarke, *Old English*, 132; lords justices to Vane, 7 June 1641, PRO, SP 63/259: 147.

34 Johnston, "Plantation of Fermanagh," 72, 207–8.

35 Gillespie, "End of an Era," 207.

36 Clarke, "Irish Economy," 169.

37 MacCarthy-Morrogh, "English Presence in Early Seventeenth Century Munster," 179.

38 Inventory of goods and chattels of the earl of Thomond, 7 Aug. 1639, Huntingdon Record Office, Manchester MSS dd. M7/23.

39 Ibid.

40 Brown, "Aristocratic Finances," 51; Cork to Warwick, 25 Feb. 1642, BL, Egerton MSS 80: 32; Perceval-Maxwell, *Scottish Migration*, 107.

41 Gillespie, *Transformation of the Irish Economy*, 21; McNeill and Otway-Ruthven, eds., *Dowdall Deeds*, 325–6; Cregan, "Social and Cultural Background of a Counter-Reformation Episcopate," 101; Nugent to Vitelleschi, 25 Aug. 1641, Irish Jesuit Archives, MSS A: no. 247; Gilbert, ed., *Contemporary History*, 1, ii: 489; lords justices to Vane, 30 June 1641, PRO, SP 63/259: 198.

42 A note on the hired servants at Castlewarning, BL, Add. MSS 46924: 152.

43 Cooke to Northumberland, 23 Aug. 1638, BL, Alnwick MSS, Mic. 285.

44 Clarke, "Irish Economy," 181; Conway's letter book, Aug. 1623, PRO, SP 14/214: 39.

45 BL, Harleian MSS 2138: 168–168v.

46 Wentworth to Hamilton, 14 May 1639, SRO, GD 406/1/1162. I am grateful to Conrad Russell for directing me to the Hamilton papers.

47 Lowther to Richard Powley, 11 Sept. 1640, in Hainsworth, *Commercial Papers of Sir Christopher Lowther*, 81.

48 Gillespie, *Colonial Ulster*, 81.

49 BL, Harleian MSS 2138: 164, 172–3, 176, 179v., 188; SCL, Wentworth Woodhouse MSS 24–5: no. 174.

50 Gillespie, *Colonial Ulster*, 81.

51 Antrim to Hamilton, 14 Jan. 1639, SRO, GD 406/1/652; Rawdon to Conway, 6 and 24 July, 1639, *Cal. SP Ireland, 1633–47*, 220; Edward Chichester to Wentworth, 16 Aug. 1639, SCL, Wentworth Woodhouse MSS 19: no. 92; Rawdon to Conway, 5 Dec. 1639, *Cal. SP Ireland, 1633–47*, 228; Wandesford to Ormond, 6 May 1640, Bodl., Carte MSS 1: 190v.; Montgomery and Clandeboye to lords justices, 16 Apr. 1641, PRO, SP 63/258: 269; Chichester to Ormond, 4 May 1641, Bodl., Carte MSS 1: 379.

52 Wentworth to Vane, 19 June 1639, SCL, Wentworth Woodhouse MSS 10b: 97.

53 Bramhall to Wandesford, 16 Apr. 1640, HMC, *Hastings MSS*, 4: 86.

54 Thornton to Ormond, 6 Apr. 1641, and Peisley to Ormond, 8 May 1641, Bodl., Carte MSS 1: 367, 385.

55 Gillespie, *Colonial Ulster*, 81–2; Perceval-Maxwell, "Strafford and the Covenanters," 448–9; Wandesford to ———, 30 Aug. 1641, Bodl., Carte MSS 80: 652. This last reference was to a part of Ireland outside Ulster.

56 "Faults in Ireland," PRO, SP 63/276: 33–33v.

57 PRO, SP 63/274: 17–18, 120; *A True Relation of the proceedings of the Scottish Armie now in Ireland* ... , BL, Thomason Tract, E. 149(12); Rushworth, *Tryal*, 420. In pressing for the tenth Grace, which permitted the transport of corn without licence, it was noted that in parts of Ulster "wheat is scarce" and that the concession might therefore apply to oats, oatmeal, barley, and malt (PRO, SP 63/274: 17–18). The military references complained that fodder for horses was not available in the north of Ireland till two or three weeks after it had become available farther south.

58 Robinson, *Plantation of Ulster*, 34, 145–7, 178–80; Perceval-Maxwell, *Scottish Migration*, 295–300; Huntingdon Record Office, Manchester MSS dd. M 70/30.

59 Gillespie, "O'Farrells and Longford," 14. I am grateful to Raymond Gillespie for letting me see this article in proof.

60 Gillespie, "End of an Era," 194–5; Clarke, "Genesis of the Ulster Rising," 36–7; Wentworth to Windebank, 2 Mar. 1639, Bodl., Clarendon MSS 15: 169; Windebank to ——, c. 1640, PRO, SP 63/273: 10. Lord Iveagh passed an income of £900 per annum to his heir after a jointure for his widow had been supplied and there were £4,500 in outstanding debts (Antrim to Hamilton, 6 Jan. [1640], SRO, GD 406/1/1171).

61 Canny, *The Upstart Earl*, 47–8; Cork to Ormond, 16 Mar. 1640, Bodl., English History MSS C 37: 6; Gillespie, *Colonial Ulster*, 202, 216–17; Dwyer, *Diocese of Killaloe*, 191; TCD MSS 836: 171.

62 Two petitions from the Irish gentry to the Irish Commons, [c. Feb. 1641], PRO, SP 63/274: 1–7; Gilbert, ed., *Contemporary History*, 1, i: 365. The petitions were debated in the Commons on 23 February 1641 (*Commons' journ. Ireland*, 1: 180).

63 Gillespie, "O'Farrells and Longford," 21.

64 Gillespie, "End of an Era," 195.

65 PRONI, D 3632/1: 1–1v.

66 Canny, "In Defence of the Constitution?" 31–2.

67 Bramhall to Wandesford, 16 Apr. 1640, HMC, *Hastings MSS*, 4: 86–8.

CHAPTER TWO

1 The literature on this subject is substantial, but see particularly: Russell, *Parliaments and English Politics*; Russell, ed., *Origins of the English Civil War*; and Sharpe, ed., *Faction and Parliament*. For the way in which Ireland became involved in English faction during the sixteenth century, see: Ellis, *Tudor Ireland*; Bradshaw, *Irish Constitutional Revolution*; Canny, *Elizabethan Conquest of Ireland*.

2 Laud to Wentworth, 23 Nov. 1637, SCL, Wentworth Woodhouse MSS 7: 75v.

3 Account of the rebellion ascribed to Nicholas Plunkett, HMC, *Appendix to the 2nd Report*, 230; Whitaker, ed., *Life of Radcliffe*, 228–33.

4 Whitaker, ed., *Life of Radcliffe*, 228–33.

5 Wedgwood, *Strafford*, 320, 364; Ashton, *English Civil War*, 135; Macray, ed., *Clarendon's History*, 1: 207, 217, 225.

6 Stevenson, *Scottish Revolution*, 56–7.

7 Livingstone, *Life of Livingstone*, 76, 83, 85, 87–8, 96–8; see above 24–5; Keeler, *Long Parliament*, 348–9; *DNB*, 12: 46, 33: 1–2, 48: 119, 50: 223, 52: 223.

8 Bramhall to Laud, c. June 1637, HMC, *Hastings MSS*, 4: 73.

9 Knowler, ed., *Strafforde's Letters*, 2: 107; Wentworth to Laud, 27 Sept. 1637, SCL, Wentworth Woodhouse MSS 7: 45–6; Hervey, *Life of Arundel*, 348, 351; Clarke, *Old English*, 108; Kearney, *Strafford in Ireland*, 99. It is possible that this Barr was the person called Parr in Sir George Wentworth's account of the plot against his brother.

10 Laud to Wentworth, 7 Oct. 1637, and same to same, 24 Oct. 1637, SCL, Wentworth Woodhouse MSS 7: 57, 58–9.

11 Laud to Wentworth, 1 Nov. 1637, ibid., 71v.–72. Bramhall, who delivered this letter to Wentworth, reached Dublin on 26 December.

12 Wentworth to English council, 29 Dec. 1637, ibid., 11a: 38; Perceval-Maxwell, "Strafford and the Covenanters," 530.

13 Laud to Wentworth, 14 May 1638, SCL, Wentworth Woodhouse MSS 7: 100–1.

14 Baillie to Spang, 5 Apr. 1638, in Laing, ed., *Letters of Baillie*, 1: 64; Perceval-Maxwell, "Strafford and the Covenanters," 529; Reid, *Presbyterian Church in Ireland*, 1: 221; Traquair to Hamilton, 17 May 1638, in Yorke, ed., *Hardwicke State Papers*, 2: 107.

15 See above, 26.

16 Perceval-Maxwell, "Strafford and the Covenanters," 531–6; Wentworth to Boswell, 26 Oct. 1638, SCL, Wentworth Woodhouse MSS 11a: 129; Laud to Wentworth, 30 May 1638, in Scott and Bliss, eds., *Works of Laud*, 7: 444; Wentworth to [Windebank], 30 Nov. 1638, SCL, Wentworth Woodhouse MSS 11a: 148–50.

17 Moody, *Londonderry Plantation*, 397.

18 SRO, GD 406/1/377, 384, 387, 512, 8381; *Cal. SP Ireland, 1633–47*, 152.

19 Moody, *Londonderry Plantation*, 358, 394; Wedgwood, *Strafford*, 248.

20 Wentworth to Laud, 1 Mar. 1638, SCL, Wentworth Woodhouse MSS 7: 70v.

21 Perceval-Maxwell, "Strafford and the Covenanters," 531; Bramhall to Laud, 23 Feb. 1638, *Cal. SP Ireland, 1633–47*, 182.

22 Moody, *Londonderry Plantation*, 395; Bramhall to Laud, 23 Feb. 1638, *Cal. SP Ireland, 1633–47*, 181–2.

23 Wentworth to Laud, 26 Apr. 1638, Wentworth to Coke, 30 Oct. 1638, and Wentworth to king, 1 Nov. 1638, SCL, Wentworth Woodhouse MSS 7: 93, 11a: 138, 3: (2).

24 See above, 31.

25 Wentworth to Laud, 7 Aug. 1638, in Knowler, ed., *Strafforde's Letters*, 2: 195–6.

26 Hill, *MacDonnells of Antrim*, 253–4; Clarke, "Earl of Antrim and the First Bishop's War," 108–9; Stevenson, *Scottish Revolution*, 99–100; Perceval-Maxwell, "Strafford and the Covenanters," 533; Laud to Wentworth, 27 June 1638, Wentworth to Laud, 11 Aug. 1638, and same to same, 3 Nov. 1638, SCL, Wentworth Woodhouse MSS 7: 118, 128, 134; Wentworth to king, 28 July 1638, in Knowler, ed., *Strafforde's Letters*, 2: 187–8; Laud to Wentworth, 10 Sept. 1638, in Scott and Bliss, eds., *Works of Laud*, 7: 482–4.

27 Moody, *Londonderry Plantation*, 395, 446; Perceval-Maxwell, "Strafford and the Covenanters," 531; Paul, ed., *Diary of Sir Archibald Johnston*, 2: 351; Stevenson, *Scottish Revolution*, 98; *Cal. SP Ireland, 1633–47*, 194–5.

28 Donald, "The King and the Scottish Troubles," 180–5.

29 Keeler, *Long Parliament*, 10, 136; Perceval-Maxwell, "Protestant Faction," 235; Perceval-Maxwell, "Strafford and the Covenanters," 535; Loeber, "Downing's and Winthrop's Plantation in Ireland," passim. I thank Rolf Loeber for permitting me to cite this unpublished typescript.

30 Stevenson, *Scottish Revolution*, 126–88; Gardiner, *History*, 9: 73–7.

31 Cited in Young, *Servility and Service*, 259.

32 Macray, ed., *Clarendon's History*, 1: 164.

33 *Privy Council Registers in Facsimile*, 6: 296.

34 Ibid., 5: 1–2 and passim. Sir Thomas Edmonds also attended frequently, but he appears to have had no political influence. The king attended only three times during this period.

35 Ibid., 8: 1.

36 Clarke, "Sir Piers Crosby," 142–53; Wedgwood, *Strafford*, 239–44, 246–7.

37 Laud to Wentworth, [17 May], received 5 June 1638, SCL, Wentworth Woodhouse MSS 7: 113. Cf. Scott and Bliss, eds., *Works of Laud*, 7: 433, where the cipher seems to be slightly misinterpreted.

38 Laud to Wentworth, 19 May 1638, Wentworth to Laud, 27 Nov. 1638, and Laud to Wentworth, 21 Nov. 1638, SCL, Wentworth Woodhouse MSS 7: 101, 144–5, 146.

39 Macray, ed., *Clarendon's History*, 1: 150.

40 Wentworth to Northumberland, 28 Feb. 1639, in Firth, "Papers Relating to Wentworth," 10.

41 Macray, ed., *Clarendon's History*, 1: 150; Wedgwood, *Strafford*, 257; Snow, *Essex*, 200–1.

42 Laud to Wentworth, 31 Mar. 1639, in Scott and Bliss, eds., *Works of Laud*, 7: 550.

43 Wentworth to Laud, 10 Apr. 1639, SCL, Wentworth Woodhouse MSS 7: 180v.; Young, *Servility and Service*, 259.

44 Wedgwood, *King's Peace*, 280; Knowler, ed., *Strafforde's Letters*, 2: 374; *Privy Council Registers in Facsimile*, 7: 646.

45 Windebank to Hopton, 29 Sept. 1639, *Calendar of Clarendon State Papers*, 1: 185.

46 *Privy Council Registers in Facsimile*, 8: 73.

47 Howarth, *Arundel and His Circle*, 209.

48 Young, *Servility and Service*, 254; Lady Leicester to Leicester, 8 Jan. 1639, HMC, *De L'Isle and Dudley MSS*, 6: 158.

49 Laud to Wentworth, 27 Feb. 1639, SCL, Wentworth Woodhouse MSS 7: 172. See also Scott and Bliss, eds., *Works of Laud*, 7: 529.

50 Laud to Wentworth, 27 Feb. 1639, in Scott and Bliss, eds., *Works of Laud*, 2: 562; Wentworth to Laud, 10 May 1639, in Knowler, ed., *Strafforde's Letters*, 2: 36–7.

51 Wentworth to Laud, 10 Apr. 1639, SCL, Wentworth Woodhouse MSS 7: 182; Hamilton to the king, 15 June 1638, SRO, GD 406/1/10775.

52 Hamilton-Vane correspondence, c. 1631, SRO, GD 406/1/157, 180, 182, 184; king to Hamilton, 18 Apr. 1639, SRO, GD 406/1/10543.

53 Wentworth to Laud, 11 Feb. 1639, SCL, Wentworth Woodhouse MSS 7: 162; Laud to Wentworth 1 May 1639, in Scott and Bliss, eds., *Works of Laud*, 7: 571.

54 Laud to Wentworth, 1 May 1639, and same to same, [March] 1639, SCL, Wentworth Woodhouse MSS 7: 186v., 173v.

55 Wentworth to Laud, 11 Feb. 1639, ibid., 166v.

56 Laud to Wentworth, 1 May 1639, ibid., 187v.

57 Wentworth to Laud, 19 June 1638, ibid., 109v.

58 Laud to Wentworth, 30 July 1638, in Scott and Bliss, eds., *Works of Laud*, 7: 469.

59 Stevenson, *Scottish Revolution*, 103–4; Wentworth to Laud, 4 Sept. 1638, and 27 Nov. 1638, SCL, Wentworth Woodhouse MSS 7: 131, 147v.

60 John Castle to Bridgwater, 6 Dec. 1639, Huntington Library, Ellesmere MSS 7814. Clarendon says that the decision to call parliament was made on 6 December, but it was almost certainly taken before this. On 5 December the countess of Carlisle reported that the calling of a parliament was being discussed secretly. (Macray, ed., *Clarendon's History*, 1: 172; HMC, *De L'Isle and Dudley MSS*, 6: 207).

61 Hawkins to Leicester, 29 Aug. 1639, HMC, *De L'Isle and Dudley MSS*, 6: 180.

62 Lady Carlisle to Leicester, 10 Oct. 1639, ibid., 195.

63 Lady Carlisle to Leicester, 21 Nov. 1639, ibid., 204.

64 Lady Carlisle to Leicester, 26 Sept. 1639, ibid., 192; Northumberland to Leicester, 4 Sept. 1639, ibid., 182.

65 Lady Carlisle to Lady Leicester, 12 Dec. 1639, ibid., 211.

66 Lady Carlisle to Lady Leicester, 12 Dec. 1639, ibid., 211.

67 Lady Carlisle to Lady Leicester, 5 Dec. 1639, ibid., 208.

68 Young, *Servility and Service*, 262.

69 Laud to Wentworth, 1 May 1639, in Scott and Bliss, eds., *Works of Laud*, 7: 568.

70 Lady Carlisle to Leicester 24 Dec. 1639, HMC, *De L'Isle and Dudley MSS*, 7: 215.

71 Macray, ed., *Clarendon's History*, 1: 161; Lady Carlisle to Leicester, 5 Dec. 1639, ibid., 207–8.

72 Wedgwood, *King's Peace*, 311–12.

73 John Castle to Bridgwater, 28 Jan. 1640, Huntington Library, Ellesmere MSS 7819; Macray, ed., *Clarendon's History*, 1: 165–6.

74 Macray, ed., *Clarendon's History*, 1: 113.

CHAPTER THREE

1 Parts of this chapter have already appeared as an article: see Perceval-Maxwell, "Protestant Faction," 235–55.

2 Lodge, *Peerage of Ireland*, 4: 159–64; Cokayne and Gibbs, eds., *Complete Peerage*, 11: 125.

3 See above, 17.

4 Ranger, "Richard Boyle," 228–9, 248–50, 366–70; Grosart, ed., *Lismore Papers*, 2nd ser., 4: 86.

5 Lodge, *Peerage of Ireland*, 1: 153n; Parsons to Cork, 10 Sept. 1639, Chatsworth, Lismore MSS 20: no. 110; Joshua Boyle to [Cork], 27 Apr. 1639, 3 June 1639, and 19 Aug. 1639, NLI MSS 13237: nos. 22, 23, 24.

6 Bodl., Carte MSS 64: 478; PROI, 1A. S3. S4: 402; Grosart, ed., *Lismore Papers*, 2nd ser., 3: 249; Ranger, "Strafford in Ireland," 284–6.

7 Joshua Boyle to [Cork], 27 Apr. 1639, NLI MSS 13237: no. 22.

8 Cork to Wentworth, endorsed 16 Mar. 1640, in Grosart, ed., *Lismore Papers*, 2nd ser., 4: 107.

9 Walley to Cork, 28 Sept. 1639, NLI MSS 13237: no. 24.

10 BL, Add. MSS 46924: 48, and Add. MSS 46926: 25; Cork to Joshua Boyle, 13 Jan. 1639, NLI MSS 13238: no. 2.

11 Clarke, *Old English*, 127–42; Clarke, "Breakdown of Authority," 277–87; Kearney, *Strafford in Ireland*, 189–98. For use of this technique in an English context, see: Glow, "Manipulation of Committees," 31–52; Sharpe, "Introduction: Parliamentary History 1603–1629," 25–6.

12 Radcliffe to Conway, 1 Jan. 1640, *Cal. SP Ireland, 1633–47*, 232; Hawkins to Leicester, 6 Feb. 1640, HMC, *De L'Isle and Dudley MSS*, 6: 230.

13 Clarke, *Old English*, 126; Notestein, ed., *Journal of D'Ewes*, 13–14, 14n.

14 Cork to Wentworth, endorsed 16 Mar. 1640, in Grosart, ed., *Lismore Papers*, 2nd ser., 4: 107; *Cal. SP Ireland, 1633–47*, 237.

15 Clarke, "Policies of the Old English," 88; Kearney, *Strafford in Ireland*, 223–63; McGrath, "Membership of the Irish House of Commons," 24; I have revised Kearney's figures slightly – Valentine Browne, for instance, was a Catholic, not a Protestant: see MacCarthy-Morrogh, *Munster Plantation*, 263. For the English stress upon consensus, see: Kishlansky, *Parliamentary Selection*, 6, 16–17, 108; Russell, *British Monarchies*, 118; Russell, *Parliaments and English Politics*, 5, 39–41. The quotation is from Kishlansky, "Consensus Politics," 52.

16 Cork to Ormond, 16 Mar. 1640, and Ormond to Cork, c. Apr. 1640, Bodl., English History MSS C 37: 5, 8; Maynard to Windebank, 19 Mar. 1640, *Cal. SP Domestic, 1639–40*, 560–1.

17 Kishlansky, *Parliamentary Selection*, 16–17, 108, 122, 128.

18 Petition, 30 Aug. 1641, Birr Castle, Rosse MSS A/1: no. 35.

19 *Cal. SP Ireland, 1633–47*, 269–70.

20 MacCarthy-Morrogh, *Munster Plantation*, 264, 266.

21 Kearney, *Strafford in Ireland*, 260–3.

22 Ranger, "Strafford in Ireland," 373n, 374n.

23 Cork to Ormond, 16 Mar. 1640. Bodl., English History MSS C 37: 5–6.

24 Perceval-Maxwell, "Protestant Faction," 247; PROI, Betham's Genealogical Abstracts, BET. 1: 21; *Cal. SP Ireland, 1647–60*, 348.

25 Clarke, *Old English*, 127–8; Wedgwood, *Strafford*, 275–7; *Commons' journ. Ireland*, 1: 138–9; Cromwell to Conway, 31 Mar. 1640, *Cal. SP Domestic, 1639–40*, 608; PRO, SP 63/258: 51–64.

26 Irish council to [Nicholas], 23 Mar. 1640, PRO, SP 63/258: 35; *Cal. SP Ireland, 1633–47*, 239; *Commons' journ. Ireland*, 1: 141.

27 *Commons' journ. Ireland*, 1: 218, 238–9, 285, 295.

28 The leaders could have been defined as those who sat on three or more committees, in which case there would have been sixteen Protestant leaders, and eight Catholic ones. Here the criterion for leadership status has been set at membership of four or more committees because of the need to bear in mind the problem of identifying leaders in six sessions of parliament. The number of committees varied considerably from one session to another, and membership on committees tended to be spread more widely the more there were. Tables 3 to 5 list as leaders those who sat on at least four of the seven committees that were formed in the first session (over half), six or more out of the eighteen committees appointed during the second session (one-third), and six or more of the twenty-four committees (one-quarter) established during the third session.

29 Perceval-Maxwell, "Protestant Faction," 241–2. Three Protestants were active in this session but held no office: Anthony Dopping, Sir Audley Mervin, and Sir Hardress Waller.

30 Clarke, *Old English*, 45, 84, 88, 129; Perceval-Maxwell, "Protestant Faction," 248.

31 Chatsworth, Lismore MSS 21: no. 98.

32 Northumberland to Leicester, 2 Apr. 1640, Kent Archives Office, De L'Isle MSS U 1475/C85/11.

33 Northumberland to Leicester, 19 Mar. 1640, and 16 Apr. 1640, ibid., U 1500/C2/41, and U 1475/C85/12; Cope and Coates, eds., *Proceedings of the Short Parliament*, 191–4, 196, 205–8, 240; Wedgwood, *Strafford*, 280–4; Russell, *British Monarchies*, 90–123, but particularly 119.

34 Northumberland to Leicester, 21 May 1640, HMC, *De L'Isle and Dudley MSS*, 4: 269–70.

35 Macray, ed., *Clarendon's History*, 1: 181–2.

36 Clarke, *Old English*, 131; Clarke, "Breakdown of Authority," 278; Wandesford to Ormond, 6 May 1640, Bodl., Carte MSS 1: 190; [Bramhall to Wandesford], 16 Apr. 1640, HMC, *Hastings MSS*, 4: 86–7. See also chapter 1.

37 Wandesford to Ormond, 16 May 1640, and 30 June 1640, Bodl., Carte MSS 1: 194, 211.

38 Kearney, *Strafford in Ireland*, 189–91; Clarke, "Breakdown of Authority," 276–7; Clarke, *Old English*, 129–31; Ranger, "Strafford in Ireland," 288; Perceval-Maxwell, "Protestant Faction," 243; *Commons' journ. Ireland*, 1: 144–51; PRO, SP 63/273: 17. Calendar of events by Sir James Ware, Public Library, Dublin, Gilbert MSS 169: 219. I am grateful to Rolf Loeber for having brought this calendar to my attention.

39 Perceval-Maxwell, "Protestant Faction," 243; Rawdon to [Conway], 10 June 1640, PRO, SP 63/258: 8ov.; *Cal. SP Ireland, 1633–47*, 242–3; *Lords' journ. Ireland*, 1: 120–4; *Commons' journ. Ireland*, 1: 148.

40 Kearney, *Strafford in Ireland*, 193; Wandesford to Ormond, 16 May 1640, Bodl., Carte MSS 1: 194v.; *Commons' journ. Ireland*, 1: 142–4; PRO, SP 63/258: 65; *Cal. SP Ireland, 1633–47*, 240.

41 See Table 3. Carte, *Ormonde*, 1: 101; list of army officers, 23 Apr. 1640, Bodl., Carte MSS 1: 181–5.

42 Perceval-Maxwell, "Protestant Faction," 244; *Commons' journ. Ireland*, 1: 145.

43 Account of the War and Rebellion in Ireland, NLI MSS 345: 48; HMC, *Appendix to the 2nd Report*, 230.

44 Wandesford to [Radcliffe], 12 June 1640, in Whitaker, ed., *Life of Radcliffe*, 249–51; Kearney, *Strafford in Ireland*, 190.

45 Wandesford to [Radcliffe], 21 June 1640, Bodl., Add. MSS C 286: 28v.

46 *Cal. SP Ireland, 1633–47*, 240.

47 See Table 4.

48 Jackson, *Intermarriage*, 22; Kearney, *Strafford in Ireland*, 195; Ranger, "Richard Boyle," 250; Perceval-Maxwell, "Protestant Faction," 246–7; Lodge, *Peerage of Ireland*, 1: 153n. and 7: 257; *Cal. SP Ireland, 1633–47*, 388; Knowler, ed., *Strafforde's Letters*, 2: 414–15.

49 *Cal. SP Ireland, 1633–47*, 388.

50 Perceval-Maxwell, "Protestant Faction," 247; Lodge, *Peerage of Ireland*, 1: 153n; Rushworth, *Tryal*, 176; That Cork received information from within the Irish council shows how deeply interested in the politics of the council he was. No letter from Davies to the earl has survived, which suggests that we do not possess all of Cork's political correspondence.

51 *DNB*, 20: 584–6; Lodge, *Peerage of Ireland*, 6: 16; Strafford to Radcliffe, 5 Nov. 1640, in Whitaker, ed., *Life of Radcliffe*, 206; MacCarthy-Morrogh, "Munster Plantation 1583–1641," 347–8.

52 Perceval-Maxwell, "Protestant Faction," 248; *Commons' journ. Ireland*, 1: 144–5.

53 *Commons' journ. Ireland*, 1: 145.

54 *Commons' journ. Ireland*, 1: 149. Sir Adam Loftus was noticeably absent from this committee, but Nicholas Loftus was present.

55 John Castle to Bridgwater, 26 June 1640, Huntington Library, Ellesmere MSS 7840.

56 John Castle to Bridgwater, 1 July 1640, ibid., Ellesmere MSS 7841; Northumberland to Leicester, 22 July 1640, BL, Alnwick MSS, Mic. 286; Hawkins to Leicester, 2 July 1640, HMC, *De L'Isle and Dudley MSS*, 6: 293.

57 Stevenson, *Scottish Revolution*, 196–211; St Leger to Ormond, 21 July 1640, Bodl., Carte MSS 1: 214; Wandesford to Ormond, 21 Aug. 1640, PRO, 31/1/1: 141; Capt. Tavener's demands, PRO, 31/1/1: 206–7. I have cited transcripts here as I could not find these items in the Carte MSS in the Bodleian.

58 *Lords' journ. Ireland*, 1: 143; Perkins to Cork, 25 Aug. 1640, Chatsworth, Lismore MSS 21: no. 41; "Propositions Scots, rejected by me [Radcliffe]," in Whitaker, ed., *Life of Radcliffe*, 206–10.

59 Clarke, *Old English*, 133–4; Kearney, *Strafford in Ireland*, 201–2.

60 *Commons' journ. Ireland*, 1: 155–7, 164; Bramhall to Laud, 4 Nov. 1640, HMC, *Hastings MSS*, 4: 90.

61 *Lords' journ. Ireland*, 1: 126; Montgomery and Clandeboye to lords justices, 16 Apr. 1641, PRO, SP 63/258: 268–9v.

62 *Commons' journ. Ireland*, 1: 157, 162; SCL, Wentworth Woodhouse MSS 24–5: no. 138.

63 Radcliffe to Wentworth, 28 Oct. 1640, and Wentworth to Radcliffe, 5 Nov. 1640, in Whitaker, ed., *Life of Radcliffe*, 210–11, 204–5.

64 Clarke, *Old English*, 135; *Commons' journ. Ireland*, 1: 165–6; "A Brief Relation of the Progress of the Irish Committee," Bodl., Carte MSS 67: 53v.

65 *Commons' journ. Ireland*, 1: 162–5.

66 Kearney, *Strafford in Ireland*, 202; Russell, "British Background to the Irish Rebellion," 171; *Commons' journ. Ireland*, 1: 162–3.

67 Segrave to Lord Hastings, 13 Nov. 1640, HMC, *Hastings MSS*, 2: 81.

68 Bramhall to Laud, 4 Nov. 1640, ibid., 4: 90.

69 *Commons' journ. England*, 2: 26–7; Laing, ed., *Letters of Baillie*, 1: 273; Notestein, ed., *Journal of D'Ewes*, 534; Society of Antiquaries, London, Proclamation, 18 Nov. 1640. By 23 November a committee of the privy council was discussing the Remonstrance with Strafford (*Cal. SP Ireland, 1633–47*, 247).

70 BL, Egerton MSS 1048: 13–14 (endorsed rec. 20 Nov.); Gilbert, ed., *Facsimiles of National Manuscripts of Ireland*, 2, iv: no. 51; *Commons' journ. England*, 2: 39. The two Irish MPs who presented the Humble Petition and Remonstrance to the English Commons were Oliver Cashell and John Bellew. These two men were appointed to an Irish Commons committee on 10 November. It is likely, therefore, that they left Ireland on the eleventh or, at latest, the twelfth.

71 Clarke, *Old English*, 135. Cokayne and Gibbs, eds., *Complete Peerage*, 9: 441, is misleading in that it dates the death of Muskerry to February 1640. In fact he died in February 1641 (*Lords' journ. Ireland*, 1: 173).

72 *Commons' journ. Ireland*, 1: 165.

73 Whitaker, ed., *Life of Radcliffe*, 232; Kearney, *Strafford in Ireland*, 203–4; HMC, *Egmont MSS*, 1: 123–4.

74 *DNB*, 20: 816–17.

75 HMC, *Appendix to the 2nd Report*, 230; Kearney, *Strafford in Ireland*, 39, 88; Ranger, "Richard Boyle," 250.

76 BL, Egerton MSS 1048: 13; Whitaker, ed., *Life of Radcliffe*, 232; Kearney, *Strafford in Ireland*, 203–4; HMC, *Egmont MSS*, 1: 123–4; *Commons' journ. Ireland*, 1: 244. For Denny, see MacCarthy-Morrogh, *Munster Plantation*, 246–7n.; for Travers and for Cole and Montgomery, see Lodge, *Peerage of Ireland*, 1: 145, and 6: 46, respectively; Hill, ed., *Montgomery Manuscripts*, 158, 343. Cole married the daughter of Sir Laurence Parsons, Sir William's brother.

77 Rawdon to Conway, 1 Dec. 1640, PRO, SP 63/258: 116v.

78 *Commons' journ. Ireland*, 1: 162, 164.

79 Whitaker, ed., *Life of Radcliffe*, 211.

80 Clarke, *Old English*, 135; *Lords' journ. Ireland*, 1: 139, 142, 148–9, 151, 173. We know that Muskerry had reached England by this time because he died there in February 1641, to be replaced on the Lords

committee by the Protestant Viscount Baltinglass (Cokayne and Gibbs, eds., *Complete Peerage*, 9: 440; *Lords' journ. Ireland*, 1: 173).

81 *Commons' journ. Ireland*, 1: 165; PRO, SO 3/12, 28 Feb. 1641: 138v. The commitment of the MacCarthy family to Catholicism was lukewarm: Sir Donough's father was buried in Westminster Abbey.

82 Laing, ed., *Letters of Baillie*, 1: 281; Rawdon to Conway, 3 Dec. 1640, PRO, SP 63/258: 118; Hawkins to Leicester, 10 Dec. 1640, HMC, *De L'Isle and Dudley MSS*, 6: 348.

83 Fr John Barnewall to Fr Hugh Burgo, 18 Dec. 1640, in Jennings, ed., *Louvain Papers*, 132.

CHAPTER FOUR

1 Fletcher, *Outbreak of the English Civil War*; Russell, ed., *Origins of the English Civil War*; Russell, *Causes of the English Civil War*; Russell, *British Monarchies*; Ashton, *English Civil War*; Aylmer, *King's Servants*; Hirst, *Authority and Conflict*; Underdown, *Revel, Riot, and Rebellion*; Morrill, *Revolt of the Provinces*; Sharpe, "Crown, Parliament, and the Locality."

2 Nalson, *Impartial Collection*, 1: 437–8.

3 Stevenson, *Scottish Revolution*, 218; Saye to Hamilton, n.d., and 13 Nov. 1641, SRO, GD 406/1/1508 and 1507.

4 Ranger, "Richard Boyle," 371.

5 Ibid., 368–70; Canny, *The Upstart Earl*, 58–9, 107–8; Townshend, *Life and Letters of Cork*, 297.

6 *Privy Council Registers in Facsimile*, 11 and 12 passim.

7 Clotworthy had married Mary Jones, Ranelagh's daughter, and was brother-in-law to Edward Rowley, one of the Irish MPs sent to England. His sister had married Pym's brother-in-law's brother. Wedgwood, *Strafford*, 312; Keeler, *Long Parliament*, 10, 136; *Commons' journ. England*, 2: 24; Macray, ed., *Clarendon's History*, 1: 224; Kearney, *Strafford in Ireland*, 203; Clarke, "Breakdown of Authority," 279.

8 Kearney, *Strafford in Ireland*, 182–3; Wentworth to Radcliffe, 5 Nov. 1640, in Whitaker, ed., *Life of Radcliffe*, 214–22. A papal informant described Bristol at this time as an "amphibious animal" with one foot in tempestuous parliamentary waters and the other on the ground defending the royal prerogative (Vatican Library, Barbarini MSS 8671: no. 92).

9 Notestein, ed., *Journal of D'Ewes*, 2–3; BL, Add. MSS 35838: 164.

10 Notestein, ed., *Journal of D'Ewes*, 2–3; *Commons' journ. England*, 2: 1.

11 Notestein, ed., *Journal of D'Ewes*, 12, 546.

12 Ibid., 13–14.

13 Ibid., 25–9; Wedgwood, *Strafford*, 314.

14 Notestein, ed., *Journal of D'Ewes*, 29n, 534; *Commons' journ. England*, 2: 27; Laing, ed., *Letters of Baillie*, 1: 273; Hawkins to Leicester, 19 Nov. 1640, HMC, *De L'Isle and Dudley MSS*, 6: 342.

15 Notestein, ed., *Journal of D'Ewes*, 72; Laing, ed., *Letters of Baillie*, 1: 273; *Commons' journ. England*, 2: 26, 38.

16 Stevenson, *Scottish Revolution*, 216; Laing, ed., *Letters of Baillie*, 1: 280.

17 NLS, Advocates' MSS 34.2.9: 157–157v.

18 Nalson, *Impartial Collection*, 1: 686–8.

19 Rushworth, *Tryal*, 20–2. For a full consideration of the nature of the charges, and particularly the fifteenth and the twenty-third, see Russell, "Theory of Treason," 30–50.

20 Petition of Gormanston and Sarsfield, received 19 Feb. 1641, PRO, SP 63/258: 183–4; *Cal. SP Ireland, 1633–47*, 262–3; The Scottish commissioners' declaration, 24 Feb. 1641, NLS, Advocates' MSS 33.4.6: 131.

21 Rushworth, *Tryal*, 22–32; Notestein, ed., *Journal of D'Ewes*, 410.

22 Andrew Honeyman to ———, 3 Mar. 1641, NLS, Advocates' MSS 29.2.9: 151–151v. I thank Kevin Sharpe for this reference.

23 Sir J. Coke jn. to ———, 24 Apr. 1641, HMC, *Cowper MSS*, 2: 280; Wentworth to Ormond, 3 Feb. 1641, Bodl., Carte MSS 1: 349; Wedgwood, *Strafford*, 326; Snow, *Essex*, 261.

24 Northumberland to Leicester, 10 Dec. 1640, Kent Archives Office, De L'Isle MSS U 1500/C2/45.

25 Whitaker, ed., *Life of Radcliffe*, 232; Rushworth, *Tryal*, 429.

26 Sir J. Coke jn. to ———, 28 Apr. 1641, HMC, *Cowper MSS*, 2: 281; Laing, ed., *Letters of Baillie*, 1: 317, 319, 323, 327; Wedgwood, *Strafford*, 320, 342.

27 *Lords' journ. England*, 4: 236–7, 240; Christianson, "'Obliterated' Portions of the House of Lords Journals," 351–2; Rushworth, *Tryal*, 554; Laing, ed., *Letters of Baillie*, 1: 342; Wentworth to Hamilton, 24 Apr. 1641, SRO, GD 406/1/1335.

28 Wedgwood, *Strafford*, 346; Laing, ed., *Letters of Baillie*, 1: 341; Rushworth, *Tryal*, 543.

29 *Cal. SP Domestic, 1640–41*, 541.

30 BL, Add. MSS 35838: 170v. This is ascribed to the earl of Manchester.

31 Wentworth to Sir A. Loftus, 15 Dec. 1640, and 4 Feb. 1641, in Knowler, ed., *Strafforde's Letters*, 2: 414, 415; BL, Add. MSS 46189: 87v.–8; Rushworth, *Tryal*, 198, 228, 469, 497. It may be significant that in 1643 both Parsons and Loftus sided with parliament against Ormond (HMC, *Ormond MSS*, n.s., 2: 106).

32 Wentworth to Sir A. Loftus, 15 Dec. 1640, in Knowler, ed., *Strafforde's Letters*, 2: 414; Rushworth, *Tryal*, 111, 173, 186, 216; Laing, ed., *Letters of Baillie*, 1: 323, 327.

33 Bodl., Carte MSS 67: 54v.; Rushworth, *Tryal*, 442; *Privy Council Registers in Facsimile*, 12: 99; Loftus to [Vane], 14 June 1641, *Cal. SP Ireland, 1633–47*, 302. After Strafford's death, the attitude of the council seems to have changed as the king ordered the new lord lieutenant to investigate the "scandalous speeches" of Henry Dillon against Ranelagh and to order the lords justices to secure Dillon: *Cal. SP Ireland, 1633–47*, 301.

34 Henry Dillon's petition, n.d., PRO, SP 63/274: 59–61; Lodge, *Peerage of Ireland*, 4: 185–7; Notestein, ed., *Journal of D'Ewes*, 546; Rushworth, *Tryal*, 186.

35 Rushworth, *Tryal*, 111, 170, 236, 401, 469; Proceedings against Thomas Wentworth, Huntingdon Record Office, Manchester MSS dd. M28/2: 3.

36 Rushworth, *Tryal*, 157, 158, 175, 186, 216, 223; BL, Egerton MSS 3383: 19v.; NLI MSS 12813: 702.

37 Percival to Barry, 13 Mar. 1641, HMC, *Egmont MSS*, 1: 131.

38 Temple to Leicester, 5 Feb. 1640, BL, Add. MSS 24023: 17–17v.; Northumberland to Leicester, 5 Mar. 1639–40, ACLS MSS project, Cambridge 752: no. 38; Northumberland to Leicester, 28 May 1640, BL, Alnwick MSS, Mic. 286.

39 Northumberland to Leicester, 12 Mar. 1640, ACLS MSS project, Cambridge 752: no. 37; Northumberland to Leicester, 7 May 1640, and 21 May 1640, Kent Archives Office, De L'Isle MSS U 1500/C2/42, and U 145/C85/15; Lady Carlisle to Leicester, 21 May 1640, HMC, *De L'Isle and Dudley MSS*, 6: 270.

40 Northumberland to Leicester, 4 June 1640, ACLS MSS project, Cambridge 752: no number; king to Strafford, 20 June 1640, *Cal. SP Ireland, 1633–47*, 242. "Concealed" lands were those that were discovered by survey to be included in an estate although they were not specifically granted by the crown in the original patent. They, therefore, reverted to the crown and were available to be held, sold, or granted under a new patent.

41 Fletcher, *Outbreak of the English Civil War*, 89; John Castle to Bridgwater, 1 July 1640, Huntington Library, Ellesmere MSS 7841; Leicester to Vane 21/11 Sept. 1640, ACLS MSS project, Cambridge 752: no number; Northumberland to Leicester, 13 Nov. 1640, Kent Archives Office, De L'Isle MSS U 145/C85/19; Northumberland to [Leicester], fragment of letter, 26 Nov. 1640, ACLS MSS project, Cambridge 752: no number.

42 Northumberland to Leicester, 3 Dec. 1640, Kent Archives Office, De L'Isle MSS U 145/C85/22; same to same, 17 Dec. 1640, BL, Alnwick MSS, Mic. 286; William Aylesbury to Hyde, 24 Dec. 1640, Bodl., Clarendon MSS 19: no. 1476.

43 Lady Carlisle to Lady Leicester, 17 Dec. 1640, HMC, *De L'Isle and Dudley MSS*, 6: 350; Wentworth to Ormond, 17 Dec. 1640, Bodl., Carte MSS 1: 294.

44 BL, Sloan MSS 1008: 368v.; petition from committee of Irish Commons to king, PRO, SP 63/273: 26; Northumberland to Leicester, 17 Dec. 1640, BL, Alnwick MSS, Mic. 286; Carre to Bramhall, 23 Jan. 1641, in Berwick, ed., *Rawdon Papers*, 69.

45 Northumberland to Leicester 31 Dec. 1640, BL, Alnwick MSS, Mic. 286.

46 Temple to Leicester, 7 Jan. 1641, HMC, *De L'Isle and Dudley MSS*, 6: 360.

47 Temple to Leicester, 14 Jan. 1641, 21 Jan. 1641, 27 Jan. 1641, 18 Feb. 1641, and 25 Feb. 1641, in ibid., 362–3, 366–7, 369, 382, 386.

48 Zagorin, *Court and Country*, 214–15.

49 Temple to Leicester, 18 Mar. 1641, HMC, *De L'Isle and Dudley MSS*, 6: 391.

50 Temple to Leicester, 4 Feb. 1641, 11 Feb. 1641, 18 Feb. 1641, and 4 Mar. 1641, in ibid., 375, 379, 382–3, 388; Aylesbury to Hyde, 19 Feb./2 Mar. 1641, Bodl., Clarendon MSS 20: 65; Zagorin, *Court and Country*, 212–14. According to Clarendon, yet another contender for the post was Hamilton, but there is no direct evidence for this (Macray, ed., *Clarendon's History*, 1: 411).

51 Temple to Leicester, 18 Mar. 1641, HMC, *De L'Isle and Dudley MSS*, 6: 390–1; Barry to Percival, 8 Mar. 1641, HMC, *Egmont MSS*, 1: 128–9. It is interesting to note that Barry reported that "the whole body of the committee" objected to Bourke's and Plunkett's behaviour; thus he implied that some Catholics objected as strongly as did the Protestants.

52 Temple to Leicester, 1 Apr. 1641, 8 Apr. 1641, 15 Apr. 1641, and 22 Apr. 1641, HMC, *De L'Isle and Dudley MSS*, 6: 394–5, 397–8, 399, 400–1; NLI, 12813(3): 178; PRO, SO 3/12: 148v.

53 Russell, "British Problem," 412.

54 Clarke, "Breakdown of Authority," 270–88.

55 Temple to Ormond, 7 June 1641, Bodl., Carte MSS 1: 423; Temple to Leicester, 22 July 1641, 29 July 1641, 5 Aug. 1641, and 11 Aug. 1641, HMC, *De L'Isle and Dudley MSS*, 6: 405, 406, 407–8, 410.

56 Temple to Leicester, 27 Aug. 1641, HMC, *De L'Isle and Dudley MSS*, 6: 411.

57 Temple to Leicester, 29 July 1641, and 5 Aug. 1641, ibid., 407, 408.

58 Gilbert, ed., *Contemporary History*, 1, ii: 450, 453.

59 Wentworth to Coke, 28 Nov. 1636, in Knowler, ed., *Strafforde's Letters*, 2: 39.

60 Nalson, *Impartial Collection*, 1: 495.

61 Hibbard, *Popish Plot*.

62 Gonzalez to Peregra, 15 Jan. 1639, Irish Jesuit Archives, transcripts of MSS A. This letter was not found among the original letters.

63 Nugent to Vitelleschi, 24 Apr. 1642, ibid., MSS A: no. 77.

64 Nugent to Vitelleschi, 1 Oct. 1640, ibid., no. 70.

65 Notestein, ed., *Journal of D'Ewes*, 11, 13, 31, 61n, 277, 285, 286–7, 301, 347; Edmund Percival to Philip Percival, 26 Jan. 1641, BL, Add. MSS 46924: 173; BL, Add. MSS 31954: 185.

66 Notestein, ed., *Journal of D'Ewes*, 346–8, 366n; BL, Harleian MSS 164: 116, 119.

67 NLS, Advocates' MSS 33.1.1: no. 82.

68 Nalson, *Impartial Collection*, 1: 686–8.

69 Stevenson, *Scottish Revolution*, 216; Russell, "British Problem," 407.

70 Articles three and five to eight. Nalson, *Impartial Collection*, 1: 686–8; Stevenson, *Scottish Revolution*, 216–17.

71 Blair to Northumberland, 26 Jan. 1641, BL, Alnwick MSS, Mic. 286.

72 NLS, Advocates' MSS 33.4.6: 131–131v. and 133v.; NLS, Wodrow MSS Quarto 25: no. 147; Laing, ed., *Letters of Baillie*, 1: 306.

73 "Desires concerning unity in religion ... as a special mean for conserving peace in his majesty's dominions," 10 Mar. 1641, NLS, Advocates' MSS 33.4.6: 142–3; Bodl., Nalson MSS Deposit C, 172N: 67–73. I thank Conrad Russell for directing me to the last source.

74 BL, Stowe MSS 187: 53v.

75 Notestein, ed., *Journal of D'Ewes*, 442.

76 Laing, ed., *Letters of Baillie*, 1: 306.

77 Gardiner, ed., *Constitutional Documents*, 137; Fletcher, *Outbreak of the English Civil War*, 92–3, 102–5.

78 Ussher to Bramhall, 19 June 1641, PRONI, T415: 22; Reid, *Presbyterian Church in Ireland*, 1: 282n.

79 Petition of the British inhabitants of counties Down, Antrim, Tyrone, and Armagh, PRO, SP 63/274: 75.

80 Owen O'Connolly's deposition, 26 Mar. 1641, BL, Egerton MSS 2541: 236.

81 Reid, *Presbyterian Church in Ireland*, 1: 291. The first petition does not seem to have been published at the time it was compiled, the second was: see Bodl., Wood pamphlets 507(4) and Huntington Library, 58750.

82 Russell, "British Background to the Irish Rebellion," 176.

83 Gilbert, ed., *Contemporary History*, 1, ii: 453.

84 Stevenson, *Scottish Revolution*, 219–21; NLS, Wodrow MSS Quarto 25: no. 150; BL, Stowe MSS 187: 50–52v.

85 Stevenson, *Scottish Revolution*, 222; BL, Add. MSS 6521: 58, 67, 67v.; BL, Harleian MSS 163: 209v.

86 *Acts Parliament Scotland*, 5: 342.

87 Ibid., 343.

88 Ibid. These provisions in the treaty were being pressed by the Scots during the spring, see: NLS, Wodrow MSS Quarto 25: no. 151; BL, Stowe MSS 187: 54v.; Scottish commissioners' paper, "For the conserving of peace betwixt both kingdoms," 8 Apr. 1641, Bodl., Nalson MSS Deposit C, 172N: 88–88v. Note that the Scots made reference to only two kingdoms.

89 BL, Harleian MSS 163: 209v.

90 Stevenson, *Scottish Revolution*, 222, 234–5; *Lords' journ. England*, 4: 356.

91 Nugent to Vitelleschi, 12 Nov. 1640, Irish Jesuit Archives, MSS A: no. 71.

92 Nugent to Vitelleschi, [Nov. 1640] and E. Archerus to Vitelleschi, 27 Nov. 1640, ibid., nos. 72, 73.

93 Barry to Percival, 24 Nov. 1640, HMC, *Egmont MSS*, 1: 122.

94 John Barnewall to Hugh Burgo, 18 Dec. 1640, in Jennings, ed., *Louvain Papers*, 132.

95 Honeyman to ———, 3 Mar. 1641, NLS, Advocates' MSS 29.2.9: 151–151v.; Barry to Percival, 31 May 1641, and O'Brien to Percival, 27 Sept. 1641, HMC, *Egmont MSS*, 1: 136, 142.

CHAPTER FIVE

1 William Wandesford to Sir Rowland Wandesford, 22 Jan. 1641, Bodl., Carte MSS 80: 636.

2 *Privy Council Registers in Facsimile*, 12: 4.

3 Most recently in Clarke, *Old English*, 125–52; Clarke, "Breakdown of Authority," 270–88; Kearney, *Strafford in Ireland*, 185–215.

4 *Lords' journ. Ireland*, 1: 143–6; *Commons' journ. Ireland*, 1: 166–7; Clarke, *Old English*, 140; Eustace to [committee], 30 Jan. 1641, Armagh Public Library MSS G.1.11.

5 *Lords' journ. Ireland*, 1: 146; lords justices to Vane, 8 Mar. 1641, PRO, SP 63/258: 171; *Cal. SP Ireland, 1633–47*, 251, 259–60. The letter of 4 January was read to the Commons on 10 February.

6 *Commons' journ. Ireland*, 1: 173–83.

7 *Lords' journ. Ireland*, 1: 146, 152. Cf. *Commons' journ. Ireland*, 1: 162–3.

8 *Lords' journ. Ireland*, 1: 153; *Commons' journ. Ireland*, 1: 178–9.

9 *Lords' journ. Ireland*, 1: 155, 157–8; *Commons' journ. Ireland*, 1: 176–7.

10 James Acheson to Montgomery and Fitzgerald, 11 Jan. 1641, Armagh Public Library MSS G.1.11.

11 "What was thought fit by the Irish councillors to be presently granted," c. May 1641, PRO, SP 63/274: 95–6; *Cal. SP Ireland, 1633–47*, 322;

Richard Barnewall, William Plunkett, et al. to committee, 23 Apr. 1641, Armagh Public Library MSS G.1.11.

12 Petitions of the Irish [Feb. 1641], PRO, SP 63/274: 1–7; *Commons' journ. Ireland*, 1: 180.

13 *Commons' journ. Ireland*, 1: 181–2.

14 Clarke, *Old English*, 140; *Commons' journ. Ireland*, 1: 183.

15 *Lords' journ. Ireland*, 1: 65–6.

16 *Commons' journ. Ireland*, 1: 199.

17 *Lords' journ. Ireland*, 1: 145.

18 Cokayne and Gibbs, eds., *Complete Peerage*, 2: 320.

19 *Lords' journ. Ireland*, 1: 145, 147.

20 Ibid., 146.

21 Ibid., 169.

22 Ibid., 173. Mayo was added to the grievance committee on 15 February (ibid., 148–9), and it was he who proposed Viscount Baltinglass for the English committee, which suggests that he supported that committee's reformist mission.

23 Petition of the Lords to the king, n.d., PRO, SP 63/274: 29.

24 *Lords' journ. Ireland*, 1: 147–8, 150–1, 153, 155.

25 Ibid., 165.

26 Ibid., 166, 168, 172. The other cause of friction between the two houses concerned an MP, John Fitzgerald, whom the Commons permitted to sit despite a suit pending against him by Lord Kerry.

27 Ibid., 178. Bishops did not participate in "matters of blood," but the judges ruled that this particular issue was not such a matter.

28 *Commons' journ. Ireland*, 1: 218, 228, 239, 285.

29 Ibid., 206, 224, 232, 234, 242, 263–4, 266.

30 Ibid., 229–31. Seven of those who were appointed to other committees at about the same time were not appointed to this group of committees on 10 June. We cannot assume, therefore, that those who were appointed to committees on 10 June represent an exact list of those who voted two weeks later.

31 Lords justices to Vane, 12 May 1641, and Sir Adam Loftus to Vane, 14 June 1641, PRO, SP 63/259: 74, 167; Parsons to Vane, 3 Aug. 1641, PRO, SP 63/260: 35v.

32 Ulster petition, PRO, SP 63/274: 17.

33 Richard Barnewall, John Dungan, William Plunkett, Stephen Stephens, Patrick Barnewall, and Alan Cooke to committee, 23 Apr. [1641], Armagh Public Library MSS G.1.11.

34 Eustace to [committee], 6 Mar. 1641, ibid.

35 Rushworth, *Tryal*, 164–5, 186, 198, 216.

36 Kearney, *Strafford in Ireland*, 212; *Commons' journ. Ireland*, 1: 333.

37 Newman, *Royalist Officers*, 278; Burke, *Vicissitudes of Families*, 1: 129–31. I thank Vera Rutledge for this last reference.

38 Vesey, *Works of Bramhall*, no page number.

39 *Commons' journ. Ireland*, 221–2, 246, 266, 269, 273. The bishop concerned was John Leslie.

40 Prendergast, "Account of Sir Audley Mervyn," 421–9, 450–1; *DNB*, 13: 299–301; Clarke, "Breakdown of Authority," 281.

41 Mervin to Ormond, 4 Feb. 1644, NLI MSS 2559: 227. I thank Robert Hunter for this reference.

42 Prendergast, "Account of Sir Audley Mervyn," 434; Mervin to Ormond, 24 May 1644, Bodl., Carte MSS 10: 789–789v.; Sir R. Stewart to Ormond, 26 May 1644, Bodl., Carte MSS 11: 3.

43 Temple, *Irish Rebellion*, 76.

44 Kearney, *Strafford in Ireland*, 194; Ball, *Judges in Ireland*, 1: 353.

45 *Cal. SP Ireland, 1633–47*, 485; Gilbert, ed., *Irish Confederation*, 4: 358, and 6: 57; Lodge, *Peerage of Ireland*, 2: 88n; Perceval-Maxwell, "Protestant Faction," 247; *Commons' journ. Ireland*, 1: 131.

46 Lodge, *Peerage of Ireland*, 2: 88n.

47 Ibid., 2: 100, and 3: 355; *DNB*, 7: 479–81; Cokayne and Gibbs, eds., *Complete Peerage*, 11: 166; Genealogical Office, Dublin, Funeral entries, 69: 11. This Richard Parsons must have been the son of the lord justice as the son of Sir Laurence Parsons, also called Richard, had died by this time.

48 Richard Barnewall et al. to committee, 23 Apr. 1641, Armagh Public Library MSS G.1.11; *Commons' journ. Ireland*, 1: 129–31.

49 Cokayne and Gibbs, eds., *Complete Peerage*, 2: 320; Lodge, *Peerage of Ireland*, 2: 88n.

50 Grosart, ed., *Lismore Papers*, 2nd ser., 3: 291, 308; Clarke, *Old English*, 46.

51 Clarke, *Old English*, 136, 142, 175, 179, 187, 205–7; Cregan, "Confederation of Kilkenny," 88–91.

52 *Lords' journ. Ireland*, 1: 151.

53 Clarke, *Old English*, 138; *Cal. SP Ireland, 1633–47*, 269–70.

54 Snow, *Essex*, 201, 239, 243–5.

55 Gormanston's and Kilmallock's petition, PRO, SP 63/258: 183–5.

56 Ibid.

57 Temple to Leicester, 18 Mar. 1641, HMC, *De L'Isle and Dudley MSS*, 6: 390–1.

58 Acheson to Montgomery and Fitzgerald, 11 Jan. 1641, Armagh Public Library MSS G.1.11.

59 Bodl. Carte MSS 67: 53–4; lords justices to Vane, 8 Mar. 1641, PRO, SP 63/258: 171; Temple to Leicester, 7 Jan. 1641, HMC, *De L'Isle and Dudley MSS*, 6: 360.

60 *Privy Council Registers in Facsimile*, 12: 82.

61 Bodl. Carte MSS 67: 54v.; Russell, "British Background to the Irish Rebellion," 172.

62 PRO, SP 63/258: 158–158v.

63 Eustace to committee, 6 Mar. 1641, Armagh Public Library MSS G.1.11.

64 Barry to Percival, 8 Mar. 1641, HMC, *Egmont MSS*, 1: 129.

65 Radcliffe's opinion on the Act of Limitations, endorsed 11 Mar. 1641, BL, Egerton MSS 2541: 225–225v.

66 Temple to Leicester, 4 Mar. 1641, HMC, *De L'Isle and Dudley MSS*, 6: 388–9.

67 *Privy Council Registers in Facsimile*, 12: 107.

68 King to lords justices, 3 Apr. 1641, PRO, SP 63/258: 227–227v.; *Cal. SP Ireland, 1633–47*, 268–9; Clarke, *Old English*, 138.

69 Percival to Barry, 15 Mar. 1641, HMC, *Egmont MSS*, 1: 130.

70 S. Digby to committee, 7 May 1641, Armagh Public Library MSS G.1.11.

71 Ibid.

72 Licence to Muskerry to pass into Ireland, 28 Feb. 1641, PRO, SO 3/12; Grosart, ed., *Lismore Papers*, 1st ser., 5: 171. I thank Michael Mac-Carthy-Morrogh for this last reference.

73 S. Digby to committee, 7 May 1641, Armagh Public Library MSS G.1.11.

74 Committee to Eustace, 12 May, 17 June, ? June, 25 June, 8 July, 9 July 1641, Duchy of Cornwall Office, Bound MSS T/M/3. I thank Conrad Russell for directing me to this set of documents.

75 *Cal. SP Ireland, 1633–47*, 269–70.

76 Kearney, *Strafford in Ireland*, 203–4; Whitaker, ed., *Life of Radcliffe*, 232; HMC, *Egmont MSS*, 1: 123.

CHAPTER SIX

1 Clarke, *Old English*, 140–52; Clarke, "Breakdown of Authority," 284–8. See also Clarke, "Policies of the Old English," 85–102.

2 Temple, *Irish Rebellion*, 76.

3 Lords justices to Vane, 2 Apr. 1641, PRO, SP 63/258: 223; *Cal. SP Ireland, 1633–47*, 268. According to Temple, the king consulted nobody about Ireland save Vane, who understood "nothing." This was not quite true as Charles consulted Radcliffe (Temple to Leicester, 18 Feb. 1641, HMC, *De L'Isle and Dudley MSS*, 6: 383).

4 Lords justices to king, 2 Apr. 1641, BL, Egerton MSS 2533: 104–115.

5 Lords justices to Vane, 3 Mar. 1641, PRO, SP 63/258: 171; *Cal. SP Ireland, 1633–47*, 259–60; Temple, *Irish Rebellion*, 13.

6 Clandeboye to lords justices, 16 Apr. 1641, PRO, SP 63/258: 268; *Cal. SP Ireland, 1633–47*, 274–5; Edward Chichester to Ormond, 4 May

1641, and Thornton to Ormond, 6 Apr. 1641, Bodl., Carte MSS 1: 379, 367; Perceval-Maxwell, "Strafford and the Covenanters," 548; Gillespie, "End of an Era," 207.

7   Walley to Cork, 14 Apr. 1641, Chatsworth, Lismore MSS 22: no. 6.

8   Lords justices to Vane, 8 May 1641, PRO, SP 63/259: 62; *Cal. SP Ireland, 1633–47*, 281; lords justices to Vane, 12 May 1641, PRO, SP 63/259: 74.

9   Richard Barnewall et al. to committee, 23 Apr. 1641, Armagh Public Library MSS G.1.11.

10   Draft, king to lords justices, 29 Apr. 1641, PRO, SP 63/258: 298; *Cal. SP Ireland, 1633–47*, 280. See also BL, Egerton MSS 2541: 227–227v.

11   Lords justices to English council, 12 May 1641, PRO, SP 63/259: 74; *Cal. SP Ireland, 1633–47*, 285.

12   *Commons' journ. Ireland*, 1: 204; Digby to committee, 7 May 1641, Armagh Public Library MSS G.1.11. The addition of the lawyers in the house would not have created a Catholic majority. The Catholic lawyer, Patrick Darcy, would have joined the committee, but so would Protestants like Sambach, the Bysse brothers, and Oliver Jones.

13   Lords justices to Vane, 18 May 1641, PRO, SP 63/259: 90; *Commons' journ. Ireland*, 1: 288–9.

14   *Commons' journ. Ireland*, 1: 203, 206, 208, 209, 214. This last committee was formed in two stages, thirteen Catholics and twenty Protestants being appointed on 14 May and an additional five Catholics and fifteen Protestants on 24 May.

15   Ibid., 212–13. Strafford had recognized in 1634 that the judicial power of the Irish parliament could probably not be denied. See Clarke, "History of Poynings' Law," 213.

16   Ibid., 213, 239.

17   Eustace to committee, c. 24 May 1641, Duchy of Cornwall Office, Bound MSS T/M/3.

18   *Commons' journ. Ireland*, 1: 215.

19   Ibid., 1: 217. The members representing Leinster were the Catholics Adam Cusack and Patrick Barnewall; Connacht's members were Sir Richard Blake (Catholic) and Oliver Jones (Protestant); Munster was represented by two Protestants, Sir Richard Osborne and Sir Edward Denny, and Ulster by an English and an Irish Protestant, Arthur Hill and Brian O'Neill.

20   These three were Patrick Barnewall, Sir Edward Denny, and Sir Richard Osborne. The presence of Hill on this committee suggests that he was a constitutionalist. He first appeared in the house in January.

21   *Commons' journ. Ireland*, 1: 219–20.

22   Ibid., 220–1, 223; Darcy, *Argument*.

23   *Commons' journ. Ireland*, 1: 229, 231.

24 Ibid., 232; Eustace to committee, 11 June 1641, Duchy of Cornwall Office, Bound MSS/T/M/3. I use the term Declaration of 10 June to distinguish this declaration from others.

25 PRO, SP 63/259: 171–171v.; *Cal. SP Ireland, 1633–47*, 303.

26 *Commons' journ. Ireland*, 1: 227.

27 Eustace to committee, 11 June 1641, Duchy of Cornwall Office, Bound MSS T/M/3.

28 Committee in England to Eustace, n.d. [c. 10 June], ibid.; Eustace to committee, 22 June 1641, Armagh Public Library MSS G.1.11. This last letter stated that the undated letter had arrived on 17 June. The next letter sent by the committee was dated 17 June, and it refers to the letter sent by Darcy's son "ten days sithence."

29 Clarke, *Old English*, 140; *Commons' journ. Ireland*, 1: 233–4.

30 See above, 127.

31 Lords justices to Vane, 30 June 1641, PRO, SP 63/259: 200v.; *Cal. SP Ireland, 1633–47*, 308.

32 Loftus to [Vane], 14 June 1641, PRO, SP 63/259: 167–167v.; *Cal. SP Ireland, 1633–47*, 302–3.

33 Lords justices to Vane, 30 June 1641, PRO, SP 63/259: 200v.; *Cal. SP Ireland, 1633–47*, 308.

34 The following MPS who signed the November Petition were also present during the fifth session although they do not qualify as leaders: R. Brice, Sir W. Brownlow, A. Champion, D. Crosby, J. Edgeworth, A. Hamilton, T. Hill, R. Leventhorp, H. Moore, J. Moore, W. Parsons (the son), W. Plunkett, H. Reynolds, W. Somers, S. Stephens, and R. Wingfield.

35 Lords justices to Vane, 30 June 1641, PRO, SP 63/259: 200v.

36 *Commons' journ. Ireland*, 1: 239.

37 Ibid. Both Peregrine Banister, a Protestant, and Sir Richard Blake, a Catholic leader, thanked Weldon for his good service.

38 Committee to Eustace, 12 May 1641 and [c. 7 June 1641], Duchy of Cornwall Office, Bound MSS T/M/3; *Cal. SP Ireland, 1633–47*, 298; *Privy Council Registers in Facsimile*, 12: 134.

39 Committee to Eustace, 17 June 1641, Duchy of Cornwall Office, Bound MSS T/M/3.

40 Committee to Eustace, 25 June 1641, ibid; *Privy Council Registers in Facsimile*, 12: 131.

41 *Commons' journ. Ireland*, 1: 244, 251, 254.

42 Committee to Eustace, 9 July 1641, Duchy of Cornwall Office, Bound MSS T/M/3.

43 Temple to Leicester, 22 July 1641, HMC, *De L'Isle and Dudley MSS*, 6: 404. Leicester had returned to his ambassadorial post in France at Charles's request.

44 "Things demanded by his majesty for the improvement ... of the revenue of Ireland," PRO, SP 63/259: 252; *Cal. SP Ireland, 1633–47*, 316; Russell, *British Monarchies*, 391.

45 *Privy Council Registers in Facsimile*, 12: 145–70; *Cal. SP Ireland, 1633–47*, 317–22, 326.

46 Russell, "British Background to the Irish Rebellion," 176; *Lords' journ. England*, 4: 339, 348; Temple to Leicester, 5 Aug. 1641, HMC, *De L'Isle and Dudley MSS*, 6: 408.

47 Temple to Leicester, 5 Aug. 1641, HMC, *De L'Isle and Dudley MSS*, 6: 407.

48 Temple to Leicester, 11 Aug. 1641, ibid., 410.

49 Grosart, ed., *Lismore Papers*, 1st ser., 5: 183; *Privy Council Registers in Facsimile*, 12: 178; T. Dillon to Vane, 27 Aug. 1641, and Loftus to Vane, 26 Aug 1641, PRO, SP 63/260: 107, 102; Temple, *Irish Rebellion*, 15; Russell, "British Background to the Irish Rebellion," 175; Russell, *British Monarchies*, 391–2. I thank Michael MacCarthy-Morrogh for the reference to the dinner with Cork.

50 *Commons' journ. Ireland*, 1: 263.

51 Ibid., 265, 269–71, 272, 274, 276.

52 Ibid., 285.

53 Parsons to Vane, 3 Aug. 1641, lords justices to Vane, 26 Aug. 1641, and Loftus to Vane, 26 Aug. 1641, PRO, SP 63/260: 35v., 98, 102; *Cal. SP Ireland, 1633–47*, 328, 339. Parsons also reported to Cork on 20 July that there were great divisions between Catholics and Protestants (Grosart, ed., *Lismore Papers*, 1st ser., 5: 208). Temple accepted that, at the end of the session, the "Popish party" had gained control in both houses (Temple, *Irish Rebellion*, 15).

54 Humble Remonstrance of the Northern Catholics, in Lodge, ed., *Desiderata Curiosa Hibernica*, 2: 97; Catholic Confederates to king's commissioners, 1642–3, in Gilbert, ed., *Irish Confederation*, 2: 231–2. Emphasis added.

55 Clarke, "A Discourse between two Councillors of State," 161–75.

56 Petition, 30 Aug. 1641, Birr Castle, Rosse MSS A/1: no. 35.

57 *Commons' journ. Ireland*, 1: 262–86. If all thirty-one committees that were selected during this period are counted, a higher proportion of committees had Protestant majorities than I have indicated in the text, but I have tried to ensure that extraneous issues do not weight the figures. It is worth noting that the total sitting on one or more committees during this period was 103, or within three of the total number of MPS voting on the last day of the session.

58 Walley to Cork, 25 June 1641, NLI MSS 12813: 579. St Leger, however, served as a teller with Sir Adam Loftus on 7 August, which suggests that he favoured adjournment.

59 Sir Thomas Tempest reported that Sambach did what he could in the house for the king though his vote was always included with the decision of the majority (Tempest to Littleton, 19 Aug. 1641, in McNeill, ed., *Tanner Letters*, 127–8).

60 Gilbert, ed., *Contemporary History*, 1, i: 12, 22.

61 "What was thought fit by the Irish councillors to be presently granted," n.d., PRO, SP 63/274: 95–6.

62 Lords justices to Vane, 8 May 1641, PRO, SP 63/259: 62; *Cal. SP Ireland, 1633–47*, 281–2; Richard Barnewall et al. to committee, 23 Apr. 1641, Armagh Public Library MSS G.1.11; lords justices to Vane, 24 Apr. 1641, PRO, SP 63/258: 273–82v.; *Cal. SP Ireland, 1633–47*, 275–8.

63 Loftus to ———, 26 Apr. 1641, and 29 Apr. 1641, PRO, SP 63/258: 294v., 296–296v; *Cal. SP Ireland, 1633–47*, 279.

64 Russell, "British Problem," 409.

65 Lords justices to Vane, 11 May 1641, PRO, SP 63/259: 62; *Cal. SP Ireland, 1633–47*, 281–3; S. Digby to committee, 7 May, Armagh Public Library MSS G.1.11.

66 Loftus to Vane, 14 June 1641, PRO, SP 63/259: 167; *Cal. SP Ireland, 1633–47*, 302–3. The calendar records this letter as saying: "The Connacht business should be settled at once," the opposite of what the letter says.

67 Loftus to Vane, 1 July 1641, PRO, SP 63/259: 215; *Cal. SP Ireland, 1633–47*, 311.

68 Loftus to Vane, 26 Aug. 1641, PRO, SP 63/260: 102; *Cal. SP Ireland, 1633–47*, 339. See above, 153–4.

69 PRO, SO 3/12: 168v.

70 Parsons to Vane, 3 Aug. 1641, PRO, SP 63/260: 35.

71 Ibid.; lords justices to Vane, 26 Aug. 1641, PRO, SP 63/260: 98.

72 Loftus to Vane, 26 Aug. 1641, ibid., 102.

73 Vane to [Nicholas], n.d. [after 9 Aug.], ibid., 112.

74 *Privy Council Registers in Facsimile*, 12: 188–9; *Cal. SP Ireland, 1633–47*, 341.

75 Lords justices to Leicester, 22 Nov. 1641, HMC, *Ormond MSS*, n.s., 2: 19; Vane to Nicholas, 20 Oct. 1641, in Warner, ed., *Nicholas Papers*, 1: 57.

76 Russell, "British Background to the Irish Rebellion," 173.

CHAPTER SEVEN

1 In this chapter, I have drawn on my article, "Ireland and the Monarchy in the Early Stuart Multiple Kingdom."

2 Clarke, *Old English*, 146.

3 Knowler, ed., *Strafforde's Letters*, 1: 65–7; *Commons' journ. Ireland*, 1: 163.

4 Clarke, *Old English*, 106; Wedgwood, *King's Peace*, 287.

5 Castle to Bridgwater, 12 Nov. 1639, Huntington Library, Ellesmere MSS 7811.

6 Perceval-Maxwell, "Ireland and the Monarchy," 288. For the English financing of Strafford's new army, see Russell, "British Background to the Irish Rebellion," 173n.31.

7 See above, 111–12, 115.

8 See above, 86, 95, and 101.

9 *Commons' journ. Ireland*, 1: 162.

10 Ibid., 191.

11 Ibid., 189, 191. The only reference to the Queries in the correspondence between the speaker and the committee in England is in a letter from the speaker to the committee telling it that he enclosed a copy of the Queries "whereunto the solutions of the judges here is desired." (Eustace to committee, 24 Feb. 1641, Armagh Public Library MSS G.1.11).

12 BL, Add. MSS 6521: 73v.

13 Laing, ed., *Letters of Baillie*, 1: 336.

14 Bruce, ed., *Verney Papers*, 60, 64. Perceval-Maxwell, "Ireland and the Monarchy," 290. Russell accepts that Ireland's status was similar to the Channel Islands and the Isle of Man as they, too, were subject to the king but not to the English parliament, but this is to suggest that Ireland's possession of a crown of its own had no significance (Russell, "British Background to the Irish Rebellion," note 9).

15 Notestein, ed., *Journal of D'Ewes*, 442–3.

16 Ibid., 487.

17 *Commons' journ. England*, 2: 104.

18 Clarke, *Old English*, 148–9.

19 See above, 83–4; *Commons' journ. Ireland*, 1: 164.

20 Ibid., 166–7; Eustace to [committee], 30 Jan. 1641, Armagh Public Library MSS G.1.11; Clarke, *Old English*, 140–1.

21 *Cal. SP Ireland, 1633–47*, 286.

22 *Privy Council Registers in Facsimile*, 12: 188–9.

23 Perceval-Maxwell, "Ireland and the Monarchy," 293.

24 Clarke, "History of Poynings' Law," 211.

25 *Commons' journ. Ireland*, 1: 185–6. On the larger committee we find, besides Mervin, Oliver Jones, Sir Faithful Fortescue, Sir Richard Osborne, Dr Alan Cooke, Stephen Stephens, Brian O'Neill (the initiator of the charge against Bramhall), Sir Robert Forth, and the two remaining Parsons in the house, Richard and William. The presence of these last two may reflect the acceptance of the process by the lords justices in February. There was much overlap in the membership of the

two committees, but it may be noted that the Bysse brothers sat on the smaller one but not on the larger.

26 Ibid., 198.

27 Mervin, *Speech Made by Captaine Audley Mervin … March 4 …* , BL, Thomason Tracts E. 196(37).

28 Bramhall's apology, 6 Mar. 1641, Huntington Library, Hastings MSS 14065; answers of Bolton, Bramhall, and Lowther, n.d., Duchy of Cornwall Office, Bound MSS T/M/3. These answers were prepared by 13 May (*Commons' journ. Ireland*, 1: 205).

29 Order of council, 26 Mar. 1641, BL, Egerton MSS 2541: 227–227v. There is no surviving copy of the king's letter. The Commons was given one, but did not, as was its custom with other letters, place a copy in its records, an indication perhaps of its distaste for the contents. There are, however, references to it: *Commons' journ. Ireland*, 1: 213; petition of the Lords and Commons to king, 10 July 1641, PRO, SP 63/259: 244; *Cal. SP Ireland, 1633–47*, 315.

30 Clarke, "Breakdown of Authority," 285.

31 *Commons' journ. Ireland*, 1: 205; lords justices to Vane, 18 May 1641, PRO, SP 63/259: 91v.; *Cal. SP Ireland, 1633–47*, 289.

32 *Commons' journ. Ireland*, 1: 212–13; PRO, SP 63/259: 133; *Cal. SP Ireland, 1633–47*, 296–7.

33 Mervin, *Captaine Audley Mervin's Speech … May 24 1641*, 1–2, 3–4, 5–7, 36, 9, 11–12, 14, 15, 16.

34 *Commons' journ. Ireland*, 1: 212–13; Eustace to committee, 25 May 1641, Duchy of Cornwall Office, Bound MSS T/M/3.

35 *Commons' journ. Ireland*, 1: 236, 249, 253; PRO, SP 63/259: 244. The committee to draw up more specific charges, which was listed on 19 June and 7 July, had eight Catholic members and eight Protestants. The Protestants were: Mervin, Simon Digby, Archibald Hamilton, Oliver Jones, Peregrine Banister, Brian O'Neill, William Cadogan, and Mathew Derenzey. It may be noted that the two Parsons were no longer dealing with the issue.

36 Russell, *Parliaments and English Politics*, 14–15. For examples of the way Ireland was tied up with English court politics, see: Bradshaw, *Irish Constitutional Revolution*; Canny, *Elizabethan Conquest of Ireland*; Rutledge, "Court-Castle Faction and the Irish Viceroyalty," 233–49.

37 Parsons to one of the secretaries of state, 21 July 1641, *Cal. SP Ireland, 1633–47*, 323–4.

38 Committee to Eustace, 25 June 1641, Duchy of Cornwall Office, Bound MSS T/M/3.

39 Koenigsberger, "Monarchies and Parliaments in Early Modern Europe," 191–217; Russell, "British Problem," 395–415.

40 Kearney, *Strafford in Ireland*, 210; Clarke, *Old English*, 145; Perceval-Maxwell, "Ireland and the Monarchy," 292.

41 *Commons' journ. Ireland*, 1: 174–5.

42 Ibid., 191.

43 Ibid., 205, 216, 218–19.

44 Darcy, *Argument*, 19–21.

45 Ibid., 23–5.

46 Kearney, *Strafford in Ireland*, 211.

47 Darcy, *Argument*, 130–43.

48 Clarke, *Old English*, 148–9.

49 *Lords' journ. Ireland*, 1: 161.

50 See above, 153.

51 Darcy, *Argument*, 67.

52 Ibid., 43, 46, 74, 91, 95–6, 105.

53 Ibid., 110, 111.

54 *Commons' journ. Ireland*, 1: 269–71.

55 Clarke, *Old English*, 146.

56 Mervin also made a speech on the subject of the Queries and apparently supported them, although the speech was even more obtuse than his others. Mervin, *Sixteen Queres Propounded by the Parliament of Ireland*.

57 *Commons' journ. Ireland*, 1: 188–9, 191, 219–20, 284.

58 Ibid., 269–71. There was some opposition in the Commons to the Queries because Sir Thomas Tempest, the Irish attorney-general, urged legal arguments against them, but, he reported, "I could not prevail." Sir William Sambach also opposed them. Tempest to Edward Littleton, 19 Aug. 1641, in McNeill, ed., *Tanner Letters*, 127–8.

59 *Privy Council Registers in Facsimile*, 12: 183, 188–9.

60 Nicholas to Vane, 27 Oct. 1641, Surrey Record Office, Bray MSS 85/5/2(23). The council's letter had been received by the king by 15 October.

61 [Leicester to Ward?], 14 Oct. 1641, *Cal. SP Domestic, 1641–43*, 139.

62 —— to Vane, 7 Oct. 1641, Surrey Record Office, Bray MSS 85/5/2(10a).

63 Kent Archives Office, De L'Isle MSS U 1475/z1/9.

64 Lords justices to Leicester, 22 Nov. 1641, HMC, *Ormond MSS*, n.s., 2: 19.

CHAPTER EIGHT

1 Borlase, *Execrable Rebellion*, 8; Cárdenas to Charles, 21 Nov. 1641, PRO, SP 94/42: 242. I thank R.A. Stradling, both for sending me this reference and for his translation of the relevant passage.

2 Montgomery to king, 24 Oct. 1641, *Cal. SP Ireland, 1633–47*, 341.

3 Clarke, "Genesis of the Ulster Rising," 40.

4 Ibid., 39–40.
5 Russell, "British Background to the Irish Rebellion," 173; St Leger to
   Ormond, 21 July 1640, Bodl., Carte MSS 1: 214; lords justices to king,
   2 Apr. 1641, BL, Egerton MSS 2533: 115; PRO, E 405/285: 143.
6 Lords justices to Vane, 8 Mar. 1641, and 10 Apr. 1641, PRO, SP 63/258:
   171, 240v.; Lords' journ. Ireland, 1: 126; Strafford to Radcliffe, 5 Nov.
   1640, in Whitaker, ed., Life of Radcliffe, 220.
7 Notestein, ed., Journal of D'Ewes, 213.
8 Ibid., 229.
9 Ibid., 301, 327, 346–7, 351, 454, 461, 498; Commons' journ. England, 2:
   82–3, 91, 102–4, 113, 117, 127; Lords' journ. England, 4: 167, 187–91;
   BL, Harleian MSS 6424: 19, 23v., 24v., 25v.; BL, Harleian MSS 164: 119;
   BL, Add. MSS 6521: 58, 67v., 68, 101; Laing, ed., Letters of Baillie, 304;
   Cal. SP Domestic 1640–41, 524; Jansson, ed., Two Diaries, 4, 20, 25, 107,
   129–30.
10 Jansson, ed., Two Diaries, 107; Commons' journ. England, 2: 104; Notestein, ed., Journal of D'Ewes, 486–7.
11 Lords justices to Vane, 8 Mar. 1641, state of the Irish revenue, 17 Mar.
   1641, and lords justices to Vane, 10 Apr. 1641, PRO, SP 63/258: 176v.,
   214, 239–42; Cal. SP Ireland, 1633–47, 270–1. The king's demands
   have to be interpreted from the reply because his letter has not survived.
12 Commons' journ. England, 2: 127; BL, Add. MSS 37343: 225v.
13 Rushworth, Historical Collections, 4: 238; BL, Add. MSS 37343: 225v.;
   Commons' journ. England, 2: 131 (this source dates the king's response
   as 29 April); BL, Add. MSS 6521: 130–130v.; BL, Harleian MSS 163:
   113; BL, Harleian MSS 6424: 57.
14 Resolution for disbanding the new Irish army, 7 May 1641, PRO, SP 63/
   259: 60; Lords' journ. England, 4: 239.
15 PRO, SO 1/3: 217v.
16 Barry to Percival, 4 May 1641, HMC, Egmont MSS, 1: 134; PRO, SP 63/
   259: 60.
17 Russell, "First Army Plot," 85–106; Hibbard, Popish Plot, 193–4; HMC,
   Egmont MSS, 1: 134; Rushworth, Historical Collections, 4: 240, 255; BL,
   Add. MSS 6521: 141, 190v., 195v.
18 Cregan, "An Irish Cavalier," 78; Cal. SP Ireland 1633–47, 331.
19 Russell, "First Army Plot," 103; Rushworth, Historical Collections, 4: 255.
20 BL, Harleian MSS 477: 27v.
21 Vane to Ormond, 8 May 1641, and king to Ormond, 8 May 1641,
   Bodl., Carte MSS 1: 383, 381; order of lords justices, 17 May 1641,
   PRO, 31/1/1: 247.
22 Ormond to [Vane], 9 June 1641, PRO, SP 63/259: 163. This information
   had been received in England by 22 June.

23 PRO, SP 63/259: 60; Grosart, ed., *Lismore Papers*, 1st ser., 5: 174–6; lords justices to Vane, 1 June 1641, PRO, SP 63/259: 125v. Those who initially put up bonds for the money included Cork, Bath, Ranelagh, Sir Adam Loftus, Sir Robert King, Sir John Clotworthy, and the Old Englishman, Nicholas Barnewall.

24 Jennings, ed., *Wild Geese*, 279–310; Cuvelier et al., eds., *Correspondance de la cour d'Espagne*, 6: 319–22.

25 1.2 million Spanish crowns. Velada to Philip IV, 23 May 1640, and Wentworth's proposal, 25 May 1640, in Jennings, ed., *Wild Geese*, 317, 318; Windebank to Hopton, 24 July 1640, Bodl., Clarendon MSS 18: 237; Radcliffe to Ormond, 22 July 1640, Bodl., Carte MSS 1: 216.

26 Giovanni Giustinian to doge and Senate, 11 Jan. 1641, *Cal. SP Venice, 1640–42*, 112; Taylor to Windebank, 29 Oct. 1640, *Cal. SP Domestic, 1640–41*, 201.

27 Cárdenas to Don Ferdinand, 18 Jan. 1641, and Don Ferdinand to Philip, 28 Apr. 1641, in Jennings, ed., *Wild Geese*, 330, 337; Cuvelier et al., eds., *Correspondance de la cour d'Espagne*, 3: 405.

28 Jennings, ed., *Wild Geese*, 334–7.

29 PRO, SP 63/259: 60–60v. Those who received commissions at this time were: Garret Barry, John Barry, Christopher Belling, John Butler, Sir Lawrence Carey, Sir James Dillon, Theobald Taafe (listed as Tibbatah), and a Colonel Winter.

30 King to Ormond, 13 May 1641, Bodl., Carte MSS 1: 391, 393, 395, 397, 399, 401, 403; PRO, 31/1/1: 240. Only seven names were sent to Ormond; Winter's and Carey's were omitted and do not appear later in the records. These men replaced by Plunkett and Porter. Sir James Dillon's name was not sent to Ormond, but this seems to have been an oversight as he certainly continued to participate in the scheme. These letters sometimes tell us when the colonels arrived as they delivered them to Ormond themselves and in some instances the date on which the commissions were received in Ireland is indicated. Belling, for instance, had arrived by 18 May.

31 Bodl., Carte MSS 1: 403; lords justices to [Vane], 24 May 1641, and 30 June 1641, PRO, SP 63/259: 139, 198; *Cal. SP Ireland, 1633–47*, 307.

32 Barry to Percival, 31 May 1641, HMC, *Egmont MSS*, 1: 136; Jennings, ed., *Wild Geese*, 342. An additional name appeared on the list of officers at this stage, Dermot O'Brien, but he was never mentioned again and seems to have been replaced by John Bermingham (Jennings, ed., *Wild Geese*, 349).

33 Jennings, ed., *Wild Geese*, 346. Cárdenas described the Irish merchant as wealthy, a Catholic, a native of Galway, and a member of the Irish parliament. Brown is the only western Catholic who fits the description; his father had been mayor of Galway (Clarke, *Old English*, 127).

34 Bodl., Carte MSS 1: 395, 397, 401; PRO, 31/1/1: 242–3, 245; Cárdenas
    to Don Ferdinand, 12 July 1641 and 20 July 1641, in Jennings, ed.,
    Wild Geese, 347, 349. John Barry was clearly one of those who had
    arrived by 20 July as his was one of the commissions received by
    Ormond though, in his case, the endorsement is undated.

35 Porter to Cárdenas, July 1641, and Plunkett to Cárdenas, 19 July 1641,
    in Jennings, ed., *Wild Geese*, 349.

36 *Commons' journ. Ireland*, 1: 272–3, 276–7.

37 Ibid., 276–7; BL, Egerton MSS 2541: 262–262v.

38 Parliament stated that 16,000 men were about to be embarked; the jus-
    tices put the figure at 9,000 and licences had been issued for only
    8,000. Borlase, *Execrable Rebellion*, 8; Irish council to [English council],
    3 Aug. 1641, BL, Egerton MSS 2533: 121.

39 Parsons to Vane, 3 Aug. 1641, PRO, SP 63/260: 35v.; *Cal. SP Ireland,
    1633–47*, 328–9.

40 PRO, SP 63/260: 38; *Cal. SP Ireland, 1633–47*, 330.

41 Lady Barrymore to Cork, 18 Aug. 1641, Chatsworth, Lismore MSS 22:
    no. 53; lords justices to Vane, 24 Aug. 1641, and Thomas Dillon to
    Vane, 27 Aug. 1641, PRO, SP 63/260: 92, 98, 107; *Cal. SP Ireland,
    1633–47*, 338, 340.

42 Lords justices to Vane, 24 Aug 1641, PRO, SP 63/260: 92; *Cal. SP Ire-
    land, 1633–47*, 338; bond of Barry and Percival to Cárdenas, 8 Sept.
    1641, BL, Add. MSS 46925: 137, 139; HMC, *Egmont MSS*, 1: 141.

43 Venetian ambassador to Spain to doge and Senate, 1 Oct. 1641, *Cal.
    SP Venice, 1640–42*, 221.

44 Witnessed certification, 25 Nov. 1641 and acknowledged by Cárdenas,
    27 Nov., BL, Add. MSS 46925: 139v.; HMC, *Egmont MSS*, 1: 141.

45 St Leger to Percival, 8 Nov. 1641, HMC, *Egmont MSS*, 1: 145; lords jus-
    tices to Leicester, 26 Nov. 1641, HMC, *Ormond MSS*, n.s., 2: 27.

46 TCD MSS 809: 129.

47 Bourke, *Memoirs and Letters of Clanricarde*, 17, 30.

48 Borlase, *Execrable Rebellion*, 9; Clarke, "Genesis of the Ulster Rising," 40.

49 Philip to Miguel de Salamanca, 14 July 1641, in Jennings, ed., *Wild
    Geese*, 347; *Cal. SP Venice, 1640–42*, 214.

50 Cárdenas to Don Ferdinand, 14 June 1641, Don Ferdinand to Philip,
    15 June 1641, Cárdenas to Salamanca, 17 July 1641, in Jennings, ed.,
    Wild Geese, 343, 344, 348; *Cal. SP Venice, 1640–42*, 164. Clarendon also
    believed that the French ambassador was involved (Macray, ed., *Claren-
    don's History*, 1: 382).

51 PRO, SO 3/12: 160; BL, Add. MSS 6521: 238; BL, Harleian MSS 6424:
    83v.; *Lords' journ. England*, 4: 321.

52 BL, Harleian MSS 6424: 87–88v.; *Lords' journ. England*, 4: 331, 340,
    345. The wording was that the house "inclines" towards 4,000 men.

53   BL, Harleian MSS 164: 57v.–58. Cf. *Commons' journ. England*, 2: 240.

54   BL, Harleian MSS 164: 57v.–58. The speaker also thought that consent had been given, but found no such order in the records (ibid., 29v.).

55   Cárdenas to Don Ferdinand, 16 Aug. 1641, in Jennings, ed., *Wild Geese*, 353.

56   Nicholas to Vane, 11 Aug 1641, in Warner, ed., *Nicholas Papers*, 1: 4–5; Vane to Ormond, 20 Aug. 1641, Bodl., Carte MSS 1: 436.

57   BL, Harleian MSS 6424: 89; BL, Harleian MSS 164: 25v.; BL, Harleian MSS 5047: 71; *Lords' journ. England*, 4: 364.

58   Cárdenas to Salamanca, 9 Aug. 1641, in Jennings, ed., *Wild Geese*, 352. See also: Russell, "British Background to the Irish Rebellion," 178.

59   King to Nicholas, 19 Aug. 1641, in Bray, ed., *Correspondence of Evelyn*, 4: 73.

60   Lords justices to Vane, 24 Aug. 1641, PRO, SP 63/260: 92; *Cal. SP Ireland, 1633–47*, 338.

61   *Commons' journ. England*, 2: 266.

62   BL, Harleian MSS 164: 58.

63   Ibid., 72v.; Russell, *British Monarchies*, 393; Fletcher, *Outbreak of the English Civil War*, 64.

64   Nicholas to king, 28 Aug. 1641, in Bray, ed., *Correspondence of Evelyn*, 4: 80–1; Giustinian to doge and Senate, 30 Aug. 1641, *Cal. SP Venice, 1640–42*, 207; Loomie, "Alonso de Cárdenas," 293.

65   *Commons' journ. England*, 2: 285.

66   Note in king's hand on Nicholas to king, 25 Oct. 1641, in Bray, ed., *Correspondence of Evelyn*, 4: 112; Hibbard, *Popish Plot*, 214. D'Ewes, Vane, and Nicholas himself expressed similar, if less outspoken, sentiments (Bray, ed., *Correspondence of Evelyn*, 121, 125; Coates, ed., *Journal of D'Ewes*, 78–9; *Cal. SP Domestic, 1641–43*, 154).

CHAPTER NINE

1   Gardiner, *History*, 10: 7–8, 49–51; Beckett, *Cavalier Duke*, 18–19; Clarke, *Old English*, 158–9, 165–8; Clarke, "Genesis of the Ulster Rising," 39–40; Corish, "1641 and the Catholic Confederacy," 290; Stevenson, *Alasdair MacColla*, 74; Casway, *Owen Roe O'Neill*, 50; Hibbard, *Popish Plot*, 214; Ohlmeyer, *Randal MacDonnell*, 96–9.

2   Russell, "British Background to the Irish Rebellion," 179.

3   Hill, *MacDonnells of Antrim*, 449–51. See also Lowe, "Negotiations between Charles and the Confederation of Kilkenny," 1–8.

4   TCD MSS 809: 5–12; Hickson, ed., *Ireland in the Seventeenth Century*, 1: 326–40.

5   Hill, *MacDonnells of Antrim*, 449–51.

6   Russell, "British Background to the Irish Rebellion," 179.

7 Examination of Antrim, 23 July 1661, PRO, SP 63/307: 270–1; *Cal. SP Ireland, 1660–62*, 384. In 1663 Antrim claimed in a petition that in 1640 Charles had commanded him to try to bring "those Irishmen" to serve the king, but this could not be a reference to the summer of 1641. It is entirely possible that Charles asked Antrim to work with Strafford in 1640 (summary of petition from Antrim, 24 Feb. 1663, PRO, SP 44/13: 221; *Cal. SP Ireland, 1663–65*, 29–30). I am grateful to Jane Ohlmeyer for directing me to the later evidence: see Ohlmeyer, "The 'Antrim Plot' of 1641," in which Antrim's account is examined in detail and accepted. Nevertheless, I maintain that no reliable contemporary evidence exists to support the view that Charles was plotting with the Irish during the summer, and the onus of proof lies on those who say he was. The contemporary evidence, indeed, points in the other direction.

8 PRO, SP 63/259: 65v., 66, 127, 150, 169v., 175, 201, 212, 240, 255, 267, 275. He signed no council letter after 31 July till 15 November (PRO, SP 63/260: 42, 103, 118, 158v.). In August Ormond does seem to have gone to the country (Carrick-on-Suir, Tipperary), where he was when the rebellion broke out (Carte, *Ormonde*, 1: 192).

9 Ormond to Percival, 3 Mar. 1642, BL, Add. MSS 46926: 34.

10 Antrim to Hamilton, 3 June 1641, SRO, GD 406/1/1355.

11 Antrim to king, 8 June 1641, SRO, GD 406/1/1356 i.

12 Antrim to Hamilton, 19 July 1641, SRO, GD 406/1/1389.

13 Ibid.

14 See above, 185–6.

15 Hill, *MacDonnells of Antrim*, 278. The receipt of this pension tends to undermine the idea that Antrim was framed.

16 Gardiner, *History*, 9: 401–3; Hibbard, *Popish Plot*, 202.

17 Rossetti to Barberini, 4/14 June 1641, Vatican Library, Barberini MSS 8650, pt 1: 5–8v.

18 Gardiner, *History*, 9: 403.

19 Rossetti to Barberini, 9/19 July 1641, Vatican Library, Barberini MSS 8650, pt 1: 89–93.

20 Gardiner, *History*, 10: 8n, 92; Rossetti to Barberini, 21 Nov./1 Dec. 1641, Vatican Library, Barberini MSS 8650, pt 2: 361–2. Rossetti's letter was written from Cologne and refers to a conversation with the queen mother about the rebellion. It makes reference to Irish forces ("forze dell Hibernia"), but it supplies no evidence of the queen's involvement in a plot with the Irish or Old English, let alone one involving the king. What it does reveal is that the queen was concerned that the topic of her earlier conversation with Rossetti might be discovered. She had every reason to be concerned because, had it emerged that in June she had been discussing freedom of conscience for Catholics in Ireland

(one of the Irish demands), it would have been difficult to explain to parliament that she had not encouraged the Irish to pursue these aims by force.

21 Giblin, "Vatican Library: MSS Barberini Latini," 130.

22 Cregan, "An Irish Cavalier," 89–91.

23 Rossetti to Barberini, 9/19 July 1641, Vatican Library, Barberini MSS 8650, pt 1: 92v.

24 [E. Bowles], *Mysterie of Iniquitie*. BL, Thomason Tracts, E. 76(25).

25 Ibid., 28.

26 Ibid., 23, 35. The account can be shown to be false in one detail. Twice it included Muskerry as one of Charles's accomplices during the summer, yet we know that the elder Muskerry died in February 1641, and his successor, Sir Donough MacCarthy, who was a member of the Commons committee, returned to Ireland on his father's death. (Licence to Muskerry to pass to Ireland, 28 Feb. 1641, PRO, SO 3/12.)

27 Extract of letter from some of the rebels to Dillon, 10 Nov. 1641, PRO, SP 63/260: 157v.; lords justices to speaker of the English Commons, 11 May 1642, BL, Add. MSS 19398: 135.

28 Lodge, *Peerage of Ireland*, 4: 177; Gilbert, ed., *Contemporary History*, 1, ii: 611; Thomas Maule to Ormond, 18 Oct. 1641, NLI MSS 2307: 125; Wemys to Ormond, 25 Sept. 1641, Bodl., Carte MSS 1: 457.

29 *Commons' journ. England*, 2: 281, 284.

30 Wemys to Ormond, 25 Sept. 1641, Bodl., Carte MSS 1: 457; Russell, *British Monarchies*, 396–7.

31 Wemys to Ormond, 19 Oct. 1641, Bodl., Carte MSS 1: 466v.; Russell, *British Monarchies*, 396–7. The issue with which Wemys was entrusted concerned rights to certain liberties in County Limerick, and his original instructions were to approach the king only through Vane, which suggests Ormond was close to the secretary. Ormond's reasons for not going to Edinburgh were that he had to attend parliament (an indication that he did not know its meeting had been postponed) and because of "some other difficulties." (Ormond to Wemys, 19 Oct. 1641, Bodl., Carte MSS 1: 475.) My interpretation of the Ormond-Wemys correspondence differs somewhat from Russell's. Charles renewed his plan to go to Ireland in April 1642 but was opposed by the English parliament (Russell, *British Monarchies*, 488).

32 Carte, *Ormonde*, 1: 150–2.

33 Ormond to king, 1 Dec. 1641, PRO, SP 63/260: 190.

34 TCD MSS 836: 130; TCD MSS 809: 6.

35 Clarke, *Old English*, 228; Clarke, "Genesis of the Ulster Rising," 40; Casway, *Owen Roe O'Neill*, 50.

36 Macray, ed., *Clarendon's History*, 1: 411n. Clarendon, however, was not aware that the Old English abandoned their plan to rebel, and he perceived this plot to be the same one that started the rebellion.

37 Letter from London, 14/24 May 1641, Vatican Library, Barberini MSS
    8671: no. 114.
38 Letter from London, 16/26 July 1641, ibid., no. 125.
39 *Cal. SP Ireland, 1633–47*, 307; *Commons' journ. Ireland*, 1: 276–7.
40 Bodl., Carte MSS 1: 294. See above, 104.
41 PRO, SO 3/12: 148v.
42 Temple to Leicester, 22 July 1641, and 29 July 1641, HMC, *De L'Isle and
    Dudley MSS*, 4: 405, 406.
43 Temple to Leicester, 5 Aug. 1641, and 11 Aug. 1641, ibid., 407–8, 410.
44 Temple to Nicholas, 27 Aug. 1641, Christ Church College, Evelyn MSS,
    Nicholas box. I thank Conrad Russell for directing me to this source.
45 Hickson, ed., *Ireland in the Seventeenth Century*, 2: 341–54.
46 Gilbert, ed., *Contemporary History*, 1, i: 396–400.
47 Meehan, *Fate and Fortune of Hugh O'Neill*, 545–7.
48 Hickson, ed., *Ireland in the Seventeenth Century*, 2: 190–1.
49 TCD MSS 809: 5–12; Hickson, ed., *Ireland in the Seventeenth Century*, 1:
    326–40.
50 Corish, "1641 and the Catholic Confederacy," 289–90; Casway, *Owen
    Roe O'Neill*, 29–36.
51 TCD MSS 809: 5; Hickson, ed., *Ireland in the Seventeenth Century*, 1: 327,
    and 2: 343; Gilbert, ed., *Contemporary History*, 1, i: 396; Casway, *Owen
    Roe O'Neill*, 34. For the genealogy of the O'Neill family, see Casway,
    Owen Roe O'Neill, appendices 1 and 2.
52 TCD MSS 809: 5.
53 Hickson, ed., *Ireland in the Seventeenth Century*, 2: 341–3; Clarke, *Old
    English*, 156; Casway, *Owen Roe O'Neill*, 44.
54 Hickson, ed., *Ireland in the Seventeenth Century*, 2: 342.
55 TCD MSS 809: 5v.; Hickson, ed., *Ireland in the Seventeenth Century*, 1:
    327–8 and 2: 343, 348.
56 Hickson, ed., *Ireland in the Seventeenth Century*, 2: 343–4.
57 Ibid., 2: 343; Gilbert, ed., *Contemporary History*, 1, i: 396; Cárdenas to
    Salamanca, 20 Apr. 1641, in Jennings, ed., *Wild Geese*, 335.
58 Gilbert, ed., *Contemporary History*, 1, i: 396; *Cal. SP Ireland, 1633–47*,
    313. Other officers were given similar permission but were raising
    forces for the French.
59 O'Neill to Wadding, 8 July 1641, in Meehan, *Fate and Fortune of Hugh
    O'Neill*, 545–6; Casway, *Owen Roe O'Neill*, 46.
60 Lords justices to Vane, 30 June 1641, PRO, SP 63/259: 198; *Cal. SP Ire-
    land, 1633–47*, 307.
61 Hickson, ed., *Ireland in the Seventeenth Century*, 2: 344.
62 Ibid.; *Commons' journ. Ireland*, 1: 276.
63 Hickson, ed., *Ireland in the Seventeenth Century*, 2: 345.
64 Ibid. In 1644 an English lawyer, in commenting upon Maguire's rela-
    tion, remarked that all the colonels save Taffe, John Barry, and Porter

joined the Irish soon after the rebellion broke out (Gilbert, ed., *Contemporary History*, 1, ii: 611). Of Richard Plunkett it was remarked that on 26 October in Cavan he had declared that he "had a contract under the hand of all the Catholic lords in Ireland for joining in that action" (ibid.). Obviously he had no such contract. Clarke (*Old English*, 158) included John Barry among the colonels who were involved but Maguire made no mention of him. Sir Phelim, in his examination taken in 1653, implicated Barry, stating that he was at the meetings and that he was one of those assigned to take Dublin Castle. However, as Maguire said, confirmed by Maxwell, Sir Phelim was not privy to the plot till September, and could not have known who was involved during August. Barry had, as we know, gone to Scotland and thence to London. Very possibly he had returned to Ireland by 20 September, by which time Sir Phelim had begun to take part in the negotiations with the colonels, but we have Maguire's word that by then the only two colonels who retained any enthusiasm for the scheme were Hugh Byrne and Plunkett. The most reliable evidence points away from Barry's involvement.

65 Hickson, ed., *Ireland in the Seventeenth Century*, 2: 345–7.
66 Plunkett to Cárdenas, 19 July 1641, in Jennings, ed., *Wild Geese*, 349.
67 Hickson, ed., *Ireland in the Seventeenth Century*, 2: 347–8; Gilbert, ed., *Contemporary History*, 1, i: 397.
68 Hickson, ed., *Ireland in the Seventeenth Century*, 2: 349. According to Antrim's initial statement to the Commonwealth officials, it was the king who first proposed the seizure of Dublin Castle (Hill, *MacDonnells of Antrim*, 449). There is no other evidence to support this idea and, if true, would mean either that Charles was working in league with Owen Roe O'Neill, which is preposterous, or that the two men had had the same idea at the same time independently.
69 Hickson, ed., *Ireland in the Seventeenth Century*, 2: 349.
70 Ibid., 350–2. Raymond Gillespie believes that Sir Phelim was not enthusiastic about the plan to seize Dublin Castle and remained aloof from it, but the decision to start the rising in Ulster at the same time as the Dublin venture points to a co-ordinated plan (Gillespie, "End of an Era," 203–4).
71 Gilbert, ed., *Contemporary History*, 1, i: 353–4, 357–9.
72 I thank Lee Matthews for pointing this out to me.
73 Gilbert, ed., *Contemporary History*, 1, i: 357.

CHAPTER TEN

1 O'Mellan's journal, TCD MSS 1071: 16–19; Perceval-Maxwell, "Ulster Rising of 1641," 149.

2 Carte, *Ormonde*, 1: 185; TCD MSS 836: 128.

3 *Cal. SP Ireland, 1633–47*, 342.

4 Chichester to king, 24 Oct. 1641, and Montgomery to king, 24 Oct. 1641, ibid., 341–2.

5 Hickson, ed., *Ireland in the Seventeenth Century*, 1: 224; TCD MSS 836: 14, 37; lords justices to Ormond, 2 Nov. 1641, Bodl., Carte MSS 2: 8; lords justices to English council, 5 Nov. 1641, HMC, *Ormond MSS*, n.s., 2: 8.

6 Fitzpatrick, "Sack of 'the Lurgan',", 170–87; Perceval-Maxwell, "Ulster Rising of 1641," 152–3; *Cal. SP Ireland, 1633–47*, 341–2; Carte, *Ormonde*, 1: 185–6; lords justices to Leicester, 25 Nov. 1641, HMC, *Ormond MSS*, n.s., 2: 22; Anonymous, ed., "A Brief Relation," 242–5; Commencement of the Troubles in Ireland, BL, Sloan MSS 1008: 337–337v.; Montgomery to Ormond, 5 Dec. 1641, Bodl., Carte MSS 2: 148; Galbraith to Percival, HMC, *Egmont MSS*, 1: 145–6.

7 *Cal. SP Ireland, 1633–47*, 344: BL, Sloan MSS 1008: 337v.; TCD MSS 839: 22v.

8 TCD MSS 835: 2, 3, 71, 73, 143v., 255, 259, 262; Gilbert, ed., *Contemporary History*, 1, i: 465–8, 527. Another source, BL, Sloan MSS 1008: 35, indicates that Maguire began the rising at Lisgoole.

9 Gilbert, ed., *Contemporary History*, 1, i: 399.

10 O'Neill to Stewart, no date, PRO, SP 63/274: 100; Gilbert, ed., *Contemporary History*, 1, ii: 466; TCD MSS 839: 1; Perceval-Maxwell, "Ulster Rising of 1641," 155–9.

11 TCD MSS 835: 71, 73, 91v., 109.

12 TCD MSS 832: 89v.

13 TCD MSS 835: 30, 82; TCD MSS 839: 15.

14 TCD MSS 836: 64.

15 Touchet, *Memoirs of Castlehaven*, 14; TCD MSS 834: 57, 103; TCD MSS 835: 189; TCD MSS 839: 8, 132v.

16 O'Neill to Sir Robert Knight, 22 Nov. 1641, in Gilbert, ed., *Contemporary History*, 1, i: 371. The date of this letter suggests that the incident took place about the middle of this month. For another Irish reference to the massacre near Augher, see Account of Irish Affairs, 6 Jan. 1642, Irish Jesuit Archives, MSS A, transcripts 3: 248B, in which the number of Scottish deaths is inflated to 7,000. For British references to this incident, see TCD MSS 839: 14v., 21, where the number killed is given as 300 to 400 men.

17 TCD MSS 835: 158. See also TCD MSS 839: 30, 70v.

18 The original of the declaration and the forged commission have not survived. The copies I have used are TCD MSS 836: 18 and Bodl., Nalson MSS Deposit C 174N: 3–3v. I thank Conrad Russell for directing me to the Nalson copy.

19 Ibid. The forgery of the commission is established in Dunlop, "Forged Commission of 1641," 527–33.

20 Carte, *Ormonde*, 1: 172–3; TCD MSS 834: 54–60; lords justices to Leicester, 25 Oct. 1641, HMC, *Ormond MSS*, n.s., 2: 3.

21 *Cal. SP Ireland, 1633–47*, 344; PRO, SP 63/260: 141; TCD MSS 839: 125–50: Gilbert, ed., *Contemporary History*, 1, ii: 472–3.

22 TCD MSS 834: 16, 20; McNeill and Otway-Ruthven, eds., *Dowdall Deeds*, 329. Bellings confirms that the advance south occurred as Sir Phelim pressed his attack on Lisburn (Gilbert, ed., *Irish Confederation*, 1: 23). Sir Phelim testified a decade later that it was only after the lords of the Pale had joined the siege of Drogheda that he was invited to participate. This concurs with what we know of his movements during November. The decision to divide the Irish forces in this manner seems to have been reached at a council of war held in Monaghan attended by Philip O'Reilly, Colonel Brian MacMahon, Sir Phelim, and Rory Maguire and others soon after the rebellion began (Gilbert, ed., *Contemporary History*, 3: 367).

23 TCD MSS 832: 96; TCD MSS 816: 235, 480–1. Gilbert, ed., *Contemporary History*, 1, ii: 477–8.

24 Gilbert, ed., *Contemporary History*, 1, ii: 529. See also TCD MSS 832: 74.

25 Gilbert, ed., *Contemporary History*, 1, ii: 526.

26 Ibid., 1, i: 372–3. The Longford depositions show that here, too, the Irish succeeded in driving a wedge between the English and the Scots (TCD MSS 817: 291–2).

27 Gilbert, ed., *Contemporary History*, 1, ii: 486.

28 Ibid., 494–7; TCD MSS 817: 187v., 291–2v.

29 Gilbert, ed., *Contemporary History*, 1, ii: 526–7. Plunkett's presence at Virginia at this time is credible in that he was reported to be near Navan on 26 October (TCD MSS 816: 223).

30 Gilbert, ed., *Contemporary History*, 1, ii: 480–1.

31 Ibid., ii: 481, and i: 364–5. Jones had reached Dublin with the Remonstrance by 6 November, which enables us to date its composition approximately. Jones, on whom we must rely for information on the background to the Cavan Remonstrance, was hostile to the Irish cause.

32 Ibid., 1, i: 364–5.

33 *Commons' journ. Ireland*, 1: 289.

34 Gilbert, ed., *Contemporary History*, 1, i: 365–7, and ii: 482. Jones's delay in returning with the response may have been because he wished to wait till parliament had met and discussed the rebellion.

35 Ibid., ii: 482–4; Bodl., Carte MSS 2: 39, 86, 90, 116v.; Carte, *Ormonde*, 1: 238–9; Christopher Barnewall's and William More's examinations, July 1642, McNeill and Otway-Ruthven, eds., *Dowdall Deeds*, 329–30; lords justices to Leicester, 22 Nov. 1641, HMC, *Ormond MSS*, n.s., 2: 20.

Carte argues that the Louth gentry had no choice but to join the Irish as they had no weapons and could not expect help from the Dublin authorities (Carte, *Ormonde*, 1: 238). Barnewall's and More's examinations do not bear this out; they made no mention of these concerns, but reported only that MacMahon declared that "most of the nobility and gentry of the kingdom was privy to the present rebellion." They were given three days to raise troops to join the Irish, "which accordingly for the most" was done, and they quickly appointed officers to command these men. This suggests an ability to organize militarily very quickly when the will was there.

36 Francis Lloyd to Lord Herbert, 2 Dec. 1641, in Smith, ed., *Herbert Correspondence*, 112–13. Other accounts of Julianstown are to be found in Wemys to Ormond, 29 Nov. 1641, Bodl., Carte MSS 2: 124; lords justices to Leicester, 30 Nov. 1641, HMC, *Ormond MSS*, n.s., 2: 31; account of Irish affairs, 6 Jan. 1642, Irish Jesuit Archives, MSS A, transcripts 3: 248A, where it is stated that the Irish numbered only 400 men, who attacked so fiercely that the English did not have time to load their muskets. An Englishman held captive by the Irish at the time heard that the Irish numbered 700 (Bodl., Carte MSS 2: 346v.). Creighton also heard that the English did not fire (Gilbert, ed., *Contemporary History*, 1, ii: 533). According to yet another account, not only was the wrong order given, but this was also misinterpreted, for it sounded in Irish as though it was a cry of "being lost" and some of those fighting for the British were Irish (H[ogan], ed., *History of the Warr*, 15).

37 Gilbert, ed., *Contemporary History*, 1, ii: 533. For similar feelings expressed in Monaghan, see TCD MSS 834: 183.

38 Lords justices to Leicester, 25 Nov. 1641, HMC, *Ormond MSS* n.s., 2: 23; TCD MSS 816: passim.

39 For those who made reference to Cavan men, see TCD MSS 816: 132, 141.

40 Ibid., 132.

41 TCD MSS 814: 114v.–15.

42 TCD MSS 816: 223–4. Fox may not have been Old English, but Gaelic Irish with the name "Sionnach" which had been Anglicized. I am grateful to Steven Ellis for pointing this out to me. However, the first name, "Arthur," suggests Old English origin.

43 TCD MSS 817: passim.

44 Ibid., 2–2v., 5.

45 Ibid., 8v.–9.

46 Hill, *MacDonnells of Antrim*, 258.

47 ——— to Ormond, 20 Nov. 1641, Bodl., Carte MSS 2: 74; lords justices to Leicester, 22 Nov. 1641, and 25 Nov. 1641, HMC, *Ormond MSS*, n.s., 2: 21, 22.

48 TCD MSS 821: 181v., 188, 191v., 194.
49 Lords justices to English council, 5 Nov. 1641, HMC, *Ormond MSS*, n.s., 2: 7.
50 TCD MSS 831: 2–31.
51 TCD MSS 817: passim from fol. 132.
52 O'Farrells to Dillon, 10 Nov. 1641, in Gilbert, ed., *Contemporary History*, 1, i: 367–8. See also Bodl., Nalson MSS Deposit C 164N: 5–6.
53 See above, 153.
54 O'Farrells to Dillon, 10 Nov. 1641, in Gilbert, ed., *Contemporary History*, 1, i: 368.
55 Gillespie, "O'Farrells and Longford," 14.
56 Lords justices to Leicester, 27 Nov. 1641, HMC, *Ormond MSS*, n.s., 2: 29.
57 Canny, "In Defence of the Constitution?" 35–40; Gillespie, "End of an Era," 195, 208, 212. For references to debt, see TCD MSS 812: 73; TCD MSS 814: 121; TCD MSS 809: 263. The depositions have been the cause of much debate. Some historians, starting with Temple, have used them to exaggerate the number of British killed and thus to justify a harsh English policy in Ireland. Others have dismissed them as sources without properly examining them. For a description of the depositions and their background, see Clarke, "The 1641 Depositions," 111–22. For a summary of the debate, see Perceval-Maxwell, "Ulster Rising of 1641," 144–8.
58 For example: Gilbert, ed., *Contemporary History*, 1, ii: 527; TCD MSS 839: 2, 3, 30, 51, 91v.; TCD MSS 836: 89, 107; TCD MSS 835: 13v., 95, 109, 191, 209, 234, 248, 249; TCD MSS 833: 4.
59 TCD MSS 835: 2, 13v., 91, 109, 248; TCD MSS 834: 56, 59.
60 TCD MSS 836: 172.
61 Ibid., 102; TCD MSS 832: 50.
62 TCD MSS 839: 7v., 132; TCD MSS 817: 39, 204; TCD MSS 836: 228; HMC, *Ormond MSS*, n.s., 2: 18.
63 TCD MSS 833: 295–6; TCD MSS 834: 184v.; TCD MSS 836: 2, 7, 32, 35, 35v., 66, 73, 87v., 177; TCD MSS 839: 14v., 43.
64 TCD MSS 836: 35; TCD MSS 839: 14v., 21, 43.
65 Dongan, "Codes and Conduct in the English Civil War," 73–6.
66 TCD MSS 834: 66, 81v., 83.
67 Ibid., 4; TCD MSS 836: 37v., 102v.; TCD MSS 839: 9, 40v., 41, 43v.; Casway, *Owen Roe O'Neill*, 64–5.
68 TCD MSS 834: 15, 56; TCD MSS 836: 95; TCD MSS 839: 91v.; Gillespie, "End of an Era," 211.
69 Gillespie, "End of an Era," 209; Stevenson, *Alasdair MacColla*, 74–9; H[ogan], ed., *History of the Warr*, 8–9; Chichester et al. to Ormond, 28 Dec. 1641, Bodl., Carte MSS 2: 203.

70 The following are but a sample of the references that could be cited: TCD MSS 816: 143; TCD MSS 817: 144v., 150v., 156, 157v.; TCD MSS 831: 3v.; TCD MSS 839: 45v.

71 Account of Irish affairs, 6 Jan. 1642, Irish Jesuit Archives, MSS A, transcripts 3: 248B.

72 Cited in Mooney, "Golden Age of the Irish Franciscans," 30.

73 TCD MSS 817: 37v.; TCD MSS 834: 54, 56, 184; TCD MSS 836: 109.

74 TCD MSS 834: 15, 184–5v.; TCD MSS 835: 251; TCD MSS 836: 173v.; TCD MSS 839: 1, 39, 91v.; Account of the Irish that Preserved the English at the Beginning of the Rebellion, Bodl., Carte MSS 63: 126–126v.

75 Gillespie, "End of an Era," 195, 208, 212; Canny, "In Defence of the Constitution?" 31–2.

76 TCD MSS 817: 4.

77 TCD MSS 835: 95, 201v.

78 TCD MSS 834: 17v.

79 TCD MSS 832: 91v.; TCD MSS 835: 210v.

80 Lords justices to Vane, 22 Nov. 1641, HMC, *Ormond MSS*, n.s., 2: 18.

81 TCD MSS 812: 89v.; TCD MSS 814: 60; TCD MSS 817: 39v.; TCD MSS 832: 53v., 79v., 87, 137; TCD MSS 833: 236; TCD MSS 834: 62, 79; TCD MSS 836: 35v. The women may not have had as much personal contact with the settlers as the men, and, if so, this would bear out Canny's point that Irish hostility to the settlers was related to the extent of personal knowledge of them.

82 TCD MSS 834: 62.

83 TCD MSS 832: 58v.

84 Lords justices to Leicester, 22 Nov. 1641, HMC, *Ormond MSS*, n.s., 2: 20; TCD MSS 831: 151, 153.

85 Evans, *Criminal Prosecution and Capital Punishment of Animals*; Cohen, "Law, Folklore and Animal Lore," 10, 30, 33. Trials of animals took place throughout Europe and in Brazil and Canada.

86 TCD MSS 809: 7; Canny, "In Defence of the Constitution?" 23, 39–40.

87 Temple to the king, 12 Dec. 1641, PRO, SP 63/260: 192v.; account of Irish affairs, 6 Jan. 1642, Irish Jesuit Archives, MSS A, transcripts 3: 248A; TCD MSS 832: 74v., 182; TCD MSS 816: 97v.

88 Gilbert, ed., *Contemporary History*, 1, i: 14.

89 TCD MSS 829: 304–304v.

90 Gilbert, ed., *Contemporary History*, 1, ii: 527. William Cadogan also reported a comment of Plunkett's, though his information came second hand. According to him, Plunkett had told an Old English family that no harm would come to them and that only the British and Protestants were to be pillaged and expelled from the kingdom.

91 TCD MSS 809: 2v.–3v.; TCD MSS 814: 61–61v.; TCD MSS 817: 144v.

92 TCD MSS 809: 3–3v.

93 —— to papal secretariat, 13/23 Nov. 1641, Vatican Library, Barberini MSS 8671: no. 154.

94 Lords justices and council to English council, 5 Nov. 1641, HMC, *Ormond MSS*, n.s., 2: 8.

95 TCD MSS 809: 3v.–4v. The Dublin government reported that the Irish intended to send an army of 30,000 to England as soon as Ireland was won (lords justices to Leicester, 3 Dec. 1641, HMC, *Ormond MSS*, n.s., 2: 34).

96 Gilbert, ed., *Irish Confederation*, 1: 289.

CHAPTER ELEVEN

1 Cole to lords justices, 11 October 1641, in Nalson, *Impartial Collection*, 2: 519–20.

2 Gilbert, ed., *Contemporary History*, 1, i: 354; Matthews, "Anglo-Irish Relations 1640–1642," 70.

3 Clarke, *Old English*, 163; HMC, *Ormond MSS*, n.s., 2: 4.

4 Lords justices to Leicester, 25 Oct. 1641, HMC, *Ormond MSS*, n.s., 2: 1.

5 Clarke, *Old English*, 163, 169; Ogle to Ormond, 19 Oct. 1641, Bodl., Carte MSS 63: 41; Temple to Ormond, 28 Oct. 1641, and the king to Ormond, 31 Oct. 1641, Bodl., Carte MSS 2: 5, 13.

6 Clarke, *Old English*, 163, 169; St Leger to Ormond, 8 and 13 Nov. 1641, Bodl., Carte MSS 2: 26, 37; St Leger to [Percival], 8 Nov. 1641, BL, Add. MSS 46925: 181.

7 Lords justices to Leicester, 25 Oct. 1641, lords justices to English council, 5 Nov. 1641, lords justices to Leicester, 13 Nov. 1641, and lords justices to Leicester, 26 Nov. 1641, HMC, *Ormond MSS*, n.s., 2: 5, 8–9, 14, 26. Parsons's information on Irish aims was derived from a set of demands "dropped under a stall in Drogheda" and obtained by Sir Faithful Fortescue.

8 Gilbert, ed., *Irish Confederation*, 1: 18–20, 32.

9 Lords justices to Vane, 27 Nov. 1641, HMC, *Ormond MSS*, n.s., 2: 29; Parsons to Cork, 20 June 1642, BL, Egerton MSS 80: 20–1.

10 Gilbert, ed., *Irish Confederation*, 1: 21; Carte, *Ormonde*, 1: 238–9; Clarke, *Old English*, 162, 175.

11 Clarke, *Old English*, 162–3; lords justices to Leicester, 25 Oct. 1641, and 14 Dec. 1641, HMC, *Ormond MSS*, n.s., 2: 4, 36; Tichborne to Ormond, 18 Nov. 1641, Bodl., Carte MSS 2: 64; TCD MSS 834: 28; McNeill and Otway-Ruthven, eds., *Dowdall Deeds*, 329–30.

12 Hugh Bourke to [Wadding], 22 Feb. 1642, HMC, *Franciscan MSS*, 119.

13 Clanricard to Ormond, 13 Nov. 1643, in Lowe, ed., *Letter-book of Clanricarde*, 16.

14 See above, 159. Lords justices to Leicester, 22 Nov. 1641, HMC, *Ormond MSS*, n.s., 2: 19.

15 Ibid., 18–19; Gilbert, ed., *Irish Confederation*, 1: 26–8; *Commons' journ. Ireland*, 1: 289; Clarke, *Old English*, 171–2. The Old English argued that the adjournment in August had contributed to the outbreak of the rising as it delayed the implementation of the Graces. This was disingenuous in that the king had not agreed to redress the main grievance of the Irish; he had agreed only to have it investigated. Thus the ending of the session in August could not have affected the Irish one way or the other, but the use of this argument by the Old English underlines their sensitivity to the August prorogation and to any further delay.

16 Gilbert, ed., *Irish Confederation*, 1: 28.

17 *Commons' journ. Ireland*, 1: 291.

18 Ibid., 29; Clarke, *Old English*, 173.

19 *Commons' journ. Ireland*, 1: 294.

20 Ibid., 295.

21 Clanricard to lords justices 30 Oct. 1641, in Bourke, *Memoirs and Letters of Clanricarde*, 5.

22 *Commons' journ. Ireland*, 1: 295.

23 Lords justices to Leicester, 3 Dec. 1641, HMC, *Ormond MSS*, n.s., 2: 34.

24 Carte, *Ormonde*, 1: 228–9; lords justices to Leicester, 26 Nov. 1641, HMC, *Ormond MSS*, n.s., 2: 25.

25 Lords justices to Leicester, 26 Nov. 1641, HMC, *Ormond MSS*, n.s., 2: 25; Coates, ed., *Journal of D'Ewes*, 328.

26 Clarke, *Old English*, 179–82; Gilbert, ed., *Irish Confederation*, 1: 34–7, 299–301.

27 Bourke, *Memoirs and Letters of Clanricarde*, 38.

28 Lords justices et al. to Leicester, 26 Nov. 1641, HMC, *Ormond MSS*, n.s., 2: 24–7.

29 Carte, *Ormonde*, 1: 227–8. Carte listed Richard Bolton, Lancelot Bulkeley (bishop of Dublin), Martin (bishop of Meath), Ormond, Henry Leslie (bishop of Down and Connor), Lord Robert Dillon, and Sir Gerard Lowther as the moderates, on the grounds that they were on the council though they did not sign the letter of 26 November. On the same grounds we should add Sir Piers Crosby and Viscount Dillon of Costello-Galen, who, although on his way to England by the twenty-sixth, was present during the session. Such a group would have constituted a majority of the council and it is unlikely that Parsons and his friends would have prevailed against such a large group. It is more likely that the moderates consisted of a smaller group and that some members avoided taking sides on the issue.

30 Edmund Butler et al. to Ormond, 18 Nov. 1641, Bodl., Carte MSS 2: 66.

31 Lords justices, 26 Nov. 1641, HMC, *Ormond MSS*, n.s., 2: 26.

32 Tichborne to Ormond, 16 Nov. 1641, Bodl., Carte MSS 2: 49; Ormond to the king, 1 Dec. 1641, PRO, SP 63/260: 178; *Cal. SP Ireland, 1633–47*, 352.

33 Ormond to the king, 12 Dec. 1641, PRO, SP 63/260: 190; *Cal. SP Ireland, 1633–47*, 353; St Leger to Ormond, 19 Dec. 1641, Bodl., Carte MSS 2: 184. Temple to ——, 10 Dec. 1641, in McNeill, ed., *Tanner Letters*, 135. We know of Ormond's letter to St Leger of 10 December only by the reply.

34 Ormond to the king, 12 Dec. 1641, PRO, SP 63/260: 190; *Cal. SP Ireland, 1633–47*, 353–4.

35 TCD MSS 831: 2–31, 153v. See above, 225.

36 Bourke, *Memoirs and Letters of Clanricarde*, 1–2.

37 Ibid., 1–2.

38 Ibid., 1, 4, 17–18.

39 Ibid., 30. See also TCD MSS 831: 67.

40 TCD MSS 831: 5v.–6.

41 Gillespie, "Mayo and the Rising of 1641," 39.

42 Bourke, *Memoirs and Letters of Clanricarde*, 13, 20.

43 TCD MSS 831: 145v., 150v., 162, 165v., 211. The spread of the rebellion in this county seems to have been uneven because one or two of the deponents indicated that the rebellion began only in December. This variation in the evidence from the same county may rest on the question of when disorder becomes rebellion. The answer is that it is impossible to draw such fine distinctions. In trying to trace the spread of the rebellion, I have adopted the view that "rebellion" had broken out when established authority could no longer keep the peace and robbery became frequent, even if it cannot be shown that the gentry were backing the incidents recorded. Thus, substantial reported robbery (not just one or two incidents) is assumed to reflect the spread of a process which, if it had not been formally declared a rebellion, was one, and one which quickly attracted men to lead it once it had started. Certainly, many of the deponents were in no doubt that the rebellion had begun once they began to be robbed.

44 Ibid., 145v.

45 Gillespie, "Mayo and the Rising of 1641," 40; Lynch, *Portrait of a Pious Bishop*, 109; TCD MSS 831: 152, 170–71v.

46 TCD MSS 831: 145–7; Gilbert, ed., *Contemporary History*, 1, ii: 611. Lord Maguire reported that Rory O'More told him that Viscount Mayo was one of the plotters. This information was almost certainly false (Gilbert, ed., *Contemporary History*, 1, ii: 503).

47 Except where indicated, the information on Sligo is derived from the typescript of chapter 7 of Mary O'Dowd's *Power, Politics and Land*, 105–

30. I am very grateful to her for letting me see this material before publication.

48 TCD MSS 831: 5, 34, 35, 143v., 145.

49 O'Dowd, *Power, Politics and Land*, 118; Bourke, *Memoirs and Letters of Clanricarde*, 36.

50 TCD MSS 831: 68, 70, 73.

51 Bourke, *Memoirs and Letters of Clanricarde*, 3–4, 6.

52 Ibid., 21–2, 26–7.

53 Ibid., 32–3.

54 Clanricard to Ormond, 9 Dec. 1641, Bodl., Carte MSS 2: 162.

55 Bourke, *Memoirs and Letters of Clanricarde*, 18–19, 20, 26–7.

56 Ibid., 12–15, 29, 32–3, 50.

57 TCD MSS 814: passim; A book of the memorable things done by the garrison of the command of Capt. William Parsons, 9 Nov. 1641, Birr Castle, Rosse MSS A/9.

58 Bourke, *Memoirs and Letters of Clanricarde*, 15.

59 Ibid., 14.

60 Lowe, ed., *Letter-book of Clanricarde*, 16.

61 Two out of thirty-one cases of robbery were reported as occurring in Carlow during October. There were two such instances in Tipperary out of fifty cases, and six out of fifty cases in Limerick, but these last seem to have been references to when the rebellion began in Ulster.

62 The percentages of incidents reported for Offaly, Kildare, and Kilkenny during the 1 November to 15 November period, for instance, were 13, 9, and 9 respectively. The percentages for the second half of the month were 41, 41, and 45 respectively. Those for December were 44, 46, and 45.

63 The rebellion seems to have started somewhat later in Waterford than in Tipperary and Limerick, but earlier than in Cork. As indicated, 28 per cent of the incidents were reported for December, by contrast to 58 per cent for Limerick, 54 per cent for Tipperary, and 6 per cent for Cork. Fourteen per cent of the incidents in Waterford were dated January 1642 and 54 per cent post-January. This heavy occurrence in 1642 places this county alongside Cork and Kerry, but the frequency of robberies reported for December warrants the inclusion of Waterford with Clare, Limerick, and Tipperary.

64 TCD MSS 821: 187–91.

65 TCD MSS 829: passim.

66 Underdown, *Revel, Riot, and Rebellion*, 109.

67 TCD MSS 812: 74.

68 HMC, *Ormond MSS*, n.s., 2: 16, 18; TCD MSS 812, passim. By 9 November word had reached County Offaly of the outbreak of the rebellion in Wicklow, and a fairly large number of Irish were operating

there under the command of Colonel Luke Byrne by 12 November (TCD MSS 814: 90; TCD MSS 811: 54; TCD MSS 815: 99).

69 TCD MSS 812: 116–16v., 122v.

70 TCD MSS 813: 298.

71 Ibid., 302.

72 HMC, *Ormond MSS*, n.s., 2: 33; TCD MSS 813: 10, 23, 306.

73 HMC, *Ormond MSS*, n.s., 2: 37; TCD MSS 813: 330v.

74 TCD MSS 812: 200, 209, 211–12.

75 Edmund Butler et al. to Ormond, 18 Nov. 1641, Bodl., Carte MSS 2: 66.

76 St Leger to Cork, 2 Dec. 1641, NLI MSS 12813: 591; TCD MSS 812: 213, 219–20, 271.

77 Bodl., Carte MSS 2: 78; TCD MSS 812: 200, 221. Edmund Butler, Mountgarret's son, was supposed to convoy English refugees to Waterford, but according to his own account, he developed ague while doing so and abandoned them, with the result that they were attacked and robbed (TCD MSS 812: 271, 328).

78 TCD MSS 812: 191v.; TCD MSS 821: 31.

79 Bodl., Carte MSS 2: 76. See also Canny, *The Upstart Earl*, 126.

80 TCD MSS 821: 30, 31, 221, 255, 257.

81 St Leger to [Percival], 8 Nov. 1641, BL, Add. MSS 46925: 181.

82 St Leger to Ormond, 4 Dec. 1641, Bodl., Carte MSS 63: 17.

83 TCD MSS 824, 828: passim. All of the Kerry depositions date from 1654.

84 St Leger to [Percival], 8 Nov. 1641, and Percival to Ormond, 25 Feb. 1642, Bodl., Carte MSS 2: 181, 374. But see Mountgarret to Edmund Butler, 17 Mar. 1642, Bodl., Carte MSS 2: 476, in which Mountgarret indicated that he was not aware that Barry had joined the rebellion.

85 Muskerry to Barrymore, 17 Mar. 1642, BL, Add. MSS 25277: 58–58v. I thank Raymond Gillespie for having brought this letter to my attention.

86 For example: TCD MSS 814: 59v., 109v.; TCD MSS 815: 7v., 47, 191.

87 Among the "neutrals" were Barnaby Dun (TCD MSS 810: 14v.), Barnewall of Turvie, fled to Wales (TCD MSS 810: 206), Sir John Dungan, the MP (TCD MSS 810: 206), Sir Thomas Butler, the rival of Walter Bagenal, and others. Ten men are listed as "neutrals" in Offaly (TCD MSS 814: 59). For a Catholic denial of culpability, see Clarke, ed., "A Discourse between two Councillors of State," 172.

88 It was reported in Kilkenny that the plot to take Dublin Castle was known before the rebellion (TCD MSS 812: 205).

89 R. Nugent to Vitelleschi, 24 Mar. 1642, Irish Jesuit Archives, MSS A, 3: no. 76. I have used the English translation attached to the original Latin document.

90 James Butler to Edmund Butler, 1 Mar. 1642, Bodl., Carte MSS 2: 388.

91 Nugent to Vitelleschi, 8 May 1642, Irish Jesuit Archives, MSS A: no. 78.
92 Cork to Warwick, 25 Feb. 1642, BL, Egerton MSS 80: 31, 33. See also HMC, *Ormond MSS*, n.s., 2: 34.
93 Carte, *Ormonde*, 1: 261; HMC, *Ormond MSS*, n.s., 2: 67.

CHAPTER TWELVE

1 Apart from Clarendon, I am particularly dependent on Stevenson, *Scottish Covenanters* and *Scottish Revolution*; Fletcher, *Outbreak of the English Civil War*; Gardiner, *History*, vol. 10; Bottigheimer, *English Money and Irish Land*; Hazlett, "Military Forces Operating in Ireland"; Matthews, "Anglo-Irish Relations 1640–1642"; McCormack, "Irish Adventurers and the English Civil War," 21–58; Lindley, "Impact of the 1641 Rebellion upon England and Wales," 143–76; Russell, "British Background to the Irish Rebellion," 166–82 and *British Monarchies*.
2 Bottigheimer, *English Money and Irish Land*, 35.
3 Nicholas to Row, 19 Feb. 1642, *Cal. SP Domestic, 1641–43*, 288.
4 Balfour, *Historical Works*, 3: 119–20; Stevenson, *Scottish Covenanters*, 43.
5 King's note on Nicholas to the king, 25 Oct. 1641, in Bray, ed., *Correspondence of Evelyn*, 4: 112.
6 Balfour, *Historical Works*, 3: 128–9.
7 Ibid., 145; Stevenson, *Scottish Covenanters*, 51–2; Macray, ed., *Clarendon's History*, 1: 399.
8 Stevenson, *Scottish Covenanters*, 51–2; Dillingham to Montagu, 27 Jan. 1642, HMC, *Montagu MSS*, 144–5.
9 *Cal. SP Domestic, 1641–43*, 181; Coates, ed., *Journal of D'Ewes*, 363, 363n; *Commons' journ. England*, 2: 361.
10 *Lords' journ. England*, 4: 459.
11 *The Kings Maiesties Speech ... 14. day of Decemb. 1641*, Huntington Library pamphlet 58381.
12 Coates, ed., *Journal of D'Ewes*, 286, 288; Gardiner, *History*, 10: 99; Bottigheimer, *English Money and Irish Land*, 36–7.
13 Fletcher, *Outbreak of the English Civil War*, 167.
14 Bodl., Clarendon MSS 20: 133; BL, Sloan MSS 1008: 37.
15 Bottigheimer, *English Money and Irish Land*, 37; Smith to Penington, 10 Dec. 1641, *Cal. SP Domestic, 1641–43*, 194.
16 Lords justices to Leicester, 14 Dec. 1641, HMC, *Ormond MSS*, n.s., 2: 43.
17 Fletcher, *Outbreak of the English Civil War*, 344; *Lords' journ. England*, 4: 547; *Commons' journ. England*, 2: 400.
18 Loudon to Henderson, 10 Feb. 1642, NLS, Wodrow MSS Folio 66: 199; Leicester to Ormond, 15 Feb. 1642, Bodl., Carte MSS 2: 357.
19 Russell, *British Monarchies*, 488; Bottigheimer, *English Money and Irish Land*, 40; *Lords' journ. England*, 4: 709; *Cal. SP Domestic, 1641–43*, 306.

20 Stevenson, *Scottish Covenanters*, 43–4.

21 Gardiner, *History*, 10: 42; Fletcher, *Outbreak of the English Civil War*, 135.

22 Stevenson, *Scottish Covenanters*, 49; Coates, ed., *Journal of D'Ewes*, 96–7; *Cal. SP Venice, 1640–42*, 241; Nicholas to the king, 10 Nov. 1641, in Bray, ed., *Correspondence of Evelyn*, 4: 132.

23 Gardiner, *History*, 10: 55.

24 *Statutes Ireland*, 1: 274.

25 [J. Elphinstone], *Lord Balmerino's Speech In the ... Parliament in Scotland, ... Novemb. 4 1641*, 3, Huntington Library pamphlet 283901; Hazlett, "Military Forces Operating in Ireland," 1: 211.

26 *Commons' journ. England*, 2: 305–6; Coates, ed., *Journal of D'Ewes*, 84, 92–4; *Lords' journ. England*, 4: 423. The English Commons only heard of the offer of 10,000 troops on 11 November.

27 SRO, PA 13/2: 104v.; Stevenson, *Scottish Covenanters*, 64.

28 Coates, ed., *Journal of D'Ewes*, 91.

29 Ibid., 118–19, 125, 130; *Commons' journ. England*, 4: 313–14.

30 Coates, ed., *Journal of D'Ewes*, 130.

31 Ibid., 138; Holland Diary, ibid., 138n.

32 Hazlett, "Military Forces Operating in Ireland," 1: 213.

33 Nicholas to Penington, 18 Nov. 1641, *Cal. SP Domestic, 1641–43*, 167.

34 Stevenson, *Scottish Covenanters*, 55–6; *Lords' journ. England*, 4: 467, 482, 484–6; *Commons' journ. England*, 2: 354; *Cal. SP Domestic, 1641–43*, 211; Coates, ed., *Journal of D'Ewes*, 324–5.

35 Bere to Penington, 23 Dec. 1641, *Cal. SP Domestic, 1641–43*, 211.

36 *Cal. SP Venice, 1640–42*, 265, 267.

37 Stevenson, *Scottish Covenanters*, 56; *Lords' journ. England*, 4: 491.

38 Stevenson, *Scottish Covenanters*, 56–7; *Lords' journ. England*, 4: 492.

39 Commissioners to Scottish council, 4 Jan. 1642, SRO, PA 13/3: 1v.; *Commons' journ. England*, 2: 375–6; Loudon to Johnston, 19 Feb. 1642, NLS, Wodrow MSS Folio 66: 204. *Cal. SP Venice, 1640–42*, 267.

40 Commissioners to Scottish council, 4 Jan. 1642, SRO, PA 13/3: 1v.

41 Viscount Montgomery to Eglinton, 31 Dec. 1642, HMC, *Eglinton MSS*, 49–51; Scottish council to commissioners, 27 Jan. 1642, SRO, PA 13/3: 7.

42 Scottish council to commissioners, 15 Feb. 1642, SRO, PA 13/3: 12.

43 Stevenson, *Scottish Covenanters*, 61; SRO, PA 13/3: 38v.

44 *Lords' journ. England*, 4: 506.

45 Commissioners to Scottish council, 26 Jan. 1642, SRO, PA 13/3: 4v.–5.

46 Ibid., 5.

47 Stevenson, *Scottish Covenanters*, 58, 60, 72, 103; Scottish council to commissioners, 2 Apr. 1642, SRO, PA 13/2: 49.

48 Stevenson, *Scottish Covenanters*, 62; Stevenson, *Alasdair MacColla*, 81–2; *Lords' journ. England*, 4: 604.

49 Commissioners to Scottish council, SRO, PA 13/2: 38; Stevenson, *Scottish Covenanters*, 60–5, 122, 139.

50 Baillie to Sprang, [Jan.?] 1642, in Laing, ed., *Letters of Baillie*, 1: 396.

51 Russell, "British Background to the Irish Rebellion," 166; Nicholas to Webb, 12 Oct. 1641, Surrey Record Office, Bray MSS 52/2/19; Bristol to Row, 2 Oct. 1641, *Cal. SP Domestic, 1641–43*, 130. But for a more pessimistic outlook, see Wiseman to Penington, 7 Oct. 1641, *Cal. SP Domestic, 1641–43*, 134. Wiseman believed that, because of the "general distempers of the whole kingdom," there was little hope for "prince, church, or people."

52 Russell, "British Background to the Irish Rebellion," 166–7.

53 [Dillingham] to Montagu, 6 Nov. 1641, HMC, *Montagu MSS*, 132–3; Coates, ed., *Journal of D'Ewes*, 58–63.

54 Gilbert, ed., *Contemporary History*, 1, i: 353–4, 357–9; Dillingham to Montagu, 6 Nov. 1641, HMC, *Montagu MSS*, 134.

55 Smith to Penington, 4 Nov. 1641, *Cal. SP Domestic, 1641–43*, 157.

56 Wiseman to Penington, 4 Nov. 1641, ibid., 157–8.

57 HMC, *Montagu MSS*, 133; *Cal. SP Domestic, 1641–43*, 156–8.

58 Macray, ed., *Clarendon's History*, 1: 409n.; Vane to Nicholas, 3 Nov. 1641, *Cal. SP Domestic, 1641–43*, 154.

59 Cárdenas to king, 11/21 Nov. 1641, *Cal. SP Domestic, 1641–43*, 162.

60 Lindley, "Impact of the 1641 Rebellion upon England and Wales," 143–5.

61 Fortescue, *Catalogue of the Pamphlets ... Collected by George Thomason, 1640–1661*, vol. 1; Matthews, "Anglo-Irish Relations 1640–1642," 63–5. For a discussion of the dating of the Thomason Tracts, see Greenberg, "Dating Civil War Pamphlets," 387–401; Mendle, "Thomason Collection: Reply to Greenberg," 85–93; Greenberg, "Rebuttal to Mendle," 95–8. Fortescue dated pamphlets according to when the event described in a pamphlet occurred, which accounts for the items dated October, but it remains true that the dates printed on the pamphlets are often inconsistent with their contents.

62 *The true Demands of the Rebells in Ireland*, BL, Thomason Tracts, E. 135(4).

63 *The Petition of Sir* Philomy Oneale, BL, Thomason Tracts, E. 137(14).

64 Fortescue, ed., *Catalogue of the Pamphlets ... Collected by George Thomason 1640–1661*, 1: 82–3.

65 Lindley, "Impact of the 1641 Rebellion upon England and Wales," 146.

66 Percival to Ormond, 25 Jan. 1642, and 5 Feb. 1642, Bodl., Carte MSS 2: 317, 336; Ormond to Percival, 3 Mar. 1642, HMC, *Egmont MSS*, 1, i:

165–6. It may be noted that Ormond was accused of having had deal-
ings with Nicholas, Lord Nettirvill, as well as Dillon. In his denial of
the various allegations, Ormond referred to "pamphlets spread of me."
One of those who spread the stories about Ormond was the son of a
Scottish planter, Sir John Wishart. He subsequently withdrew his allegations.

67 Aldis, *List of Books Printed in Scotland before 1700*, no. 1046.

68 Information reaching Hugh Bourke, commissary of the Irish Friars
Minors in Germany and Belgium, at Antwerp was that Antrim
remained neutral but "will not fail when the proper time comes." Information reaching the Irish on the continent was often wrong and
tended to exaggerate the support for their cause. Even if Bourke's
information on Antrim was correct, he would not have signed a
defence of Irish actions. (Delan to Bourke, 25 Jan. 1642, HMC, *Franciscan MSS*, 116).

69 Coates, ed., *Journal of D'Ewes*, 164.

70 *Commons' journ. Ireland*, 2: 396.

71 HMC, *Appendix to the 4th Report*, 113.

72 Cust, "News and Politics in Early Seventeenth Century England," 60–
90.

73 Wiseman to Penington, 11 Nov. 1641, *Cal. SP Domestic, 1641–43*, 163.

74 *Bloody Newes from Norwich*, BL, Thomason Tracts, E. 179(10).

75 Lindley, "Impact of the 1641 Rebellion upon England and Wales," 147–
55; Society of Antiquaries, London, Broadsides, Chas. I, 1634–48, no.
392, 1637–48, no. 377, and 1637–42, no. 317.

76 *Worse and Worse Newes from Ireland*, BL, Thomason Tracts, E. 180(15).
The date on which Partington is supposed to have written the letter
was 27 November. There may, indeed, have been such a letter. Par-
tington was an unusual name in Ireland, but we find that one of the
Dublin deponents was called Henry Partington (TCD MSS 810: 20v.).
Thomas Partington may have been a relative.

77 Newsletter, 16 Dec. 1641, HMC, *Montagu MSS*, 135–6.

78 Coates, ed., *Journal of D'Ewes*, 182.

79 Ibid., 347. For other such letters, see 62, 97, 118, 137, 179, 219, 227,
251, 253, 283.

80 MacCormack, "Irish Adventurers and the English Civil War," 21–2.

81 Coates, ed., *Journal of D'Ewes*, 121.

82 *Lords' journ. England*, 4: 484–5.

83 Ibid., 485.

84 Northumberland to [Row], 12 Nov. 1641, *Cal. SP Domestic, 1641–43*,
165.

85 Bottigheimer, *English Money and Irish Land*, 32.

86 Fletcher, *Outbreak of the English Civil War*, 166.

87 Coates, ed., *Journal of D'Ewes*, 62–4.

88 Ibid., 67–8.

89 Ibid., 71.

90 Ibid., 76; *Commons' journ. England*, 2: 304.

91 Coates, ed., *Journal of D'Ewes*, 78.

92 Ibid., 78–9.

93 *Cal. SP Venice, 1640–42*, 250.

94 HMC, *Montagu MSS*, 134.

95 Leicester to Ormond, 15 Feb. 1642, Bodl., Carte MSS 2: 357; *Commons' journ. England*, 2: 430; *Statutes of the Realm*, 5: 138–9. Under the act, impressment beyond a man's county was permitted only between 1 December 1641 and 1 November 1642.

96 *Commons' journ. England*, 2: 305; *Lords' journ. England*, 4: 424; Coates, ed., *Journal of D'Ewes*, 86.

97 *Lords' journ. England*, 4: 429, 444; *Commons' journ. England*, 2: 308.

98 Coates, ed., *Journal of D'Ewes*, 110–11.

99 Ibid., 94.

100 Ibid., 104.

101 HMC, *Ormond MSS*, n.s., 2: 34, 56.

102 Coates, ed., *Journal of D'Ewes*, 121, 128.

103 Ibid., 133.

104 Ibid., 164.

105 Ibid., 256, 284–5. Some of the £400,000 was to be spent on the payment of debts.

106 Ibid., 121, 284.

107 Ibid., 179, 251.

108 Ibid., 285, 351; *Cal. SP Venice, 1640–42*, 265.

109 *Lords' journ. England*, 4: 537–8; Coates et al., eds., *Private Journals of the Long Parliament*, 168.

110 HMC, *Ormond MSS*, n.s., 2: 43.

111 *Lords' journ. England*, 4: 422; Coates, ed., *Journal of D'Ewes*, 82n.

112 Gardiner, ed., *Constitutional Documents*, 205; Bottigheimer, *English Money and Irish Land*, 39.

113 *Commons' journ. England*, 2: 330.

114 —— to ——, [29] Dec. 1641, NLS, Wodrow MSS Folio 25: no. 9. The catalogue lists this letter as being from A. Borthwick to Robert Douglas. Parts of the letter are very difficult to read and I acknowledge with thanks the assistance of Elspeth Yeo in deciphering it.

115 *Statutes of the Realm*, 5: 168; *Commons' journ. England*, 2: 425.

116 Bottigheimer, *English Money and Irish Land*, 40; Coates et al., eds., *Private Journals of the Long Parliament*, 369, 387.

117 Coates et al., eds., *Private Journals of the Long Parliament*, 266, 268, 274, 300.

118 *Lords' journ. England*, 4: 569.
119 Coates et al., eds., *Private Journals of the Long Parliament*, 370–1. The other MPs chosen as commissioners were: Sir Walter Earle, Sir Robert Harley, Sir Robert Cooke, Robert Wallop, Sir Richard Cave, and Sir Robert Parkhurst. The lords included Northumberland, Pembroke, Holland, Saye, and Mandeville (Kimbolton), all of whom opposed the king.
120 *Cal. SP Ireland, 1633–47*, 366. This paragraph is to a considerable extent based on Matthews, "Anglo-Irish Relations 1640–1642," 87–90.
121 BL, Harleian MSS 163: 66v., 68, 71v., 80v.
122 Baxter, *Reliquiae Baxterianae*, 37.

CONCLUSION

1 Clarke, "Ireland and the General Crisis," 86, cited in Russell, *Causes of the English Civil War*, 26.
2 TCD MSS 809: 6–6v.
3 Ibid., 6.
4 Beckett, "The Confederation of Kilkenny Reviewed," 33.
5 Ibid., 32.
6 Barnard, "Uses of 23 October 1641," 889–920; Barnard, "Crises of Identity among Irish Protestants," 39–83.

Bibliography

MANUSCRIPT MATERIAL

England

Bodleian Library, Oxford (Bodl.)
Additional MSS C: 286 (Wandesford Papers)
Carte MSS: 1; 2; 10; 11; 63; 64; 67; 80; 118
Clarendon MSS: 15; 17; 18; 19; 20
English History MSS C 37 (Ormond Papers)
Nalson MSS Deposit C

British Library, London (BL)
Additional MSS: 6521 (Proceedings, English House of Commons)
19398 (Turner MSS)
24023 (Miscellaneous Papers)
25277 (Montagu MSS)
31954 (Nicholas Papers)
34253 (Montagu MSS)
35838 (Hardwicke Papers)
37343 (Whitelocke's Annals)
41844A (Middleton Papers)
46189 (Jessop Papers)
46924–6 (Egmont or Perceval Papers)
Alnwick MSS: Microfilm 285, 286 (Northumberland Papers)
Egerton MSS: 80 (Miscellaneous Papers)
1048 (Parliamentary Documents)
2533 (Nicholas Papers)
2541 (Nicholas Papers)
3383 (Leeds Papers)

Harleian MSS: 162–4 (D'Ewes's Journal)
                477 (More's Journal)
                2138 (Historical Miscellanies concerning Ireland)
                6424 (Diary of a bishop)
Sloan MSS: 1008 (Edmund Borlase Papers)
                3838 (Condition of Ireland from 1640)
Stowe MSS: 187 (Negotiations of the Scots commissioners)

Chatsworth House, Derbyshire
Lismore MSS: 20; 21; 22

Christ Church College, Oxford
Evelyn MSS, Nicholas box

Duchy of Cornwall Office, London
Bound MSS T/M/3 (Political Tracts and Treatises: Subsidies and the Irish
   Grievances)

Huntingdon Record Office
Manchester MSS: dd. M7/23; dd. M28/2; dd. M70/30

Kent Archives Office, Maidstone
De L'Isle MSS: U 145/C85; U 1475/C85; U 1475/Z1; U 1500/C2

Public Record Office, London
E 405/285 (Exchequer)
SO 1/3 (Signet Office)
   3/12 (Signet Office)
SP 14/214 (State Papers, domestic)
   63/258, 259, 260, 273, 274, 276, 307 (State Papers, Ireland)
   94/42 (State Papers, Spain)
31/1/1 (Transcripts of the Carte MSS)

Society of Antiquaries, London
Proclamations
Broadsides

Sheffield City Library
Wentworth Woodhouse MSS: 3; 7; 10b, 11a, 19, 24–5 (Strafford's Papers)

Surrey Record Office, Guildford
Bray MSS: 85/5/2; 52/2/19

Ireland

Armagh Public Library, Armagh
Armagh Public Library MSS: G.1.11 (Lodge Papers)

Birr Castle, Co. Offaly
Rosse MSS: A/1; A/4; A/9

Genealogical Office, Dublin
Funeral entries: 69

Irish Jesuit Archives, Dublin
MSS A, and Transcripts and Translations

National Library of Ireland (NLI)
NLI MSS: 345 (A Treatise or Account of the War and Rebellion in Ireland
          ascribed to Nicholas Plunkett)
          2307 (Miscellaneous Papers)
          2559 (Irish army lists)
          12813 (Calendar of Lismore Papers)
          13237 (Lismore Papers)
          13238 (Lismore Papers)

Public Library, Dublin
Gilbert MSS: 169 (Sir John Ware's diary)

Public Record Office of Ireland, Dublin (PROI)
Betham's Genealogical Abstracts, BET. 1
Lodge Manuscripts, records of the rolls, 1A. S3. S4

Public Record Office of Northern Ireland, Belfast (PRONI)
D 282/2 (Antrim Papers)
D 3632/1 (Drapers' Papers)
T 415 (Transcripts of Bramhall Papers)

Trinity College, Dublin
Counties listed refer to "The Depositions" for those counties.
TCD MSS: 809 (Dublin)
          810 (Dublin)
          811 (Wicklow)
          812 (Carlow and Kilkenny)
          813 (Kildare and Offaly or King's)

814 (Kildare and Offaly or King's)
815 (Laois or Queen's)
816 (Meath)
817 (Westmeath and Longford)
821 (Waterford and Tipperary)
823 (Cork)
824 (Cork)
828 (Cork and Kerry)
829 (Clare and Limerick)
830 (Roscommon and Galway)
831 (Leitrim, Sligo, and Mayo)
832 (Cavan)
833 (Cavan)
834 (Louth and Monaghan)
835 (Fermanagh)
836 (Armagh)
838 (Antrim)
839 (Tyrone, Londonderry, and Donegal)
840–1 (Supplementary)
1071 (Transcript of O'Mellan's Journal)

Italy

Vatican Library, Rome
Barberini MSS (microfilm): 8650, pt 1; 8650, pt 2; 8671

Scotland

Scottish Record Office, Edinburgh
PA 13/2 (Proceedings of the Scots commissioners in England)
PA 13/3 (Register of letters relating to the Scots commissioners in England)
GD 406/1 (Hamilton MSS)

National Library of Scotland, Edinburgh
Advocates' MSS: 29.2.9 (Miscellaneous Papers)
    33.1.1 (Johnstone's calendar of correspondence 1639–41)
    33.4.6 (Minutes of the conferences between the English and Scots commissioners)
    34.2.9 (Historical Miscellanies concerning the troubles, 1638–51)
Wodrow MSS: Quarto 25 (Scottish Reports from London, 1641)
    Folio 25 (Church and State Papers, 1631–51)
    Folio 66 (Miscellaneous Letters, 1606–42)

United States

American Council of Learned Societies (ACLS)
British Project, Cambridge 752 Microfilm (Northumberland and Temple Correspondence)

Huntington Library, San Marino, California
Ellesmere MSS: 7811; 7814; 7819; 7840–1
Hastings MSS: 14065

PRINTED PRIMARY AND CONTEMPORARY MATERIAL

Acts of the Parliament of Scotland. Edited by T. Thomson and C. Innes. 12 vols. 1814–75.

Acts of the Privy Council of England. Edited by J.R. Dasent. 32 vols. London, 1890–1907.

Adair, P. *A True Narrative of the Rise and Progress of the Presbyterian Church in Ireland (1623–70).* Edited by W.D. Killen. Belfast: C. Aitchison 1866.

Anonymous, ed. "A Brief Relation of the Miraculous Victory there [Lisburn] that day [28 November 1641]." *Ulster Journal of Archaeology,* 1st series, 1 (1853): 242–5.

Baxter, R. *Reliquiae Baxterianae.* London, 1696. [Written 1664.]

Balfour, Sir J. *The Historical Works of Sir James Balfour.* Edited by J. Haig. 3 vols. Edinburgh: A. Constable 1824.

Berwick, E., ed. *Rawdon Papers.* London, 1819.

Bloody Newes from Norwich: Or, A True Relation of a bloody attempt of the Papists in Norwich, *to consume the whole City by fire … Likewise here is added the last bloody Newes from* Ireland. London, 1641. British Library, Thomason Tracts E. 179(10).

Borlase, E. *The History of the Execrable Rebellion 1641–1660.* London, 1680.

Bourke, U. *The Memoirs and Letters of Ulick, Marquiss of Clanricarde.* London, 1757.

[Bowles, E.]. *The Mysterie of Iniquitie, Yet Working* In the Kingdomes of *England, Scotland, and Ireland,* for the destruction of Religion truly Protestant. Edinburgh, 24 Nov. 1643/London, 11 Dec. 1643. British Library, Thomason Tracts E. 76(25).

Bray, W., ed. *Diary and Correspondence of John Evelyn.* 4 vols. London: Bickers & Son 1879.

Bruce, J., ed. *Verney Papers: Notes of Proceedings in the Long Parliament temp. Charles I … from Memoranda … by Sir Ralph Verney.* Camden Society, 1st series, vol. 31. London: The Society 1845.

Calendar of Clarendon State Papers. Edited by O. Ogle et al. 3 vols. Oxford, 1869–76.

Calendar of State Papers, Domestic Series, 1639–40, 1640, 1640–1, 1641–3. Edited by W. Douglas Hamilton. London, 1877, 1880, 1882, 1887.

Calendar of State Papers Relating to Ireland, 1509–1670. Edited by C.W. Russell et al. 24 vols. London, 1860–1912.

Calendar of State Papers and Manuscripts Relating to English Affairs, Preserved in the Archives of Venice and North Italy 1640–42. Edited by A. Hinds. London, 1924.

Clarke, A., ed. "A Discourse between two Councillors of State, the One of England and the Other of Ireland (1642)." *Analecta Hibernica* 26 (1970): 161–75.

Coates, W.H., ed. *The Journal of Sir Simonds D'Ewes from the first Recess of the Long Parliament to the Withdrawal of King Charles from London*. New Haven: Yale University Press 1942.

Coates, W.H., et al., eds. *The Private Journals of the Long Parliament 3 January to 5 March 1642*. New Haven: Yale University Press 1982.

Cope, E.S., and W.H. Coates, eds. *Proceedings of the Short Parliament of 1640*. Camden Society, 4th series, vol. 19. London: The Society 1977.

Cuvelier, J., et al., eds. *Correspondance de la cour d'Espagne sur les affaires des Pays-Bas au XVIIe siècle*. 6 vols. Brussels: Commission Royale d'Histoire 1937.

Darcy, P. *An Argument Delivered ... by the Express Order of the House of Commons in the Parliament of Ireland, 9 Junii, 1641*. Waterford, 1643.

[Elphinstone, J., Lord Balmerino]. *The Lord Balmerino's Speech In the High Court of Parliament in Scotland, Spoken Novemb. 4 1641 Concerning the levying of an army against the papists in Ireland. Describing their Conspiracies, which have a long time insulted and continued against these two Kingdomes of England and Scotland*. London, 1641. Huntington Library Pamphlet 283901.

Firth, C.H. "Papers Relating to Thomas Wentworth, First Earl of Strafford. From the MSS of Dr William Knowler." In *Camden Society Miscellany*. Camden Society, new series, vol. 53. Westminster: The Society 1895, vol. 9: 1–31.

Gardiner, S.R., ed. *The Constitutional Documents of the Puritan Revolution 1625–1660*. Oxford: Clarendon Press 1906.

Gilbert, J.T., ed. *A Contemporary History of Affairs in Ireland from 1641 to 1652*. 3 vols. Dublin: Irish Archaeological and Celtic Society 1879–80.

– ed. *History of the Irish Confederation and the War in Ireland, 1641–1643*. 7 vols. Dublin: M.H. Gill & Son, 1882–91.

– ed. *Facsimiles of National Manuscripts of Ireland*. 2 vols. London: Longmans 1884.

Grosart, A.B., ed. *Lismore Papers*. 1st and 2nd series. 10 vols. London: privately printed, 1886–88.

Hainsworth, D.R., ed. *Commercial Papers of Sir Christopher Lowther 1611–1644*. Gateshead: Surtees Society, 1977, vol. 189.

Hervey, M.F.S. *The Life, Correspondence and Collections of Thomas Howard, Earl of Arundel*. Cambridge: Cambridge University Press 1921.

Hickson, M., ed. *Ireland in the Seventeenth Century; or, the Irish Massacres of 1641–2, their Causes and Results*. 2 vols. London: Longmans Green 1884.

Hill, G., ed. *The Montgomery Manuscripts (1603–1706)*. Belfast: James Cleeland & Thomas Dargan 1849.

Historical Manuscripts Commission (HMC). London: His/Her Majesty's Stationery Office.

Appendix to the 2nd Report, 1871

Appendix to the 4th Report, 1874

Cowper MSS, vol. 2, 1888

De L'Isle and Dudley MSS, vol. 6, 1966

Eglinton MSS, 1885

Egmont MSS, vol. 1, 1905

Franciscan MSS, 1906

Hastings MSS, vols. 2 and 4, 1930 and 1947

Montagu MSS, 1900

Ormond MSS, vol. 2, new series, 1903

Various Collections, vol. 8, 1913

H[ogan], E., ed. *The History of the Warr of Ireland from 1641 to 1653. By a British Officer, of the Regiment of Sir John Clotworthy*. Dublin: McGlashan & Gill 1873.

Jansson, M., ed. *Two Diaries of the Long Parliament*. New York: St Martin's Press 1984.

Jennings, B., ed. *Louvain Papers 1606–1827*. Dublin: Irish Manuscripts Commission 1968.

– ed. *Wild Geese in Spanish Flanders 1582–1700*. Dublin: Irish Manuscripts Commission 1964.

Journals of the House of Commons [of England], vol. 2. London, 1803.

Journals of the House of Commons of the Kingdom of Ireland, vol. 1. Dublin, 1796.

Journals of the House of Lords [of England], vol. 4. London, n.d.

Journals of the House of Lords [of Ireland], vol. 1. Dublin, 1779.

The Kings Maiesties Speech In the House of Lords in Parliament on … the 14. day of Decemb. 1641. for the raising of Forces to reduce the Irish Rebels … Also a letter sent by the Lord Chief Justices of Ireland. London, 1641. Huntington Library Pamphlet 58381.

Knowler, W., ed. *The Earl of Strafforde's Letters and Dispatches*. 2 vols. Dublin, 1739.

Laing, D., ed. *The Letters and Journals of Robert Baillie 1637–1662.* 3 vols. Edinburgh: Bannatyne Club 1841.

Livingstone, J. *A Brief Historical Relation of the Life of Mr John Livingston.* Edited by T. Houston. Edinburgh: J. Johnstone 1848.

Lodge, J., ed. *Desiderata Curiosa Hibernica or a Select Collection of State Papers.* 2 vols. Dublin, 1772.

Lowe, W.J., ed. *Letter-book of the Earl of Clanricarde.* Dublin: Irish Manuscripts Commission 1983.

McNeill, C., ed. *The Tanner Letters.* Dublin: Irish Manuscripts Commission 1943.

– and Otway-Ruthven, A.J., eds. *Dowdall Deeds.* Dublin: Irish Manuscripts Commission 1960.

Macray, W.D., ed. *[Clarendon's] The History of the Rebellion and Civil Wars in England.* 6 vols. Oxford: Clarendon Press 1888.

Mervin, Sir A. *Captaine Audley Mervin's Speech, Delivered in the Upper House to the Lords in Parliament,* May 24 1641. London, 1641.

– *Sixteen Queres Propounded by the Parliament of Ireland to the Judges of the said Kingdome.* [London], 1641.

– *Speech Made by Captaine* Audley Mervin *to the Upper House of Parliament in* Ireland, March 4. 1640[–1]. [London], 1641. British Library, Thomason Tracts E. 196(37).

Nalson, J. *An Impartial Collection of the Great Affairs of State, from the Beginning of the Scotch Rebellion in the Year 1639 to the Murther of Charles I.* 2 vols. London, 1682.

Notestein, W., ed. *The Journal of Sir Simonds D'Ewes from the Beginning of the Long Parliament to the Opening of the Trial of the Earl of Strafford.* New Haven: Yale University Press 1923.

Paul, G.M., ed. *Diary of Sir Archibald Johnston of Wariston 1632–1639.* Scottish History Society, 1st series, vol. 61. Edinburgh: The Society 1911.

The Petition of Sir Philomy Oneale *Knight, Generall of the Rebels, in* Ireland, *and the Lords, Nobility and Commanders of the Army of the Catholiques in that Kingdome Presented to … the Lords and Commons in Ireland.* London, 1642. British Library, Thomason Tracts E. 137(14).

Privy Council Registers Preserved in the Public Record Office, Reproduced in Facsimile. 12 vols. London: HMSO, 1967–8.

Rushworth, J. *Historical Collections of Private Passages of State, Weighty Matters of Law, Remarkable Proceedings in Five Parliaments.* 8 vols. London, 1680–1701.

– *The Tryal of Thomas, Earl of Strafford.* London, 1680.

Scott, W., and J. Bliss, eds. *The Works of the Most Reverend Father in God William Laud.* 7 vols. Oxford: "Library of Anglo-Catholic Theology" 1847–60.

Smith, W.J., ed. *Herbert Correspondence: the Sixteenth and Seventeenth Century*

Letters of the Herberts of Chirbury, Powis Castle and Delguog, formerly at Powis Castle in Montgomeryshire. Dublin: Irish Manuscripts Commission and the University of Wales 1963.

The Statutes at Large Passed in the Parliament held in Ireland (1310–1800). 20 vols. Dublin, 1786–1801.

Statutes of the Realm [of England to 1713]. Edited by T.E. Tomlins et al. 11 vols. London, 1810–28.

Temple, Sir J. *The Irish Rebellion: or, an History of the Beginnings and first Progresse of the Generall Rebellion Raised within the Kingdom of Ireland, upon the three and twentieth day of October, in the Year, 1641*. 1646.

Touchet, James, earl of Castlehaven, *Memoirs of James, Lord Audley, Earl of Castlehaven. His Engagement and Carriage in the Wars of Ireland from the year 1642 to the year 1651*. Dublin: G. Mullens 1815.

The true Demands of the Rebells in Ireland. Declaring The Causes of their taking up Armes. Sent into England *by Sir* Phelom O-Neale, *their Generall: To the Honorable and High Court* of Parliament. [London], 1642. British Library, Thomason Tracts E. 135(4).

Vesey, J. *The Works of the Most Reverend Father in God, John Bramhall D.D. Late Lord Archbishop of Ardmagh ... with the life of the Author*. Dublin, 1677.

Warner, G.F., ed. *The Nicholas Papers: Correspondence of Sir Edward Nicholas, Secretary of State*. 3 vols. Camden Society, new series. London: The Society 1886–97.

Whitaker, T.D., ed. *The Life and Correspondence of Sir George Radcliffe*. London, 1810.

Worse and Worse Newes from Ireland being The Coppy Of A Letter read in the House of Parliament, the 14. of this instant Moneth of December, wherein is contained such unheard of Cruelties, committed by the Papists against the Protestants, not sparing Age nor sex, that would make a Christians heart to bleede. London, 1641. British Library, Thomason Tracts E. 180(15).

Yorke, P., ed. *Hardwicke State Papers*. 2 vols. London, 1778.

SECONDARY SOURCES

Andrews, K.R. *Trade, Plunder and Settlement: Maritime Enterprise and the Genesis of the British Empire, 1480–1630*. Cambridge: Cambridge University Press 1984.

Aldis, H. *List of Books Printed in Scotland before 1700*. Edinburgh: National Library of Scotland 1970.

Ashton, R. *The English Civil War: Conservatism and Revolution 1603–1649*. London: Weidenfeld and Nicolson 1978.

Aylmer, G.E. *The King's Servants: The Civil Service of Charles I, 1622–1642*. New York: Columbia University Press 1961.

Ball, F.E. *The Judges in Ireland 1221–1921.* 2 vols. London: John Murray 1926.

Barnard, T.C. "Crises of Identity among Irish Protestants 1641–1685." *Past and Present* 127 (1990): 37–83.

– "The Uses of 23 October 1641 and Irish Protestant Celebration." *English Historical Review* 106 (1991): 889–920.

Beckett, J.C. *The Cavalier Duke: A Life of James Butler, 1st Duke of Ormond.* Belfast: Pretani Press 1990.

– "The Confederation of Kilkenny Reviewed." In *Historical Studies,* edited by M. Roberts. London: Bowes and Bowes 1959, vol. 2: 29–41.

– *The Making of Modern Ireland.* London: Faber and Faber 1966.

Bossy, J. "The Counter-Reformation and the People of Ireland, 1596–1641." In *Historical Studies,* edited by T.W. Williams. Dublin: Gill and MacMillan 1971, vol. 8: 155–69.

Bottigheimer, K.S. *English Money and Irish Land: the "Adventurers" in the Cromwellian Settlement of Ireland.* Oxford: Clarendon Press 1971.

– "The Failure of the Reformation in Ireland: *une question bien posée.*" *Journal of Ecclesiastical History* 36 (1985): 196–207.

– "The Reformation in Ireland Revisited." *Journal of British Studies* 15 (1976): 140–9.

Bradshaw, B. "The Beginnings of Modern Ireland." In *The Irish Parliamentary Tradition,* edited by B. Farrell. Dublin: Gill and Macmillan 1973, 102–15.

– *The Irish Constitutional Revolution of the Sixteenth Century.* Cambridge: Cambridge University Press 1979.

– "Sword, Word and Strategy in the Reformation in Ireland." *Historical Journal* 21 (1978): 475–502.

Brown, K.M. "Aristocratic Finances and the Origins of the Scottish Revolution," *English Historical Review* 104 (1989): 46–87.

Bush, M.L. *The Government Policy of Protector Somerset.* Montreal: McGill-Queen's University Press 1975.

Burke, Sir B. *Vicissitudes of Families.* 2 vols. London: Longmans 1869.

Canny, N.P. *The Elizabethan Conquest of Ireland: A Pattern Established 1565–76.* Hassocks, Sussex: Harvester Press 1976.

– "In Defence of the Constitution? The Nature of Irish Revolt in the Seventeenth Century." In *Culture et pratiques politiques en France et en Irlande XVI-XVIIIᵉ siècle: Actes du Colloque de Marseille,* edited by L. Bergeron and L. Cullen. Paris, 1991, 23–40.

– "The Irish Background to Penn's Experiment." In *The World of William Penn,* edited by R.S. Dunn and M.M. Dunn. Philadelphia: University of Philadelphia Press 1986, 139–56.

– *Kingdom and Colony: Ireland and the Atlantic World 1560–1800.* Baltimore: Johns Hopkins University Press 1988.

- "Migration and Opportunity: Britain, Ireland and the New World." *Irish Economic and Social History* 12 (1985), 7–32.
- *The Upstart Earl: A Study of the Social and Mental World of Richard Boyle, First Earl of Cork, 1566–1643.* Cambridge: Cambridge University Press 1982.
- "Why the Reformation Failed in Ireland: *une question mal posée.*" *Journal of Ecclesiastical History* 30 (1979): 423–50.

Carte, T. *An History of the Life of James Duke of Ormonde, from his Birth in 1610, to his Death in 1688.* 3 vols. London, 1736.

Casway, J.I. *Owen Roe O'Neill and the Struggle for Catholic Ireland.* Philadelphia: University of Pennsylvania Press 1984.
- "Two Phelim O'Neills." *Seanchas Ardmhacha* 21 (1985): 331–41.

Christianson, P. "The 'Obliterated' Portions of the House of Lords Journals dealing with the Attainder of Strafford 1641." *English Historical Review* 95 (1980): 339–53.

Clarke, A. "Breakdown of Authority, 1640–41." In *A New History of Ireland*, edited by T.W. Moody, F.X. Martin, and F.J. Byrne. Oxford: Clarendon Press 1976, vol. 3: 270–88.
- "The Earl of Antrim and the First Bishop's War." *Irish Sword* 6 (1963–64): 108–15.
- "The Genesis of the Ulster Rising of 1641." In *Plantation to Partition*, edited by P. Roebuck. Belfast: Blackstaff Press 1981, 27–45.
- "The History of Poynings' Law, 1615–41." *Irish Historical Studies* 18 (1972): 207–22.
- "Ireland and the General Crisis." *Past and Present* 48 (1970): 79–99.
- "The Irish Economy, 1600–60." In *A New History of Ireland*, edited by T.W. Moody, F.X. Martin, and F.J. Byrne. Oxford: Clarendon Press 1976, vol. 3: 168–86.
- *The Old English in Ireland, 1625–42.* London: MacGibbon & Kee 1966.
- with R. Dudley Edwards. "Pacification, Plantation, and the Catholic Question, 1603–23." In *A New History of Ireland*, edited by T.W. Moody, F.X. Martin, and F.J. Byrne. Oxford: Clarendon Press, 1976, vol. 3: 187–232.
- "The Policies of the Old English in Parliament, 1640–41." In *Historical Studies*, edited by J.L. McCracken. London: Bowes 1965, vol. 5: 85–102.
- "Selling Royal Favours, 1624–32." In *A New History of Ireland*, edited by T.W. Moody, F.X. Martin, and F.J. Byrne. Oxford: Clarendon Press 1976, vol. 3: 233–42.
- "Sir Piers Crosby, 1590–1646: Wentworth's 'tawney ribbon'." *Irish Historical Studies* 26 (1988): 142–60.
- "The 1641 Depositions." In *Treasures of the Library of Trinity College Dublin*, edited by P. Fox. Dublin: The Royal Irish Academy for the Library of Trinity College Dublin 1986, 111–22.

Cohen, E. "Law, Folklore and Animal Lore." *Past and Present* 110 (1986): 6–37.

Cokayne, G.E., and V. Gibbs, eds., *The Complete Peerage of England Scotland Ireland Great Britain and the United Kingdom.* 13 vols. London: St Catherine Press 1910–40.

Cooper, J.P. "The Fortune of Thomas Wentworth, Earl of Strafford." In *Land, Men and Beliefs: Studies in Early-Modern History*, edited by G.E. Aylmer and J.S. Morrill. London: Hambledon Press 1983, 148–75.

Corish, P.J. *The Catholic Community in the Seventeenth and Eighteenth Centuries.* Dublin: Helicon Press 1981.

– "The Cromwellian Regime, 1650–60." In *A New History of Ireland*, edited by T.W. Moody, F.X. Martin, and F.J. Byrne. Oxford: Clarendon Press 1976, vol. 3: 353–86.

– "The Rising of 1641 and the Catholic Confederacy, 1641–5." In *A New History of Ireland*, edited by T.W. Moody, F.X. Martin, and F.J. Byrne. Oxford: Clarendon Press 1976, vol. 3: 289–335.

Cregan, D.F. "The Confederation of Kilkenny: Its Organisation, Personnel and History," Ph.D. dissertation, University College, Dublin, 1947.

– "An Irish Cavalier: Daniel O'Neill." *Studia Hibernica* 3 (1963): 60–100; 4 (1964): 104–33; 5 (1965): 42–77.

– "The Social and Cultural Background of a Counter-Reformation Episcopate, 1618–60." In *Studies in Irish History Presented to R. Dudley Edwards*, edited by A. Cosgrove and D. McCartney. Dublin: University College, Dublin, 1979, 85–117.

Cullen, L.M. "Economic Trends, 1660–91." In *A New History of Ireland*, edited by T.W. Moody, F.X. Martin, and F.J. Byrne. Oxford: Clarendon Press 1976, vol. 3: 387–407.

Cunningham, B. "Native Culture and Political Change in Ireland, 1580–1640." In *Natives and Newcomers*, edited by C. Brady and R. Gillespie. Dublin: Irish Academic Press 1986, 148–70.

Cust, R. "News and Politics in Early Seventeenth Century England." *Past and Present* 112 (1986): 60–90.

Dictionary of National Biography. Edited by L. Stephen and S. Lee. 63 vols. London, 1885–1900.

Dietz, F.C. *English Public Finance 1558–1641.* 2 vols. London: Frank Cass 1964.

Donald, P.H. "The King and the Scottish Troubles, 1637–1641." Ph.D. dissertation, Cambridge University, 1988.

– *An Uncounselled King: Charles I and the Scottish Troubles 1637–1641.* Cambridge: Cambridge University Press 1990.

Dongan, B. "Codes and Conduct in the English Civil War." *Past and Present* 118 (1988): 65–95.

Dunlop, R. "The Forged Commission of 1641." *English Historical Review* 2 (1887): 527–33.

- "A Note on the Export Trade of Ireland in 1641, 1665 and 1669." *English Historical Review* 22 (1907): 754–5.

Dwyer, P. *The Diocese of Killaloe from the Reformation to the Close of the Eighteenth Century.* Dublin: Hodges, Fosher 1878.

Edwards, R.D. and T.W. Moody, "The History of Poynings' Law: Part I, 1494–1615." *Irish Historical Studies* 2 (1941): 415–24.

Ellis, S. "Parliament and Community in Yorkist and Tudor Ireland." In *Historical Studies*, edited by A. Cosgrove and D. McCartney. Belfast: Appletree Press 1983, vol. 14: 43–68.

- *Tudor Ireland: Crown, Community and the Conflict of Cultures 1470–1603.* London: Longman 1985.

Evans, E.P. *The Criminal Prosecution and Capital Punishment of Animals: The Lost History of Europe's Animal Trials.* London: Faber and Faber 1987. First published 1906.

Fitzpatrick, T. "The Sack of 'the Lurgan'." *Ulster Journal of Archaeology*, 2nd series, 10 (1904): 170–87.

Fletcher, A. *The Outbreak of the English Civil War.* London: Edward Arnold 1981.

Ford, A. *The Protestant Reformation in Ireland, 1590–1641.* Frankfurt-am-Main: Verlag Peter Lang 1985.

Fortescue, G.K., ed. *Catalogue of the Pamphlets, Books, Newspapers, and Manuscripts relating to the Civil War, the Commonwealth, and Restoration, Collected by George Thomason, 1640–1661.* 2 vols. London: Longmans 1908.

Gardiner, S.R. *History of England from the Accession of James I to the Outbreak of the Civil War, 1603–1642.* 10 vols. London: Longmans, Green 1883–4.

Giblin, C. "Vatican Library: MSS Barberini Latini." *Archivium Hibernicum: Irish Historical Records* 18 (1955): 67–144.

Gillespie, R. *Colonial Ulster: The Settlement of East Ulster 1600–1641.* Cork: Cork University Press 1985.

- "The End of an Era: Ulster and the Outbreak of the 1641 Rising." In *Natives and Newcomers: Essays on the Making of Irish Colonial Society, 1534–1641*, edited by C. Brady and R. Gillespie. Dublin: Irish Academic Press 1986, 191–213.

- "Mayo and the Rising of 1641." *Cathair na Mart* 5 (1985): 38–44.

- "Migration and Opportunity: A Comment." *Irish Economic and Social History* 13 (1986): 90–5.

- "A Question of Survival: The O'Farrells and Longford in the Seventeenth Century." In *Longford: Essays in County History*, edited by R. Gillespie and G. Moran. Dublin: Lilliput Press 1990, 13–29.

- *The Transformation of the Irish Economy 1550–1700.* [Dublin]: Economic and Social History Society of Ireland 1991.

Glow, L. "Manipulation of Committees in the Long Parliament, 1641–1642." *Journal of British Studies* 5 (1965): 31–52.

Greenberg, S. "Dating Civil War Pamphlets, 1641–1644." *Albion* 20 (1988): 387–401.
– "The Thomason Collection: Rebuttal to Michael Mendle." *Albion* 22 (1990): 95–8.
Hayes-McCoy, G.A. "Conciliation, Coercion, and the Protestant Reformation, 1547–71." In *A New History of Ireland*, edited by T.W. Moody, F.X. Martin, and F.J. Byrne. Oxford: Clarendon Press 1976, vol. 3: 69–93.
Hazlett, H. "A History of the Military Forces Operating in Ireland 1641–1649." Ph.D. dissertation, Queen's University, Belfast, 1938.
Hibbard, C. *Charles I and the Popish Plot.* Chapel Hill: University of North Carolina Press 1983.
Hill, G. *An Historical Account of the MacDonnells of Antrim: including notices of some other Septs, Irish and Scottish.* Belfast: Archer & Sons 1873.
Hirst, D. *Authority and Conflict: England, 1603–1658.* Cambridge, MA: Harvard University Press 1986.
Howarth, D. *Lord Arundel and His Circle.* New Haven: Yale University Press 1985.
Jackson, D. *Intermarriage in Ireland 1550–1650.* Montreal: Cultural and Educational Productions 1970.
Johnston, D.J. "The Plantation of County Fermanagh," M.A. dissertation, Queen's University, Belfast, 1976.
Kearney, H.F. "Ecclesiastical Politics and the Counter-Reformation in Ireland, 1618–1648." *Journal of Ecclesiastical History* 2 (1960): 202–12.
– *Strafford in Ireland 1633–41: A Study in Absolutism.* Manchester: Manchester University Press 1959.
Keeler, M. *The Long Parliament, 1640–1641: A Biographical Study of Its Members.* Philadelphia: American Philosophical Society 1954.
Kishlansky, M.A. "Consensus Politics and the Structure of Debate at Putney." *Journal of British Studies* 20 (1981): 50–69.
– *Parliamentary Selection: Social and Political Choice in Early Modern England.* Cambridge: Cambridge University Press 1986.
Koenigsberger, H.G. "Monarchies and Parliaments in Early Modern Europe: *dominium regale* or *dominium politicum et regale.*" *Theory and Society* 5 (1978): 191–217.
Lindley, K.J. "The Impact of the 1641 Rebellion upon England and Wales, 1641–5." *Irish Historical Studies* 18 (1972): 143–76.
Lodge, J. *The Peerage of Ireland, revised by M. Archdall.* 7 vols. Dublin: 1789.
Loeber, R. "Downing's and Winthrop's Plantation in Ireland." Unpublished typescript.
Loomie, A.J. "Alonso de Cárdenas and the Long Parliament, 1640–1648." *English Historical Review* 97 (1982): 289–307.
Lowe, J. "The Negotiations between Charles I and the Confederation of Kilkenny 1642–1649." Ph.D. dissertation, London University, 1960.

Lynch, J. *The Portrait of a Pious bishop; or, the Life and Death of the Most Rev. Francis Kirwan, Bishop of Killala*. Dublin: J. Duffy 1884.

MacCarthy-Morrogh, M. "The English Presence in Early Seventeenth Century Munster." In *Natives and Newcomers*, edited by C. Brady and R. Gillespie. Dublin: Irish Academic Press 1986, 171–90.

– *The Munster Plantation: English Migration to Southern Ireland 1583–1641*. Oxford: Clarendon Press 1986.

– "The Munster Plantation 1583–1641," Ph.D. dissertation, London University, London, 1983.

MacCormack, J.R. "The Irish Adventurers and the English Civil War." *Irish Historical Studies* 10 (1956): 21–58.

McCracken, E. *The Irish Woods since Tudor Times*. Newton Abbot: David and Charles 1971.

McGrath, B. "The Membership of the Irish House of Commons, 1613–15." M.Litt. dissertation, Trinity College, Dublin, 1985.

Matthews, L.V. "Anglo-Irish Relations: The English Militia and the Irish Rebellion 1640–1642." M.A. dissertation, McGill University, 1983.

Meehan, C.P. *The Fate and Fortune of Hugh O'Neill, Earl of Tyrone and Rory O'Donnell, Earl of Tyrconnell*. Dublin: J. Duffy 1886.

Mendle, M. "The Thomason Collection: A Reply to Stephen J. Greenberg." *Albion* 22 (1990): 85–93.

Moody, T.W. *Londonderry Plantation 1609–41: The City of London and the Plantation in Ulster*. Belfast: William Mullan 1939.

Mooney, C. "The Golden Age of the Irish Franciscans, 1615–50." In *Measgra I gCuimhne Mhichil Uí CHLEIRIGH, Miscellany of Historical and Linguistic Studies in Honour of Brother Michael O Cleirigh, O.F.M. Chief of the Four Masters*, edited by S. O'Brien. Dublin: Assisi Press 1944, 21–33.

Morrill, J.S. *The Revolt of the Provinces: Conservatives and Radicals in the English Civil War 1630–1650*. London: George Allen & Unwin 1976.

Newman, P.R. *Royalist Officers in England and Wales, 1642–1660: A Biographical Dictionary*. New York: Garland Publishing 1981.

O'Dowd, M. *Power, Politics and Land: Early Modern Sligo 1568–1688*. Belfast: Institute of Irish Studies, Queen's University of Belfast, 1991.

– "Rebellion and War." Typed manuscript.

Ohlmeyer, J.H. "The 'Antrim Plot' of 1641 – a Myth?" *Historical Journal* 35 (1992): 905–19.

– *Civil War and Restoration in the Three Stuart Kingdoms: The Career of Randal MacDonnell, marquis of Antrim, 1609–1683*. Cambridge: Cambridge University Press 1993.

– "A Seventeenth Century Survivor: The Political Career of Randal MacDonnell, First Marquis and Second Earl of Antrim (1609–83)." Ph.D. dissertation, Trinity College, Dublin, 1990.

O'Sullivan, H. "Franciscans in Dundalk." *Seanchas Ardhmaca* 4 (1960–61): 33–71.

Perceval-Maxwell, M. "Ireland and the Monarchy in the Early Stuart Multiple Kingdom." *Historical Journal* 34 (1991): 279–95.

– "Protestant Faction, the Impeachment of Strafford and the Origins of the Irish Civil War." *Canadian Journal of History* 17 (1982): 235–55.

– *The Scottish Migration to Ulster in the Reign of James I.* London: Routledge & Kegan Paul 1973.

– "Strafford, the Ulster Scots, and the Covenanters." *Irish Historical Studies* 18 (1973): 524–51.

– "The Ulster Rising of 1641, and the Depositions." *Irish Historical Studies* 21 (1978): 144–67.

Prendergast, J.P. "Some Account of Sir Audley Mervyn, His Majesty's Prime Sergeant and Speaker in the House of Commons in Ireland, from 1661 till 1666." *Transactions of the Royal Historical Society*, 1st series, 4 (1874): 421–54.

Ranger, T.O. "The Career of Richard Boyle, First Earl of Cork in Ireland, 1588–1642." D.Phil. dissertation, Oxford University, 1959.

– "Strafford in Ireland: A Revaluation." In *Crisis in Europe 1560–1660*, edited by T. Aston. London: Routledge & Kegan Paul 1965, 271–94.

Reid, J.S. *History of the Presbyterian Church in Ireland.* 3 vols. Belfast: William Mullan 1867.

Robinson, P. *The Plantation of Ulster: British Settlement in an Irish Landscape, 1600–1670.* Dublin: Gill and Macmillan 1984.

Russell, C. "The British Background to the Irish Rebellion of 1641." *Historical Research* 61 (1988): 166–82.

– "The British Problem and the English Civil War." *History* 72 (1987): 395–415.

– *The Causes of the English Civil War.* Oxford: Clarendon Press 1990.

– *The Fall of the British Monarchies 1637–1642.* Oxford: Clarendon Press 1991.

– "The First Army Plot of 1641." *Transactions of the Royal Historical Society* 38 (1988): 85–106.

– *Parliaments and English Politics 1621–1629.* Oxford: Clarendon Press 1979.

– "The Theory of Treason in the Trial of Strafford." *English Historical Review* 80 (1965): 30–50.

– ed. *Origins of the English Civil War.* London: Macmillan 1973.

Rutledge, V.L. "Court-Castle Faction and the Irish Viceroyalty: The Appointment of Oliver St John as Lord Deputy of Ireland in 1616." *Irish Historical Studies* 26 (1989): 233–49.

Sharpe, K. "Crown, Parliament, and Locality: Government and Communications in Early Stuart England." *English Historical Review* 101 (1986): 321–50.

– "Introduction: Parliamentary History 1603–1629." In *Faction and Parliament*, edited by K. Sharpe. Oxford: Clarendon Press 1978, 1–42.

– ed. *Faction and Parliament*. Oxford: Clarendon Press 1978.

Sheehan, A.J. "Irish Towns in a Period of Change, 1558–1625." In *Natives and Newcomers*, edited by C. Brady and R. Gillespie. Dublin: Irish Academic Press 1986, 93–119.

Snow, V.F. *Essex the Rebel: The Life of Robert Devereux, the Third Earl of Essex 1591–1646*. Lincoln: University of Nebraska Press 1970.

Stevenson, D. *Alasdair MacColla and the Highland Problem in the Seventeenth Century*. Edinburgh: John Donald 1980.

– *Scottish Covenanters and Irish Confederates: Scottish-Irish Relations in the Mid-Seventeenth Century*. Belfast: Ulster Historical Foundation 1981.

– *The Scottish Revolution, 1637–44: The Triumph of the Covenanters*. Newton Abbot: David & Charles 1973.

Townshend, D.B. *The Life and Letters of the Great Earl of Cork*. London: Duckworth 1904.

Treadwell, V. "Irish Financial Administrative Reform under James I: The Customs and State Regulation of Trade." Ph.D. dissertation, Queen's University, Belfast, 1961.

Underdown, D. *Revel, Riot, and Rebellion: Popular Politics and Culture in England 1603–1660*. Oxford: Clarendon Press 1985.

Watts, J. "Thomas Wentworth, Earl of Strafford." In *Statesmen and Politicians of the Stuart Age*, edited by T. Eustace. London: Macmillan 1985, 83–114.

Wedgwood, C.V. *The King's Peace*. London: Collins 1955.

– *Thomas Wentworth, First Earl of Strafford, 1593–1641: A Revaluation*. New York: Macmillan 1962.

Young, M.B. *Servility and Service: The Life and Work of Sir John Coke*. London: Royal Historical Society 1986.

Zagorin, P. *The Court and the Country: The Beginning of the English Revolution*. London: Routledge & Kegan Paul 1969.

Index